Patterns for College Writing

A Rhetorical Reader and Guide

John Wojtusik   785-1758
29 Laura Dr. Latham
        12110

Patterns for College Writing

A Rhetorical Reader
and Guide

Second Edition

LAURIE G. KIRSZNER
Philadelphia College of Pharmacy and Science
STEPHEN R. MANDELL
Drexel University

St. Martin's Press   New York

Acknowledgments

NARRATION

Maya Angelou, "Finishing School." From *I Know Why the Caged Bird Sings,* by Maya Angelou. Copyright © 1969 by Maya Angelou. Reprinted by permission of Random House, Inc.

Donna Smith-Yackel, "My Mother Never Worked." Copyright © 1975 by *Women: A Journal of Liberation,* 3028 Greenmount Avenue, Baltimore, Md. 21218.

Richard Rodriguez, "Aria: A Memoir of a Bilingual Childhood." From *Hunger of Memory* by Richard Rodriguez. Copyright © 1981 by Richard Rodriguez. Reprinted by permission of David R. Godine, Publisher.

Martin Gansberg, "38 Who Saw Murder Didn't Call the Police." © 1964 by The New York Times Company. Reprinted by permission.

George Orwell, "Shooting an Elephant." From *Shooting an Elephant and Other Essays* by George Orwell, copyright 1950 by Sonia Brownell Orwell; renewed 1978 by Sonia Pitt-Rivers. Reprinted by permission of Harcourt Brace Jovanovich, Inc.

DESCRIPTION

Roger Angell, "On the Ball." From *Five Seasons* by Roger Angell, Copyright © 1972, 1973, 1974, 1975, 1976, 1977. Reprinted by permission of Simon & Schuster, a Division of Gulf & Western Corporation.

Maxine Hong Kingston, "Photographs of My Parents." From *The Woman Warrior: Memoirs of a Girlhood Among Ghosts,* by Maxine Hong Kingston. Copyright © 1975, 1976 by Maxine Hong Kingston. Reprinted by permission of Alfred A. Knopf, Inc.

Joan Didion, "Rock of Ages." Reprinted by permission of Farrar, Straus and Giroux, Inc. "Rock of Ages" from *Slouching Towards Bethlehem* by Joan Didion, Copyright © 1967, 1968 by Joan Didion.

Acknowledgments and copyrights continue at the back of the book on pages 433–35, which constitute an extension of the copyright page.

Preface

In preparing the second edition of *Patterns for College Writing,* we have made many changes large and small, but our original purpose and approach remain the same. As before, our main concern is practical: to help students prepare for writing assignments not only in the English classroom but beyond it in their other college courses. Our approach combines precept and example: discussions of writing procedure and rhetorical pattern are immediately illustrated by one or more annotated student papers and then followed by a series of professionally written pieces for analysis and discussion in the classroom.

Many instructors have found that in a single volume *Patterns* answers their needs both for a writing textbook and for an anthology—with the extra benefit that the two are coordinated. We are confident that these instructors will find the second edition significantly improved in both aspects—its discussions fuller and clearer, its readings more varied and more interesting. The many other instructors who have used *Patterns* mainly as an anthology will find the second edition still very manageable for that purpose and considerably strengthened by the new selections.

As before, the book begins with a comprehensive introductory chapter devoted to the writing process, and we have carefully revised this chapter in response to suggestions from users of the first edition. Here we explain to students how they can move confidently through the process of invention by understanding their assignment, establishing general boundaries, narrowing a subject to a workable topic, brainstorming to generate ideas, and formulating a thesis. The chapter goes on to discuss arrangement, analyzing the parts of the essay in some detail. Finally, the chapter deals with writing and revising and examines two successive versions of a sample student essay. In this new edition, we have especially taken care to strengthen the first chapter's discussions of the paragraph, of outlining, and of revising.

The balance of *Patterns for College Writing* consists of nine chapters, each discussing and illustrating a rhetorical pattern that students will use in their college writing assignments: narration, description, exemplification, process, cause and effect, comparison and contrast, classification and division, definition, and argumentation. Each chapter begins with a comprehensive introduction that first defines and illustrates the rhetorical pattern and then provides a thorough analysis of an annotated student paper to show how the chapter's concepts can be applied to a particular college writing situation. Each of these introductions has been rewritten in the interests of greater completeness and clarity. Those who know the first edition will find the greatest changes in the treatments of cause and effect, classification, and argumentation—patterns which are notoriously difficult to teach but which are among the most important for academic work.

Each chapter then goes on to illustrate the pattern with a number of selections, diverse in subject and style, by professional writers. Like the student examples in the introductions these essays are not intended to be imitated (though they may serve as stimuli for student writing). Rather, in the possibilities they offer for arranging material and developing ideas, they are meant to be analyzed and understood. In this edition we have retained the essays that our colleagues felt were most useful to their students and that our own students enjoyed the most. We have replaced other, less favored readings with some classics (Orwell's "Politics and the English Language" and E. B. White's "Once More to the Lake," for example) and with fresh, timely selections that will interest students (Jonathan Schell's "The Fate of the Earth," Stephen Jay Gould's "A Biological Homage to Mickey Mouse," and Joseph Epstein's "Runners vs. Smokers," for instance). Our selections now encompass an even greater variety of styles and periods than before, while offering a more evenly balanced representation of subject matter from different fields of study.

Each reading selection is followed by three types of questions designed to help students measure their comprehension of the essay's content, their understanding of the author's purpose and audience, and their recognition of the stylistic and structural techniques used to shape the essay. Finally, with every selection we include a "Writing Workshop" of suggestions for student writing. Many of these ask students to respond to a specific situation and to consider a specific audience and purpose, thus making their assignments not only more concrete but more interesting.

We hope that by offering interesting and accessible reading selections, by fully analyzing student writing that represents many academic disciplines, by stressing the importance of purpose and audience in our questions and assignments, and by presenting writing as a flexible, individualized process, we may encourage students to approach college writing not as a chore but as a challenge. Our own students have taught us that when writing is presented as a skill that can be learned and applied to projects in many fields, they will work to master that skill.

Friends, colleagues, students, and family all helped this project along. Of particular value were the seventy-three responses to a questionnaire sent to users of the first edition, and we thank each of the perceptive, thoughtful teachers who responded so frankly and helpfully to our questions. We are grateful to John W. N. Francis for his help and encouragement in our revision, and to Marcia Muth for her careful copy editing. We also wish to thank our typist, Lee Endicott, for helping us meet our deadlines. Above all, on the home front we thank Mark, Adam, and Rebecca Kirszner and Demi, David, and Sarah Mandell.

Laurie G. Kirszner
Stephen R. Mandell

Contents

"No other small package comes as close to the ideal in design and utility. It is a perfect object for a man's hand. Pick it up and it instantly suggests its purpose."

"Chinese do not smile for photographs. Their faces command relatives in foreign lands—'Send money'—and posterity forever—'Put food in front of this picture.' My mother does not understand Chinese-American snapshots. 'What are you laughing at?' she asks."

"Any child could imagine a prison more like a prison than Alcatraz looks, for what bars and wires there are seem perfunctory, beside the point; the island itself was the prison. . . . It is precisely what they called it: the Rock."

"He is seventeen. He had worked as a box boy at a supermarket in a middle-class suburb on the outskirts of Los Angeles. 'People come to the counter and you put things in their bags for them. And carry things to their cars. It was a grind.' "

"Summertime, oh summertime, pattern of life indelible, the fadeproof lake, the woods unshatterable, the pasture with the sweetfern and the juniper forever and ever, summer without end."

"Didn't I know she was working hard every day in the
hot kitchens of the white folks to make money to take
care of me? When was I ever going to learn to be a good
boy? She couldn't be bothered with my fights."

"My Principle is the key to an understanding of all
hierarchal systems, and therefore to an understanding of
the whole structure of civilization."

"He worked six days a week, five of them until eight or
nine at night, during a time when his own company had
begun the four-day week for everyone but the executives.
He worked like the Important People."

"I have lived all my life with an embarrassment of
squirrels in my backyard, they are all over the place, all
year long, and I have never seen, anywhere, a dead
squirrel."

"It is a bright and melancholy story, the age-old desire of
the male for the female, the age-old desire of the female
to be amused and entertained."

5. PROCESS   153

"Each man was a mass culture hero to his generation, but
it tells us something of the difference between
generations that each man's admirers would be hard-
pressed to understand why the other could mean very
much to his devotees."

"When Ulysses S. Grant and Robert E. Lee met in the
parlor of a modest house at Appomattox Court House,
Virginia, on April 9, 1865, to work out the terms for the
surrender of Lee's Army of Northern Virginia, a great
chapter in American life came to a close, and a great new
chapter began."

"The ambiguity and multiplicity of meanings possessed
by words are an obstacle to the scientist but a resource to
the poet. Where the scientist wants singleness of meaning, the poet wants richness of meaning."

"The most cheering thing about good health is that it allows one not to think about one's health. Think too
closely about it, dwell on it too long, and, lo, it will depart."

"Now when I had mastered the language of this water,
and had come to know every trifling feature that bordered
the great river as familiarly as I knew the letters of the
alphabet, I had made a valuable acquisition. But I had
lost something, too."

10. ARGUMENTATION   363

Thematic Guide to the Contents
Arranged by Subject

HISTORY AND POLITICS

SCIENCE AND TECHNOLOGY

LANGUAGE AND LITERATURE

ETHICS, JUSTICE, AND RELIGION

SOCIETY AND CULTURE

1

The Writing Process

Every essay in this book is the result of a struggle between a writer and his or her material. Every writer starts with an idea or an assignment and then must work to translate his or her thoughts about the subject into a clear and easily read essay. If the writer's struggle is successful, the finished essay is welded together without a seam, and the reader has no sense of the writer's frustration while hunting for the right word or rearranging the ideas. Writing is no easy business, and even a professional writer can have a very difficult time. Still, although there is no simple formula for good writing, some ways of writing are easier and more productive than others.

At this point, you may be asking yourself, "So what? What has this got to do with me? I'm not a professional writer." True enough, but during the next few years you will be doing a good deal of writing. Throughout your college career, you may need to write midterms, final exams, quizzes, lab reports, short essays, summaries, progress reports, proposals, personal letters, business correspondence, memos, or résumés. As diverse as these assignments seem, they have something in common: they can be made easier if you are familiar with the writing process—the way in which successful writers begin with a subject, come up with a thesis or unifying idea, and eventually put together an essay.

In general, the writing process has three stages. During *invention,* sometimes called *prewriting,* you decide exactly what you will write about. Then you accumulate ideas and information to support or explain what you want to say. During the next stage, *arrangement,* you decide how you are going to organize your ideas. And finally, during *writing and revision,* you write your essay, progressing through several drafts as you refine ideas as well as style, structure, and mechanics.

1

When you write, you need not finish one stage before starting another. Because the three stages often overlap, most writers engage in some aspects of invention, arrangement, and writing and revision simultaneously—finding ideas, considering possible methods of organization, and looking for the right words all at the same time. And even as writers draft or revise their essays, they may discover ideas that had not occurred to them before.

In fact, no two writers approach the writing process in exactly the same way. Some people outline; others do not. Some take elaborate notes during the invention stage; others keep track of everything in their heads. But regardless of the differences in their particular systems, almost all successful writers work in some orderly way. If you, too, can approach your writing in college as an orderly process, it will be easier for you to carry out your assignments and to become a more efficient, competent, and relaxed writer. The rest of this chapter will look at the writing process more closely in order to suggest techniques that may work for you.

STAGE ONE: INVENTION

Invention, or prewriting, is a crucial part of the writing process. Oddly enough, many people totally ignore this stage, either because they underestimate the importance of preparation or because they simply do not know how to plan to write. In college and afterward, you will often be told what to write about, at least in general, and you may be tempted to plunge into a first draft immediately. Before writing, however, you should probe your subject and decide what you are going to say about it.

Your first step should be to make sure you understand your assignment. Next, you should limit your subject by considering your essay's length, purpose, audience, and occasion, as well as what you know about the subject. You can then move from your subject, which may be very broad, to a manageably narrow topic. When you have settled on a topic, you need to gather and organize ideas and facts until, finally, you are prepared to formulate a thesis—the main idea of your essay, the point you want to make.

Assignments

Almost everything you write in college will begin as an assignment. Some assignments will be direct and easy to understand:

Write about an experience that changed your life.

Discuss the procedure you used in this experiment.

But others will be difficult and complex:

> According to Wayne Booth, point of view is central to the understanding of modern fiction. In a short essay discuss how Henry James uses point of view in his *Turn of the Screw*.

Therefore, before you begin to write, you need to understand what you are being asked to do. If the assignment is a written question, read it carefully several times. You might even underline its most important parts. If the assignment is dictated to you by your instructor, be sure to copy it accurately since a missed word can make quite a difference. Whatever the case, don't be afraid to ask your instructor for clarification if you are confused. Remember that an essay, no matter how well written, will be unacceptable if it doesn't fulfill the assignment.

Setting Limits

Once you are certain you understand your assignment, you must consider its length, purpose, audience, and occasion, as well as your own knowledge of the subject. Each of these considerations limits what you can say—or want to say—and simplifies your writing task.

Length. Often your instructor will specify an approximate length for a paper, or your writing situation will determine how much you can write. For example, you would need a narrower topic for a two- or three-page essay than you would for a ten-page paper. Similarly, during an hour exam you could not discuss a question as thoroughly as you might in a paper prepared over several days.

If your instructor sets no length, consider how other aspects of the assignment might indirectly determine length. A summary of a chapter or an article, for instance, should be much shorter than the original, whereas an analysis of a poem usually will be longer than the poem itself. If your instructor says that the length of your paper should suit your topic and you are uncertain what this means, discuss your ideas for the paper with your instructor rather than ask for a page limit.

Purpose. Your purpose for writing sets another limit to what you say and how you say it. For example, if you were to write to a prospective employer about a summer job, you would emphasize different aspects of your college life than you would in a letter to a friend. In the first case, you would want to persuade your reader to hire you. In the second, you would want to inform and perhaps entertain. In college, you write to demonstrate your mastery of the subject matter, your reasoning ability, and your competence as a writer. When you are assigned a college paper, your instructor may give you some guidelines about purpose. Often an assignment (such as a discussion of three economic causes of the Spanish-American War) may seem to require only an informational paper. But the successful paper will do more than provide information. It will convince your reader that you know what you are talking about and that your point deserves thoughtful attention.

Audience. To be effective, your essay should be written with a particular audience in mind. Audiences, however, can be extremely varied. An audience can be an *individual*—your instructor, for example—or it can be a *group,* like your classmates or co-workers. Your essay could address a *specialized* audience, like a group of medical doctors or economists, or a *general* or *universal* audience that has no particular expertise, like the readers of a newspaper or newsmagazine.

When you write for a college assignment, your audience is your instructor, and your purpose is to convince him or her that your facts are valid and your conclusions are reasonable and intelligent. Other audiences may be harder to define. Considering the age and sex of your audience, its political and religious values, its social and educational level, and its knowledge about and interest in your subject may help you to define it. For example, if you were selling life insurance, the sales letters you prepare for people with young children would probably differ from those you prepare for single people. Likewise, you might promote a local park from one angle for retired people and from another for working couples.

Many times, even after all these considerations, you may find that your audience is just too diverse to be categorized. In such cases, many writers imagine a universal audience and write for it, making points that they think will appeal to many different readers. Sometimes, writers try to think of one typical individual in the audience—perhaps a person they know—so that they can write to someone specific. At other times, writers solve this problem by finding a common denominator, a role that interests or involves all those in the audience. For example, when a report on toy safety asserts, "Now is the time for concerned consumers to demand that dangerous toys be removed from the market," it automatically casts its audience in the role of "concerned consumers."

Occasion. In academic writing, the occasion is most often a classroom writing exercise or a take-home assignment. Although these situations may seem artificial, they serve as valuable practice for writing you do outside the classroom—writing a memo or a report for your job, writing a letter to your representative in Congress, or preparing a flyer for an organization. Each of these occasions, in or out of college, requires a special approach to your writing. A memo to your co-workers, for instance, might be more informal than a report to your company's president. A notice about a meeting, sent to your fellow beer-can collectors, might be strictly informational, whereas a letter to your senator about preserving a local historical landmark would be persuasive as well as informational. Similarly, when you are writing a classroom exercise, remember that there are different kinds of classes, each with different occasions for writing. A response suitable for a psychology class or a history class might not be acceptable for an English class, just as a good answer on a quiz might be insufficient on a midterm.

Knowledge. What you know (and don't know) about a subject obviously limits what you can say about it. Different assignments or writing situations require different kinds of knowledge. A personal essay may draw on your own experiences and observations; a term paper will probably require you to acquire new knowledge through research. Although your experience riding city buses might be sufficient for an English composition essay, you might need to research rapid transit for an urban sociology paper. Sometimes you will be able to increase your knowledge about a particular topic easily because of your strong background in the general subject. At other times, when a subject is new to you, you will need to select a topic particularly carefully so that you do not get out of your depth. Often, the time allowed to do the assignment and its page limit will guide you as you consider what you already know and what you need to learn before you can write knowledgeably.

EXERCISES

1. Decide if the following topics are appropriate for the limits noted next to them. Write a few sentences for each topic to justify your conclusions.

   a. *A five-hundred-word paper:* A history of the Louisiana American Civil Liberties Union

   b. *A final exam:* The role of France and Germany in the American Revolutionary War

   c. *A one-hour in-class essay:* An interpretation of Andy Warhol's painting of Campbell's soup cans

   d. *A letter to your college paper:* A discussion of your school's investment practices

2. Make a list of the different audiences to whom you speak or write in your daily life. (Consider all the different types of people you see regularly, such as your family, your roommate, your instructors, your boss, your friends, and so on.)

   a. Do you speak or write to each in the same way and about the same things? If not, how do your approaches to these people differ?

   b. Name some subjects that would interest some of these people but not others. How do you account for these differences?

   c. Choose a subject, such as your English class or local politics, and describe how you would speak or write to each audience about it.

From Subject to Topic: Questions for Probing

Once you have considered the limits of your assignment, you need to narrow your subject to a workable topic within those limits. Many writing assignments begin as broad areas of interest or concern. These *general subjects* always need to be narrowed or limited to specific *topics* that can be reasonably discussed. For example, a subject like DNA recombinant research is certainly interesting. But it is too vast a subject to write about except in a vague and generalized way. You need to narrow such a subject down into a topic that you can cover specifically within the time and space available to you.

Subject	Topic
DNA recombinant research	Some uses of DNA recombinant research
Herman Melville's *Billy Budd*	Billy Budd as a Christ figure
Constitutional law	One result of the Miranda ruling
Home computers	A comparison of the Apple III and IBM home computers

To narrow a general subject, you need to explore what topics it contains that fall within your limits and what you have to say about each topic. Do not make the mistake of skipping this stage of the writing process, hoping that a topic will suddenly come to you. Not only will you waste time with this haphazard approach, but you also may fail to realize the potential of your subject. Instead, you can use two of the most productive techniques—questions for probing and brainstorming—to help you to narrow your topic and generate ideas. Like most other writers, you will probably discover by trial and error what method of invention works best for you.

When you probe your subject, try asking the following questions about it. These questions are useful because they reflect ways in which the mind operates: finding similarities and differences, for instance, or dividing a whole into its parts. By running through the list of questions, you can probe your subject systematically. Of course, not all questions will work for every subject. Still, any question may lead to many different answers, and each answer is a possible topic for your essay.

What happened?
When did it happen?
Where did it happen?
What does it look like?
What are its characteristics?
What are some typical cases or examples of it?
How did it happen?
What makes it work?
How is it made?
Why did it happen?
What caused it?
What does it cause?
What are its effects?
How is it related to something else?
How is it like other things?
How is it different from other things?
What are its parts or types?
How can its parts or types be separated or grouped?
Do its parts or types fit into a logical order?
Into what categories can its parts or types be arranged?
On what basis can it be categorized?
What is it?
How does it resemble other members of its class?
How does it differ from other members of its class?
What are its limits?

Even a few of these questions can yield many workable topics—

some you might never have considered had you not asked the questions. By applying this approach to a general subject, such as "the Brooklyn Bridge," you can generate more ideas and topics than you need:

What happened? A short history of the Brooklyn Bridge
What does it look like? A description of the Brooklyn Bridge
How is it made? The construction of the Brooklyn Bridge
What are its effects? The effect of the Brooklyn Bridge on American writers
How does it differ from other members of its class? Innovations in the design of the Brooklyn Bridge

At this point in the writing process, you mainly want to explore possible topics, and the more ideas you have, the wider your choice. So write down all the topics you think of. You can even repeat the process of probing several times to uncover topics that are still more limited. For instance, you might begin probing the subject of television programs and decide you are interested in writing about game shows. But that topic is still very broad, so you might probe again, arriving at a narrower topic: types of game-show contestants. Once you have generated many topics, eliminate those that do not interest you or that go beyond your knowledge or are too complex or too simple to fit the limits of the assignment. When you have discarded these weaker ideas, you will still have several left, and you can select from these possible topics the one that best suits your paper's length, purpose, audience, and occasion, as well as your knowledge of the subject.

EXERCISES

1. Indicate whether the following are general subjects or limited topics. Be prepared to explain your decisions.
   a. An argument for gun control
   b. A comparison of metal and fiberglass skis
   c. Supply-side economics
   d. Two creation stories in the Book of Genesis
   e. Waterfowl and fresh-water plants
   f. The Haber process for the fixation of atmospheric nitrogen
   g. Michelangelo's Sistine Chapel paintings
   h. The advantages of term over whole life insurance
   i. Skiing

    j. An analysis of the McDonald's television marketing strategy
    k. The Book of Genesis

2. Choose two of the following subjects, and generate topics from each by using as many of the questions for probing as you can. (Assume that the essay you are preparing is due in three days for your English class and that it should be about one thousand words long.)
    a. Television programs
    b. Computers
    c. Pocket calculators
    d. Ads and commercials
    e. Teachers
    f. Video games
    g. Styles of clothing
    h. Doctors
    i. Motorcycles
    j. Radio stations
    k. Diets
    l. Fatherhood or motherhood
    m. Grading
    n. Social problems
    o. Politics

Finding Something to Say: Brainstorming

After you have decided on a topic, you still have to find something to say about it. Brainstorming is a method of invention that can help you do this. To brainstorm, quickly write down every fact, idea, or association you can think of that relates to your topic. Your list might include words, phrases, statements, or questions. Jot them down in whatever order you think of them, allowing your thoughts to wander freely. Some of the items may be inspired by notes you took in class; others may be ideas you got from talking with friends or things you heard in class but didn't write down. Still others may be things you have begun to wonder about, points you thought of while working toward your topic, or ideas that spontaneously occur to you as you brainstorm.

An engineering student planning to write for his composition class a short paper on the advantages and disadvantages of alternate energy sources made these brainstorming notes:

Alternate Energy Sources

Solar
Fusion
Wind

Tidal
Nuclear
Nuclear technology already exists and is widely used
Nuclear plants can leak radioactivity
Synthetic fuels
Steam power plants
Free fuel source for solar
Solar technology exists but is not widely used
Inefficiency of solar collectors
Efficiency of fusion reaction
Difficulty of containing fusion reaction
Solar collectors safe
Disposal of nuclear wastes—dangerous
Proliferation of plutonium
Breeder reactors
Sophisticated technology still not developed for fusion
Fusion relatively clean—little radioactive waste
Unlimited fuel source for fusion—H_2O
Limited uranium resources
Solar—no waste—no pollution
Oil will run out by 2020
Limited energy resources
Long lines at gas stations
Congress and president worried
Development money
Certain alternate sources still too expensive
Coal gasification
Shale oil
Decontrol
Raising prices
Rationing
Heating
Cars and transportation
Electricity

The student who wrote this list was obviously at no loss for ideas. Because the assignment was due in two days and was to be only about three pages long, he realized that he would have to cut his list down. After reading it over several times, he decided that he would concentrate on the advantages and disadvantages of the three alternate energy sources about which he knew the most: nuclear, solar, and fusion. They would require no research, would fit the limitations of time and space, and could be clearly explained in nontechnical language for his English composition instructor and classmates.

Grouping Related Ideas

The next step is to organize your ideas by grouping the items from your brainstorming list under a few broad headings. Here is how the engineering student grouped his ideas about the advantages and disadvantages of nuclear, solar, and fusion power:

Nuclear
Nuclear technology already exists and is widely used
Nuclear plants can leak radioactivity
Limited uranium resources
Disposal of nuclear wastes—dangerous

Solar
Solar technology exists but is not widely used
Inefficiency of solar collectors
Solar collectors safe
Free fuel source
No waste—no pollution

Fusion
Sophisticated technology still not developed
Difficulty of containing fusion reaction
Unlimited fuel source—H_2O
Relatively clean—little radioactive waste

This type of grouping is sometimes called a "scratch outline," because it is jotted down quickly and informally. Based on the three groups here, the student can sum up in one sentence his main idea: "Although nuclear, solar, and fusion power are promising energy sources, each also has serious disadvantages."

EXERCISES

Imagine that your English composition instructor has given you the following list of subjects and told you to select one for a five-hundred-word essay, due in two days. Prepare at least three of these subjects following the procedures for invention just discussed. First, use the questions for probing. Next, pick the best topic developed from each subject, and then brainstorm

about it. Finally, select the ideas about each topic that you would use if you were actually writing the paper, and group them into a scratch outline.
    a. Grandparents
    b. Science-fiction movies
    c. Gay rights
    d. Divorce
    e. The draft
    f. Fast-food restaurants
    g. Music
    h. Religion
    i. The death penalty
    j. Cats
    k. Television comedy

Formulating a Thesis

Once you have decided what your essay is going to discuss, your next job is to formulate a thesis. Your topic determines what your essay is about; your thesis states your essay's main idea, the specific point you want to make about the topic. A thesis is usually a single sentence and most often appears at the beginning of an essay.

Three things characterize a good thesis. First, it should be so *clear* that it leaves no doubt in your mind, or in your reader's, about what you are going to discuss in your essay.

Subject:	Coeducational dormitories
Topic:	An examination of the pros and cons of coeducational dormitories
Thesis:	Despite predictions to the contrary from parents and church groups, coeducational college dormitories have not proved to be hotbeds of promiscuity.

Here, the general subject, "coeducational dormitories," has been limited to a narrower topic. The thesis is narrower still. It shows that the paper will be concerned mainly with one issue: the lack of promiscuity in the dorms. Moreover, the thesis statement explicitly reveals the writer's position on the issue.

This is the second characteristic of a good thesis—it *takes a stand*. It is an idea that your readers can agree or disagree with. In either case, your thesis should generate a serious discussion in your essay and prompt a serious consideration by your reader. A thesis, therefore, is much more than a title of an essay or an announcement of its subject.

Title: Alternate Energy Sources
Announcement: This paper will explore three alternatives to
                    oil, gas, and electricity as energy sources.
Title: Orwell's "A Hanging"
Announcement: In this paper I will discuss George Orwell's
                    essay, "A Hanging."

Neither of these examples is a thesis statement. Although each tells what the writer is going to discuss, none indicates what the writer's stand will be. These examples can be revised into the following thesis statements:

Thesis: Although nuclear, solar, and fusion power are
          promising energy sources, each also has serious
          disadvantages.
Thesis: In "A Hanging," George Orwell shows that capital
          punishment is not only immoral, but unnatural.

The third requirement for a good thesis statement is that it be *specific* enough to give your essay a good, strong push in the direction you want to go. For example, the statement "The president has failed to control unemployment" indicates the writer's topic and general stand, but it stops there. With additional specific detail this thesis can be much more dynamic. Here is a revised version:

Thesis: Though the president has repeatedly promised to
          control unemployment, his three major programs to
          date have failed to solve the problem.

The writer is now committed to a point and can easily move ahead to the facts and reasoning that will support it. Furthermore, readers, having been shown where the essay is headed, will not have to puzzle out just what the writer means to say.

A clear, specific thesis that takes a stand unifies an essay and establishes its direction and purpose. Every piece of writing should have this clear sense of purpose, this unifying idea that draws different details into a logical whole. Not every kind of writing, however, requires an explicitly stated thesis. Sometimes, a thesis may only be implied. Like an explicit thesis, an implied thesis is clear and specific and takes a stand, but it is not directly stated in a single sentence. Instead, it is suggested by the selection and arrangement of the essay's details. Although an implied thesis requires that a writer plan and organize especially carefully, many of the professional writers whose essays are included in this book prefer this technique because it is more subtle than stating a thesis. In most college writing, however, since you want to avoid any risk of being misunderstood, you will usually state your thesis explicitly.

Some types of writing do not need a thesis and should not be given one. A lab report describing the process of typing blood, for instance, merely provides factual information for its own sake. The author has no point to argue and therefore no thesis. Trying to force an argumentative thesis on such an assignment (for example, "Typing blood can be fun") may distort your purpose and distract your readers from the solid information you are presenting. When a piece of writing has—and needs—no thesis, what keeps it heading in the right direction is the writer's topic and purpose. Often, these should be announced openly: "This paper describes the correct procedure for typing blood."

No fixed rules determine when you formulate your thesis; it depends on the type of assignment, your knowledge of the subject, and your own method of writing. Sometimes you may prefer to formulate a tentative thesis statement before brainstorming or even probing a subject for a topic. At other times you may wait until later—slowly reviewing all the material and then drawing it together into a single statement. Occasionally, your assignment may specify a thesis statement by telling you to take this or that position on a given topic. Whatever the case, you should arrive at your thesis before you begin to write your first draft.

Keep in mind that the thesis you develop at this point does not have to be final, but because it gives you guidance and purpose, some thesis is necessary at this stage of the writing process. If the direction of your essay changes as you write, you should change your thesis accordingly.

EXERCISES

1. Assess the strengths and weaknesses of the following as thesis statements. Note which ones would most effectively establish the direction of an essay.
   a. Myths and society.
   b. Myths serve an important function in society.
   c. Contrary to popular assumptions, myths are more than fairy stories; they are tales that express the underlying attitudes a society has toward important issues.
   d. Today, almost two marriages in four will end in divorce.
   e. Skiing, a popular sport for millions, is a major cause of winter injuries.

   f. If certain reforms are not instituted immediately, our company will be bankrupt within two years.

   g. Early childhood is an important period.

   h. By using the proper techniques, parents can significantly improve the learning capabilities of their preschool children.

   i. Science fiction can be used to criticize society.

   j. Science fiction, in the hands of an able writer, can be a powerful tool for social reform.

2. For three of the following general subjects and topics, go through as many steps as you need to formulate workable thesis statements.

   a. The importance of your family

   b. Writing

   c. Space exploration

   d. The difficulty of adjusting to college

   e. One thing you would change about your life

   f. Air pollution

   g. Gasoline prices

   h. Humor in television commercials

   i. The objectivity of newspaper reporting

   j. Television evangelism

STAGE TWO: ARRANGEMENT

So far, this chapter has progressed through the following steps:

- Understanding the assignment
- Establishing the limits of the subject
- Moving from subject to topic by using questions for probing
- Brainstorming to generate ideas
- Selecting and grouping ideas
- Formulating a thesis

Each of these steps represents a series of choices you have to make about your topic and your material. Now, before you actually begin writing, you have another choice to make—how to arrange your material into an essay. This extremely important choice determines how clear your essay will be and how your audience will react to it.

Sometimes deciding how to arrange your ideas will be easy because your assignment specifies a particular pattern of development. This may often be the case in your freshman English class where your instructor may assign, say, a descriptive or a narrative essay. Also, certain assignments or examination questions imply how your material should be structured. Probably no one except an

English composition instructor will say to you, "Write a narrative," but you will have assignments in other courses that begin, "Give an account of . . ." Likewise, few teachers will directly assign a process essay, but they will do so indirectly when they ask you to explain how something works. An examination question might ask you to trace the events leading up to an event. If you are perceptive, you will realize that this question calls for a narrative or cause-and-effect answer. The important thing is to recognize the clues that such assignments give or those you find in your topic or thesis, and to structure your essay accordingly.

Here are some of those clues. You will recognize them as the same questions you used to probe for a topic:

What happened? When did it happen? Where did it happen?	Narration
What does it look like? What are its characteristics?	Description
What are some typical cases or examples of it?	Exemplification
How did it happen? What makes it work? How is it made?	Process
Why did it happen? What caused it? What does it cause? What are its effects? How is it related to something else?	Cause and Effect
How is it like other things? How is it different from other things?	Comparison and Contrast
What are its parts or types? How can its parts or types be separated or grouped? Do its parts or types fit into a logical order? Into what categories can its parts or types be arranged? On what basis can it be categorized?	Classification and Division

What is it?
How does it resemble other members of
    its class?
How does it differ from other members
    of its class?
What are its limits?

} Definition

The names in the right column—narration, description, and so on—
identify some useful patterns of development that help you order
your ideas. As you will see, the rest of this book explains and illustrates these patterns, one by one. If, when you probed your subject,
you found questions under narration most helpful, your essay should
be organized as a narrative. This is true of process, cause and effect,
and all the other categories in this list.

Outlines

Once you have prepared a scratch outline, formulated a thesis,
and selected a pattern of development, you may want to construct
a "formal" outline for your essay. Formal outlines range from sketchy
lists that simply remind the writer what points to make in which
order to multilevel, highly detailed constructions in which every
item is expressed in a complete sentence. The complexity of your
assignment will determine the type of outline that you need; just
remember that the more material you include in your outline, the
easier your first draft will be.

Your outline maps the shape of the body of your paper, detailing
everything except the introduction and the conclusion, which usually are not developed until later. You group each of your major
categories under Roman numerals. You use capital letters for major
points and numbers for subtopics. Compare the following formal
outline with the scratch outline in which the writer simply grouped
his notes under three general headings:

Alternate Energy Sources

   I. Introduction
  II. Nuclear energy
     A. Advantages
       1. Existing technology
       2. Widely used technology
     B. Disadvantages
       1. Limited uranium resources
       2. Dangerous disposal of nuclear wastes
       3. Possible radioactive leaks from plants

III. Solar energy
  A. Advantages
    1. Safe solar collectors
    2. Free fuel source
    3. No waste—no pollution
  B. Disadvantages
    1. Existing technology but not widely used
    2. Inefficiency of solar collectors
IV. Fusion energy
  A. Advantages
    1. Unlimited fuel source—H_2O
    2. Relatively clean—little radioactive waste
  B. Disadvantages
    1. Sophisticated technology still not developed
    2. Difficulty of containing fusion reaction
V. Conclusion

This outline is only moderately complicated, but it is sufficient for this knowledgeable author's needs. It will remind the writer how to order his points so that both the advantages and the disadvantages are clear for each of the three energy sources.

Parts of the Essay

A piece of writing should have a beginning, a middle, and an end. This is true no matter which pattern of development you use. As noted earlier, these parts are called the introduction, the body, and the conclusion.

The Introduction.   The opening of your essay, usually one paragraph and rarely more than two, introduces your subject, engages your reader's interest, and states your thesis or announces your purpose. But in so short a space, there is obviously no room for an in-depth discussion or even a summary of your topic.

You can introduce an essay and engage your reader's interest in a number of ways. Here are several you can employ.

1. You can move directly to your thesis. This approach works well whenever you know that your audience is already interested in your topic and that there is no reason not to come directly to the point. It is especially useful for exams, where there is no need or time for subtlety.

With double-digit inflation taking its toll, it is understandable that many companies have been forced to raise prices, and the oil industry should be no exception. But well-intentioned individuals begin wondering whether high rates are justified when increases occur every week. It is at this point that we should start examining the pricing policies of the major American oil companies.

(economics take-home exam)

2. You can introduce an essay with a definition of a relevant term or concept. This technique is especially useful for research papers or examinations where the meaning of a specific term is crucial.

Democracy is a form of government in which the ultimate authority is vested in and exercised by the people. This may be so in theory, but recent elections in our city have caused much concern for the future of democracy here. Extensive voting machine irregularities and ghost voting have seriously jeopardized the people's faith in the democratic process.

(political science paper)

3. You can begin your essay with an anecdote or story that is an example supporting your thesis.

Upon meeting the famous author James Joyce, a young student stammered, "May I kiss the hand that wrote *Ulysses?*" "No!" said Joyce. "It did a lot of other things, too." As this exchange shows, Joyce was an individual who valued humor. This tendency is also present in his final work, *Finnegan's Wake,* where comedy is used to comment upon the human condition.

(English literature paper)

4. You can begin with a question.

What was it like to live through the holocaust? Elie Wiesel, in *One Generation After,* answers this question. As he does so, he challenges many of the assumptions we hold in our somewhat smug and highly materialistic society.

(sociology book report)

5. Finally, you can begin with a quotation. If it is well chosen, it can interest your audience in reading further.

"The rich are different," said F. Scott Fitzgerald fifty years ago. Apparently, they remain so today. As any examination of the tax laws shows, the wealthy receive many more benefits than do the middle class or the poor.

(business law essay)

No matter which method you select, your introduction should be consistent in tone and approach with the rest of your essay. If it is not, it can misrepresent your intentions to your reader and even destroy your credibility. For this reason, the introduction is often the last part of a rough draft to be written. (During an exam, of course, when time is limited, you do not have the luxury of reconsidering your opening.) A technical report, for instance, should have an introduction that reflects the formality and seriousness of the occasion. The introduction to an autobiographical essay or a personal letter, on the other hand, should have an informal and relaxed tone.

The Body Paragraphs.   The middle section, or body, of your essay supports and expands your thesis. The body paragraphs present the detail, such as examples, descriptions, and facts, that will convince your audience that your thesis is reasonable. To do their job, body paragraphs should be unified, coherent, and well developed.

Body paragraphs should be unified. Generally, each body paragraph contains a *topic sentence,* a statement that tells your audience what point you are discussing in that specific paragraph. The paragraph has unity when everything in it directly relates to the topic sentence. Like a thesis, a topic sentence acts as a guidepost and makes it easier for your reader to follow what you have to say. In an essay, topic sentences usually begin the body paragraphs and generally reflect the major divisions of your outline.

In this excerpt from a student essay, the topic sentence unifies the paragraph by summarizing its main idea.

> Built on the Acropolis overlooking the city of Athens in the fifth century B.C., the Parthenon is an excellent example of Greek architecture. It was a temple of the gods and was very important to the people. Although at first glance its structure seems to be perfect, on closer examination it becomes clear that it is a static, two-dimensional object. As long as you stand in the center of any of its four sides to look at it, its form will appear to be perfect. The strong Doric columns seem to be equally spaced, one next to another, along all four of its sides. But if you take a step to the right or left, the Parthenon's symmetry is destroyed.

This paragraph identifies the Parthenon as an excellent example of Greek architecture. The explicit topic sentence, located at the beginning of the paragraph, enables readers to grasp the writer's point immediately. The examples that follow all relate to that point. The whole paragraph is therefore focused and unified.

Body paragraphs should be coherent. If your readers are to be able to follow your ideas and understand your arguments, your support paragraphs must be composed of sentences that smoothly and logically connect to each other. Coherence can be increased through three devices. First, you can repeat key words to carry concepts from one sentence to another and to echo important terms. Second, you can use pronouns to refer back to key nouns in previous sentences. Finally, you can use transitional expressions to show chronological sequence (*then, next, after that*); cause and effect (*as a result, therefore*); addition (*first, second, and, furthermore*); comparison (*similarly*); and contrast (*but, however, still, nevertheless*). These strategies for connecting sentences can spell out for your readers exactly what the relationships among your ideas are. The following paragraph, from George Orwell's "Shooting an Elephant," uses all three techniques to achieve coherence.

> I got up. The Burmans were already racing past me across the mud. It was obvious that the elephant would never rise again, but he was not dead. He was breathing very rhythmically with long rattling gasps, his great mound of a side painfully rising and falling. His mouth was wide open—I could see far down into the caverns of pale pink throat. I waited a long time for him to die, but his breathing did not weaken. Finally I fired my two remaining shots into the spot where I thought his heart must be. The thick blood welled out of him like red velvet, but still he did not die. His body did not even jerk when the shots hit him, the tortured breathing continued without a pause. He was dying, very slowly and in great agony, but in some world remote from me where not even a bullet could damage him further. I felt that I had got to put an end to that dreadful noise. It seemed dreadful to see the great beast lying there, powerless to move and yet powerless to die, and not even to be able to finish him. I sent back for my small rifle and poured shot after shot into his heart and down his throat. They seemed to make no impression. The tortured gasps continued as steadily as the ticking of a clock.

Here Orwell keeps his narrative coherent by using transitional expressions ("already," "finally," "when the shots hit him") to signal the passing of time. He uses pronouns ("he," "his") in nearly every sentence to refer back to the elephant, the topic of his paragraph. Finally, repetition of key words like "shot" and "die" (and its variants "dead" and "dying") also link the paragraph's sentences together. The result is a coherent, cohesive whole.

Body paragraphs should be well developed. In order to support your thesis, your body paragraphs should contain as much specific information as possible that is relevant to your topic and appropriate for your audience and purpose. The material you use to support your thesis usually grows from your brainstorming list. But if you find that your list doesn't provide enough material to develop your thesis fully, you can brainstorm again, review your notes, talk with your friends and instructors, read more about your topic, or go to the library and do some research. Your assignment and your topic will determine the kind and amount of information you need. This paragraph by a student writer marshals much concrete information to support its topic sentence and the thesis of the essay from which it is excerpted.

> Just look at how our society teaches males that extravagance is a positive characteristic. Scrooge, the main character of Dickens's *A Christmas Carol,* is portrayed as an evil man until he is rehabilitated—meaning that he gives up his miserly ways and freely distributes gifts and money on Christmas day. This behavior, of course, is rewarded when people change their opinions about him and decide that perhaps he isn't such a bad person after all. Diamond Jim Brady is another interesting example. This individual was a financier who was known for his extravagant taste in women and food. In any given night, he would consume food enough to feed at least ten of the many poor who roamed the streets of late nineteenth-century New York. Yet, despite his selfishness and infantile self-gratification, Diamond Jim Brady's name has become a synonym for the good life.

This student writer provides much detail to support her assertion that society teaches males that extravagance is a positive characteristic. Her literary and historical examples are not only complete but also carefully chosen and effectively presented.

In addition to making sure that your body paragraphs are unified, coherent, and well enough developed to support your thesis, you need to arrange your material according to the pattern of development that suits it best. For instance, an essay in which you discuss the causes of Hitler's defeat in Russia could be organized following a cause-and-effect pattern:

Introduction: Thesis

Body
- Cause 1:   The Russian winter
- Cause 2:   The opening of a second front
- Cause 3:   The problem of logistics
- Cause 4:   Hitler's refusal to take advice

Conclusion

A lab report on the synthesis of aspirin could be organized like this, following a process pattern of development:

	Introduction:	Unifying idea
	Step 1:	Mix 5 g. of salicylic acid, 10 ml. of acetic anhydride, and 1–2 ml. of sulphuric acid.
Body	Step 2:	Wait for the mixture to cool. Then add 50 ml. of water and collect on a Büchner filter.
	Step 3:	Dry the residue.
	Step 4:	Recrystallize the aspirin from benzene.
	Conclusion	

These patterns, and others, will be outlined and analyzed in detail throughout the rest of this book.

The Conclusion.   Readers remember best what they read last, and so your conclusion is extremely important. Always end your essay in a way that reinforces your thesis or serves your purpose.

Like your introduction, your conclusion should be brief. In a five-hundred-word essay, it can be as short as one line and most often is no longer than a paragraph. Regardless of its length, however, your conclusion should accurately reflect or review the content of your essay. Thus, it should not introduce new points or material that you have not discussed earlier. Frequently, a conclusion will end an essay by restating the thesis.

Conclusions can be as challenging to construct as introductions. Here are several ways to conclude an essay.

1. You can conclude your essay by simply reviewing your main points and restating your thesis.

> Rotation of crops provided several benefits. It enriched soil by giving it a rest; it enabled farmers to vary their production; and it ended the cycle of "boom or bust" that had characterized the prewar South's economy when cotton was the primary crop. Of course, this innovation did not solve all the economic problems of the postwar South, but it did lay the groundwork for the healthy economy this region enjoys today.
>
> (history exam)

2. You can end a discussion of a problem by recommending a course of action.

While there is still time, American engineering has to reassess its priorities. We no longer have the luxury of exotic and wasteful experiments such as automobile airbags. Instead, we need technology grounded in common sense and economic feasibility. That Volkswagen, rather than an American company, developed an outstanding and inexpensive passive restraint system illustrates how far we have strayed from old-fashioned Yankee ingenuity.

(engineering ethics report)

3. You can conclude with a prediction. Be careful, however, that your prediction is supported by the points you have made in the essay. The conclusion is too late to make new points or change direction.

It is too late to save parts of the great swamps in northern Florida, but it is not too late to preserve the Everglades in the southern part of the state. With intelligent planning and an end of the dam building program by the Army Corps of Engineers, we will be able to halt the destruction of what the Indians called the "Timeless Swamp."

(environmental science essay)

4. Finally, you can end with a quotation. If selected carefully, it can add weight to an already strong essay.

In *Walden,* Henry David Thoreau said, "The mass of men lead lives of quiet desperation." This sentiment is reinforced when you drive through the Hill District of our city. Perhaps the work of the men and women who run the health clinic on Jefferson Street cannot totally change this situation, but it can give us hope to know that some people, at least, are working for the betterment of us all.

(public health essay)

STAGE THREE: WRITING AND REVISION

When you finally begin drafting your essay, your major concern should be getting your ideas down on paper. At this point, you should not let worries about sentence proportion or word choice interfere with your flow of ideas. All you want to do is to keep your momentum until you finish the first draft. Later, when you write the second or third draft, you can polish your writing, making sure as you revise that each part does what it should do.

Remember that revision is not something you do after your paper is finished. It is a continuing process during which you consider the logic and clarity of your ideas as well as their effective and correct expression. Thus, revision is more than proofreading or editing, crossing out one word and substituting another; it may involve extensive addition, deletion, and reordering of whole sentences or paragraphs as you reconsider what you want to communicate to your audience.

After you have written your first draft, you should put it aside for several hours or even a day or two, if you have the time. This "cooling off" period enables you to distance yourself from your essay so that you can go back to it and read it more objectively. Then, when you read it again, you can begin to revise.

If you have time, you can start your revising by setting up a revision checklist and applying it to your essay. As you move systematically from the whole essay to the individual paragraphs to the sentences and words, you can assess your paper's effectiveness. First, check your thesis statement to see if it is still accurate. Is it clear and specific? Does it take a stand? If you departed from your original goal while you were writing, you will need either to revise the thesis so that it accurately sums up the ideas and information contained in your essay or to remove any unrelated sections—or to revise them so that they are relevant to your thesis.

Next, look at your body paragraphs to see if they need strengthening. Are they unified? Coherent? Well developed? Do the points you make support your topic sentences and your thesis? Are they themselves convincingly supported? Would other points be better? You might have to add more facts or examples to one paragraph to make it as strong as the others.

Consider your introductory and concluding strategies. Are they appropriate for your material, your audience, and your purpose? Do they reinforce your thesis?

Now look over your sentences. Are they correct? Effective? Interesting? Are there any sentences that might be added or deleted or relocated?

Consider the words you use. Are there any additions or substitutions you feel you should make?

Only now, after doing all your revision, should you go back and edit your essay. Polish your sentence structure, check your spelling, and make sure your punctuation and grammar are correct. Revision can take a lot of time, so don't be discouraged if you have to go through three or four drafts of your essay before you feel it is ready to hand in.

Even if you do not have time to reconsider your written work this thoroughly, you might want to check the logic of your essay's structure by making an after-the-fact outline. Such an outline of what you have actually written can be useful as a revision tool. Either a scratch outline or a more formal one can show you whether any important points have been omitted or misplaced. An outline can also show you whether your essay follows the pattern of development you have chosen. Finally, an outline can clarify for you the relationship between your thesis and your support paragraphs.

Another revision strategy you might find helpful is to seek peer criticism—in other words, to ask a friend to read your essay and comment on it. Sometimes peer criticism can be quite formal. An instructor may require students to exchange papers and evaluate their classmates' work according to certain standards, perhaps by completing a formal checklist. More often, however, peer criticism is informal. Even if your friend is not as good a student as you are, or is unfamiliar with your material, he or she can still tell you honestly whether you are getting your point across—and maybe even advise you on how to communicate more effectively. (Of course, your friend can only be your reader, not your ghost writer.)

How you revise—what specific strategies you decide to use—depends upon your own preference, your instructor's directions, and the time you have. Like the rest of the writing process, revision varies from student to student and from assignment to assignment.

The following two drafts of an essay were written by a student, Michael Ginsberg, for his class in business management. His assignment was to choose a local corporation and, in about five hundred words, discuss two or three of its management problems. He was able to do this easily because he had already analyzed the management structure of Acme Power and Light Company for his work-study project. Michael realized that the assignment itself suggested a thesis (company X has management problems) and a pattern of development (example). As part of his process of invention, Michael prepared this outline before he began writing his essay:

Introduction:	Thesis—Acme Power and Light has management problems.
Example 1:	Too many managers
Example 2:	Long record of bad management decisions
Example 3:	Poor customer relations
Conclusion:	Restatement of thesis

Here is the rough draft of his essay:

ACME POWER AND LIGHT

Introduction: When the city said, "Let there be   1
Quotation   light," Acme was ready. Acme Power and

Thesis   Light Corporation has supplied the
city's power since 1962, when it was
formed as a city owned and subsidized
company. During the years since its inception, Acme has consistently lost
money despite a yearly subsidy by the
taxpayer. This financial trouble
is no doubt due to Acme's management
practices, which are downright
shocking.

Examples 1   Acme has too many managers and has   2
and 2   made bad decisions that have cost consumers tens of millions of dollars.
During the last ten years, the company
has increased its middle- and upper-
level management by two and one half
times and built a costly atomic power
plant to meet a projected increase in
demand for electricity. This proliferation of management has added almost $5
million in salaries and benefits to the
company's expenses, and the power plant
cost another $75 million.

Example 3   Perhaps the most blatant management   3
problem Acme has is its seemingly cal-
lous attitude toward consumers. On any
given day, Acme is flooded by hundreds
of calls about errors in billing.

Conclusion   It is clear that Acme's financial   4
problems are costing the consumer too
much.

Revising the Rough Draft

The Introduction.   The day after he wrote his draft, Michael analyzed it and decided what he wanted to revise. First, he reconsidered his catchy opening. Although he thought his opening would have been excellent in another situation, he decided it was inappropriate for his practical, business-minded audience and the no-nonsense purpose of his assignment. Next, he realized that, since all his points about Acme were negative, his neutral audience might think he was being a little too hard on the company. Instead of blaming everything on management, he decided to introduce the company's financial problems more fairly so that his thesis would seem more reasonable. He also reconsidered his title because he decided that it did not describe his essay as precisely as it might.

The Body Paragraphs.   Although Michael knew he had outlined three fairly good examples of the company's poor management practices, he discovered he had jumbled together the first two examples—too many managers and bad decisions—while he was writing. As a result, he suspected that his second paragraph blurred his ideas, and he decided to revise it so that each example was developed in its own separate paragraph. Finally, he reviewed his third example—the company's attitude toward customers—and concluded that it was insufficiently developed. Just mentioning the phone calls did not support his assertion that Acme was "callous toward customers," so he decided to add more information here.

The Conclusion.   Rather than giving his readers a feeling of closure or providing them with something to think about, Michael knew that he had simply quit writing. He felt that his single concluding sentence was too brief and abrupt. Most importantly, he realized that it did not restate his thesis about Acme's management practices. Instead, it left his readers thinking solely about Acme's financial difficulties. Since Michael knew that his audience would remain unconvinced if he let them forget the thrust of his argument, he decided to completely rewrite his last paragraph.

After his careful analysis, Michael reordered and expanded his original paper in this final draft:

THE MANAGEMENT PRACTICES OF

ACME POWER AND LIGHT

Introduction: Acme Power and Light Corporation has   1
Direct approach   supplied the city's power since 1962

when it was formed as a city owned and
subsidized company. During the years
since its inception, Acme has consistently lost money despite a sizable
yearly subsidy from the taxpayers. It
would be unfair to single Acme out for
criticism because it suffers the ills
that all public utilities face--anti-
quated equipment and increased operating costs. But there is one area where
Thesis Acme can be faulted, and this is in the
(revised) quality of its management. Even a cursory examination of this company re-
veals management practices that are
downright shocking.

Example 1   One management problem Acme has is   2
obvious--too many managers. During the
last ten years, the company has increased the number of middle- and up-
per-level management employees by two
and one half times. This increase occurred even though Acme's area of
service actually decreased. This proliferation of management has added almost $5 million in annual salaries and
benefits to the company's expenses
which, of course, the consumers are required to absorb.

Example 2   Another management problem Acme has   3
is its long record of bad decisions
that have cost consumers tens of millions of dollars. An example was the
decision ten years ago to construct an
atomic power plant to meet a projected
increase in demand for electricity. De-

spite subsequent projections of decreasing energy demands, Acme proceeded
with the project. As a result, $75 mil-
lion later thay have an atomic power
plant that operates at 25 percent capacity because the demand for electricity has gone down instead of up.

Example 3   Perhaps the most blatant management   4
problem Acme has is its inability to
handle customer complaints. On a given
day, Acme is flooded by hundreds of
calls about errors in billing, equipment malfunction, or any number of
other complaints. As a recent newspaper
article asserts, the majority of these
problems result from negligence or from
Acme's inability to supervise its employees adequately. If this were not
enough, statistics provided by the Better Business Bureau show that it takes
between two and three service calls for
Acme fully to correct most problems.
The cost of this poor management represents about 20 percent of Acme's operating budget.

Conclusion   These are just a few examples of the   5
problems that Acme Power and Light has.
Restatement In any private corporation, such inef-
of thesis   ficiency would lead to stockholder
charges of mismanagement or to bank-
ruptcy. But because Acme is owned by
the city, it is kept afloat by taxpayer
money and regular rate increases. Price
increases caused by inflation and ris-

```
ing fuel costs affect all of us, in-
cluding corporations, and must be ac-
cepted, but increases caused by
mismanagement should be unacceptable to
everyone.
```

Reviewing the Final Draft

The Introduction. Michael's introduction follows the direct approach discussed earlier. Because he felt that a paper for a management course should sound businesslike, he wisely chose to eliminate the rough draft's opening. His introduction is straightforward and simple. He begins by briefly outlining the history of Acme Power and Light Company and moves right into his thesis statement that the company has "management practices that are downright shocking." In the process, Michael demonstrates to his audience that he is reasonable by granting that Acme has some of the problems every public corporation has. Still, he maintains that poor management, the subject of his paper, is something different.

The Body Paragraphs. Michael supports his thesis by presenting examples of Acme Power and Light Company's inefficient management. He now presents each example in a separate paragraph and introduces each paragraph with a clearly stated topic sentence. Following each topic sentence are facts to support it. Perhaps the major weakness of his paper is that he could have used still more supporting data in his first and second body paragraphs. Although his third body paragraph has been adequately expanded, he presents only one example in each of the preceding paragraphs to support his assertions that Acme has too many managers and that it has a long record of bad decisions. Although they are good examples, they are not enough in themselves to convince his audience that what he asserts is reasonable.

The Conclusion. In his conclusion, Michael now not only restates his thesis but also restates his essay's main points. Because his essay is actually a report on the management status of Acme Power and Light, he wants to be sure that his audience does not forget his thesis or the implications of the material he has presented. To make sure, he ends his conclusion with a statement designed to stay with his readers. Fuel costs and inflation we have to put up with, he says, but increased costs caused by mismanagement are unacceptable to everyone.

SUMMARY

The following list can be used as a checklist when you write. Keep in mind that, as you become a more confident writer, you will develop your own approaches to the writing process.

- Make sure you understand your assignment.
- Establish the limits of your subject.
- Move from subject to topic by using questions for probing.
- Brainstorm to generate ideas.
- Select and group your ideas.
- Formulate a thesis.
- Arrange your material.
- Write and revise your essay.

Each of the essays in the chapters that follow is organized around one dominant pattern. It is not at all unusual, however, to find more than one pattern used in a single essay. For example, a narrative essay might contain an introduction that is descriptive. As you can see, these patterns are not to be followed blindly but should be adapted to your subject, your audience, and your writing occasion.

2

Narration

WHAT IS NARRATION?

A narrative tells a story by presenting a sequence of events. Narration can be the dominant pattern in many types of writing—formal, such as history, biography, autobiography, and journalism, as well as less formal, such as personal letters and entries in diaries and journals. Narration is also an essential part of casual conversation, and it may dominate tall tales, speeches, and shaggy-dog stories, as well as news and feature stories presented on television. In short, any time you "tell what happened," you are using narration.

Although a narrative may be written for its own sake—that is, simply to recount events—in most college writing narration is used for a purpose, and a sequence of events is presented to prove a point. For instance, in a narrative essay about your first date, your purpose may be to show your readers that dating is a bizarre and often unpleasant ritual. Accordingly, you do not simply "tell the story" of your date. Rather, you select and arrange details of the evening that show your readers why dating is bizarre and unpleasant.

Often, too, narrative writing may be part of an essay that is not primarily a narrative. In an argumentative essay in support of stricter gun-control legislation, for example, you may devote one or two paragraphs to a story of a child killed with a handgun. These narrative paragraphs, though only a small portion of the essay, still have a definite purpose. They support your point that stricter gun-control laws are needed.

In this chapter, however, we are concerned with narration when it is the dominant pattern in a piece of writing. During your college career, you will have many assignments that call for such writing. In an English composition class, for instance, you may be asked to write about an experience that was important to your development as an adult; in European history, you may need to relate the events that led to Napoleon's defeat at the Battle of Waterloo; in a technical writing class, you may be asked to write a letter of complaint reviewing in detail a company's negligent actions. In each of these situations (as well as in case studies for business management classes, reports for criminal justice classes, and many additional assignments), the piece of writing has a structure that is primarily narrative, and the narrative is presented not for its own sake but for a specified purpose.

The skills you develop in narrative writing will also be helpful to you in other kinds of writing. A process essay, such as an account of a laboratory experiment, is like narration in that it outlines a series of steps in chronological order; a cause-and-effect essay, such as your answer on an economics midterm that directs you to "analyze American monetary policy during the Great Depression," also resembles narrative in that it traces a sequence of events. A process essay, however, presents events to explain how to do something, and a cause-and-effect essay presents them to explain how they are related. (Process essays and cause-and-effect essays will be dealt with in chapters 4 and 5, respectively.) Writing both process and cause-and-effect essays will be easier if you master narration, telling what events took place.

Narrative Detail

Narratives, like other types of writing, need rich, specific detail to be convincing. Each detail should help form a picture for the reader; even exact times, dates, and geographical locations can be helpful. Look, for example, at the following excerpt from the essay "My Mother Never Worked," which appears in its complete form later in this chapter:

> In the winter she sewed night after night, endlessly, begging cast-off clothing from relatives, ripping apart coats, dresses, blouses, and trousers to remake them to fit her four daughters and son. Every morning and every evening she milked cows, fed pigs and calves, cared for chickens, picked eggs, cooked meals, washed dishes, scrubbed floors, and tended and loved her children. In the spring she planted a garden once more, dragging pails of water to nourish and sustain the vegetables for the family. In 1936 she lost a baby in her sixth month.

In this excerpt, the list of details makes the narrative genuine and convincing. The central figure in the narrative is a busy, productive woman, and the readers know this because they are presented with a specific list of her actions.

Narrative Variety

Because narratives are often told from one person's perspective and because they usually present a series of events in chronological order, a constant danger is that all the sentences will begin to sound alike: "She sewed dresses . . . She milked cows . . . She fed pigs . . . She fed calves . . . She cared for chickens . . ." A narrative without sentence variety may affect your readers like a ride down a monotonous stretch of highway. You can avoid this monotony by varying your sentence structure: "In the winter she sewed night after night, endlessly . . . Every morning and every evening she milked cows, fed pigs and calves, cared for chickens . . ."

Narrative Order

Most narratives present events in exactly the order in which they occurred, moving from beginning to end, from first event to last. Whether or not you follow a strict chronological order, though, depends on the purpose of your narrative. If you are writing a straightforward account of a historical event or presenting a series of poor management practices, you will probably want to move efficiently from beginning to end. Often, however, in writing personal experience essays, you may choose to engage your reader's interest by beginning with a key event from the middle of your story, or even from the end, and then presenting the events that led up to it. In fictional narratives or in personal experience essays, you may also begin in the present and then use a series of flashbacks, shifts into the past, to tell your story. Whatever ordering scheme you use, it should shape and direct your narrative. Without some plan for clear and orderly progression, your readers will be unable to follow your story.

Verb tense is an extremely important clue in writing that recounts events in a fixed order because tenses show the temporal relationships of actions—earlier, simultaneous, later. When you write a narrative, you must be especially careful to keep verb tense consistent and accurate so your reader can easily understand the time sequence. Naturally, there are times when you must shift tense to reflect an actual time shift in your narrative. For instance, a flashback may require a shift from present to past tense. But it is important to avoid unnecessary shifts in verb tense because such unwarranted shifts will make your narrative confusing.

Together with verb tenses, transitions—connecting words or phrases—are the most precise way you can show the correct sequence of events. Transitions can indicate the order in which events in a narrative occurred (*first, second, after that, next, then, later*) or their simultaneous occurrence (*at the same time, meanwhile*). Transitional words and phrases can also show how much time has passed between events (*just then* or *three years later*). Without these guides, your essay would lack coherence, and your readers would be unsure of the correct sequence of events. Other transitions commonly used to signal shifts in time include *immediately, soon, before, earlier, after, afterward, now,* and *finally.*

STRUCTURING A NARRATIVE ESSAY

Like other essays, narratives usually have an introduction, a body, and a conclusion. A pure narrative may tell a story for its own sake or in order to create a particular mood or effect, without trying to prove a point. On the other hand, most often you will want to use narrative for a particular purpose—for instance, to support an argument. Thus, each of your narrative essays will probably have an arguable thesis which, if it is explicitly stated, will appear in the *introduction*. Once the thesis or significance of your narrative is established in the introduction, the *body* of your essay will recount the series of events that makes up your narrative, following a clear and orderly plan. Finally, the *conclusion* will give your reader the sense that your story is complete, perhaps by restating your thesis if it is explicit. Thus, to plan a five-paragraph narrative essay, you would follow this outline:

¶1　Introduction—including thesis
¶2　First event or events in sequence
¶3　Next event or events in sequence
¶4　Last event or events in sequence
¶5　Conclusion—including restatement of thesis

Let's suppose that you are assigned a short history paper about the Battle of Waterloo. You plan to support the thesis that if Napoleon had kept more troops in reserve, he might have defeated the

British troops under Wellington. Based on this thesis, you decide that the best way to organize your paper is to present the five major phases of the battle in strict chronological sequence. An outline of your essay might look like this:

¶1 Introduction—thesis: Had Napoleon kept more troops in reserve, he might have broken Wellington's line with another infantry attack and thus reversed the outcome of the Battle of Waterloo.

¶2 Phase one of the battle: Napoleon attacks the Château of Hougoumont.

¶3 Phase two of the battle: The French infantry attacks the British lines.

¶4 Phase three of the battle: The French cavalry stages a series of charges aganst the British lines that had not been attacked before. Napoleon commits his reserves.

¶5 Phase four of the battle: The French capture La Haye Sainte, their first success of the day but an advantage which Napoleon, having committed troops elsewhere, could not maintain without reserves.

¶6 Phase five of the battle: The French infantry is decisively defeated by the combined thrust of the British infantry and the remaining British cavalry.

¶7 Conclusion—restatement of thesis: Had Napoleon had reinforcements ready to capitalize on his capture of La Haye Sainte, he could have broken through the British lines with another infantry attack.

By discussing the five phases of the battle in chronological order, you clearly demonstrate the validity of your thesis. In turning your outline into a historical narrative, you realize that exact details, dates, times, and geographical locations will be extremely important. Without them, your mere assertions will be open to question. In addition, you plan to select appropriate transitional words and phrases carefully and to pay special attention to verb tenses to keep your readers aware of the order in which the events of the battle took place.

The following essay is typical of the informal narrative writing many freshmen are asked to do in English composition classes. It was written by a student, Derek Wilson, in response to the assignment "Write an essay about an event which had a significant effect upon you."

DO I BELIEVE IN MIRACLES?

Introduction (implied thesis)

Do miracles still happen? Do supernatural healings still take place? Kathryn Kuhlman was known as the "love healer," and her famous words were "I believe in miracles." But these strange occurrences were reserved for famous people; everyone knows that. At least this is what I thought until I was sixteen years old—when I saw the impossible happen.

Narrative begins

It was on a Friday, just after dinner. I was reading when my mother came into the living room.

"Derek," she said, "will you take your aunt Elitia to the gospel meeting? I promised I would take her, but I'm just too busy."

"But, Mama, why would I want to go there?"

"Derek," she snapped, "I don't want any more arguments. You know your aunt is sick, and she can't go on her own. You go on, get dressed, and take her."

Flashback

Aunt Elitia had been sick for years, but during the last few months she had gotten worse. The doctor finally convinced her to go into the hospital for tests, and when they were completed he told her she had a tumor. My aunt had always been religious, but when she heard the doctor's diagnosis she stopped going to the Baptist Church and began attending a faith-healing service. I thought the whole thing was ridiculous, but I did feel sorry for the old woman, so I agreed to take her that Friday night.

Narrative continues The Faith Gospel Healing Church was [7] an old store that had been gutted, painted, and filled with chairs. We ar-rived late, and the service was in full swing. The preacher was singing a hymn, and the congregation was swaying and clapping in time to the music. As we sat down, the music ended, and the healing part of the service began. The preacher read a verse from the Bible about praying and healing and then be-gan talking about Jesus and faith. After what seemed like an hour, he asked those in the audience who wanted to be healed to stand up. My aunt struggled to her feet and leaned on me for support.

Ten women were standing. The preacher [8] began at the front of the room. He moved from person to person. He took each one by the arm. He placed his hand on each one's head and prayed. As he touched them, they would close their eyes, begin to moan or pray, and fi-nally declare loudly that they were healed.

Climax of the narrative As I watched the preacher slowly come [9] closer, I began to wonder why I had ever let my mother talk me into this. Suddenly, the preacher was standing in front of us, and every person in the

church was looking. I felt very hot,
and sweat ran down my face. I didn't
hear a word the preacher said until he
was almost finished. ". . . Father heal
this woman's tumor. In Jesus' name,
Amen."

One minute I was holding my aunt and   10
thinking I was the biggest fool in the
world, and the next I was struggling to
keep her tremendous bulk from collaps-
ing onto the seats. She had fainted.
The preacher and several men from the
congregation carried her prostrate body
to the open door of the church.

"I'm healed," she mumbled. "Praise   11
the Lord. I'm healed," she said over
and over.

"Sure you are, Aunt Elitia," I said.   12
"Just relax. You'll be all right."

Three weeks later my aunt went back   13
into the hospital for more tests. And
to everyone's surprise, except Aunt
Elitia's, the doctors found that the
tumor had receded and that there was no
need for an operation. She was positive
that a miracle had taken place and that
God, because of her faith, had healed
her.

**Conclusion
(return to
implied thesis)**   In spite of my experience, I remain   14
unconvinced. I still would rather go to
a doctor than the corner storefront
church. But I do not dismiss what I saw
three years ago with my own eyes. Whenever I see a faith healer on television

```
on Sunday morning, I no longer laugh. I
watch and listen and remember when I
saw the impossible happen.
```

Points for Special Attention

Thesis.   Because the assignment does not call for pure narrative but rather for narrative that will illustrate a point, Derek Wilson's introduction includes an implied thesis: miracles do happen. The narrative itself begins with the second paragraph.

Structure.   Derek recounts the events of his narrative in chronological order, with only one flashback. What makes his story effective is that he builds to a climax, a moment of high tension and excitement near the end. (Not all narratives require a climax, and several of the essays that follow have none. But when the story hinges on an important or spectacular event, a climax is appropriate.)

Detail.   Personal narratives, like Derek's, are especially dependent upon detail because the authors ask the audience to see and hear and feel what they did. In order to present a picture of the scene, Derek supplies all the significant details he can remember: the description of the church, the swaying of the congregation, the physical bulk of his aunt. He could have presented even more (a description of his aunt's face, her clothes, or the preacher's appearance), but he chose not to because he wanted to keep his account focused on the events that related to his thesis.

Dialogue.   Derek characterizes himself, his mother, the preacher, and Aunt Elitia through bits of dialogue. As a result, his narrative is more interesting and immediate than it would be if he simply described events. (In order to avoid confusion, Derek begins a new paragraph each time a character speaks.) Using convincing dialogue is one way to give your audience a sense of reality. Of course, dialogue is rarely used in exams or academic papers, but when it is appropriate (as it is in this personal experience essay), it gives the narrative an added dimension.

Sentence Variety.   In most of his essay, Derek's sentences are sufficiently varied to sustain reader interest. In one section, however, he could have revised to vary his sentence structure by combining some of his sentences. For instance,

Ten women were standing. The preacher began at the front of the room. He moved from person to person. He took each one by the arm. He placed his hand on each one's head and prayed.

could have become

Ten women were standing. The preacher, beginning at the front of the room, moved from person to person, taking each one by the arm, placing his hand on her head, and praying.

This version eliminates the monotonous string of choppy sentences. It puts the preacher's actions into one sentence and creates more variety by setting off the long sentence about the preacher against the short sentence about the women. The vitality and movement created by this change help to sustain and direct a reader's attention.

Verb Tense.   Derek knows that chronological order is very important in narrative and that it is essential that he avoid unwarranted shifts in verb tense that could confuse his readers. (Wouldn't you have been puzzled if he had said, "I *thought* the whole thing was ridiculous, but I *do* feel sorry for the old woman so I *agreed* to take her"?) Derek also realizes that a shift in tense is necessary to indicate a time shift in his narrative. For instance, at the beginning of the sixth paragraph he changes from the past tense of paragraph five (*snapped*) to the past perfect (*had been*). He does this in a brief flashback which introduces some background events that had occurred before the Friday evening he is writing about. The flashback and the corresponding shift in tense make clear that Aunt Elitia was sick *before* she heard the news about the tumor (Aunt Elitia *had been* sick) and also that she was religious *before* the doctor's diagnosis (My aunt *had* always *been* religious).

Transitions.   In "Do I Believe in Miracles?" Derek effectively uses transitional words like *after, then, as, when,* and *suddenly,* as well as transitional expressions like *three weeks later.* For the most part, however, he relies on chronological order to clarify the sequence of events for his reader. Still, there are places where the addition of a transitional word or phrase could have helped. For instance, compare Derek's "We arrived late, and the service was in full swing" with a possible revision, "When we arrived, the service was in full swing." On the other hand, see how effectively his "One minute I was holding my aunt . . . and the next I was struggling . . ." carries the reader along with the action of the story.

The following selections illustrate the many possibilities open to writers of narrative. Most of these selections have a thesis, but in several cases the thesis is implied rather than explicitly stated.

FINISHING SCHOOL

Maya Angelou

*Maya Angelou (originally Marguerita Johnson) was born in 1928
in St. Louis and grew up in Stamps, Arkansas, with her brother
Bailey and her grandmother ("Momma"), who owned a general store.
Later Angelou studied dance and toured Europe and Africa performing in* Porgy and Bess. *She also starred in the off-Broadway
play* The Blacks, *was Northern Coordinator for the Southern Christian Leadership Conference, worked as a newspaper reporter in Egypt
and Ghana, and wrote four autobiographical volumes and several
books of poetry. "Finishing School" is a chapter from* I Know Why
the Caged Bird Sings *(1969), Angelou's vividly evocative memoir
of her childhood. In this selection, she explores a theme she returns
to often: her inability to understand the ways of the town's whites
and their inability to understand her.*

Recently a white woman from Texas, who would quickly describe 1
herself as a liberal, asked me about my hometown. When I told her
that in Stamps my grandmother had owned the only Negro general
merchandise store since the turn of the century, she exclaimed,
"Why, you were a debutante." Ridiculous and even ludicrous. But
Negro girls in small Southern towns, whether poverty-stricken or
just munching along on a few of life's necessities, were given as
extensive and irrelevant preparations for adulthood as rich white
girls shown in magazines. Admittedly the training was not the same.
While white girls learned to waltz and sit gracefully with a tea cup
balanced on their knees, we were lagging behind, learning the mid-
Victorian values with very little money to indulge them. . . .

We were required to embroider and I had trunkfuls of colorful 2
dishtowels, pillowcases, runners and handkerchiefs to my credit. I
mastered the art of crocheting and tatting, and there was a lifetime's supply of dainty doilies that would never be used in sacheted
dresser drawers. It went without saying that all girls could iron and
wash, but the finer touches around the home, like setting a table
with real silver, baking roasts and cooking vegetables without meat,
had to be learned elsewhere. Usually at the source of those habits.
During my tenth year, a white woman's kitchen became my finishing school.

Mrs. Viola Cullinan was a plump woman who lived in a three- 3
bedroom house somewhere behind the post office. She was singu-
larly unattractive until she smiled, and then the lines around her
eyes and mouth which made her look perpetually dirty disappeared,
and her face looked like the mask of an impish elf. She usually
rested her smile until late afternoon when her women friends dropped
in and Miss Glory, the cook, served them cold drinks on the closed-
in porch.

The exactness of her house was inhuman. This glass went here 4
and only here. That cup had its place and it was an act of impudent
rebellion to place it anywhere else. At twelve o'clock the table was
set. At 12:15 Mrs. Cullinan sat down to dinner (whether her husband had arrived or not). At 12:16 Miss Glory brought out the food.

It took me a week to learn the difference between a salad plate, 5
a bread plate and a dessert plate.

Mrs. Cullinan kept up the tradition of her wealthy parents. She 6
was from Virginia. Miss Glory, who was a descendant of slaves that
had worked for the Cullinans, told me her history. She had married
beneath her (according to Miss Glory). Her husband's family hadn't
had their money very long and what they had "didn't 'mount to
much."

As ugly as she was, I thought privately, she was lucky to get a 7
husband above or beneath her station. But Miss Glory wouldn't let
me say a thing against her mistress. She was very patient with me,
however, over the housework. She explained the dishware, silverware and servants' bells. The large round bowl in which soup was
served wasn't a soup bowl, it was a tureen. There were goblets,
sherbet glasses, ice-cream glasses, wine glasses, green glass coffee
cups with matching saucers, and water glasses. I had a glass to
drink from, and it sat with Miss Glory's on a separate shelf from
the others. Soup spoons, gravy boat, butter knives, salad forks and
carving platter were additions to my vocabulary and in fact almost
represented a new language. I was fascinated with the novelty, with
the fluttering Mrs. Cullinan and her Alice-in-Wonderland house.

Her husband remains, in my memory, undefined. I lumped him 8
with all the other white men that I had ever seen and tried not to
see.

On our way home one evening, Miss Glory told me that Mrs. 9
Cullinan couldn't have children. She said that she was too delicate-
boned. It was hard to imagine bones at all under those layers of fat.
Miss Glory went on to say that the doctor had taken out all her lady
organs. I reasoned that a pig's organs included the lungs, heart and
liver, so if Mrs. Cullinan was walking around without those essen-

tials, it explained why she drank alcohol out of unmarked bottles. She was keeping herself embalmed.

When I spoke to Bailey about it, he agreed that I was right, but he also informed me that Mr. Cullinan had two daughters by a colored lady and that I knew them very well. He added that the girls were the spitting image of their father. I was unable to remember what he looked like, although I had just left him a few hours before, but I thought of the Coleman girls. They were very light-skinned and certainly didn't look very much like their mother (no one ever mentioned Mr. Coleman). 10

My pity for Mrs. Cullinan preceded me the next morning like the Cheshire cat's smile. Those girls, who could have been her daughters, were beautiful. They didn't have to straighten their hair. Even when they were caught in the rain, their braids still hung down straight like tamed snakes. Their mouths were pouty little cupid's bows. Mrs. Cullinan didn't know what she missed. Or maybe she did. Poor Mrs. Cullinan. 11

For weeks after, I arrived early, left late and tried very hard to make up for her barrenness. If she had had her own children, she wouldn't have had to ask me to run a thousand errands from her back door to the back door of her friends. Poor old Mrs. Cullinan. 12

Then one evening Miss Glory told me to serve the ladies on the porch. After I set the tray down and turned toward the kitchen, one of the women asked, "What's your name, girl?" It was the speckled-faced one. Mrs. Cullinan said, "She doesn't talk much. Her name's Margaret." 13

"Is she dumb?" 14

"No. As I understand it, she can talk when she wants to but she's usually quiet as a little mouse. Aren't you, Margaret?" 15

I smiled at her. Poor thing. No organs and couldn't even pronounce my name correctly. 16

"She's a sweet little thing, though." 17

"Well, that may be, but the name's too long. I'd never bother myself. I'd call her Mary if I was you." 18

I fumed into the kitchen. That horrible woman would never have the chance to call me Mary because if I was starving I'd never work for her. . . . 19

That evening I decided to write a poem on being white, fat, old and without children. It was going to be a tragic ballad. I would have to watch her carefully to capture the essence of her loneliness and pain. 20

The very next day, she called me by the wrong name. Miss Glory and I were washing up the lunch dishes when Mrs. Cullinan came to the doorway. "Mary?" 21

Miss Glory asked, "Who?"   22

Mrs. Cullinan, sagging a little, knew and I knew. "I want Mary   23
to go down to Mrs. Randall's and take her some soup. She's not been
feeling well for a few days."

Miss Glory's face was a wonder to see. "You mean Margaret,   24
ma'am. Her name's Margaret."

"That's too long. She's Mary from now on. Heat that soup from   25
last night and put it in the china tureen and, Mary, I want you to
carry it carefully."

Every person I knew had a hellish horror of being "called out of   26
his name." It was a dangerous practice to call a Negro anything
that could be loosely construed as insulting because of the centuries
of their having been called niggers, jigs, dinges, blackbirds, crows,
boots and spooks.

Miss Glory had a fleeting second of feeling sorry for me. Then as   27
she handed me the hot tureen she said, "Don't mind, don't pay that
no mind. Sticks and stones may break your bones, but words . . .
You know, I been working for her for twenty years."

She held the back door open for me. "Twenty years. I wasn't much   28
older than you. My name used to be Hallelujah. That's what Ma
named me, but my mistress give me 'Glory,' and it stuck. I likes it
better too."

I was in the little path that ran behind the houses when Miss   29
Glory shouted, "It's shorter too."

For a few seconds it was a tossup over whether I would laugh   30
(imagine being named Hallelujah) or cry (imagine letting some white
woman rename you for her convenience). My anger saved me from
either outburst. I had to quit the job, but the problem was going to
be how to do it. Momma wouldn't allow me to quit for just any
reason.

"She's a peach. That woman is a real peach." Mrs. Randall's maid   31
was talking as she took the soup from me, and I wondered what her
name used to be and what she answered to now.

For a week I looked into Mrs. Cullinan's face as she called me   32
Mary. She ignored my coming late and leaving early. Miss Glory
was a little annoyed because I had begun to leave egg yolk on the
dishes and wasn't putting much heart in polishing the silver. I hoped
that she would complain to our boss, but she didn't.

Then Bailey solved my dilemma..He had me describe the contents   33
of the cupboard and the particular plates she liked best. Her favorite
piece was a casserole shaped like a fish and the green glass coffee
cups. I kept his instructions in mind, so on the next day when Miss
Glory was hanging out clothes and I had again been told to serve
the old biddies on the porch, I dropped the empty serving tray. When

I heard Mrs. Cullinan scream, "Mary!" I picked up the casserole and two of the green glass cups in readiness. As she rounded the kitchen door I let them fall on the tiled floor.

I could never absolutely describe to Bailey what happened next, 34 because each time I got to the part where she fell on the floor and screwed up her ugly face to cry, we burst out laughing. She actually wobbled around on the floor and picked up shards of the cups and cried, "Oh, Momma. Oh, dear Gawd. It's Momma's china from Virginia. Oh, Momma, I sorry."

Miss Glory came running in from the yard and the women from 35 the porch crowded around. Miss Glory was almost as broken up as her mistress. "You mean to say she broke our Virginia dishes? What we gone do?"

Mrs. Cullinan cried louder, "That clumsy nigger. Clumsy little 36 black nigger."

Old speckled-face leaned down and asked, "Who did it, Viola? 37 Was it Mary? Who did it?"

Everything was happening so fast I can't remember whether her 38 action preceded her words, but I know that Mrs. Cullinan said, "Her name's Margaret, goddamn it, her name's Margaret." And she threw a wedge of the broken plate at me. It could have been the hysteria which put her aim off, but the flying crockery caught Miss Glory right over her ear and she started screaming.

I left the front door wide open so all the neighbors could hear. 39

Mrs. Cullinan was right about one thing. My name wasn't Mary. 40

COMPREHENSION

1. What is Angelou required to learn in the white woman's kitchen that serves as her finishing school? What things does she find unfamiliar in the household?

2. Why does Angelou feel sorry for Mrs. Cullinan at first? When does her attitude change?

3. Why does Mrs. Cullinan's friend recommend that Angelou be called "Mary"? Why does this upset Angelou so deeply?

4. When Angelou decides she wants to quit but realizes she can't quit "for just any reason," how does Bailey help her solve her dilemma?

5. What does Angelou actually learn through her experience? In what sense, then, does the kitchen really serve as a finishing school?

PURPOSE AND AUDIENCE

1. Is Angelou writing for Southerners, blacks, whites, or a general audience? Point to specific details to support your answer.

2. Angelou begins her narrative by summarizing a discussion between herself and a white woman. What is her purpose in doing this?

3. What is Angelou's thesis?

STYLE AND STRUCTURE

1. What image does the phrase *finishing school* usually produce? How is this ironic in view of its meaning in this selection?

2. How does Angelou signal the passage of time in this narrative? Identify some transitional phrases that show the passage of time.

3. How does the use of dialogue highlight the contrast between the black and white characters? In what way does this strengthen the narrative?

4. What details does Angelou use to describe Mrs. Cullinan and her home to the reader? How does this detailed description help advance the narrative?

5. What is Angelou's tone? Is she angry, amused, or matter-of-fact? Quote specific words and passages that illustrate the tone.

WRITING WORKSHOP

1. Think about a time in your life when an adult in a position of authority treated you unjustly. How did you react? Write a narrative essay in which you recount the situation and your responses. Would you act differently today? Explain.

2. What institution served as your "finishing school" in Angelou's sense of the words? Tell how you learned the skills you needed there.

MY MOTHER NEVER WORKED

Donna Smith-Yackel

Although this essay draws on personal experience, it makes a general point about what society thinks of "women's work." According to federal law, a woman who is a homemaker is entitled to Social Security benefits only through the earnings of her husband. Thus, a homemaker who becomes disabled receives no disability benefits, and her husband and children are allowed no survivors' benefits if she should die. Although this law is being challenged in the courts, a woman who does not work for wages outside the home is still not entitled to Social Security benefits in her own right. Without explicitly stating her thesis, Donna Smith-Yackel comments on this situation in her narrative.

"Social Security Office." (The voice answering the telephone sounds very self-assured.) 1

"I'm calling about . . . I . . . my mother just died . . . I was told to call you and see about a . . . death-benefit check, I think they call it. . . ." 2

"I see. Was your mother on Social Security? How old was she?" 3

"Yes . . . she was seventy-eight. . . ." 4

"Do you know her number?" 5

"No . . . I, ah . . . don't you have a record?" 6

"Certainly. I'll look it up. Her name?" 7

"Smith. Martha Smith. Or maybe she used Martha Ruth Smith. . . . Sometimes she used her maiden name . . . Martha Jerabek Smith." 8

"If you'd care to hold on, I'll check our records—it'll be a few minutes." 9

"Yes. . . ." 10

Her love letters—to and from Daddy—were in an old box, tied with ribbons and stiff, rigid-with-age leather thongs: 1918 through 1920; hers written on stationery from the general store she had worked in full-time and managed, single-handed, after her graduation from high school in 1913; and his, at first, on YMCA or Soldiers and Sailors Club stationery dispensed to the fighting men of World War I. He wooed her thoroughly and persistently by mail, and though she reciprocated all his feeling for her, she dreaded marriage. . . . 11

"It's so hard for me to decide when to have my wedding day— 12
that's all I've thought about these last two days. I have told you
dozens of times that I won't be afraid of married life, but when it
comes down to setting the date and then picturing myself a married
woman with half a dozen or more kids to look after, it just makes
me sick. . . . I am weeping right now—I hope that some day I can
look back and say how foolish I was to dread it all."

They married in February, 1921, and began farming. Their first 13
baby, a daughter, was born in January, 1922, when my mother was
26 years old. The second baby, a son, was born in March, 1923. They
were renting farms; my father, besides working his own fields, also
was a hired man for two other farmers. They had no capital initially,
and had to gain it slowly, working from dawn until midnight every
day. My town-bred mother learned to set hens and raise chickens,
feed pigs, milk cows, plant and harvest a garden, and can every
fruit and vegetable she could scrounge. She carried water nearly a
quarter of a mile from the well to fill her wash boilers in order to
do her laundry on a scrub board. She learned to shuck grain, feed
threshers, shock and husk corn, feed corn pickers. In September,
1925, the third baby came, and in June, 1927, the fourth child—
both daughters. In 1930, my parents had enough money to buy their
own farm, and that March they moved all their livestock and be-
longings themselves, 55 miles over rutted, muddy roads.

In the summer of 1930 my mother and her two eldest children 14
reclaimed a 40-acre field from Canadian thistles, by chopping them
all out with a hoe. In the other fields, when the oats and flax began
to head out, the green and blue of the crops were hidden by the
bright yellow of wild mustard. My mother walked the fields day
after day, pulling each mustard plant. She raised a new flock of
baby chicks—500—and she spaded up, planted, hoed, and harvested
a half-acre garden.

During the next spring their hogs caught cholera and died. No 15
cash that fall.

And in the next year the drought hit. My mother and father 16
trudged from the well to the chickens, the well to the calf pasture,
the well to the barn, and from the well to the garden. The sun came
out hot and bright, endlessly, day after day. The crops shriveled and
died. They harvested half the corn, and ground the other half, stalks
and all, and fed it to the cattle as fodder. With the price at four
cents a bushel for the harvested crop, they couldn't afford to haul
it into town. They burned it in the furnace for fuel that winter.

In 1934, in February, when the dust was still so thick in the 17
Minnesota air that my parents couldn't always see from the house

to the barn, their fifth child—a fourth daughter—was born. My father hunted rabbits daily, and my mother stewed them, fried them, canned them, and wished out loud that she could taste hamburger once more. In the fall the shotgun brought prairie chickens, ducks, pheasant, and grouse. My mother plucked each bird, carefully reserving the breast feathers for pillows.

In the winter she sewed night after night, endlessly, begging cast-off clothing from relatives, ripping apart coats, dresses, blouses, and trousers to remake them to fit her four daughters and son. Every morning and every evening she milked cows, fed pigs and calves, cared for chickens, picked eggs, cooked meals, washed dishes, scrubbed floors, and tended and loved her children. In the spring she planted a garden once more, dragging pails of water to nourish and sustain the vegetables for the family. In 1936 she lost a baby in her sixth month.

In 1937 her fifth daughter was born. She was 42 years old. In 1939 a second son, and in 1941 her eighth child—and third son.

But the war had come, and prosperity of a sort. The herd of cattle had grown to 30 head; she still milked morning and evening. Her garden was more than a half acre—the rains had come, and by now the Rural Electricity Administration and indoor plumbing. Still she sewed—dresses and jackets for the children, housedresses and aprons for herself, weekly patching of jeans, overalls, and denim shirts. She still made pillows, using the feathers she had plucked, and quilts every year—intricate patterns as well as patchwork, stitched as well as tied—all necessary bedding for her family. Every scrap of cloth too small to be used in quilts was carefully saved and painstakingly sewed together in strips to make rugs. She still went out in the fields to help with the haying whenever there was a threat of rain.

In 1959 my mother's last child graduated from high school. A year later the cows were sold. She still raised chickens and ducks, plucked feathers, made pillows, baked her own bread, and every year made a new quilt—now for a married child or for a grandchild. And her garden, that huge, undying symbol of sustenance, was as large and cared for as in all the years before. The canning, and now freezing, continued.

In 1969, on a June afternoon, mother and father started out for town so that she could buy sugar to make rhubarb jam for a daughter who lived in Texas. The car crashed into a ditch. She was paralyzed from the waist down.

In 1970 her husband, my father, died. My mother struggled to regain some competence and dignity and order in her life. At the rehabilitation institute, where they gave her physical therapy and trained her to live usefully in a wheelchair, the therapist told me: "She did fifteen pushups today—fifteen! She's almost seventy-five years old! I've never known a woman so strong!"

From her wheelchair she canned pickles, baked bread, ironed 24 clothes, wrote dozens of letters weekly to her friends and her "half dozen or more kids," and made three patchwork housecoats and one quilt. She made balls and balls of carpet rags—enough for five rugs. And kept all her love letters.

"I think I've found your mother's records—Martha Ruth Smith; 25 married to Ben F. Smith?"

"Yes, that's right." 26

"Well, I see that she was getting a widow's pension. . . ." 27

"Yes, that's right." 28

"Well, your mother isn't entitled to our $255 death benefit." 29

"Not entitled! But why?" 30

The voice on the telephone explains patiently: 31

"Well, you see—your mother never worked." 32

COMPREHENSION

1. Why wasn't Martha Smith eligible for a death benefit?

2. What kind of work did Martha Smith do while her children were growing up? How does the government define work?

PURPOSE AND AUDIENCE

1. What is the essay's thesis? Why is it never explicitly stated?

2. This essay appeared in *Ms.* magazine and other journals whose audiences are sympathetic to feminism. Could it just as easily have appeared in a magazine whose audience was not? Why or why not?

3. How can you tell that this essay's purpose is to persuade and not simply to entertain or to inform?

STYLE AND STRUCTURE

1. Is the title effective? Why or why not?

2. The author could have outlined her mother's life without framing it with the telephone conversation. Why does she include this frame?

3. This narrative piles details one on top of another almost like a list. For

instance, paragraph 13 says, "My town-bred mother learned to set hens and raise chickens, feed pigs, milk cows, plant and harvest a garden, and can every fruit and vegetable she could scrounge." Why does the author list so many details?

WRITING WORKSHOP

1. If you can, interview your mother or grandmother (or another woman you know who might remind you of Donna Smith-Yackel's mother) about her work, and write a chronological narrative based on what she tells you. Try to find a strong thesis that gives a point to your narrative.

2. Use a narrative to structure an essay that takes a stand on an issue you feel strongly about. For instance, should alimony be outlawed? Should nuclear power plants be closed? Should plagiarism be grounds for a student's expulsion from college?

3. Write Martha Smith's obituary as it might have appeared in her home-town newspaper. If you are not familiar with the form of an obituary, read a few in your local paper.

4. Write a narrative account of the worst job you ever had. Include a strong thesis.

ARIA: A MEMOIR OF A BILINGUAL CHILDHOOD

Richard Rodriguez

Born in 1944 to Mexican-American parents, Richard Rodriguez eventually went on to do graduate work in English Renaissance literature and teach at the University of California at Berkeley, often feeling he was an outsider. In a series of autobiographical essays revised and collected in The Hunger of Memory (1982), *Rodriguez explores his ambivalent feelings about what he gained—and lost— by leaving home. In this excerpt from an essay that was originally published in* The American Scholar, *Rodriguez recalls the conflicting pulls of home and school, family and outsiders, Spanish and English.*

I remember, to start with, that day in Sacramento, in a California now nearly thirty years past, when I first entered a classroom—able to understand about fifty stray English words. The third of four children, I had been preceded by my older brother and sister to a neighborhood Roman Catholic school. But neither of them had revealed very much about their classroom experiences. They left each morning and returned each afternoon, always together, speaking Spanish as they climbed the five steps to the porch. And their mysterious books, wrapped in brown shopping-bag paper, remained on the table next to the door, closed firmly behind them.

An accident of geography sent me to a school where all my classmates were white and many were the children of doctors and lawyers and business executives. On that first day of school, my classmates must certainly have been uneasy to find themselves apart from their families, in the first institution of their lives. But I was astonished. I was fated to be the "problem student" in class.

The nun said, in a friendly but oddly impersonal voice: "Boys and girls, this is Richard Rodriguez." (I heard her sound it out: *Rich-heard Road-ree-guess.*) It was the first time I had heard anyone say my name in English. "Richard," the nun repeated more slowly, writing my name down in her book. Quickly I turned to see my mother's face dissolve in a watery blur behind the pebbled-glass door. . . .

In the early years of my boyhood, my parents coped very well in America. My father had steady work. My mother managed at home. They were nobody's victims. When we moved to a house many blocks

55

from the Mexican-American section of town, they were not intimidated by those two or three neighbors who initially tried to make
us unwelcome. ("Keep your brats away from my sidewalk!") But
despite all they achieved, or perhaps because they had so much to
achieve, they lacked any deep feeling of ease, of belonging in public.
They regarded the people at work or in crowds as being very distant
from us. Those were the others, *los gringos*. That term was inter-
changeable in their speech with another, even more telling: *los
americanos*.

I grew up in a house where the only regular guests were my   5
relations. On a certain day, enormous families of relatives would
visit us, and there would be so many people that the noise and the
bodies would spill out to the backyard and onto the front porch. Then
for weeks no one would come. (If the doorbell rang, it was usually a
salesman.) Our house stood apart—gaudy yellow in a row of white
bungalows. We were the people with the noisy dog, the people who
raised chickens. We were the foreigners on the block. A few neighbors
would smile and wave at us. We waved back. But until I was seven
years old, I did not know the name of the old couple living next door
or the names of the kids living across the street.

In public, my father and mother spoke a hesitant, accented, and   6
not always grammatical English. And then they would have to strain,
their bodies tense, to catch the sense of what was rapidly said by
los gringos. At home, they returned to Spanish. The language of
their Mexican past sounded in counterpoint to the English spoken
in public. The words would come quickly, with ease. Conveyed through
those sounds was the pleasing, soothing, consoling reminder that
one was at home.

During those years when I was first learning to speak, my mother   7
and father addressed me only in Spanish; in Spanish I learned to
reply. By contrast, English (*inglés*) was the language I came to
associate with gringos, rarely heard in the house. I learned my first
words of English overhearing my parents speaking to strangers. At
six years of age, I knew just enough words for my mother to trust
me on errands to stores one block away—but no more.

I was then a listening child, careful to hear the very different   8
sounds of Spanish and English. Wide-eyed with hearing, I'd listen
to sounds more than to words. First, there were English (gringo)
sounds. So many words still were unknown to me that when the
butcher or the lady at the drugstore said something, exotic polysyllabic sounds would bloom in the midst of their sentences. Often
the speech of people in public seemed to me very loud, booming with

confidence. The man behind the counter would literally ask, "What can I do for you?" But by being so firm and clear, the sound of his voice said that he was a gringo; he belonged in public society. There were also the high, nasal notes of middle-class American speech— which I rarely am conscious of hearing today because I hear them so often, but could not stop hearing when I was a boy. Crowds at Safeway or at bus stops were noisy with the birdlike sounds of *los gringos.* I'd move away from them all—all the chirping chatter above me. . . .

But then there was Spanish: *español,* the language rarely heard 9 away from the house; *español,* the language which seemed to me therefore a private language, my family's language. To hear its sounds was to feel myself specially recognized as one of the family, apart from *los otros.* A simple remark, an inconsequential comment could convey that assurance. My parents would say something to me and I would feel embraced by the sounds of their words. Those sounds said: *I am speaking with ease in Spanish. I am addressing you in words I never use with los gringos. I recognize you as someone special, close, like no one outside. You belong with us. In the family. Ricardo.*

At the age of six, well past the time when most middle-class 10 children no longer notice the difference between sounds uttered at home and words spoken in public, I had a different experience. I lived in a world compounded of sounds. I was a child longer than most. I lived in a magical world, surrounded by sounds both pleasing and fearful. I shared with my family a language enchantingly pri- vate—different from that used in the city around us.

Just opening or closing the screen door behind me was an im- 11 portant experience. I'd rarely leave home all alone or without feel- ing reluctance. Walking down the sidewalk, under the canopy of tall trees, I'd warily notice the (suddenly) silent neighborhood kids who stood warily watching me. Nervously, I'd arrive at the grocery store to hear there the sounds of the gringo, reminding me that in this so-big world I was a foreigner. But if leaving home was never routine, neither was coming back. Walking toward our house, climbing the steps from the sidewalk, in summer when the front door was open, I'd hear voices beyond the screen door talking in Spanish. For a second or two I'd stay, linger there listening. Smil- ing, I'd hear my mother call out, saying in Spanish, "Is that you, Richard?" Those were her words, but all the while her sounds would assure me: *You are home now. Come closer inside. With us.* "Sí," I'd reply.

COMPREHENSION

1. What things made Rodriguez ill at ease on his first day of school?

2. What does Rodriguez mean when he says of his parents, "They were nobody's victims"?

3. In what ways was the Rodriguez family isolated from *los gringos*?

4. How did the sounds of English differ from the sounds of Spanish to the young Rodriguez?

5. Why did Spanish seem to Rodriguez to be a private language?

6. Why does Rodriguez say, "Just opening or closing the screen door behind me was an important experience"?

7. What traits do the English-speaking characters in Rodriguez's essay share?

PURPOSE AND AUDIENCE

1. What is Rodriguez's main point here?

2. This essay was addressed to a well-educated audience composed largely of *los gringos*. What concessions does Rodriguez make to this audience?

STYLE AND STRUCTURE

1. What is the function of the occasional words of Spanish Rodriguez uses?

2. Why are some passages italicized?

3. Rodriguez's essay does not move in a straight line from one time period or episode to the next; different periods and events blend together. How is this indefinite sense of time consistent with the aims of the essay?

4. How does the use of dialogue strengthen Rodriguez's essay?

5. In the first three paragraphs, Rodriguez uses the flashback technique to highlight an episode that occurred when he was a child. What would his essay have gained or lost if he had continued in chronological order from this early time period?

WRITING WORKSHOP

1. Think of a time when you felt like an outsider, isolated from a group. Write a narrative essay explaining what happened and how you felt.

2. Has anyone you know come from a family whose private language, unique culture, or special customs set them apart in any way from you and your family? Write a narrative explaining how these differences manifested themselves.

38 WHO SAW MURDER DIDN'T CALL THE POLICE

Martin Gansberg

*Martin Gansberg, a native of Brooklyn, New York, was born in 1920
and has been on the staff of the* New York Times *for some forty
years. He has also taught at Fairleigh Dickinson University and
written for popular magazines. The essay reprinted below was written for the* New York Times *two weeks after the murder it recounts.
The entire country was shocked by this incident, which has been
the subject of countless articles and editorials, as well as a television
movie. Indeed, the murder of Kitty Genovese is still cited today as
an example of public indifference. Gansberg's article is frequently
anthologized; its thesis, though not explicitly stated, retains its power.*

For more than half an hour 38 respectable, law-abiding citizens 1
in Queens watched a killer stalk and stab a woman in three separate attacks in Kew Gardens.

Twice their chatter and the sudden glow of their bedroom lights 2
interrupted him and frightened him off. Each time he returned,
sought her out, and stabbed her again. Not one person telephoned
the police during the assault; one witness called after the woman
was dead.

That was two weeks ago today. 3

Still shocked is Assistant Chief Inspector Frederick M. Lussen, 4
in charge of the borough's detectives and a veteran of 25 years of
homicide investigations. He can give a matter-of-fact recitation on
many murders. But the Kew Gardens slaying baffles him—not because it is a murder, but because the "good people" failed to call the
police.

"As we have reconstructed the crime," he said, "the assailant had 5
three chances to kill this woman during a 35-minute period. He
returned twice to complete the job. If we had been called when he
first attacked, the woman might not be dead now."

This is what the police say happened beginning at 3:20 A.M. in 6
the staid, middle-class, tree-lined Austin Street area:

Twenty-eight-year-old Catherine Genovese, who was called Kitty 7
by almost everyone in the neighborhood, was returning home from
her job as manager of a bar in Hollis. She parked her red Fiat in a

lot adjacent to the Kew Gardens Long Island Rail Road Station, facing Mowbray Place. Like many residents of the neighborhood, she had parked there day after day since her arrival from Connecticut a year ago, although the railroad frowns on the practice.

She turned off the lights of her car, locked the door, and started   8
to walk the 100 feet to the entrance of her apartment at 82–70 Austin Street, which is in a Tudor building, with stores in the first floor and apartments on the second.

The entrance to the apartment is in the rear of the building   9
because the front is rented to retail stores. At night the quiet neighborhood is shrouded in the slumbering darkness that marks most residential areas.

Miss Genovese noticed a man at the far end of the lot, near a   10
seven-story apartment house at 82–40 Austin Street. She halted. Then, nervously, she headed up Austin Street toward Lefferts Boulevard, where there is a call box to the 102nd Police Precinct in nearby Richmond Hill.

She got as far as a street light in front of a bookstore before the   11
man grabbed her. She screamed. Lights went on in the 10-story apartment house at 82–67 Austin Street, which faces the bookstore. Windows slid open and voices punctuated the early-morning stillness.

Miss Genovese screamed: "Oh, my God, he stabbed me! Please   12
help me! Please help me!"

From one of the upper windows in the apartment house, a man   13
called down: "Let that girl alone!"

The assailant looked up at him, shrugged, and walked down Aus-   14
tin Street toward a white sedan parked a short distance away. Miss Genovese struggled to her feet.

Lights went out. The killer returned to Miss Genovese, now trying   15
to make her way around the side of the building by the parking lot to get to her apartment. The assailant stabbed her again.

"I'm dying!" she shrieked. "I'm dying!"   16

Windows were opened again, and lights went on in many apart-   17
ments. The assailant got into his car and drove away. Miss Genovese staggered to her feet. A city bus, O–10, the Lefferts Boulevard line to Kennedy International Airport, passed. It was 3:35 A.M.

The assailant returned. By then, Miss Genovese had crawled to   18
the back of the building, where the freshly painted brown doors to the apartment house held out hope for safety. The killer tried the first door; she wasn't there. At the second door, 82–62 Austin Street, he saw her slumped on the floor at the foot of the stairs. He stabbed her a third time—fatally.

It was 3:50 by the time the police received their first call, from 19
a man who was a neighbor of Miss Genovese. In two minutes they
were at the scene. The neighbor, a 70-year-old woman, and another
woman were the only persons on the street. Nobody else came forward.

The man explained that he had called the police after much de- 20
liberation. He had phoned a friend in Nassau County for advice and
then he had crossed the roof of the building to the apartment of the
elderly woman to get her to make the call.

"I didn't want to get involved," he sheepishly told the police. 21

Six days later, the police arrested Winston Moseley, a 29-year- 22
old business-machine operator, and charged him with homicide.
Moseley had no previous record. He is married, has two children
and owns a home at 133–19 Sutter Avenue, South Ozone Park,
Queens. On Wednesday, a court committed him to Kings County
Hospital for psychiatric observation.

When questioned by the police, Moseley also said that he had 23
slain Mrs. Annie May Johnson, 24, of 146–12 133d Avenue, Ja-
maica, on Feb. 29 and Barbara Kralik, 15, of 174–17 140th Avenue,
Springfield Gardens, last July. In the Kralik case, the police are
holding Alvin L. Mitchell, who is said to have confessed that slaying.

The police stressed how simple it would have been to have gotten 24
in touch with them. "A phone call," said one of the detectives, "would
have done it." The police may be reached by dialing "O" for operator
or SPring 7–3100.

Today witnesses from the neighborhood, which is made up of one- 25
family homes in the $35,000 to $60,000 range with the exception of
the two apartment houses near the railroad station, find it difficult to
explain why they didn't call the police.

A housewife, knowingly if quite casually, said, "We thought it was 26
a lovers' quarrel." A husband and wife both said, "Frankly, we were
afraid." They seemed aware of the fact that events might have been
different. A distraught woman, wiping her hands in her apron, said,
"I didn't want my husband to get involved."

One couple, now willing to talk about that night, said they heard 27
the first screams. The husband looked thoughtfully at the bookstore
where the killer first grabbed Miss Genovese.

"We went to the window to see what was happening," he said, "but 28
the light from our bedroom made it difficult to see the street." The
wife, still apprehensive, added: "I put out the light and we were able
to see better."

Asked why they hadn't called the police, she shrugged and replied: 29
"I don't know."

A man peeked out from a slight opening in the doorway to his   30
apartment and rattled off an account of the killer's second attack. Why
hadn't he called the police at the time? "I was tired," he said without
emotion. "I went back to bed."

It was 4:25 A.M. when the ambulance arrived to take the body of   31
Miss Genovese. It drove off. "Then," a solemn police detective said,
"the people came out."

COMPREHENSION

1. How much time elapsed between when Kitty Genovese was first stabbed
   and when the people finally came out?

2. What excuses did the neighbors make for not having come to Kitty
   Genovese's aid?

PURPOSE AND AUDIENCE

1. This article appeared in 1964. What effect was it intended to have on
   its audience? Do you think it has the same impact today, or has its
   impact diminished?

2. The author of this article tells his readers very little about Kitty Genovese. Why, for instance, doesn't he tell us what she looked like? How
   might additional details have affected the impact of the essay?

3. What is the article's main idea? State it in one sentence as a thesis.

4. What is Gansberg's purpose in describing the Austin Street area as
   "staid, middle-class, tree-lined"?

5. Why does Gansberg provide the police department phone number in his
   article?

STYLE AND STRUCTURE

1. The author is very precise in this article, especially in his references to
   time, addresses, and ages. Why?

2. The objective newspaper style is dominant in this article, and yet the
   author's anger shows through. Point to words and phrases that reveal
   his attitude toward his material.

3. Identify the transitions in the article. Characterize the kinds of expressions that are used.

4. Because this article was originally set in the narrow columns of a newspaper, there are many short paragraphs. Would it be more effective if

some of these brief paragraphs were combined? If so, why? If not, why not? Give examples to support your answer.

5. Examine the dialogue. Does it strengthen the author's presentation? Would the article be more compelling without dialogue? Why or why not?

6. This article does not have a formal conclusion; nevertheless, the last paragraph sums up the author's attitude. How?

WRITING WORKSHOP

1. In your own words, write a ten-sentence summary of the article. Try to reflect the author's order and emphasis as well as his ideas.

2. Rewrite the article as if it were a diary entry of one of the thirty-eight people who watched the murder. Outline what you saw, and explain why you didn't call for help.

3. If you have ever been involved in or witnessed a situation where someone was in trouble, write a narrative essay about the incident. If people failed to help the person in trouble, note why you think no one acted. Or, if people did act, tell how.

SHOOTING AN ELEPHANT

George Orwell

Born Eric Blair in 1903 in Bengal, India, George Orwell was brought up in England and was only nineteen when he joined the British police force in Burma. Unhappy in his role as a defender of British colonialism, a system he despised, and wanting to be a writer, Orwell left Burma after five years to live and write in London and Paris; later he fought in the Spanish Civil War. As a reporter and a socialist, Orwell wrote about the living conditions of English miners and factory workers; he sought to expose the dangers of totalitarianism in his widely read novels Animal Farm *(1945) and* 1984 *(1949). He died in 1950. "Shooting an Elephant," set in Burma, relates an incident that clarified for Orwell the nature of British rule. Notice that Orwell uses an extended narrative to support his thesis and includes much specific detail to increase its impact.*

In Moulmein, in Lower Burma, I was hated by large numbers of people—the only time in my life that I have been important enough for this to happen to me. I was sub-divisional police officer of the town, and in an aimless, petty kind of way anti-European feeling was very bitter. No one had the guts to raise a riot, but if a European woman went through the bazaars alone somebody would probably spit betel juice over her dress. As a police officer I was an obvious target and was baited whenever it seemed safe to do so. When a nimble Burman tripped me up on the football field and the referee (another Burman) looked the other way, the crowd yelled with hideous laughter. This happened more than once. In the end the sneering yellow faces of young men that met me everywhere, the insults hooted after me when I was at a safe distance, got badly on my nerves. The young Buddhist priests were the worst of all. There were several thousands of them in the town and none of them seemed to have anything to do except stand on street corners and jeer at Europeans.

All this was perplexing and upsetting. For at that time I had already made up my mind that imperialism was an evil thing and the sooner I chucked up my job and got out of it the better. Theoretically—and secretly, of course—I was all for the Burmese and all against their oppressors, the British. As for the job I was doing, I hated it more bitterly than I can perhaps make clear. In a job like that you see the dirty work of Empire at close quarters. The wretched prisoners huddling in the stinking cages of the lockups, the grey, cowed faces of the long-term convicts, the scarred buttocks of the men who had been flogged with bamboos—all these oppressed me with an intolerable sense of guilt. But I could get nothing into perspective. I was young and ill-educated and I had had to think out my problems in the utter silence that is imposed on every Englishman in the East. I did not even know that the British Empire is dying, still less did I know that it is a great deal better than the younger empires that are going to supplant it.* All I knew was that I was stuck between my hatred of the empire I served and my rage against the evil-spirited little beasts who tried to make my job impossible. With one part of my mind I thought of the British Raj as an unbreakable tyranny, as something clamped down, in *saecula saeculorum,*** upon the will of prostrate peoples; with another part I thought that the greatest joy in the world would be to drive a bayonet into a Buddhist priest's guts. Feelings like these are the normal byproducts of imperialism; ask any Anglo-Indian official, if you can catch him off duty.

One day something happened which in a roundabout way was enlightening. It was a tiny incident in itself, but it gave me a better glimpse than I had had before of the real nature of imperialism— the real motives for which despotic governments act. Early one morning the sub-inspector at a police station the other end of the town rang me up on the phone and said that an elephant was ravaging the bazaar. Would I please come and do something about it? I did not know what I could do, but I wanted to see what was happening and I got on to a pony and started out. I took my rifle, an old .44 Winchester and much too small to kill an elephant, but I thought the noise might be useful *in terrorem.* Various Burmans stopped me on the way and told me about the elephant's doings. It was not, of course, a wild elephant, but a tame one which had gone "must."*** It had been chained up, as tame elephants always are when their attack of "must" is due, but on the previous night it had broken its chain and escaped. Its mahout, the only person who could manage it when it was in that state, had set out in pursuit, but had taken the wrong direction and was now twelve hours' journey away,

3

---

*EDS. NOTE—Orwell was writing in 1936, when Hitler and Stalin were in power and World War II was only three years away.

**EDS. NOTE—From time immemorial. *Raj:* sovereignty.

***EDS. NOTE—That is, gone into an uncontrollable frenzy.

and in the morning the elephant had suddenly reappeared in the town. The Burmese population had no weapons and were quite helpless against it. It had already destroyed somebody's bamboo hut, killed a cow and raided some fruit-stalls and devoured the stock; also it had met the municipal rubbish van and, when the driver jumped out and took to his heels, had turned the van over and inflicted violences upon it.

The Burmese sub-inspector and some Indian constables were waiting for me in the quarter where the elephant had been seen. It was a very poor quarter, a labyrinth of squalid bamboo huts, thatched with palm-leaf, winding all over a steep hillside. I remember that it was a cloudy, stuffy morning at the beginning of the rains. We began questioning the people as to where the elephant had gone, and, as usual, failed to get any definite information. That is invariably the case in the East; a story always sounds clear enough at a distance, but the nearer you get to the scene of events the vaguer it becomes. Some of the people said that the elephant had gone in one direction, some said that he had gone in another, some professed not even to have heard of an elephant. I had almost made up my mind that the whole story was a pack of lies, when we heard yells a little distance away. There was a loud, scandalized cry of "Go away, child! Go away this instant!" and an old woman with a switch in her hand came round the corner of a hut, violently shooing away a crowd of naked children. Some more women followed, clicking their tongues and exclaiming; evidently there was something that the children ought not to have seen. I rounded the hut and saw a man's dead body sprawling in the mud. He was an Indian, a black Dravidian coolie, almost naked, and he could not have been dead many minutes. The people said that the elephant had come suddenly upon him round the corner of the hut, caught him with its trunk, put its foot on his back and ground him into the earth. This was the rainy season and the ground was soft, and his face had scored a trench a foot deep and a couple of yards long. He was lying on his belly with arms crucified and head sharply twisted to one side. His face was coated with mud, the eyes wide open, the teeth bared and grinning with an expression of unendurable agony. (Never tell me, by the way, that the dead look peaceful. Most of the corpses I have seen looked devilish.) The friction of the great beast's foot had stripped the skin from his back as neatly as one skins a rabbit. As soon as I saw the dead man I sent an orderly to a friend's house nearby to borrow an elephant rifle. I had already sent back the pony, not wanting it to go mad with fright and throw me if it smelled the elephant.

The orderly came back in a few minutes with a rifle and five ⁵ cartridges, and meanwhile some Burmans had arrived and told us that the elephant was in the paddy fields below, only a few hundred yards away. As I started forward practically the whole population of the quarter flocked out of the houses and followed me. They had seen the rifle and were all shouting excitedly that I was going to shoot the elephant. They had not shown much interest in the elephant when he was merely ravaging their homes, but it was different now that he was going to be shot. It was a bit of fun to them, as it would be to an English crowd; besides they wanted the meat. It made me vaguely uneasy. I had no intention of shooting the elephant—I had merely sent for the rifle to defend myself if necessary—and it is always unnerving to have a crowd following you. I marched down the hill, looking and feeling a fool, with the rifle over my shoulder and an ever-growing army of people jostling at my heels. At the bottom, when you got away from the huts, there was a metalled road and beyond that a miry waste of paddy fields a thousand yards across, not yet ploughed but soggy from the first rains and dotted with coarse grass. The elephant was standing eight yards from the road, his left side towards us. He took not the slightest notice of the crowd's approach. He was tearing up bunches of grass, beating them against his knees to clean them and stuffing them into his mouth.

I had halted on the road. As soon as I saw the elephant I knew ⁶ with perfect certainty that I ought not to shoot him. It is a serious matter to shoot a working elephant—it is comparable to destroying a huge and costly piece of machinery—and obviously one ought not to do it if it can possibly be avoided. And at that distance, peacefully eating, the elephant looked no more dangerous than a cow. I thought then and I think now that his attack of "must" was already passing off; in which case he would merely wander harmlessly about until the mahout came back and caught him. Moreover, I did not in the least want to shoot him. I decided that I would watch him for a little while to make sure that he did not turn savage again, and then go home.

But at that moment I glanced round at the crowd that had fol- ⁷ lowed me. It was an immense crowd, two thousand at the least and growing every minute. It blocked the road for a long distance on either side. I looked at the sea of yellow faces above the garish clothes—faces all happy and excited over this bit of fun, all certain that the elephant was going to be shot. They were watching me as they would watch a conjurer about to perform a trick. They did not like me, but with the magical rifle in my hands I was mo-

mentarily worth watching. And suddenly I realized that I should
have to shoot the elephant after all. The people expected it of me
and I had got to do it; I could feel their two thousand wills pressing me forward, irresistibly. And it was at this moment, as I stood
there with the rifle in my hands, that I first grasped the hollow-
ness, the futility of the white man's dominion in the East. Here
was I, the white man with his gun, standing in front of the unarmed native crowd—seemingly the leading actor of the piece; but
in reality I was only an absurd puppet pushed to and fro by the
will of those yellow faces behind. I perceived in this moment that
when the white man turns tyrant it is his own freedom that he
destroys. He becomes a sort of hollow, posing dummy, the conven-
tionalized figure of a sahib. For it is the condition of his rule that
he shall spend his life in trying to impress the "natives," and so
in every crisis he has got to do what the "natives" expect of him.
He wears a mask, and his face grows to fit it. I had got to shoot
the elephant. I had committed myself to doing it when I sent for
the rifle. A sahib has got to act like a sahib; he has got to appear
resolute, to know his own mind and do definite things. To come
all that way, rifle in hand, with two thousand people marching at
my heels, and then to trail feebly away, having done nothing—no,
that was impossible. The crowd would laugh at me. And my whole
life, every white man's life in the East, was one long struggle not
to be laughed at.

But I did not want to shoot the elephant. I watched him beating   8
his bunch of grass against his knees, with that preoccupied grand-
motherly air that elephants have. It seemed to me that it would be
murder to shoot him. At that age I was not squeamish about killing
animals, but I had never shot an elephant and never wanted to.
(Somehow it always seems worse to kill a *large* animal.) Besides,
there was the beast's owner to be considered. Alive, the elephant
was worth at least a hundred pounds; dead, he would only be worth
the value of his tusks, five pounds, possibly. But I had got to act
quickly. I turned to some experienced-looking Burmans who had
been there when we arrived, and asked them how the elephant had
been behaving. They all said the same thing: he took no notice of
you if you left him alone, but he might charge if you went too close
to him.

It was perfectly clear to me what I ought to do. I ought to walk   9
up to within, say, twenty-five yards of the elephant and test his
behavior. If he charged I could shoot, if he took no notice of me it
would be safe to leave him until the mahout came back. But also I
knew that I was going to do no such thing. I was a poor shot with

a rifle and the ground was soft mud into which one would sink at every step. If the elephant charged and I missed him, I should have about as much chance as a toad under a steam-roller. But even then I was not thinking particularly of my own skin, only of the watchful yellow faces behind. For at that moment, with the crowd watching me, I was not afraid in the ordinary sense, as I would have been if I had been alone. A white man mustn't be frightened in front of "natives"; and so, in general, he isn't frightened. The sole thought in my mind was that if anything went wrong those two thousand Burmans would see me pursued, caught, trampled on and reduced to a grinning corpse like that Indian up the hill. And if that happened it was quite probable that some of them would laugh. That would never do. There was only one alternative. I shoved the cartridges into the magazine and lay down on the road to get a better aim.

The crowd grew very still, and a deep, low, happy sigh, as of   10
people who see the theatre curtain go up at last, breathed from innumerable throats. They were going to have their bit of fun after all. The rifle was a beautiful German thing with cross-hair sights. I did not then know that in shooting an elephant one would shoot to cut an imaginary bar running from ear-hole to ear-hole. I ought, therefore, as the elephant was sideways on, to have aimed straight at his ear-hole; actually I aimed several inches in front of this, thinking the brain would be further forward.

When I pulled the trigger I did not hear the bang or feel the   11
kick—one never does when a shot goes home—but I heard the devilish roar of glee that went up from the crowd. In that instant, in too short a time, one would have thought, even for the bullet to get there, a mysterious, terrible change had come over the elephant. He neither stirred nor fell, but every line on his body had altered. He looked suddenly stricken, shrunken, immensely old, as though the frightful impact of the bullet had paralyzed him without knocking him down. At last, after what seemed a long time—it might have been five seconds, I dare say—he sagged flabbily to his knees. His mouth slobbered. An enormous senility seemed to have settled upon him. One could have imagined him thousands of years old. I fired again into the same spot. At the second shot he did not collapse but climbed with desperate slowness to his feet and stood weakly upright, with legs sagging and head drooping. I fired a third time. That was the shot that did for him. You could see the agony of it jolt his whole body and knock the last remnant of strength from his legs. But in falling he seemed for a moment to rise, for as his hind

legs collapsed beneath him he seemed to tower upwards like a huge rock toppling, his trunk reaching skywards like a tree. He trumpeted, for the first and only time. And then down he came, his belly towards me, with a crash that seemed to shake the ground even where I lay.

I got up. The Burmans were already racing past me across the   12
mud. It was obvious that the elephant would never rise again, but he was not dead. He was breathing very rhythmically with long rattling gasps, his great mound of a side painfully rising and falling. His mouth was wide open—I could see far down into the caverns of pale pink throat. I waited a long time for him to die, but his breathing did not weaken. Finally I fired my two remaining shots into the spot where I thought his heart must be. The thick blood welled out of him like red velvet, but still he did not die. His body did not even jerk when the shots hit him, the tortured breathing continued without a pause. He was dying, very slowly and in great agony, but in some world remote from me where not even a bullet could damage him further. I felt that I had got to put an end to that dreadful noise. It seemed dreadful to see the great beast lying there, powerless to move and yet powerless to die, and not even to be able to finish him. I sent back for my small rifle and poured shot after shot into his heart and down his throat. They seemed to make no impression. The tortured gasps continued as steadily as the ticking of a clock.

In the end I could not stand it any longer and went away. I heard   13
later that it took him half an hour to die. Burmans were bringing dahs* and baskets even before I left, and I was told they had stripped his body almost to the bones by the afternoon.

Afterwards, of course, there were endless discussions about the   14
shooting of the elephant. The owner was furious, but he was only an Indian and could do nothing. Besides, legally I had done the right thing, for a mad elephant has to be killed, like a mad dog, if its owner fails to control it. Among the Europeans opinion was divided. The older men said I was right, the younger men said it was a damn shame to shoot an elephant for killing a coolie, because an elephant was worth more than any damn Coringhee coolie. And afterwards I was very glad that the coolie had been killed; it put me legally in the right and it gave me a sufficient pretext for shooting the elephant. I often wondered whether any of the others grasped that I had done it solely to avoid looking a fool.

*EDS. NOTE—Heavy knives.

COMPREHENSION

1. Why was Orwell "hated by large numbers of people" in Burma?

2. Orwell had mixed feelings toward the Burmese people. Explain why.

3. Why did the local officials want something done about the elephant?

4. Why did the crowd want Orwell to shoot the elephant?

5. Why did Orwell finally decide to kill the elephant? What made him hesitate at first?

6. Why does Orwell say at the end that he was glad the coolie had been killed?

PURPOSE AND AUDIENCE

1. One of Orwell's purposes in telling his story is to show how it gave him a glimpse of "the real nature of imperialism." How does the story illustrate this?

2. Do you think Orwell wrote this essay to inform or to persuade his audience? How did Orwell expect his audience to react to his ideas? How can you tell?

3. What is the essay's thesis?

STYLE AND STRUCTURE

1. What is the function of Orwell's first paragraph? Where does the introduction end and the narrative itself begin?

2. Orwell uses a good deal of descriptive detail in this essay. Locate some details that you think are particularly vivid or strong. Why is detail so important?

3. Point out some of the transitional words and phrases Orwell uses to indicate the passing of time. Why are they so important in this essay?

4. The essay includes almost no dialogue. Why do you think Orwell's voice as narrator is the only one the reader hears? Is this a strength or a weakness? Explain why.

5. Why does Orwell devote so much attention to the elephant's misery (paragraphs 11 and 12)?

6. Orwell's essay includes a number of editorial comments inserted into his text between parentheses or pairs of dashes. What kind of comments are these? Why are they set off from the text?

WRITING WORKSHOP

1. Orwell says that even though he hated British imperialism and sympathized with the Burmese people, he found himself a puppet of the system. Write a narrative essay about a time when you had to do something that went against your beliefs or convictions.

2. Orwell's experience taught him something not only about himself but also about something beyond himself—the way imperialism worked. Write a narrative essay that reveals how an incident in your life taught you something about yourself and about some larger social or political force.

3

Description

WHAT IS DESCRIPTION?

We are surrounded by persons, places, and objects—all of which have their own qualities and all of which affect us in different ways. We begin to understand our world by observing these things that make it up. Usually we describe what we observe before we make judgments about the world, before we compare or contrast or classify our experiences. Scientists observe and describe whenever they conduct experiments, and you do the same thing whenever you write a paper. In a comparison-and-contrast essay, for example, you may describe the performance of two cars to show that one is superior to another. In an argumentative essay, you may describe a fish kill in a local river to show that factory pollution is a problem. Through description, you introduce your view of the world to your readers. If your readers come to understand or share your view, they are more likely to accept your conclusions and judgments as well. Thus, for almost every essay you write, knowing how to describe effectively is important. In this chapter, we go even further; we examine descriptive writing as a strategy for a whole essay.

A narrative essay presents a series of events; it tells a story. A descriptive essay, on the other hand, tells what something looks like, what it feels like, smells like, sounds like, or tastes like. Description can also do more than convey sense impressions. If you are describing a city, for example, you might describe the kinds of people living there, including their life styles, their backgrounds, or their attitudes. When you write description, you use your observations to create a vivid impression for your reader. As we mentioned in chapter 2, a good narrative may depend heavily on descriptive details. It is important, however, not to confuse these two types of writing. A narrative always presents events in time, in some sort of chronological order, whereas a description tells about things in spatial rather than temporal order.

Like a narrative essay, a descriptive essay may or may not have a thesis. You can describe a person, place, or thing for its own sake, simply to share your sensory observations with your reader. You can also use description to support an implied or explicit thesis. Whether or not your description has a thesis, its details should be tailored to create a particular dominant impression. In college writing situations, you are most likely to use description to support an idea or assertion, as this thesis for an architectural design paper suggests: "The sculptures that adorn Philadelphia's City Hall form a catalogue of nineteenth-century artistic styles."

Objective and Subjective Descriptions

There are two basic approaches to description: objective and subjective. In an *objective* description, you focus on the object you are portraying rather than on your personal reactions to it. Many writing situations require precise descriptions of apparatus or conditions, and in these cases your goal is to supply information—to construct as accurate a picture as you can for your audience. A biologist describing what he sees through a microscope and a historian describing a Civil War battlefield would both write objectively. The biologist would not, for instance, say how exciting his observations were, nor would the historian say how surprising she thought the outcome of the battle was. Newspaper reporters also try to achieve this cameralike objectivity, and so do writers of technical reports, scientific papers, and certain types of business correspondence. Of course, objectivity is an ideal that writers aim for but never achieve. Any time writers select some details and eliminate others, they cannot be completely objective.

In the following descriptive passage, Thomas Marc Parrott tries to achieve objectivity by giving his readers all the factual information they need to visualize Shakespeare's theater.

When James Burbage built the Theatre in 1576 he naturally designed it along the lines of inn-yards in which he had been accustomed to play. The building had two entrances—one in front for the audience; one in the rear for actors, musicians, and the personnel of the theatre. Inside the building a rectangular platform projected far out into what was called "the yard"—we know the stage of the Fortune ran halfway across the "yard," some twenty-seven and a half feet.

Note that Parrott is not interested in responding to or evaluating the environment he describes. Instead, he uses impersonal words that are calculated to convey sizes, shapes, and distances. His choice of adjectives such as *two* and *rectangular* reflects this intent. Only one word in the paragraph—*naturally*—suggests that the author is expressing a personal opinion.

In contrast to objective description is *subjective* or *impressionistic* description, which discloses your responses to what you see and tries to get your readers to share them. These responses are not expressed directly, through a straightforward statement of your opinion or perspective. Rather, they are revealed indirectly, through your choice of words and phrasing. For instance, if an assignment in freshman English asked you to describe a place that had special meaning for you, you would write about your topic by selecting and emphasizing details that showed your feelings about the place. Similarly, editorial writers on newspapers are expected to use their personal feelings and opinions to shape their descriptions; their function is to interpret, to give their impressions of the events they describe.

Thus, a subjective or impressionistic description should convey not just a factual record of sights and sounds but also their meaning or significance. For example, if you objectively described a fire, you might include its temperature, its duration, and its dimensions. In addition to these quantifiable details, you might describe, as accurately as possible, its color, its movement, and its intensity. If you subjectively described the fire, however, you would include more than these unbiased observations about it. Through your choice of language and your phrasing, you would try to re-create for your audience a sense of how the fire made you feel: your reactions to the crackling noise, to the dense smoke, to the sudden destruction.

In the following passage, Mark Twain subjectively describes the Mississippi River.

> I still kept in mind a certain wonderful sunset which I witnessed when steamboating was new to me. A broad expanse of the river was turned to blood; in the middle distance the red hue brightened into gold, through which a solitary log came floating, black and conspicuous; in one place a long, slanting mark lay sparkling upon the water; in another the surface was broken by boiling, tumbling rings, that were as many-tinted as an opal.

In this passage, Twain uses language that has emotional connotations—"wonderful"—and comparisons that suggest great value ("gold," "opal," even "blood"), to convey his feelings to the reader.

By emphasizing the red color, the solitary log "black and conspic-uous," and the "boiling, tumbling rings," he shares with his readers his vivid perception of the river's beauty.

Neither of the two approaches to description exists independ-ently. Objective description is always the product of a subjective selection of details; subjective description captures reactions to an objective reality. The skillful writer, however, adjusts the balance between objectivity and subjectivity to suit the topic, thesis, audi-ence, purpose, and occasion of an essay.

Objective and Subjective Language

As the passages by Parrott and Twain illustrate, objective and subjective descriptions are characterized by different uses of lan-guage. Both depend on specific and concrete words to convey, as precisely as possible, a picture of the person, place, or thing that the observer is describing. Objective descriptions rely on language that is as unbiased and impersonal as possible. They describe things with words and phrases so unambiguous that many observers could agree that the descriptions were appropriate and exact. Ideally, their language conveys identical meanings to all readers. Subjective de-scriptions, however, generally rely on richer and more suggestive language than objective descriptions. Subjective descriptions are more likely to play on the connotations of language, on the emotional associations of words. They may deliberately provoke the individual reader's imagination with striking phrases or vivid comparisons. For example, a subjective description might liken the behavior of an exotic peacock spreading its feathers to that of a pet Siamese cat posturing and posing, thus evoking a lively image in the reader's mind.

When you write such descriptions, you can use several kinds of comparisons. You can compare two similar things, using the famil-iar parakeet to describe the unfamiliar peacock. Or, instead of com-paring two things that are alike, you can find similarities between things that are unlike, such as the peacock and the cat, and provide a fresh view of both. Such special comparisons are known as *figures of speech*. Three of the most common are simile, metaphor, and personification.

A *simile* compares two things that are unlike using *like* or *as*. These comparisons occur constantly in everyday speech when, for example, someone claims to be "happy as a clam," "slow as molas-ses," or "hungry as a bear." Effective writers, however, strive to use more original similes than these. For instance, in his short story "A & P," John Updike likens people going through the checkout aisle of a store to balls dropping down a slot in a pinball machine.

A *metaphor* identifies two unlike things without using *like* or *as*. Instead of saying that something is like something else, a metaphor says that it *is* something else. Twain uses a metaphor when he says that "a broad expanse of the river was turned to blood."

Personification endows animals or objects with the qualities of human beings. If you say that the wind whispered or that the engine died, you are personifying them.

Your purpose and audience determine whether you should use predominantly objective or subjective description. Legal, medical, technical, business, and scientific writing assignments frequently require objective descriptions, but even in these areas you may be encouraged to tailor your descriptions so that they develop your own interpretations and arguments. Still, in all these instances, your primary purpose is to give your audience factual information about your subject. On the other hand, an assignment that specifically asks for your reactions demands a subjective or impressionistic description.

Sometimes inexperienced writers load their subjective descriptions with words like *beautiful, tasty, disgusting,* or *scary.* They may confuse their own reactions to an object with the qualities of the object itself. For an effective description, however, it is not enough just to *say* something is wonderful. The writer should try to make it seem wonderful to the reader, as Twain does with the sunset. Twain does in fact use the word *wonderful* at the beginning of his description, but he then goes on to give many concrete details that make the experience vivid and specific for us.

Selection of Detail

All good descriptive writing, whether objective or subjective, relies heavily on specific details which enable readers to visualize what you are describing. Your aim is not simply to *tell* your readers what something looks like but to *show* them. Every person, place, or thing has its special characteristics, and you must use your powers of observation to detect them. Then, you must select the concrete words that will enable your readers to see, feel, hear, taste, touch, or smell what you are describing as you do. Don't be satisfied with "he looked angry" when you can say, "His face flushed, and one corner of his mouth twitched as he tried to control his anger." What's the difference? In the first case, you simply name the man's emotional state. In the second, you describe his appearance in enough detail that readers can tell not only that he was angry but also how he revealed the intensity of his anger. Of course, you could have provided even more detail by noting the man's beard or his wrinkles or any number of other features. In a given description, however, not all details are equally useful or desirable. Only those that add to the *dominant impression* you wish to create should be included. In describing a man's face to show how angry he was, you would probably not describe the shape of his nose or the color of his hair. (After all, the color of somebody's hair doesn't change when he or she gets angry.) The number of details you use is less important than their quality. In order to avoid an indiscriminate list, you must select and use only those specific details that are relevant to your purpose.

STRUCTURING A DESCRIPTIVE ESSAY

When you write a descriptive essay, you will probably begin with a brainstorming list of details that need to be organized. You don't want to present them randomly, of course, but rather to arrange them in a way that advances your thesis or unifying idea. For example, you can move from a specific description of an object to a general description of other things around it. Or you can reverse this order, beginning with the general and proceeding to the specific. You can progress from the least important feature to a more important feature until you finally focus on the most important one. You can also move from the smallest to the largest item or from the least unusual to the most unusual detail. Finally, you can present the details of your description in a straightforward spatial order, moving from left to right or right to left, from top to bottom or bottom to top. The particular *organizing scheme* you choose depends upon the dominant impression you want to convey to your readers, your thesis or unifying idea, and your purpose and audience.

Let's suppose that your English composition instructor has assigned a short essay describing a person, place, or thing. After thinking about the subject for a day or two, you decide to write an objective description of the Air and Space Museum in Washington, D.C., since you have just visited it and many details are fresh in your mind. Because the museum is so large and has so many different exhibits, you realize at once that you will not be able to describe them all. Therefore, you decide to concentrate on one, the heavier-than-air flight exhibit, and you choose as the topic for your essay the particular display that you remember most vividly: Charles Lindbergh's airplane, *The Spirit of St. Louis.* You brainstorm to recollect all the details you can, and when you read over your list, you immediately see that the order of presentation in your essay could be based on your actual experience in the museum. You decide to present the details of the airplane in the order in which the eye takes them in, from front to rear. The dominant impression you wish to create is how small and fragile *The Spirit of St. Louis* appears. The outline for your essay might look like this:

¶1   Introduction—thesis: It is startling that a plane as small as *The Spirit of St. Louis* was able to fly across the Atlantic.
¶2   Front of plane: single engine, tiny cockpit
¶3   Middle of plane: wing span, extra gas tanks
¶4   Rear of plane: limited cargo space filled with more gas tanks
¶5   Conclusion—restatement of thesis

The following student essays both illustrate the principles of effective description. The first one, by Joseph Tessari, is an objective description of the light microscope. The second, by Mary Lim, is a subjective description of an area in Burma.

THE LIGHT MICROSCOPE

Introduction   The simple light microscope is widely   1
used in the scientific community. The
basic function of the microscope is to
view in great detail objects or biological specimens that would otherwise be
invisible to the naked eye. Light microscopes come in a variety of shapes
and sizes, all having different degrees
of magnification and complexity. Most
microscopes, however, are made of metal
or plastic (primarily metal) and stand
approximately ten to thirteen inches
tall.

Description of stand

There are several integrated parts in a simple light microscope. The largest piece is the stand. The stand (black in this example) is composed of a single metal structure that has vertical and horizontal sections. The horizontal piece sits on the tabletop and is wishbone–shaped. The vertical section stands approximately nine inches tall and is shaped like a question mark. These two sections join at the base of the wishbone. [2]

Description of optic tube

Attached at the top of the vertical piece of the stand is a black metal tube approximately three to four inches long. One entire side of this optic tube is attached to the end of the vertical stand and, therefore, sits in front of the stand when viewed from the side. [3]

Description of eyepiece

Sitting directly on top of this tube is a silver cylinder called the eyepiece. The eyepiece is slightly smaller in diameter than the optic tube and approximately two inches in length. The top of the eyepiece is covered with a clear glass lens called the fixed lens. The lens and the cylinder together make up the entire eyepiece. [4]

Description of coarse adjustment knobs

On the stand, adjacent to the point where it meets the optic tube, are two silver knobs––one on each side of the microscope. These knobs are termed the coarse adjustment knobs. When rotated, [5]

they raise and lower the optic tube.
This raising and lowering of the tube
serves to focus the object being
viewed.

**Description of
objective lens**

Attached to the bottom of the optic   6
tube is a movable disc which, when
viewed from the side, makes a forty-
five degree angle with the front of the
optic tube. The side of the disc in the
front of the microscope is higher than
the back of the disc. Two small silver
cylinders are attached, one hundred
eighty degrees apart from each other,
to the bottom of this movable disc.
These cylinders have small glass lenses
covering the unattached ends. Each cylinder lens is of a different magnification power. This entire piece (disc and
lenses) is called the objective lens.
When the objective lens is in place,
the eyepiece, optic tube, and objective
lens fall in a vertical line.

**Description of
viewing stage**

Sitting directly below the objective   7
lens, attached to the bend in the question mark of the vertical stand, is a
horizontal metal plate. The plate,
termed the viewing stage, is square in
shape with a small hole cut out in the
center. This circular hole is approximately the same diameter as the objective lens and is also along the same
vertical line. On either side of the
hole, attached to the back of the

stage, are metal clips that hold the
specimen in place.

Description of
diaphragm

Connected to the underside of the   8
stage is a flat circular diaphragm that
can be rotated to vary the amount of
light passing through the hole in the
stage.

Description
of mirror

A few inches below the stage, sitting   9
in the opening of the wishbone base, is
a small circular mirror. The mirror is
centered along the vertical line of the
eyepiece, optic tube, objective lens,
and stage opening. The mirror can pivot
around a horizontal axis and is attached to the stand by a Y-shaped
structure. (The mirror sits in the
opening of the Y.) When the mirror is
moved, light from some source (usually
the sun) can be reflected off the mirror's surface up into the viewing apparatus (objective lens, optic tube, and
eyepiece).

Conclusion

The simple light microscope has been   10
an extremely useful biological tool for
many years and has been responsible for
a significant number of important scientific advancements, such as pasteuri-
zation, immunization, sterilization,
cures for diseases, and better understanding of human anatomy and physiol-
ogy. With modern technology, newer and
more complex microscopes, such as the
electron microscope, are being devel-

oped to further aid members of the scientific community in their research.

Points for Special Attention

Objective Description.   Joseph Tessari, a toxicology major, wrote
this paper for a class in scientific writing. His assignment was to
write a detailed, factual description of an instrument, mechanism,
or piece of apparatus or equipment used in his study of his major
field. Because he was to write an objective description, his essay
does not react subjectively to the microscope, or tell how it works,
or stress its advantages and disadvantages. Instead, his essay simply details the microscope's physical features. Since his purpose here
is to describe, the essay has no thesis.

Objective Language.   Because his essay is written for a class
in scientific writing, Joseph keeps his objective description technical. His factual, concrete language concentrates on the size, shape,
and composition of each part, and on each part's physical relationship to the other parts and to the whole. He does not use unusual
imagery or elaborate figures of speech.

Structure.   In organizing his essay, Joseph chose to describe the
microscope piece by piece. He starts at the bottom of the microscope
with its largest part—the stand. He next directs the reader's attention upward from the optic tube to the eyepiece and then downward
past the coarse adjustment knobs to the bottom of the optic tube
(where the objective lens is located), down to the viewing stage, the
diaphragm, the mirror, and the light source. In the essay's introduction, Joseph comments on the microscope's purpose and general
appearance; in his conclusion, he summarizes the microscope's past
achievements and briefly considers its future.

Selection of Detail.   Joseph Tessari's assignment identified his
audience as a group of well-educated nonscientists. Thus, while he
could assume that his readers would generally know what a microscope looked like, he realized that he would have to describe the
unfamiliar individual components in some detail.

Unlike "The Light Microscope," Mary Lim's essay uses subjective
description so that the reader can share, as well as understand, her
experience.

THE VALLEY OF WINDMILLS

Introduction   In my native country of Burma,   1
strange happenings and strange scenery
are not unusual. For it is a strange
land that in some areas seems to have
been ignored by time. Mountains stand
jutting their rocky peaks into the
clouds as they have for thousands of
years. Jungles are so dense with exotic
vegetation that human beings or large
animals cannot even enter. But one of
the strangest areas in Burma is the
Description   Valley of Windmills, nesting between
(moving
toward the   the tall mountains near the fertile and
valley)   beautiful city of Taungaleik. In this
valley there is beautiful and breath-
taking scenery, but there are also old,
massive, and gloomy structures that can
disturb a person deeply. The road to
Taungaleik twists out of the coastal
flatlands into those heaps of slag,
shale, and limestone that are the Tennesserim Mountains in the southern part
of Burma. The air grows rarer and
cooler, the stones become grayer, the
highway a little more precarious at its
edges until ahead, standing in ghostly
Description   sentinel across the lip of a pass, is a
(immediate
view)   line of squat forms. They straddle the
road and stand at intervals up the
hillsides on either side. Are they
boulders? Are they fortifications? Are
they broken wooden crosses on graves in
an abandoned cemetery?

These dark figures are windmills   2
standing in the misty atmosphere. They
are immensely old and distinctly evil,
some merely turrets, some with remnants
of arms hanging derelict from their
snouts, and most of them covered with
dark green moss. Their decayed but
still massive forms seem to turn and

Description (more distant view) sneer at visitors. Down the pass on the
other side is a circular green plateau
that lies like an arena below, where
there are still more windmills. Massed
in the plain behind them, as far as the
eye can see, in every field, above
every hut, stand ten thousand iron
windmills, silent and sailless. They
seem to await only a call from a watchman to clank, whirr, flap, and groan
into action. Visitors suddenly feel
cold. Perhaps it is a sense of loneliness, the cool air, the desolation, or
the weirdness of the arcane windmills—
but something chills them.

Description (immediate view contrasted with city) As you stand at the lip of the val-   3
ley, contrasts rush as if to overwhelm
you. Beyond, glittering on the mountainside like a solitary jewel, is
Taungaleik in the territory once occupied by the Portuguese. Below, on rolling hillsides, are the dark windmills,
still enveloped in morning mist. These

Conclusion (implied thesis) ancient windmills can remind you of the
impermanence of life and the mystery
that still surrounds these hills. In an

odd way, the scene in the valley can
disturb you, but it also can give you
an insight into the darkness that seems
to define our lives here in Burma.

Points for Special Attention

Subjective Description. One of the first things you notice when you read Mary's essay is her use of vivid details. The road to Taungaleik is described in specific terms: it twists "out of the coastal flatlands" into the mountains which are "heaps of slag, shale, and limestone." The iron windmills are decayed and stand "silent and sailless" on a green plateau that "lies like an arena." Using language in this way, Mary creates her dominant impression of the Valley of Windmills as dark, mysterious, and disquieting. Thus her language is no less specific than Joseph Tessari's, but she uses it to create a different kind of dominant impression and to support a different kind of thesis. The point of her essay, stated in the last paragraph, is that the Valley of Windmills embodies the contrasts that characterize life in Burma.

Subjective Language and Figures of Speech. Mary conveys the sense of foreboding she felt by describing the windmills in several different ways. Upon first introducing them, she questions whether these "squat forms" are "boulders," "fortifications," or "broken wooden crosses," each of which has a menacing connotation. After telling the reader what they are, she personifies the windmills by describing them as dark, evil, sneering figures with "arms hanging derelict." She sees them as ghostly sentinels awaiting a call from a watchman to spring into action. Through this figure of speech, Mary masterfully re-creates the unearthly quality of the scene she witnessed in Burma.

Structure. Mary's purpose in writing this paper was to create the sensation of actually being in the Valley of Windmills in Burma. She uses an organizing scheme that takes the reader along the road to Taungaleik, up into the Tennesserim Mountains, and finally to the pass where the windmills are. From the perspective of the lip of the valley, she describes the details closest to her and then those farther away, as if following the movement of her eyes. She ends by bringing her reader back to the lip of the valley and contrasts Taungaleik "glittering on the mountainside" with the windmills "enveloped in morning mist." Through her description, she helps the reader learn something about the point of her essay, the nature of life in Burma. She withholds the explicit statement of this point until her last paragraph, when the reader has been fully prepared for it.

The following essays illustrate different types and uses of description, sometimes more than one in the same essay. Pay particular attention to the difference between objective and subjective descriptions.

ON THE BALL

Roger Angell

Roger Angell was born in 1920 in New York City. He is currently the fiction editor at The New Yorker, *where he regularly contributes short stories, humor, and verse. He is perhaps best known for his insightful and imaginative articles on baseball, a game to which he admits being hopelessly addicted. His sports pieces appear in* The New Yorker *and have been collected in* The Summer Game, Five Seasons, *and, most recently,* Late Innings. *In this selection from* Five Seasons *(1977), Angell describes the most fundamental item of the game, the baseball itself. At first objective and then subjective, this description conveys not only a good deal of information but also the author's involvement and fascination with the game.*

It weighs just over five ounces and measures between 2.86 and 2.94 inches in diameter. It is made of a composition-cork nucleus encased in two thin layers of rubber, one black and one red, surrounded by 121 yards of tightly wrapped blue-gray wool yarn, 45 yards of white wool yarn, 53 more yards of blue-gray wool yarn, 150 yards of fine cotton yarn, a coat of rubber cement, and a cowhide (formerly horsehide) exterior, which is held together with 216 slightly raised red cotton stitches. Printed certifications, endorsements, and outdoor advertising spherically attest to its authenticity. Like most institutions, it is considered inferior in its present form to its ancient archetypes, and in this case the complaint is probably justified; on occasion in recent years it has actually been known to come apart under the demands of its brief but rigorous active career. Baseballs are assembled and hand-stitched in Taiwan (before this year the work was done in Haiti, and before 1973 in Chicopee, Massachusetts), and contemporary pitchers claim that there is a tangible variation in the size and feel of the balls that now come into play in a single game; a true peewee is treasured by hurlers, and its departure from the premises, by fair means or foul, is secretly mourned. But never mind: any baseball is beautiful. No other small package comes as close to the ideal in design and utility. It is a perfect object for a man's hand. Pick it up and it instantly suggests its purpose; it is meant to be thrown a considerable distance—thrown hard and with precision. Its feel and heft are the beginning of the sport's critical dimensions; if it were a fraction of an inch larger or smaller, a few centigrams heavier or lighter, the game of baseball would be utterly different. Hold a baseball in your hand. As it happens, this one is not brand-new. Here, just to one side of the curved surgical welt of stitches, there is a pale-green grass smudge, darkening on one edge almost to black—the mark of an old infield play, a tough grounder now lost in memory. Feel the ball, turn it over in your hand; hold it across the seam or the other way, with the seam just to the side of your middle finger. Speculation stirs. You want to get outdoors and throw this spare and sensual object to somebody or, at the very least, watch somebody else throw it. The game has begun.

COMPREHENSION

1. Why are baseballs made in recent years inferior to those made in earlier years?

2. What does Angell mean when he says most pitchers mourn the loss of "a true peewee"? What does he mean by the phrase, "by fair means or foul"?

3. Why is a baseball "a perfect object for a man's hand"?

4. How would a slight change in the size or weight of a baseball change the nature of the game?

5. Angell calls the baseball a "sensual object". What does he mean?

PURPOSE AND AUDIENCE

1. What is Angell's purpose in writing this essay?

2. Does this essay have an implied or stated thesis? What is it?

3. What evidence does Angell provide to support his thesis?

4. Is Angell writing for a general audience or for an audience of baseball fans such as himself? What evidence leads you to your conclusion?

STYLE AND STRUCTURE

1. Why does Angell begin his essay with an objective description? How does this section relate to the subjective description that follows?

2. What is the effect of including so much detail in the objective description? What is the organizing scheme of this section?

3. Where and how does Angell make the transition between the objective and the subjective descriptions?

4. What is the organizing scheme of the subjective description? Is this the best scheme for the topic? Explain.

5. Why did Angell write his description as one long paragraph? What would he have gained or lost by breaking his essay into two paragraphs?

WRITING WORKSHOP

1. Choose an object that you are familiar with, and write an objective description of it. Be sure that your essay has an organizing scheme.

2. Now write a subjective description of the same object.

PHOTOGRAPHS
OF MY PARENTS

Maxine Hong Kingston

Maxine Hong Kingston was born in Stockton, California, in 1940. She graduated from the University of California at Berkeley and taught high school English and mathematics in California and Hawaii, where she now teaches creative writing at the University of Honolulu. Her first book, The Woman Warrior: Memories of a Girlhood Among Ghosts *(1975), won the National Book Critics Circle Award. Her second book,* China Men *(1980), also received critical praise. In "Photographs of My Parents," an excerpt from* The Woman Warrior, *Kingston describes some old photographs of her mother and father. By doing so she conveys their strength and dignity as well as the cultural differences that separate China from America.*

Once in a long while, four times so far for me, my mother brings 1
out the metal tube that holds her medical diploma. On the tube are
gold circles crossed with seven red lines each—"joy" ideographs in
abstract.* There are also little flowers that look like gears for a gold
machine. According to the scraps of labels with Chinese and American addresses, stamps, and postmarks, the family airmailed the
can from Hong Kong in 1950. It got crushed in the middle, and
whoever tried to peel the labels off stopped because the red and gold
paint came off too, leaving silver scratches that rust. Somebody
tried to pry the end off before discovering that the tube pulls apart.
When I open it, the smell of China flies out, a thousand-year-old
bat flying heavy-headed out of the Chinese caverns where bats are
as white as dust, a smell that comes from long ago, far back in the
brain. Crates from Canton, Hong Kong, Singapore, and Taiwan have
that smell too, only stronger because they are more recently come
from the Chinese.

Inside the can are three scrolls, one inside another. The largest 2
says that in the twenty-third year of the National Republic, the To
Keung School of Midwifery, where she has had two years of instruction and Hospital Practice, awards its Diploma to my mother, who
has shown through oral and written examination her Proficiency in
Midwifery, Pediatrics, Gynecology, "Medecine," "Surgary," Therapeutics, Ophthalmology, Bacteriology, Dermatology, Nursing and

---

*Eds. note—That is, stylized Chinese characters for the word *joy*.

93

Bandage. This document has eight stamps on it: one, the school's English and Chinese names embossed together in a circle; one, as the Chinese enumerate, a stork and a big baby in lavender ink; one, the school's Chinese seal; one, an orangish paper stamp pasted in the border design; one, the red seal of Dr. Wu Pak-liang, M.D., Lyon, Berlin, president and "Ex-assistant étranger à la clinique chirugicale et d'accouchement de l'université de Lyon";* one, the red seal of Dean Woo Yin-kam, M.D.; one, my mother's seal, her chop mark** larger than the president's and the dean's; and one, the number 1279 on the back. Dean Woo's signature is followed by "(Hackett)." I read in a history book that Hackett Medical College for Women at Canton was founded in the nineteenth century by European women doctors.

The school seal has been pressed over a photograph of my mother at the age of thirty-seven. The diploma gives her age as twenty-seven. She looks younger than I do, her eyebrows are thicker, her lips fuller. Her naturally curly hair is parted on the left, one wavy wisp tendrilling off to the right. She wears a scholar's white gown, and she is not thinking about her appearance. She stares straight ahead as if she could see me and past me to her grandchildren and grandchildren's grandchildren. She has spacy eyes, as all people recently from Asia have. Her eyes do not focus on the camera. My mother is not smiling; Chinese do not smile for photographs. Their faces command relatives in foreign lands—"Send money"—and posterity forever—"Put food in front of this picture." My mother does not understand Chinese-American snapshots. "What are you laughing at?" she asks.

The second scroll is a long narrow photograph of the graduating class with the school officials seated in front. I picked out my mother immediately. Her face is exactly her own, though forty years younger. She is so familiar, I can only tell whether or not she is pretty or happy or smart by comparing her to the other women. For this formal group picture she straightened her hair with oil to make a chinlength bob like the others'. On the other women, strangers, I can recognize a curled lip, a sidelong glance, pinched shoulders. My mother is not soft; the girl with the small nose and dimpled underlip is soft. My mother is not humorous, not like the girl at the end who lifts her mocking chin to pose like Girl Graduate. My mother does not have smiling eyes; the old woman teacher (Dean Woo?) in front crinkles happily, and the one faculty member in the western suit

---

*EDS. NOTE—Foreign ex-assistant (teacher) at the surgical and maternity clinic of the University of Lyons (France).

**EDS. NOTE—Chinese seal.

smiles westernly. Most of the graduates are girls whose faces have not yet formed; my mother's face will not change anymore, except to age. She is intelligent, alert, pretty. I can't tell if she's happy.

The graduates seem to have been looking elsewhere when they pinned the rose, zinnia, or chrysanthemum on their precise black dresses. One thin girl wears hers in the middle of her chest. A few have a flower over a left or a right nipple. My mother put hers, a chrysanthemum, below her left breast. Chinese dresses at that time were dartless, cut as if women did not have breasts; these young doctors, unaccustomed to decorations, may have seen their chests as black expanses with no reference points for flowers. Perhaps they couldn't shorten that far gaze that lasts only a few years after a Chinese emigrates. In this picture too my mother's eyes are big with what they held—reaches of oceans beyond China, land beyond oceans. Most emigrants learn the barbarians' directness—how to gather themselves and stare rudely into talking faces as if trying to catch lies. In America my mother has eyes as strong as boulders, never once skittering off a face, but she has not learned to place decorations and phonograph needles, nor has she stopped seeing land on the other side of the oceans. Now her eyes include the relatives in China, as they once included my father smiling and smiling in his many western outfits, a different one for each photograph that he sent from America.

He and his friends took pictures of one another in bathing suits at Coney Island beach, the salt wind from the Atlantic blowing their hair. He's the one in the middle with his arms about the necks of his buddies. They pose in the cockpit of a biplane, on a motorcycle, and on a lawn beside the "Keep Off the Grass" sign. They are always laughing. My father, white shirt sleeves rolled up, smiles in front of a wall of clean laundry. In the spring he wears a new straw hat, cocked at a Fred Astaire angle. He steps out, dancing down the stairs, one foot forward, one back, a hand in his pocket. He wrote to her about the American custom of stomping on straw hats come fall. "If you want to save your hat for next year," he said, "you have to put it away early, or else when you're riding the subway or walking along Fifth Avenue, any stranger can snatch it off your head and put his foot through it. That's the way they celebrate the change of seasons here." In the winter he wears a gray felt hat with his gray overcoat. He is sitting on a rock in Central Park. In one snapshot he is not smiling; someone took it when he was studying, blurred in the glare of the desk lamp.

There are no snapshots of my mother. In two small portraits, however, there is a black thumbprint on her forehead, as if someone had inked in bangs, as if someone had marked her.

"Mother, did bangs come into fashion after you had the picture   8
taken?" One time she said yes. Another time when I asked, "Why
do you have fingerprints on your forehead?" she said, "Your First
Uncle did that." I disliked the unsureness in her voice.

The last scroll has columns of Chinese words. The only English   9
is "Department of Health, Canton," imprinted on my mother's face,
the same photograph as on the diploma. I keep looking to see whether
she was afraid. Year after year my father did not come home or
send for her. Their two children had been dead for ten years. If he
did not return soon, there would be no more children. ("They were
three and two years old, a boy and a girl. They could talk already.")
My father did send money regularly, though, and she had nobody
to spend it on but herself. She bought good clothes and shoes. Then
she decided to use the money for becoming a doctor. She did not
leave for Canton immediately after the children died. In China there
was time to complete feelings. As my father had done, my mother
left the village by ship. There was a sea bird painted on the ship to
protect it against shipwreck and winds. She was in luck. The following ship was boarded by river pirates, who kidnapped every passenger, even old ladies. "Sixty dollars for an old lady" was what the
bandits used to say. "I sailed alone," she says, "to the capital of the
entire province." She took a brown leather suitcase and a seabag
stuffed with two quilts.

COMPREHENSION

1. What did Kingston's mother study in China?

2. Kingston says that in a photograph her mother has "spacy eyes." What
   does she mean? Why don't Chinese smile for photographs?

3. What is the "barbarians' directness" that Kingston mentions? What does
   the use of this term show?

4. How do the photographs of Kingston's father show him to be different
   from his wife?

5. What qualities of Kingston's mother and father do the photographs reveal? What do they conceal?

PURPOSE AND AUDIENCE

1. What preconceptions does Kingston feel her audience has about Chinese
   men and women?

2. Does Kingston identify with her audience or her parents? Explain.

3. What is Kingston's purpose in writing this essay? What ideas does she wish to convey?

4. In your own words, state the thesis of this essay.

STYLE AND STRUCTURE

1. What is the organizing scheme for this description?

2. Why does Kingston spend so much time describing the stamps on her mother's diploma?

3. What effect does Kingston achieve by describing the single and group portraits one after the other?

4. How does Kingston use the photographs to fill in bits of her parents' history?

5. What is the dominant impression that Kingston wants to create with her description?

WRITING WORKSHOP

1. Select several pictures from a family album, and describe them. Try to organize in a way that links your pictures together.

2. Find a picture of a famous person in a book or magazine. Describe the picture, inferring as many character traits as you can from the expression or attitude of the subject.

ROCK OF AGES

Joan Didion

Joan Didion was born in 1934 in Sacramento, California. After graduating from the University of California at Berkeley, she worked as an editor for Vogue *and then for the* Saturday Evening Post, National Review, *and* Esquire. *Author of three novels, Didion is best known for* Slouching Towards Bethlehem *(1968), a collection of essays that examines the political and social unrest of the 1960s. "Rock of Ages" is taken from this collection and presents Didion's reactions to Alcatraz Island. Here she demonstrates how even the once infamous federal prison known as "The Rock" can yield a detailed and psychologically revealing subjective description.*

Alcatraz Island is covered with flowers now: orange and yellow nasturtiums, geraniums, sweet grass, blue iris, black-eyed Susans. Candytuft springs up through the cracked concrete in the exercise yard. Ice plant carpets the rusting catwalks. "WARNING! KEEP OFF! U.S. PROPERTY," the sign still reads, big and yellow and visible for perhaps a quarter of a mile, but since March 21, 1963, the day they took the last thirty or so men off the island and sent them to prisons less expensive to maintain, the warning has been only *pro forma,* the gun turrets empty, the cell blocks abandoned. It is not an unpleasant place to be, out there on Alcatraz with only the flowers and the wind and a bell buoy moaning and the tide surging through the Golden Gate, but to like a place like that you have to want a moat.

I sometimes do, which is what I am talking about here. Three people live on Alcatraz Island now. John and Marie Hart live in the same apartment they had for the sixteen years that he was a prison guard; they raised five children on the island, back when their neighbors were the Birdman and Mickey Cohen, but the Birdman and Mickey Cohen are gone now and so are the Harts' children, moved away, the last married in a ceremony on the island in June 1966. One other person lives on Alcatraz, a retired merchant seaman named Bill Doherty, and, between them, John Hart and Bill Doherty are responsible for the General Services Administration for maintaining a twenty-four-hour watch over the twenty-two-acre island. John Hart has a dog named Duffy, and Bill Doherty has a dog named Duke, and although the dogs are primarily good company they are also the first line of defense on Alcatraz Island. Marie Hart has a corner window which looks out to the San Francisco skyline, across a mile and a half of bay, and she sits there and paints "views" or plays her organ, songs like "Old Black Joe" and "Please Go 'Way and Let Me Sleep." Once a week the Harts take their boat to San Francisco to pick up their mail and shop at the big Safeway in the Marina, and occasionally Marie Hart gets off the island to visit her children. She likes to keep in touch with them by telephone, but for ten months recently, after a Japanese freighter cut the cable, there was no telephone service to or from Alcatraz. Every morning the KGO traffic reporter drops the San Francisco *Chronicle* from his helicopter, and when he has time he stops for coffee. No one else comes out there except a man from the General Services Administration named Thomas Scott, who brings out an occasional congressman or somebody who wants to buy the island or, once in a while, his wife and small son, for a picnic. Quite a few people would like to buy the island, and Mr. Scott reckons that it would bring about five million dollars in a sealed-bid auction, but the General Services Administration is powerless to sell it until Congress acts on a standing proposal to turn the island into a "peace park." Mr. Scott says that he will be glad to get Alcatraz off his hands, but the charge of a fortress island could not be something a man gives up without ambivalent thoughts.

I went out there with him a while ago. Any child could imagine a prison more like a prison than Alcatraz looks, for what bars and wires there are seem perfunctory, beside the point; the island itself was the prison, and the cold tide its wall. It is precisely what they called it: the Rock. Bill Doherty and Duke lowered the dock for us, and in the station wagon on the way up the cliff Bill Doherty told Mr. Scott about small repairs he had made or planned to make. Whatever repairs get made on Alcatraz are made to pass the time, a kind of caretaker's scrimshaw, because the government pays for no upkeep at all on the prison; in 1963 it would have cost five million dollars to repair, which is why it was abandoned, and the $24,000 a year that it costs to maintain Alcatraz now is mostly for surveillance, partly to barge in the 400,000 gallons of water that Bill Doherty and the Harts use every year (there is no water at all on Alcatraz, one impediment to development), and the rest to heat two apartments and keep some lights burning. The buildings seem quite literally abandoned. The key locks have been ripped from the cell doors and the big electrical locking mechanisms disconnected. The tear-gas vents in the cafeteria are empty and the paint is buckling everywhere, corroded by the sea air, peeling off in great scales of pale green and ocher. I stood for a while in Al Capone's cell, five by nine feet, number 200 on the second tier of B Block, not one of the view cells, which were awarded on seniority, and I walked through the solitary block, totally black when the doors were closed. "Snail Mitchell," read a pencil scrawl on the wall of Solitary 14. "The only man that ever got shot for walking too slow." Beside it was a calendar, the months penciled on the wall with the days scratched off, May, June, July, August of some unnumbered year.

Mr. Scott, whose interest in penology dates from the day his office   4 acquired Alcatraz as a potential property, talked about escapes and security routines and pointed out the beach where Ma Barker's son Doc was killed trying to escape. (They told him to come back up, and he said he would rather be shot, and he was.) I saw the shower room with the soap still in the dishes. I picked up a yellowed program from an Easter service (*Why seek ye the living among the dead? He is not here, but is risen*) and I struck a few notes on an upright piano with the ivory all rotted from the keys and I tried to imagine the prison as it had been, with the big lights playing over the windows all night long and the guards patrolling the gun galleries and the silverware clattering into a bag as it was checked in after meals, tried dutifully to summon up some distaste, some night terror of the doors locking and the boat pulling away. But the fact of it was that I liked it out there, a ruin devoid of human vanities, clean of human illusions, an empty place reclaimed by the weather where a woman plays an organ to stop the wind's whining and an old man plays ball with a dog named Duke. I could tell you that I came back because I had promises to keep, but maybe it was because nobody asked me to stay.

COMPREHENSION

1. Why does Didion visit Alcatraz Island?

2. Why did the government decide to close Alcatraz prison?

3. What duties do John and Marie Hart and Bill Doherty carry out on the island?

4. Why can't the General Services Administration sell Alcatraz Island?

5. What did Didion like about Alcatraz Island? What is the meaning of the last sentence of the essay?

PURPOSE AND AUDIENCE

1. What knowledge about Alcatraz does Didion assume her audience has?

2. Underline the sentence that best expresses Didion's thesis.

3. What is the focus of this essay—Alcatraz or Didion? Cite several examples to support your position.

STYLE AND STRUCTURE

1. What is the meaning of this essay's title? How does it express Didion's feelings about Alcatraz Island? ("Rock of Ages" is also the title of a hymn.)

2. Why does Didion begin her essay about Alcatraz with a description of flowers?

3. Why does so little of this essay describe the prison and its former inmates?

4. What details does Didion choose to focus on? What is the organizing scheme of her description?

5. At what point in her conclusion does Didion restate her thesis?

WRITING WORKSHOP

1. Write a subjective description of the home in which you grew up.

2. Walk through your campus or neighborhood, and find a building that has some unusual feature. Prepare to write your essay by jotting down as many significant details as possible. After reviewing your notes, write *either* an objective or subjective description of the building.

BRETT HAUSER:
SUPERMARKET BOX BOY

Studs Terkel

Studs Terkel was born in 1912 in Chicago. He graduated from the University of Chicago in 1932 and then from Chicago Law School in 1934. Since then he has traveled all over the world and held a variety of jobs. He has acted in radio soap operas, been a disc jockey, and conducted television interviews. Perhaps as a result of these experiences, Terkel has developed a keen interest in oral history. In his writing he attempts to present history through the words of the ordinary people who lived it. His books include Division Street: America, Hard Times: An Oral History of the Great Depression, Working, *and* Talking to Myself. *In "Brett Hauser: Supermarket Box Boy," Terkel presents his edited version of an interview with a supermarket box boy who talks about his job. Hauser's account, like the others in Terkel's book* Working, *is a subjective description that reveals his attitude toward the work he does. By editing the interview to emphasize certain details and to focus on selected incidents, Terkel enables his readers to grasp Brett Hauser's contradictory feelings about his work.*

He is seventeen. He had worked as a box boy at a supermarket in a middle-class suburb on the outskirts of Los Angeles. "People come to the counter and you put things in their bags for them. And carry things to their cars. It was a grind." 1

You have to be terribly subservient to people: "Ma'am, can I take your bag?" "Can I do this?" It was at a time when the grape strikers were passing out leaflets. They were very respectful people. People'd come into the check stand, they'd say, "I just bought grapes for the first time because of those idiots outside." I had to put their grapes in the bag and thank them for coming and take them outside to the car. Being subservient made me very resentful. 2

It's one of a chain of supermarkets. They're huge complexes with bakeries in them and canned music over those loudspeakers—Muzak. So people would relax while they shopped. They played selections from *Hair*. They'd play "Guantanamera," the Cuban Revolution song. They had *Soul on Ice*, the Cleaver book, on sale. They had everything dressed up and very nice. People wouldn't pay any attention to the music. They'd go shopping and hit their kids and talk about those idiots passing out anti-grape petitions. 3

102

Everything looks fresh and nice. You're not aware that in the   4
back room it stinks and there's crates all over the place and the
walls are messed up. There's graffiti and people are swearing and
yelling at each other. You walk through the door, the music starts
playing, and everything is pretty. You talk in hushed tones and are
very respectful.

You wear a badge with your name on it. I once met someone I   5
knew years ago. I remembered his name and said, "Mr. Castle, how
are you?" We talked about this and that. As he left, he said, "It was
nice talking to you, Brett." I felt great, he remembered me. Then I
looked down at my name plate. Oh shit. He didn't remember me at
all, he just read the name plate. I wish I put "Irving" down on my
name plate. If he'd have said, "Oh yes, Irving, how could I forget
you . . .?" I'd have been ready for him. There's nothing personal
here.

You have to be very respectful to everyone—the customers, to   6
the manager, to the checkers. There's a sign on the cash register
that says: Smile at the customer. Say hello to the customer. It's
assumed if you're a box boy, you're really there 'cause you want to
be a manager some day. So you learn all the little things you have
absolutely no interest in learning.

The big thing there is to be an assistant manager and eventually   7
manager. The male checkers had dreams of being manager, too. It
was like an internship. They enjoyed watching how the milk was
packed. Each manager had his own domain. There was the ice cream
manager, the grocery manager, the dairy case manager . . . They
had a sign in the back: Be good to your job and your job will be
good to you. So you take an overriding concern on how the ice cream
is packed. You just die if something falls off a shelf. I saw so much
crap there I just couldn't take. There was a black boy, an Oriental
box boy, and a kid who had a Texas drawl. They needed the job to
subsist. I guess I had the luxury to hate it and quit.

When I first started there, the manager said, "Cut your hair.   8
Come in a white shirt, black shoes, a tie. Be here on time." You get
there, but he isn't there. I just didn't know what to do. The checker
turns around and says, "You new? What's your name?" "Brett." "I'm
Peggy." And that's all they say and they keep throwing this down
to you. They'll say, "Don't put it in that, put it in there." But they
wouldn't help you.

You had to keep your apron clean. You couldn't lean back on the   9
railings. You couldn't talk to the checkers. You couldn't accept tips.
Okay, I'm outside and I put it in the car. For a lot of people, the
natural reaction is to take out a quarter and give it to me. I'd say,

"I'm sorry, I can't." They'd get offended. When you give someone a tip, you're sort of suave. You take a quarter and you put it in their palm and you expect them to say, "Oh, thanks a lot." When you say, "I'm sorry, I can't," they feel a little put down. They say, "No one will know." And they put it in your pocket. You say, "I really can't." It gets to a point where you have to do physical violence to a person to avoid being tipped. It was not consistent with the store's philosophy of being cordial. Accepting tips was a cordial thing and made the customer feel good. I just couldn't understand the incongruity. One lady actually put it in my pocket, got in the car, and drove away. I would have had to throw the quarter at her or eaten it or something.

When it got slow, the checkers would talk about funny things 10 that happened. About Us and Them. Us being the people who worked there, Them being the stupid fools who didn't know where anything was—just came through and messed everything up and shopped. We serve them but we don't like them. We know where everything is. We know what time the market closes and they don't. We know what you do with coupons and they don't. There was a camaraderie of sorts. It wasn't healthy, though. It was a put-down of the others.

There was this one checker who was absolutely vicious. He took 11 great delight in making every little problem into a major crisis from which he had to emerge victorious. A customer would give him a coupon. He'd say, "You were supposed to give me that at the beginning." She'd say, "Oh, I'm sorry." He'd say, "Now I gotta open the cash register and go through the whole thing. Madam, I don't watch out for every customer. I can't manage your life." A put-down.

It never bothered me when I would put something in the bag 12 wrong. In the general scheme of things, in the large questions of the universe, putting a can of dog food in the bag wrong is not of great consequence. For them it was.

There were a few checkers who were nice. There was one that 13 was incredibly sad. She could be unpleasant at times, but she talked to everybody. She was one of the few people who genuinely wanted to talk to people. She was saying how she wanted to go to school and take courses so she could get teaching credit. Someone asked her, "Why don't you?" She said, "I have to work here. My hours are wrong. I'd have to get my hours changed." They said, "Why don't you?" She's worked there for years. She had seniority. She said, "Jim won't let me." Jim was the manager. He didn't give a damn. She wanted to go to school, to teach, but she can't because every day she's got to go back to the supermarket and load groceries. Yet she wasn't bitter. If she died a checker and never enriched her life, that was okay, because those were her hours.

She was extreme in her unpleasantness and her consideration. 14 Once I dropped some grape juice and she was squawking like a bird. I came back and mopped it up. She kept saying to me, "Don't worry about it. It happens to all of us." She'd say to the customers, "If I had a dime for all the grape juice I dropped . . ."

Jim's the boss. A fish-type handshake. He was balding and in his 15 forties. A lot of managers are these young, clean-shaven, neatly cropped people in their twenties. So Jim would say things like "groovy." You were supposed to get a ten-minute break every two hours. I lived for that break. You'd go outside, take your shoes off, and be human again. You had to request it. And when you took it, they'd make you feel guilty.

You'd go up and say, "Jim, can I have a break?" He'd say, "A 16 break? You want a break? Make it a quick one, nine and a half minutes." Ha ha ha. One time I asked the assistant manager, Henry. He was even older than Jim. "Do you think I can have a break?" He'd say, "You got a break when you were hired." Ha ha ha. Even when they joked it was a put-down.

The guys who load the shelves are a step above the box boys. It's 17 like upperclassmen at an officer candidate's school. They would make sure that you conformed to all the prescribed rules, because they were once box boys. They know what you're going through, your anxieties. But instead of making it easier for you, they'd make it harder. It's like a military institution.

I kept getting box boys who came up to me, "Has Jim talked to 18 you about your hair? He's going to because it's getting too long. You better get it cut or grease it back or something." They took delight in it. They'd come to me before Jim had told me. Everybody was out putting everybody down . . .

COMPREHENSION

1. What does Brett Hauser think of the supermarket customers? What is his opinion of the supermarket itself? What statements lead you to your conclusions?

2. What does Hauser think of himself?

3. What does Hauser mean when he says that the camaraderie that existed among the workers in the store "wasn't healthy"?

4. Describe Hauser's physical appearance on the job.

5. Give some examples of the "put-downs" Hauser describes.

PURPOSE AND AUDIENCE

1. Hauser's audience during this interview was Studs Terkel, but Terkel expected his collection of interviews to be read widely. (In fact, it was a best-seller.) What do you think Hauser's purpose was in talking to Terkel? What do you think Terkel's purpose was in collecting interviews about how people feel about their jobs?

2. Formulate a thesis statement for this interview.

3. Hauser states that he had the luxury to hate his job and even to quit. How does this affect your reaction to his complaints?

STYLE AND STRUCTURE

1. Studs Terkel prefaces Hauser's remarks with an introduction. Is this introductory paragraph necessary? Is it complete enough? If so, why? If not, what else do you think Terkel should tell the reader?

2. Originally this was not a written essay; Hauser told his story to Terkel. Can you tell by the style or organization that this was spoken rather than written? If so, how? Be specific.

3. Terkel has Hauser tell his own story instead of telling Hauser's story for him. Why do you think Terkel chooses this option here (and throughout the book *Working*)?

4. Does this selection have an organizing scheme? If so, what is it? If not, why not?

5. This selection contains several narrative sections. Identify them. What is their purpose?

WRITING WORKSHOP

1. Write a descriptive essay about the physical environment of the worst job you ever had. Select and order the details you use so they convey to the reader your feelings about the work you had to do.

2. Visit a supermarket or some other store to observe the employees. Describe the physical appearance or behavior of several of the people you see working there.

ONCE MORE TO THE LAKE

E. B. White

Elwyn Brooks White was born in 1899 in Mount Vernon, New York. After attending Cornell University, he became a regular contributor to The New Yorker *in 1926. Widely praised for his prose style, White wrote many editorials, features, and essays. In 1957, he moved permanently to his farm in North Brookline, Maine. He has published many books, including the children's story* Charlotte's Web *(1952),* One Man's Meat *(1944), and* The Second Tree from the Corner *(1954). His collected letters were published in 1976 and his* Essays *in 1977. In 1966, he won the presidential Medal of Freedom. "Once More to the Lake" (1941), reprinted from* One Man's Meat, *is a classic essay of personal reminiscence. Using precise detail and vivid language, he masterfully creates the lakeside camp he visited with his son.*

One summer, along about 1904, my father rented a camp on a 1
lake in Maine and took us all there for the month of August. We
all got ringworm from some kittens and had to rub Pond's Extract
on our arms and legs night and morning, and my father rolled over
in a canoe with all his clothes on; but outside of that the vacation
was a success and from then on none of us ever thought there was
any place in the world like that lake in Maine. We returned summer
after summer—always on August 1st for one month. I have since
become a salt-water man, but sometimes in summer there are days
when the restlessness of the tides and the fearful cold of the sea
water and the incessant wind which blows across the afternoon and
into the evening make me wish for the placidity of a lake in the
woods. A few weeks ago this feeling got so strong I bought myself
a couple of bass hooks and a spinner and returned to the lake where
we used to go, for a week's fishing and to revisit old haunts.

I took along my son, who had never had any fresh water up his 2
nose and who had seen lily pads only from train windows. On the
journey over to the lake I began to wonder what it would be like. I
wondered how time would have marred this unique, this holy spot—
the coves and streams, the hills that the sun set behind, the camps
and the paths behind the camps. I was sure that the tarred road
would have found it out and I wondered in what other ways it would

be desolated. It is strange how much you can remember about places like that once you allow your mind to return into the grooves which lead back. You remember one thing, and that suddenly reminds you of another thing. I guess I remembered clearest of all the early mornings, when the lake was cool and motionless, remembered how the bedroom smelled of the lumber it was made of and of the wet woods whose scent entered through the screen. The partitions in the camp were thin and did not extend clear to the top of the rooms, and as I was always the first up I would dress softly so as not to wake the others, and sneak out into the sweet outdoors and start out in the canoe, keeping close along the shore in the long shadows of the pines. I remembered being very careful never to rub my paddle against the gunwale for fear of disturbing the stillness of the cathedral.

The lake had never been what you would call a wild lake. There 3 were cottages sprinkled around the shores, and it was in farming country although the shores of the lake were quite heavily wooded. Some of the cottages were owned by nearby farmers, and you would live at the shore and eat your meals at the farmhouse. That's what our family did. But although it wasn't wild, it was a fairly large and undisturbed lake and there were places in it which, to a child at least, seemed infinitely remote and primeval.

I was right about the tar: it led to within half a mile of the shore. 4 But when I got back there, with my boy, and we settled into a camp near a farmhouse and into the kind of summertime I had known, I could tell that it was going to be pretty much the same as it had been before— I knew it, lying in bed the first morning, smelling the bedroom, and hearing the boy sneak quietly out and go off along the shore in a boat. I began to sustain the illusion that he was I, and therefore, by simple transposition, that I was my father. This sensation persisted, kept cropping up all the time we were there. It was not an entirely new feeling, but in this setting it grew much stronger. I seemed to be living a dual existence. I would be in the middle of some simple act, I would be picking up a bait box or laying down a table fork, or I would be saying something, and suddenly it would be not I but my father who was saying the words or making the gesture. It gave me a creepy sensation.

We went fishing the first morning. I felt the same damp moss 5 covering the worms in the bait can, and saw the dragonfly alight on the tip of my rod as it hovered a few inches from the surface of the water. It was the arrival of this fly that convinced me beyond any doubt that everything was as it always had been, that the years were a mirage and there had been no years. The small waves were the same, chucking the rowboat under the chin as we fished at anchor, and the boat was the same boat, the same color green and the ribs broken in the same places, and under the floor-boards the same freshwater leavings and débris—the dead helgramite,* the wisps of moss, the rusty discarded fishhook, the dried blood from yesterday's catch. We stared silently at the tips of our rods, at the dragonflies that came and went. I lowered the tip of mine into the water, tentatively, pensively dislodging the fly, which darted two feet away, poised, darted two feet back, and came to rest again a little farther up the rod. There had been no years between the ducking of this dragonfly and the other one—the one that was part of memory. I looked at the boy, who was silently watching his fly, and it was my hands that held his rod, my eyes watching. I felt dizzy and didn't know which rod I was at the end of.

We caught two bass, hauling them in briskly as though they were   6 mackerel, pulling them over the side of the boat in a businesslike manner without any landing net, and stunning them with a blow on the back of the head. When we got back for a swim before lunch, the lake was exactly where we had left it, the same number of inches from the dock, and there was only the merest suggestion of a breeze. This seemed an utterly enchanted sea, this lake you could leave to its own devices for a few hours and come back to, and find that it had not stirred, this constant and trustworthy body of water. In the shallows, the dark, water-soaked sticks and twigs, smooth and old, were undulating in clusters on the bottom against the clean ribbed sand, and the track of the mussel was plain. A school of minnows swam by, each minnow with its small individual shadow, doubling the attendance, so clear and sharp in the sunlight. Some of the other campers were in swimming, along the shore, one of them with a cake of soap, and the water felt thin and clear and unsubstantial. Over the years there had been this person with the cake of soap, this cultist, and here he was. There had been no years.

Up to the farmhouse to dinner through the teeming, dusty field,   7 the road under our sneakers was only a two-track road. The middle track was missing, the one with the marks of the hooves and the splotches of dried, flaky manure. There had always been three tracks to choose from in choosing which track to walk in; now the choice was narrowed down to two. For a moment I missed terribly the middle alternative. But the way led past the tennis court, and something about the way it lay there in the sun reassured me; the tape had loosened along the backline, the alleys were green with plan-

*EDS. NOTE—An insect larva often used as bait.

tains and other weeds, and the net (installed in June and removed in September) sagged in the dry noon, and the whole place steamed with midday heat and hunger and emptiness. There was a choice of pie for dessert, and one was blueberry and one was apple, and the waitresses were the same country girls, there having been no passage of time, only the illusion of it as in a dropped curtain—the waitresses were still fifteen; their hair had been washed, that was the only difference—they had been to the movies and seen the pretty girls with the clean hair.

Summertime, oh summertime, pattern of life indelible, the fade-proof lake, the woods unshatterable, the pasture with the sweetfern and the juniper forever and ever, summer without end; this was the background, and the life along the shore was the design, the cottages with their innocent and tranquil design, their tiny docks with the flagpole and the American flag floating against the white clouds in the blue sky, the little paths over the roots of the trees leading from camp to camp and the paths leading back to the outhouses and the can of lime for sprinkling, and at the souvenir counters at the store the miniature birch-bark canoes and the post cards that showed things looking a little better than they looked. This was the American family at play, escaping the city heat, wondering whether the newcomers in the camp at the head of the cove were "common" or "nice," wondering whether it was true that the people who drove up for Sunday dinner at the farmhouse were turned away because there wasn't enough chicken. 8

It seemed to me, as I kept remembering all this, that those times and those summers had been infinitely precious and worth saving. There had been jollity and peace and goodness. The arriving (at the beginning of August) had been so big a business in itself, at the railway station the farm wagon drawn up, the first smell of the pineladen air, the first glimpse of the smiling farmer, and the great importance of the trunks and your father's enormous authority in such matters, and the feel of the wagon under you for the long ten-mile haul, and at the top of the last long hill catching the first view of the lake after eleven months of not seeing this cherished body of water. The shouts and cries of the other campers when they saw you, and the trunks to be unpacked, to give up their rich burden. (Arriving was less exciting nowadays, when you sneaked up in your car and parked it under a tree near the camp and took out the bags and in five minutes it was all over, no fuss, no loud wonderful fuss about trunks.) 9

Peace and goodness and jollity. The only thing that was wrong now, really, was the sound of the place, an unfamiliar nervous sound of the outboard motors. This was the note that jarred, the one thing 10 that would sometimes break the illusion and set the years moving. In those other summertimes all motors were inboard; and when they were at a little distance, the noise they made was a sedative, an ingredient of summer sleep. They were one-cylinder and two-cylinder engines, and some were make-and-break and some were jump-spark, but they all made a sleepy sound across the lake. The one-lungers throbbed and fluttered, and the twin-cylinder ones purred and purred, and that was a quiet sound too. But now the campers all had outboards. In the daytime, in the hot mornings, these motors made a petulant, irritable sound; at night, in the still evening when the afterglow lit the water, they whined about one's ears like mosquitoes. My boy loved our rented outboard, and his great desire was to achieve singlehanded mastery over it, and authority, and he soon learned the trick of choking it a little (but not too much), and the adjustment of the needle valve. Watching him I would remember the things you could do with the old one-cylinder engine with the heavy flywheel, how you could have it eating out of your hand if you got really close to it spiritually. Motor boats in those days didn't have clutches, and you would make a landing by shutting off the motor at the proper time and coasting in with a dead rudder. But there was a way of reversing them, if you learned the trick, by cutting the switch and putting it on again exactly on the final dying revolution of the flywheel, so that it would kick back against compression and begin reversing. Approaching a dock in a strong following breeze, it was difficult to slow up sufficiently by the ordinary coasting method, and if a boy felt he had complete mastery over his motor, he was tempted to keep it running beyond its time and then reverse it a few feet from the dock. It took a cool nerve, because if you threw the switch a twentieth of a second too soon you could catch the flywheel when it still had speed enough to go up past center, and the boat would leap ahead, charging bull-fashion at the dock.

We had a good week at the camp. The bass were biting well and the sun shone endlessly, day after day. We would be tired at night and lie down in the accumulated heat of the little bedrooms after the long hot day and the breeze would stir almost imperceptibly outside and the smell of the swamp drift in through the rusty screens. Sleep would come easily and in the morning the red squirrel would be on the roof, tapping out his gay routine. I kept remembering everything, lying in bed in the mornings—the small steamboat that had a long rounded stern like the lip of a Ubangi,* and how quietly

*EDS. NOTE—An African tribe whose members wear mouth ornaments that stretch their lips into a saucerlike shape.

she ran on the moonlight sails, when the older boys played their mandolins and the girls sang and we ate doughnuts dipped in sugar, and how sweet the music was on the water in the shining night, and what it had felt like to think about girls then. After breakfast we would go up to the store and the things were in the same place— the minnows in a bottle, the plugs and spinners disarranged and pawed over by the youngsters from the boys' camp, the fig newtons and the Beeman's gum. Outside, the road was tarred and cars stood in front of the store. Inside, all was just as it had always been, except there was more Coca-Cola and not so much Moxie and root beer and birch beer and sarsaparilla. We would walk out with a bottle of pop apiece and sometimes the pop would backfire up our noses and hurt. We explored the streams, quietly, where the turtles slid off the sunny logs and dug their way into the soft bottom; and we lay on the town wharf and fed worms to the tame bass. Everywhere we went I had trouble making out which was I, the one walking at my side, the one walking in my pants.

One afternoon while we were there at that lake a thunderstorm 12 came up. It was like the revival of an old melodrama that I had seen long ago with childish awe. The second-act climax of the drama of the electrical disturbance over a lake in America had not changed in any important respect. This was the big scene, still the big scene. The whole thing was so familiar, the first feeling of oppression and heat and a general air around camp of not wanting to go very far away. In midafternoon (it was all the same) a curious darkening of the sky, and a lull in everything that had made life tick; and then the way the boats suddenly swung the other way at their moorings with the coming of a breeze out of the new quarter, and the premonitory rumble. Then the kettle drum, then the snare, then the bass drum and cymbals, then crackling light against the dark, and the gods grinning and licking their chops in the hills. Afterward the calm, the rain steadily rustling in the calm lake, the return of light and hope and spirits, and the campers running out in joy and relief to go swimming in the rain, their bright cries perpetuating the deathless joke about how they were getting simply drenched, and the children screaming with delight at the new sensation of bathing in the rain, and the joke about getting drenched linking the generations in a strong indestructible chain. And the comedian who waded in carrying an umbrella.

When the others went swimming my son said he was going in 13 too. He pulled his dripping trunks from the line where they had hung all through the shower, and wrung them out. Languidly, and with no thought of going in, I watched him, his hard little body, skinny and bare, saw him wince slightly as he pulled up around his vitals the small, soggy, icy garment. As he buckled the swollen belt suddenly my groin felt the chill of death.

COMPREHENSION

1. In what ways are the author and his son alike? In what ways are they different?

2. What does White mean when he says, "I seemed to be living a dual existence"?

3. At one time White says that "there had been no years," and at another he senses that things are different. How do you account for these conflicting feelings?

4. Why does White feel disconcerted when he discovers that the road to the farmhouse had two tracks, not three? What do you make of his comment, "now the choice was narrowed down to two"?

5. What is White referring to in the last sentence?

PURPOSE AND AUDIENCE

1. What is the thesis of this essay? Is it stated or implied?

2. Does White expect the ending of his essay to be a surprise to his audience? Explain.

3. To what age group do you think this essay would appeal most? Why?

4. How does White expect his readers to react to his description of the camp?

STYLE AND STRUCTURE

1. Why does White begin his essay with a short narrative about his trip to the lake in 1904? What context does this opening provide for the entire essay?

2. What ideas and images does White repeat throughout his essay? What is the purpose of this repetition?

3. In paragraph 12, White describes a thunderstorm. How does he use language to convey the experience of the storm to his readers?

4. White goes to great lengths to describe how things look, feel, smell, taste, and sound. How does this help him achieve his purpose in this essay?

5. In what way does White's conclusion refer back to the first paragraph of the essay?

WRITING WORKSHOP

1. Write a description of a scene you remember from your childhood. In your essay discuss how your current view of the scene differs from your view as a child.

2. Write a description of a person, place, or thing in which you appeal to a reader's five senses.

4

Exemplification

WHAT IS EXEMPLIFICATION?

You have probably noticed when watching television talk shows or listening to classroom discussions that the most lively and interesting exchanges take place when those involved illustrate their general assertions with specific examples. It is one thing to say, "The mayor is corrupt and should not be reelected," and another to exemplify his corruption by saying, "The mayor should not be reelected because he has fired two city employees who refused to contribute to his campaign fund, put his family and friends on the city payroll, and used public funds to pay for improvements on his home." The same principle applies to writing, and many of the best essays extensively use examples. Exemplification is used in every kind of writing situation, either as a basic essay pattern or in combination with every other pattern of development, to explain, to add interest, and to persuade.

Examples Explain and Clarify

On a film midterm, you might say, "Even though horror movies seem modern, they really aren't." You may think your statement is perfectly clear, but don't be surprised when your exam comes back with a question mark in the margin next to this sentence. After all, your statement goes no further than making a general assertion or claim about horror movies. It is not specific, nor does it anticipate a reader's questions about the ways in which horror movies are not modern. Furthermore, it includes no examples, your best means of ensuring clarity and avoiding ambiguity. To make sure your audience knows exactly what you mean, you should state your point precisely: "Despite the fact that horror movies seem modern, the

115

most memorable ones are adaptations of nineteenth-century Gothic novels."

If you were developing a whole paper around this idea, you would illustrate your point thoroughly by analyzing specific films like *Frankenstein,* directed by James Whale, and *Dracula,* directed by Todd Browning, and by linking them with the novels on which they are based. With the benefit of these specific examples, a reader would know that you meant that the literary roots of such movies are in the past, not that their cinematic techniques or production methods are dated. Moreover, a reader would understand which literary sources you meant. With these additions, your point would be clear.

Examples Add Interest

The more relevant detail you provide for your readers, the more intriguing and engaging your essay will be. Well-chosen examples provide such detail and add life to relatively bland or straightforward statements. Laurence J. Peter and Raymond Hull skillfully use this technique in their essay "The Peter Principle," which appears later in this chapter. In itself, their assertion that each employee in a system rises to his or her level of incompetence is not particularly engrossing. It becomes intriguing, however, when supported by specific examples, such as the cases of the affable foreman who becomes the indecisive supervisor, the exacting mechanic who becomes the disorganized foreman, and the charismatic battlefield general who becomes the impotent and self-destructive field marshal.

When you use exemplification to support your assertions, look for examples that are interesting in themselves. Test the vigor of your examples by putting yourself in your reader's place. If you wouldn't find your own essay lively and interesting, you need to rewrite it with more spirited examples. After all, your goal is to communicate your ideas to your readers, and energetic, imaginative examples can make the difference between an engrossing essay and one that is a chore to read.

Examples Persuade

Although you may use examples simply to help explain an idea or to interest or entertain your readers, examples are also an effective way of convincing others that what you are saying is reasonable and true. A few well-chosen examples can eliminate pages of gen-

eral, and many times unconvincing, explanations. The old cliché
that a picture is worth a thousand words is equally true for an
example. For instance, a statement on an economics quiz that "rising costs and high unemployment have changed life for many Americans" needs such support to be convincing. Noting appropriate examples—that in a typical working-class neighborhood one out of
every six primary wage earners is now jobless and that many white-
collar workers can no longer afford to go to movies or to eat any
beef except hamburger—can persuade a reader that the statement
is valid. Similarly, a statement in a biology paper that "despite
recent moves to reverse its status, DDT should not be released to
commercial users and should continue to be banned" is unconvincing without persuasive examples like these to back it up:

- Even though DDT has been banned for more than a decade,
  traces are still being found in the eggs of various fish and water
  fowl.
- Certain lakes and streams cannot be used for sport and recre-
  ation because DDT levels are dangerously high, presumably
  because of farmland runoff.
- DDT has been found in the milk of a significant number of
  nursing mothers.
- DDT residues, apparently carried by global air currents, have
  even been found in meltwater samples from Antarctica.
- Because of its stability as a compound, DDT does not degrade
  quickly, and, therefore, existent residues will threaten the environment well into the twenty-first century.

Examples are often necessary to convince, so choosing effective
examples to support your ideas is important. When deciding which
ones to include in an essay, you should consider both the quality
and the quantity of your examples.

Examples Test Your Point

Everyone knows the old saying that "the exception proves (that
is, tests) the rule." Certain examples can help you test your ideas
as well as the ideas of others. For instance, let's suppose you plan
to write a paper for freshman composition about the decline in verbal skills of students nationwide. Your thesis is that writing well
is an inborn talent and that teachers can do little to help people
write better. But is this really true? Has it been true in your own

case? To test your point, you go back over your academic career and brainstorm about the various teachers who tried to help you improve your writing.

As you assemble your list, you remember Mrs. Colson, a teacher you had when you were a junior in high school. She was strict, required lots of writing, and seemed to accept nothing less than perfection. At the time neither you nor your classmates liked her; in fact, her nickname was Warden Colson. But looking back, you recall her private conferences, her organized lessons, and her pointed comments. You also remember her careful review of essay tests and that after your year with her, you felt much more comfortable taking such tests. After examining some papers that you saved, you are surprised to see how much your writing actually improved that year. These examples cause you to reevaluate your ideas and revise your thesis. You now feel that even though the job is difficult, a good teacher can make a difference in a person's writing.

Using Enough Examples

Unfortunately, there is no general rule to tell you whether to use one example or many to support your ideas. In some cases, one example will be sufficient, and in others, more will be needed. Simply stated, the number of examples you should use depends upon your thesis. If, for instance, your thesis is that an educational institution, like a business, needs careful financial management, a detailed consideration of your own school or university could work well. This one *extended example* could provide all the detail necessary for you to make your point. In this case, you would not need to include examples from a number of schools. In fact, too many examples could prove tedious to your readers and undercut your points.

On the other hand, if your thesis were that conflict between sons and fathers is a recurrent theme throughout the works of Franz Kafka, several examples would be necessary. One example would show only that the theme of conflict is present in *one* of Kafka's works. In this case, the more examples you include, the more effectively you prove your point. Of course, for some theses even a great number of examples would not be enough. You would, for instance, have a very difficult time finding enough examples to demonstrate convincingly that children from small families have more successful careers than children from large families. This thesis would require nothing less than a statistical study to prove its validity, certainly an impractical, if not impossible, procedure for most of us.

Selecting a sufficient range of examples is just as important as choosing an appropriate number of examples to support your ideas. If you wanted to convince a reader that Douglas MacArthur was an able general, you would choose examples from more than just the early part of his career. Likewise, if you wanted to argue that outdoor advertising was ruining the scenic view from local highways, you would discuss an area larger than your immediate neighborhood. Your object in every case is to select a cross section of examples appropriate for the boundaries of your topic.

Using Representative Examples

Just as professional pollsters take great pains to assure that their samples actually do reflect the makeup of the general public, so your examples should fairly represent the total group about which your thesis makes an assertion. If you wanted to support a ban on smoking in all public buildings, you could not base your supporting points solely on the benefits of such a ban for restaurants. To be convincing, you would have to widen your scope to include other public places such as city buildings, hospital lobbies, and movie theaters. For the same reason, one person's experience or one school's problems aren't sufficient for a conclusion about many others unless you can establish that the experience or problems are typical in some significant way.

If you decide that you cannot cite enough representative examples to support your point, reexamine your thesis. Rather than switching to a new topic, you may be able to make your thesis narrower. After all, the only way your paper will be convincing is if your readers feel that your examples and your claim about your topic correspond—that your thesis is supported by your examples and that your examples fairly represent the breadth of your topic.

Of course, your essay will be a success not simply because you use examples effectively but because you keep your essay focused on your point. A constant danger when using examples is that you may get so involved with one that you lose sight of what your paper is really about. Then the result is that you wander off into a digression. Disregarding your paper's topic in this way not only could confuse your readers but also could render much of your essay irrelevant. Thus, no matter how carefully they are developed, no matter how specific, lively, and appropriate they are, to be effective all of your examples must address the main idea of your essay.

STRUCTURING AN EXEMPLIFICATION ESSAY

Essays organized around examples usually follow a straightforward pattern. The introduction includes the thesis, which is supported by examples in the body of the essay. Each middle paragraph develops a separate example, an aspect of an extended example, or a point illustrated by several brief examples. The conclusion restates the thesis and reinforces the main idea of the essay. Of course, this pattern need not be followed rigidly. At times, variations are advisable, even necessary. For instance, beginning your paper with a striking example might stimulate your reader's interest and curiosity; ending with one might vividly reinforce your thesis.

Exemplification presents one special organizational problem. In an essay of this type, a large number of examples is not unusual. If these examples are not handled properly, your paper could become a thesis followed by a list or by ten or fifteen very brief paragraphs, resulting in a choppy, confused paper. One way to avoid this problem is to select your best examples for full development in separate paragraphs and to drop the others. Another way is to gather related examples together and to group them in paragraphs. Within each paragraph, examples could be arranged in order of increasing importance or persuasiveness, to hold and increase your audience's interest. Such an arrangement is illustrated by the following outline for a paper evaluating the nursing care at a local hospital. Notice how well the author groups his examples under four general categories: private rooms, semiprivate rooms, emergency wards, and outpatient clinics.

¶1   Introduction—thesis: The quality of nursing care at Albert Einstein Hospital is excellent.
¶2   Private rooms
       Example 1: Responsiveness
       Example 2: Effective rapport established
       Example 3: Good bedside care
¶3   Semiprivate rooms
       Example 4: Efficient use of time
       Example 5: Small ratio of nurses to patients
       Example 6: Patient-centered care
¶4   Emergency wards
       Example 7: Adequate staffing
       Example 8: Nurses circulating among patients in the waiting room

Example 9: Satisfactory working relationship between doctors and nurses
¶5 Outpatient clinics
Example 10: Nurses preparing patients
Example 11: Nurses assisting during treatment
Example 12: Nurses instructing patients after treatment
¶6 Conclusion—restatement of thesis

Exemplification is frequently used in nonacademic writing situations; fiscal reports, memos, progress reports, and proposals can be organized this way. One of the more important uses you may make of the example pattern is in applying for a job. Your letter of application to a prospective employer is usually a variation of this form.

2432 Oak Drive
Reston, Virginia 22090
February 17, 1982

Mr. R. W. Weaver
Product Safety Division
General Motors Company
Detroit, Michigan 48202

Dear Mr. Weaver:

Opening   I have learned of your opening for a   1
product safety engineer both from your
advertisement in the February <u>Journal
of Product Safety Engineering</u> and from
my work-study adviser, Dr. Jerome
Weishoff. As you know, Dr. Weishoff has
worked as a consultant to your division, and he has inspired much of my
enthusiasm about my field and about
this opportunity to work on your re-
Thesis search team. I am confident that my ed-

ucation and experience have prepared me to join General Motors as a product safety engineer.

Brief examples   At present I am a senior at Drexel University where I am majoring in electrical engineering. Throughout my academic career I have maintained a 3.65 average and have been on the dean's list every quarter but one. In addition, I have been active in the campus community as junior class president and in my professional field as secretary of the product safety engineering society. 2

Brief examples   My theoretical background corresponds to the criteria mentioned in your advertisement. Besides my electrical engineering program, which emphasized solid-state circuitry, I have taken two advanced physics classes. Moreover, through my computer courses, including systems programming, I have acquired a working knowledge of Cobol and Fortran. 3

Major example   I spent my work-study periods working in the product safety division of the Budd Company in Philadelphia. During this time, I worked closely with my supervisor, Norman Gainor, manager of the product safety division. Our special projects included a study of circuit failure in subway cars. 4

Closing   I have enclosed a résumé and will be   5
available to discuss my qualifications
any time after graduation on March 17.
I am looking forward to meeting with
you, and I hope to hear from you soon.

Sincerely,

Doris J. Miller

Points for Special Attention

Organization. Exemplification is ideally suited for letters of application. Doris Miller wants to make claims about her qualifications for the job. The only way she can support her claims persuasively is to set forth her experience and knowledge. The body of her letter is divided into three categories: educational record, theoretical background, and work-study experience. Each of the body paragraphs has a clear purpose and function, and each contains specific examples which tell the prospective employer what qualifies her for the job. In these paragraphs, she uses order of importance to arrange not only her claims but also her examples. Although her academic record is important, in this case it is not as significant to an employer as her experience. Because her practical knowledge directly relates to the position she wants, Doris considered this her strongest point and wisely chose to present it last.

Doris closes her letter with a request for an interview. In it, she not only asserts her willingness to be interviewed but also gives the date after which she will be available. Because people remember best what they read last, a strong conclusion is as essential here as it is in other writing situations. In a letter of application, the most effective strategy is to end with a request for an interview.

Persuasive Examples. In order to support a thesis convincingly, examples should convey specific information, not just judgments. Saying "I am a good student who works hard at her studies" means very little. It is better to say, as Doris Miller does, "Throughout my academic career I have maintained a 3.65 average and have been on the dean's list every quarter but one." A letter of application should show a prospective employer how your strengths and background correspond to the employer's needs, and specific examples can help such a reader reach the proper conclusions.

The following essay, by Norman Falzone, illustrates a more traditional use of the example pattern. Written for an English composition class, it answers the question, "Is there too much violence on children's television?"

SATURDAY MORNING VIOLENCE

Introduction   For the past five years, television   1
networks have come under increasing at-
tack for the violent programs that fill
their schedules. Psychologists and communications experts have formulated
scales to measure the carnage that
comes into American homes daily. Sociologists have discussed the possible
effects of this situation on the viewing public. One area that is currently
receiving attention is children's tele-
Thesis   vision. As even a cursory glance at
Saturday morning cartoon shows reveals,
children are being exposed to a steady
diet of violence that rivals that of
the prime-time shows their parents so
eagerly watch.

Brief   Children's cartoons have tradition-   2
examples ally contained much violence, and this
situation is something we have learned
to accept as normal. Consider how much
a part of our landscape the following
situations are. The coyote chases the
roadrunner and finds himself standing
in midair over a deep chasm. For a
fraction of a second he looks patheti-
cally at the audience; then he plunges
to the ground. Elmer Fudd puts his

shotgun into a tree where Bugs Bunny is hiding. Bugs bends the barrel so that, when Elmer pulls the trigger, the gun discharges into his face. A dog chases Woody Woodpecker into a sawmill and, unable to stop, slides into the whirling blade of a circular saw. As the scene ends, the two halves of the dog fall to the ground with a clatter.

Major example Where these so-called traditional cartoons depict violence as an isolated occurrence, newer cartoons portray it as a normal condition of life. The "Godzilla Super-Ninety Show" is a good example of this. Every Saturday morning, Godzilla, a prehistoric dinosaur who appears when called by his human companions, battles monsters that seem to appear everywhere. Every week the plot stays the same; only the monsters change. And every week the message to the young viewers is the same: "Only by violent action can the problems of the world be solved." For it is only when Godzilla burns, tears, crushes, drowns, or stamps his adversaries to death that the status quo can be reestablished. There is never an attempt by the human characters to help themselves or to find a rational explanation for what is happening to them.

Major example Even more shocking is the violence depicted in "Challenge of the Super-friends," a ninety-minute cartoon extravaganza that is, as its title suggests, a weekly battle between the Superfriends (the forces of good) and the Hall of Doom (the forces of evil). In this series, violence and evil are ever present, threatening to overwhelm goodness and mercy. Each week the Hall of Doom destroys cities, blows up planets, or somehow alters the conditions of our world. In one episode Lex Luthor, Superman's arch enemy, designs a ray that can bore to the center of the earth and release its molten-iron core. As the ray penetrates the earth's crust, New York crumbles, London shakes, and a tidal wave rushes toward Japan. Of course the superheroes manage to set everything right, but the precocious child viewers of the show must know, even though it isn't shown, that many people are killed when the buildings fall and the tidal wave hits.

Conclusion (restatement of thesis)

Violence on Saturday morning children's television is the rule rather than the exception. There are few shows (other than those on public television) that attempt to go beyond the simplistic formulas that cartoons follow. As a result, our children are being shown that violence is superior to reason and that conflict and threats of violent death are acceptable conditions for existence. Perhaps the recently convened government commission to study violence

5

```
will put an end to this situation, but
until it does we parents will have to
shudder every time our children sit
down in front of the television for a
Saturday morning of fun.
```

Points for Special Attention

Organization.   In his introduction, Norman Falzone establishes the context of his remarks and states his thesis. In the body of his essay, Norman presents the examples that support his thesis. In the second paragraph, he begins with a series of short examples of what he calls traditional children's cartoons, those like "The Roadrunner," "Bugs Bunny," and "Woody Woodpecker" that, although violent, are restricted in scope. He then gives examples of contemporary cartoons. In the third paragraph he uses a major example, the "Godzilla Super-Ninety Show," to illustrate his assertion that newer cartoons portray violence as a normal condition of life. The fourth paragraph presents another major example, "Challenge of the Superfriends," to show the extent to which violence pervades children's programs. In his conclusion, Norman sums up his points and ends with an emphatic statement: parents will shudder every time their children watch Saturday morning television.

Enough Examples.   Certainly no single example, no matter how graphic, could adequately support the thesis of this essay. In order to establish that children's television is violent, Norman has to use a number of examples. As a consequence, he presents three brief examples in the second paragraph and a more extensive example in each of the remaining body paragraphs.

By giving several brief examples and by not dwelling on them, Norman suggests that they represent a still larger group of examples he could have used. By examining two major examples at some length, he also shows that his case is broadly based and that he doesn't just count TV programs but can analyze them, too.

Representative Examples.   Norman is careful to ensure that his examples illustrate the full range of his subject. He draws from traditional cartoons as well as newer ones, and he presents the plots of these cartoons in enough detail to make them clear to his readers. He also makes sure that his examples are representative, that they are typical of Saturday morning cartoons. (As it happens, the "Godzilla Super-Ninety Show" and "Challenge of the Superfriends" were the top two shows when Norman wrote his essay.)

Effective Examples. All of Norman's examples support his thesis. While developing five examples, he never loses sight of his main idea. Each paragraph in the body of his essay directly addresses one aspect of his thesis. His essay does not wander or get bogged down in needlessly long plot summaries or irrelevant digressions.

The selections that appear in this chapter all depend on exemplification to explain and clarify, to add interest, or to persuade. Some essays use single extended examples; others use series of briefer illustrations.

THE ETHICS OF LIVING
JIM CROW

Richard Wright

*Richard Wright was a black writer whose work powerfully expresses
what it was like for him to grow up black in America. The brief,
informal essay which follows is an excerpt from Wright's autobiographical* Black Boy, *first published in 1937. In this selection, Wright
presents a single, emotionally moving example to support his implied thesis.*

My first lesson in how to live as a Negro came when I was quite   1
small. We were living in Arkansas. Our house stood behind the
railroad tracks. Its skimpy yard was paved with black cinders.
Nothing green ever grew in that yard. The only touch of green we
could see was far away, beyond the tracks, over where the white
folks lived. But cinders were good enough for me and I never missed
the green growing things. And anyhow cinders were fine weapons.
You could always have a nice hot war with huge black cinders. All
you had to do was crouch behind the brick pillars of a house with
your hands full of gritty ammunition. And the first woolly black
head you saw pop out from behind another row of pillars was your
target. You tried your very best to knock it off. It was great fun.

I never fully realized the appalling disadvantages of a cinder   2
environment till one day the gang to which I belonged found itself
engaged in a war with the white boys who lived beyond the tracks.
As usual we laid down our cinder barrage, thinking that this would
wipe the white boys out. But they replied with a steady bombard-
ment of broken bottles. We doubled our cinder barrage, but they
hid behind trees, hedges, and the sloping embankments of their
lawns. Having no such fortifications, we retreated to the brick pillars of our homes. During the retreat a broken milk bottle caught
me behind the ear, opening a deep gash which bled profusely. The
sight of blood pouring over my face completely demoralized our ranks.
My fellow-combatants left me standing paralyzed in the center of
the yard and scurried for their homes. A kind neighbor saw me and
rushed me to a doctor, who took three stitches in my neck.

I sat brooding on my front steps, nursing my wound and waiting   3
for my mother to come from work. I felt that a grave injustice had
been done me. It was all right to throw cinders. The greatest harm

a cinder could do was leave a bruise. But broken bottles were dangerous; they left you cut, bleeding, and helpless.

When night fell, my mother came from the white folks' kitchen. 4
I raced down the street to meet her. I could just feel in my bones that she would understand. I knew she would tell me exactly what to do next time. I grabbed her hand and babbled out the whole story. She examined my wound, then slapped me.

"How come yuh didn't hide?" she asked me. "How come yuh aw- 5
ways fightin'?"

I was outraged and bawled. Between sobs I told her that I didn't 6
have any trees or hedges to hide behind. There wasn't a thing I could have used as a trench. And you couldn't throw very far when you were hiding behind the brick pillars of a house. She grabbed a barrel stave, dragged me home, stripped me naked, and beat me till I had a fever of one hundred and two. She would smack my rump with the stave, and, while the skin was still smarting, impart to me gems of Jim Crow wisdom. I was never to throw cinders any more. I was never to fight any more wars. I was never, never, under any conditions, to fight *white* folks again. And they were absolutely right in clouting me with the broken milk bottle. Didn't I know she was working hard every day in the hot kitchens of the white folks to make money to take care of me? When was I ever going to learn to be a good boy? She couldn't be bothered with my fights. She finished by telling me that I ought to be thankful to God as long as I lived that they didn't kill me.

All that night I was delirious and could not sleep. Each time I 7
closed my eyes I saw monstrous white faces suspended from the ceiling, leering at me.

From that time on, the charm of my cinder yard was gone. The 8
green trees, the trimmed hedges, the cropped lawns grew very meaningful, became a symbol. Even today when I think of white folks, the hard, sharp outlines of white houses surrounded by trees, lawns, and hedges are present somewhere in the background of my mind. Through the years they grew into an overreaching symbol of fear.

COMPREHENSION

1. In what kind of area did Richard Wright live as a boy? What are the "appalling disadvantages of a cinder environment" that Wright refers to?

2. What does Wright mean when he says, "From that time on, the charm of my cinder yard was gone"?

3. What do the green trees and lawns of "the white folks" come to mean to Wright?

4. What is "Jim Crow" wisdom?

PURPOSE AND AUDIENCE

1. Do you think Wright was addressing his essay mainly to a white or a black audience? What evidence led you to your conclusion?

2. Do you suppose Wright's purpose in writing this essay was to inform or to persuade? Why do you think so?

3. What is Wright's implied thesis?

STYLE AND STRUCTURE

1. Notice how many times Wright refers to the colors white, black, and green in his essay. What do you think is the reason for this repetition?

2. Wright uses much detail in this essay, but he does not present detailed physical descriptions of any of the people he mentions. Why do you think he chose not to do so?

3. What words and phrases does the author use to convey the passage of time?

4. Notice how the conclusion completes the essay's frame by referring back to the cinder yard mentioned at the beginning. What effect does this frame create? How does it help the reader understand the meaning of the essay?

WRITING WORKSHOP

1. Write an essay about a time in your life when you learned a painful lesson. Use an extended example to support your thesis.

2. Write an essay about your own experiences with prejudice or discrimination. Use these experiences as examples to support your thesis.

THE PETER PRINCIPLE

Laurence J. Peter and Raymond Hull

Laurence J. Peter is a professor of education at the University of Southern California, and Raymond Hull is a writer and dramatist. Together they wrote The Peter Principle, *a book that so dramatically analyzed American organizations that its title has been absorbed into our language. This selection, the first chapter of* The Peter Principle, *presents the book's thesis along with several supporting examples.*

When I was a boy I was taught that the men upstairs knew what they were doing. I was told, "Peter, the more you know, the further you go." So I stayed in school until I graduated from college and then went forth into the world clutching firmly these ideas and my new teaching certificate. During the first year of teaching I was upset to find that a number of teachers, school principals, supervisors and superintendents appeared to be unaware of their professional responsibilities and incompetent in executing their duties. For example my principal's main concerns were that all window shades be at the same level, that classrooms should be quiet and that no one step on or near the rose beds. The superintendent's main concerns were that no minority group, no matter how fanatical, should ever be offended and that all official forms be submitted on time. The children's education appeared farthest from the administrator's mind. 1

At first I thought this was a special weakness of the school system in which I taught so I applied for certification in another province. I filled out the special forms, enclosed the required documents and complied willingly with all the red tape. Several weeks later, back came my application and all the documents! 2

No, there was nothing wrong with my credentials; the forms were correctly filled out; an official departmental stamp showed that they had been received in good order. But an accompanying letter said, "The new regulations require that such forms cannot be accepted by the Department of Education unless they have been registered at the Post Office to ensure safe delivery. Will you please remail the forms to the Department, making sure to register them this time?" 3

I began to suspect that the local school system did not have a ₄ monopoly on incompetence.

As I looked further afield, I saw that every organization contained ₅ a number of persons who could not do their jobs.

A UNIVERSAL PHENOMENON

Occupational incompetence is everywhere. Have you noticed it? ₆ Probably we all have noticed it.

We see indecisive politicians posing as resolute statesmen and ₇ the "authoritative source" who blames his misinformation on "situational imponderables." Limitless are the public servants who are indolent and insolent; military commanders whose behavioral timidity belies their dreadnought rhetoric, and governors whose innate servility prevents their actually governing. In our sophistication, we virtually shrug aside the immoral cleric, corrupt judge, incoherent attorney, author who cannot write and English teacher who cannot spell. At universities we see proclamations authored by administrators whose own office communications are hopelessly muddled, and droning lectures from inaudible or incomprehensible instructors.

Seeing incompetence at all levels of every hierarchy—political, ₈ legal, educational and industrial—I hypothesized that the cause was some inherent feature of the rules governing the placement of employees. Thus began my serious study of the ways in which employees move upward through a hierarchy, and of what happens to them after promotion.

For my scientific data hundreds of case histories were collected. ₉ Here are three typical examples.

Municipal Government File, Case No. 17. J. S. Minion[1] was ₁₀ a maintenance foreman in the public works department of Excelsior City. He was a favorite of the senior officials at City Hall. They all praised his unfailing affability.

"I like Minion," said the superintendent of works. "He has good ₁₁ judgment and is always pleasant and agreeable."

This behavior was appropriate for Minion's position: he was not ₁₂ supposed to make policy, so he had no need to disagree with his superiors.

The superintendent of works retired and Minion succeeded him. ₁₃ Minion continued to agree with everyone. He passed to his foreman

[1]Some names have been changed, in order to protect the guilty.

every suggestion that came from above. The resulting conflicts in policy, and the continual changing of plans, soon demoralized the department. Complaints poured in from the Mayor and other officials, from taxpayers and from the maintenance-workers' union.

Minion still says "Yes" to everyone, and carries messages briskly back and forth between his superiors and his subordinates. Nominally a superintendent, he actually does the work of a messenger. The maintenance department regularly exceeds its budget, yet fails to fulfill its program of work. In short, Minion, a competent foreman, became an incompetent superintendent.   14

Service Industries File, Case No. 3. E. Tinker was exceptionally zealous and intelligent as an apprentice at G. Reece Auto Repair Inc., and soon rose to journeyman mechanic. In this job he showed outstanding ability in diagnosing obscure faults, and endless patience in correcting them. He was promoted to foreman of the repair shop.   15

But here his love of things mechanical and his perfectionism became liabilities. He will undertake any job that he thinks looks interesting, no matter how busy the shop may be. "We'll work it in somehow," he says.   16

He will not let a job go until he is fully satisfied with it.   17

He meddles constantly. He is seldom to be found at his desk. He is usually up to his elbows in a dismantled motor and while the man who should be doing the work stands watching, other workmen sit around waiting to be assigned new tasks. As a result the shop is always overcrowded with work, always in a muddle, and delivery times are often missed.   18

Tinker cannot understand that the average customer cares little about perfection—he wants his car back on time! He cannot understand that most of his men are less interested in motors than in their pay checks. So Tinker cannot get on with his customers or with his subordinates. He was a competent mechanic, but is now an incompetent foreman.   19

Military File, Case No. 8. Consider the case of the late renowned General A. Goodwin. His hearty, informal manner, his racy style of speech, his scorn for petty regulations and his undoubted personal bravery made him the idol of his men. He led them to many well-deserved victories.   20

When Goodwin was promoted to field marshal he had to deal, not with ordinary soldiers, but with politicians and allied generalissimos.

He would not conform to the necessary protocol. He could not turn his tongue to the conventional courtesies and flatteries. He quarreled with all the dignitaries and took to lying for days at a time, drunk and sulking, in his trailer. The conduct of the war slipped out of his hands into those of his subordinates. He had been promoted to a position that he was incompetent to fill.

AN IMPORTANT CLUE!

In time I saw that all such cases had a common feature. The employee had been promoted from a position of competence to a position of incompetence. I saw that, sooner or later, this could happen to every employee in every hierarchy.

Hypothetical Case File, Case No. 1. Suppose you own a pill-rolling factory, Perfect Pill Incorporated. Your foreman pill roller dies of a perforated ulcer. You need a replacement. You naturally look among your rank-and-file pill rollers.

Miss Oval, Mrs. Cylinder, Mr. Ellipse and Mr. Cube all show various degrees of incompetence. They will naturally be ineligible for promotion. You will choose—other things being equal—your most competent pill roller, Mr. Sphere, and promote him to foreman.

Now suppose Mr. Sphere proves competent as foreman. Later, when your general foreman, Legree, moves up to Works Manager, Sphere will be eligible to take his place.

If, on the other hand, Sphere is an incompetent foreman, he will get no more promotion. He has reached what I call his "level of incompetence." He will stay there till the end of his career.

Some employees, like Ellipse and Cube, reach a level of incompetence in the lowest grade and are never promoted. Some, like Sphere (assuming he is not a satisfactory foreman), reach it after one promotion.

E. Tinker, the automobile repair-shop foreman, reached his level of incompetence on the third stage of the hierarchy. General Goodwin reached his level of incompetence at the very top of the hierarchy.

So my analysis of hundreds of cases of occupational incompetence led me on to formulate *The Peter Principle:*

*In a Hierarchy Every Employee Tends
to Rise to His Level of Incompetence*

A NEW SCIENCE!

Having formulated the Principle, I discovered that I had inad-   31
vertently founded a new science, hierarchiology, the study of hierarchies.

The term "hierarchy" was originally used to describe the system   32
of church government by priests graded into ranks. The contemporary meaning includes any organization whose members or employees are arranged in order of rank, grade or class.

Hierarchiology, although a relatively recent discipline, appears   33
to have great applicability to the fields of public and private administration.

THIS MEANS YOU!

My Principle is the key to an understanding of all hierarchal   34
systems, and therefore to an understanding of the whole structure
of civilization. A few eccentrics try to avoid getting involved with
hierarchies, but everyone in business, industry, trade-unionism,
politics, government, the armed forces, religion and education is so
involved. All of them are controlled by the Peter Principle.

Many of them, to be sure, may win a promotion or two, moving   35
from one level of competence to a higher level of competence. But
competence in that new position qualifies them for still another
promotion. For each individual, for *you,* for *me,* the final promotion
is from a level of competence to a level of incompetence.[1]

So, given enough time—and assuming the existence of enough   36
ranks in the hierarchy—each employee rises to, and remains at, his
level of incompetence. Peter's Corollary states:

In time, every post tends to be occupied by an employee who is   37
incompetent to carry out its duties.

WHO TURNS THE WHEELS?

You will rarely find, of course, a system in which *every* employee   38
has reached his level of incompetence. In most instances, something
is being done to further the ostensible purposes for which the hierarchy exists.

Work is accomplished by those employees who have not yet reached   39
their level of incompetence.

---

[1]The phenomena of "percussive sublimation" (commonly referred to as "being
kicked upstairs") and of "the lateral arabesque" are not, as the casual observer might
think, exceptions to the Principle. They are only pseudo-promotions. . . .

COMPREHENSION

1. What things disillusioned Laurence Peter during his first year of teaching?

2. What did Peter find out about organizations?

3. What is the Peter Principle? What happens when an employee reaches his "level of incompetence"?

4. What does Peter mean by *hierarchiology*? How did *hierarchiology* lead him to the Peter Principle?

5. If the Peter Principle operates in hierarchies, who does the work?

PURPOSE AND AUDIENCE

1. Is this essay aimed at a general or a specialized audience? What led you to your conclusion?

2. What is Peter's thesis?

3. The author places his thesis after the examples. Why does he wait so long to state it?

4. Does Peter give any indication of the purpose and occasion of this essay? If so, where?

5. How serious is Peter? What words or phrases indicate whether his theory is humorous, or serious, or something of both?

STYLE AND STRUCTURE

1. Why does the author begin the essay with an example? Why does he present a series of brief examples before introducing the "typical case histories"?

2. Why does Peter say he collected hundreds of case histories for data? Why are the three case histories analyzed here typical?

3. Do you find the organization of this essay satisfactory? How else could the points be arranged?

WRITING WORKSHOP

1. Does Laurence Peter overstate his case? Write a letter to him in the form of an exemplification essay pointing out the weaknesses of his position.

2. Study a school, business, or organization with which you are familiar. Write an exemplification essay showing how the Peter Principle applies.

3. Do you know someone who has progressed to the highest level of his or her incompetence? Write an exemplification essay showing how the Peter Principle applies.

THE COMPANY MAN

Ellen Goodman

Ellen Goodman was born in Newton, Massachusetts, in 1941. After graduating from Radcliffe College, she worked for Newsweek *and the* Detroit Free Press. *In 1971 she became a columnist for the Boston Globe, and she won a Pulitzer Prize for journalism in 1980. Currently her column is syndicated in over two hundred papers. Some of her columns are collected in* Close to Home *(1975) and* At Large *(1981). Goodman also wrote* Turning Points *(1979), in which she discusses changing life-styles. "The Company Man," from* Close to Home, *presents an example of what clinicians call a "workaholic." In this extended example Goodman creates a case study of a man who literally worked himself to death.*

He worked himself to death, finally and precisely, at 3:00 A.M. 1
Sunday morning.

The obituary didn't say that, of course. It said that he died of a 2
coronary thrombosis—I think that was it—but everyone among his
friends and acquaintances knew it instantly. He was a perfect Type
A, a workaholic, a classic, they said to each other and shook their
heads—and thought for five or ten minutes about the way they
lived.

This man who worked himself to death finally and precisely at 3
3:00 A.M. Sunday morning—on his day off—was fifty-one years old
and a vice-president. He was, however, one of six vice-presidents,
and one of three who might conceivably—if the president died or
retired soon enough—have moved to the top spot. Phil knew that.

He worked six days a week, five of them until eight or nine at 4
night, during a time when his own company had begun the four-
day week for everyone but the executives. He worked like the Important People. He had no outside "extracurricular interests," unless, of course, you think about a monthly golf game that way. To
Phil, it was work. He always ate egg salad sandwiches at his desk.
He was, of course, overweight, by 20 or 25 pounds. He thought it
was okay, though, because he didn't smoke.

On Saturdays, Phil wore a sports jacket to the office instead of a 5
suit, because it was the weekend.

139

He had a lot of people working for him, maybe sixty, and most 6
of them liked him most of the time. Three of them will be seriously
considered for his job. The obituary didn't mention that.

But it did list his "survivors" quite accurately. He is survived by 7
his wife, Helen, forty-eight years old, a good woman of no particular
marketable skills, who worked in an office before marrying and
mothering. She had, according to her daughter, given up trying to
compete with his work years ago, when the children were small. A
company friend said, "I know how much you will miss him." And
she answered, "I already have."

"Missing him all these years," she must have given up part of 8
herself which had cared too much for the man. She would be "well
taken care of."

His "dearly beloved" eldest of the "dearly beloved" children is a 9
hard-working executive in a manufacturing firm down South. In
the day and a half before the funeral, he went around the neighborhood researching his father, asking the neighbors what he was
like. They were embarrassed.

His second child is a girl, who is twenty-four and newly married. 10
She lives near her mother and they are close, but whenever she was
alone with her father, in a car driving somewhere, they had nothing
to say to each other.

The youngest is twenty, a boy, a high-school graduate who has 11
spent the last couple of years, like a lot of his friends, doing enough
odd jobs to stay in grass and food. He was the one who tried to grab
at his father, and tried to mean enough to him to keep the man at
home. He was his father's favorite. Over the last two years, Phil
stayed up nights worrying about the boy.

The boy once said, "My father and I only board here." 12

At the funeral, the sixty-year-old company president told the forty- 13
eight-year-old widow that the fifty-one-year-old deceased had meant
much to the company and would be missed and would be hard to
replace. The widow didn't look him in the eye. She was afraid he
would read her bitterness and, after all, she would need him to
straighten out the finances—the stock options and all that.

Phil was overweight and nervous and worked too hard. If he 14
wasn't at the office, he was worried about it. Phil was a Type A, a
heart-attack natural. You could have picked him out in a minute
from a lineup.

So when he finally worked himself to death, at precisely 3:00 15
A.M. Sunday morning, no one was really surprised.

By 5:00 P.M. the afternoon of the funeral, the company president 16
had begun, discreetly of course, with care and taste, to make in-

quiries about his replacement. One of three men. He asked around:
"Who's been working the hardest?"

COMPREHENSION

1. When Phil's widow is told by a friend, "I know how much you will miss
   him," she answers, "I already have." What does she mean?

2. Why did Phil's oldest son go around the neighborhood researching his
   father?

3. Why doesn't Phil's widow look the company president in the eye?

4. What does Goodman tell us about Phil's job—what he actually did at
   the office? Why?

PURPOSE AND AUDIENCE

1. What point is Goodman trying to make in this essay?

2. What assumptions does Goodman make about her readers?

3. Why does Goodman imply her thesis and not state it?

STYLE AND STRUCTURE

1. Why does Goodman state the time of Phil's death at the beginning and
   at the end of her essay?

2. Is there a reason why Goodman waits until the end of paragraph 3 before
   she uses the company man's name?

3. How does Goodman support her assertions about Phil?

4. What is the effect of the dialogue that Goodman presents?

5. Goodman tells Phil's story in a flat, impersonal way. How does this tone
   help her achieve her purpose?

WRITING WORKSHOP

1. Write an essay about the workaholic student, using an extended example. As Goodman does, use a series of details and dialogue to support
   your thesis.

DEATH IN THE OPEN

Lewis Thomas

Lewis Thomas was born in Flushing, New York, in 1913. He graduated from Princeton in 1933 and Harvard Medical School in 1937. He held posts at various medical schools and hospitals before assuming his present position in 1973 as president of the Memorial Sloan-Kettering Cancer Center in New York. He began writing a regular column for the New England Journal of Medicine *in 1971. In 1975 he won the National Book Award for a collection of his essays,* The Lives of a Cell: Notes of a Biology Watcher *(1979). "Death in the Open" is from* The Lives of a Cell *and examines the role death plays in the cycle of life. In this essay Thomas offers examples to support his assertion that death seems to be one of nature's best-kept secrets.*

Most of the dead animals you see on highways near the cities are dogs, a few cats. Out in the countryside, the forms and coloring of the dead are strange; these are the wild creatures. Seen from a car window they appear as fragments, evoking memories of woodchucks, badgers, skunks, voles, snakes, sometimes the mysterious wreckage of a deer.

It is always a queer shock, part a sudden upwelling of grief, part unaccountable amazement. It is simply astounding to see an animal dead on a highway. The outrage is more than just the location; it is the impropriety of such visible death, anywhere. You do not expect to see dead animals in the open. It is the nature of animals to die alone, off somewhere, hidden. It is wrong to seen them lying out on the highway; it is wrong to see them anywhere.

Everything in the world dies, but we only know about it as a kind of abstraction. If you stand in a meadow, at the edge of a hillside, and look around carefully, almost everything you can catch sight of is in the process of dying, and most things will be dead long before you are. If it were not for the constant renewal and replacement going on before your eyes, the whole place would turn to stone and sand under your feet.

There are some creatures that do not seem to die at all; they simply vanish totally into their own progeny. Single cells do this. The cell becomes two, then four, and so on, and after a while the last trace is gone. It cannot be seen as death; barring mutation, the descendants are simply the first cell, living all over again. The cycles of the slime mold have episodes that seem as conclusive as death, but the withered slug, with its stalk and fruiting body, is plainly the transient tissue of a developing animal; the free-swimming amebocytes use this organ collectively in order to produce more of themselves.

There are said to be a billion billion insects on the earth at any moment, most of them with very short life expectancies by our standards. Someone has estimated that there are 25 million assorted insects hanging in the air over every temperate square mile, in a column extending upward for thousands of feet, drifting through the layers of the atmosphere like plankton. They are dying steadily, some by being eaten, some just dropping in their tracks, tons of them around the earth, disintegrating as they die, invisibly.

Who ever sees dead birds, in anything like the huge numbers stipulated by the certainty of the death of all birds? A dead bird is an incongruity, more startling than an unexpected live bird, sure evidence to the human mind that something has gone wrong. Birds do their dying off somewhere, behind things, under things, never on the wing.

Animals seem to have an instinct for performing death alone, hidden. Even the largest, most conspicuous ones find ways to conceal themselves in time. If an elephant missteps and dies in an open place, the herd will not leave him there; the others will pick him up and carry the body from place to place, finally putting it down in some inexplicably suitable location. When elephants encounter the skeleton of an elephant out in the open, they methodically take up each of the bones and distribute them, in a ponderous ceremony, over neighboring acres.

It is a natural marvel. All of the life of the earth dies, all of the time, in the same volume as the new life that dazzles us each morning, each spring. All we see of this is the odd stump, the fly struggling on the porch floor of the summer house in October, the fragment on the highway. I have lived all my life with an embarrassment of squirrels in my backyard, they are all over the place, all year long, and I have never seen, anywhere, a dead squirrel.

I suppose it is just as well. If the earth were otherwise, and all the dying were done in the open, with the dead there to be looked at, we would never have it out of our minds. We can forget about it much of the time, or think of it as an accident to be avoided, somehow. But it does make the process of dying seem more exceptional than it really is, and harder to engage in at the times when we must ourselves engage.

In our way, we conform as best we can to the rest of nature. The obituary pages tell us of the news that we are dying away, while the birth announcements in finer print, off at the side of the page, inform us of our replacements, but we get no grasp from this of the enormity of scale. There are 3 billion of us on the earth, and all 3 billion must be dead, on a schedule, within this lifetime. The vast mortality, involving something over 50 million of us each year, takes place in relative secrecy. We can only really know of the deaths in our households, or among our friends. These, detached in our minds from all the rest, we take to be unnatural events, anomalies, outrages. We speak of our own dead in low voices; struck down, we say, as though visible death can only occur for cause, by disease or violence, avoidably. We send off for flowers, grieve, make ceremonies, scatter bones, unaware of the rest of the 3 billion on the same schedule. All of that immense mass of flesh and bone and consciousness will disappear by absorption into the earth, without recognition by the transient survivors.

Less than a half century from now, our replacements will have more than doubled the numbers. It is hard to see how we can continue to keep the secret, with such multitudes doing the dying. We will have to give up the notion that death is catastrophe, or detestable, or avoidable, or even strange. We will need to learn more about the cycling of life in the rest of the system, and about our connection to the process. Everything that comes alive seems to be in trade for something that dies, cell for cell. There might be some comfort in the recognition of synchrony, in the information that we all go down together, in the best of company.

COMPREHENSION

1. Why is it a shock to see death in the open?

2. Why do human beings only know about death as an abstraction?

3. What would be the effect if all dying were done in the open?

4. When it comes to death, how do human beings conform to the rest of nature?

5. Why do human beings have to give up the idea that death is a catastrophe?

PURPOSE AND AUDIENCE

1. Where does Thomas state his thesis? Why does he place it where he does?

2. This essay was originally published in the *New England Journal of Medicine*. Is it aimed at physicians or at the general public? Explain.

3. What assumptions does Thomas make about his audience's attitude toward his subject?

STYLE AND STRUCTURE

1. Make a list of the examples that Thomas presents to support his thesis. What do all his examples have in common?

2. What techniques does Thomas use to lessen the distance between his audience and himself? How does he avoid sounding as if he is preaching?

3. Although this essay deals with death, it is upbeat and optimistic. How does Thomas achieve this effect?

4. What transitions does Thomas use to link his paragraphs together? Underline these transitional words and phrases.

5. How does Thomas use statistics to support his points?

WRITING WORKSHOP

1. Write an essay in which you agree or disagree with Thomas's thesis. Use examples from your own experience to support your assertions.

2. Using examples from the local TV evening news, write an essay in which you discuss how you are affected by stories about violence and death.

3. Drawing examples from Thomas's essay and from your own experience, discuss the need for more open and humane attitudes toward the elderly and the dying.

COURTSHIP THROUGH
THE AGES

James Thurber

*James Thurber, the popular American humorist, was born in 1894
in Ohio and died in 1961. His first work appeared in 1927 in* The
New Yorker. *Through the years he has entertained readers with
his short stories, sketches, fables and reminiscences. His works include* Is Sex Necessary? *(1929), written with E. B. White,* My World
and Welcome to It *(1942), which contains the well-known story
"The Secret Life of Walter Mitty,"* Thurber Country *(1953), and*
The Male Animal *(1940), a comedy written with Elliot Nugent.
"Courtship Through the Ages" was published in* The New Yorker
and appeared in My World and Welcome to It. *In it he uses several
examples to humorously illustrate the problems that males of all
animal species have arousing the interest of females.*

Surely nothing in the astonishing scheme of life can have non-
plussed Nature so much as the fact that none of the females of any
of the species she created really cared very much for the male, as
such. For the past ten million years Nature has been busily inventing ways to make the male attractive to the female, but the
whole business of courtship, from the marine annelids up to man,
still lumbers heavily along, like a complicated musical comedy. I
have been reading the sad and absorbing story in Volume 6 (Cole
to Dama) of the *Encyclopaedia Britannica*. In this volume you can
learn all about cricket, cotton, costume designing, crocodiles, crown
jewels, and Coleridge, but none of these subjects is so interesting as
the Courtship of Animals, which recounts the sorrowful lengths to
which all males must go to arouse the interest of a lady.

We all know, I think, that Nature gave man whiskers and a
mustache with the quaint idea in mind that these would prove attractive to the female. We all know that, far from attracting her,
whiskers and mustaches only made her nervous and gloomy, so that
man had to go in for somersaults, tilting with lances, and performing feats of parlor magic to win her attention; he also had to bring
her candy, flowers, and the furs of animals. It is common knowledge
that in spite of all these "love displays" the male is constantly being
turned down, insulted, or thrown out of the house. It is rather comforting, then, to discover that the peacock, for all his gorgeous plum-

age, does not have a particularly easy time in courtship; none of the males in the world do. The first peahen, it turned out, was only faintly stirred by her suitor's beautiful train. She would often go quietly to sleep while he was whisking it around. The *Britannica* tells us that the peacock actually had to learn a certain little trick to wake her up and revive her interest: he had to learn to vibrate his quills so as to make a rustling sound. In ancient times man himself, observing the ways of the peacock, probably tried vibrating his whiskers to make a rustling sound; if so, it didn't get him anywhere. He had to go in for something else; so, among other things, he went in for gifts. It is not unlikely that he got this idea from certain flies and birds who were making no headway at all with rustling sounds.

One of the flies of the family Empidae, who had tried everything, finally hit on something pretty special. He contrived to make a glistening transparent balloon which was even larger than himself. Into this he would put sweetmeats and tidbits and he would carry the whole elaborate envelope through the air to the lady of his choice. This amused her for a time, but she finally got bored with it. She demanded silly little colorful presents, something that you couldn't eat but that would look nice around the house. So the male Empis had to go around gathering flower petals and pieces of bright paper to put into his balloon. On a courtship flight a male Empis cuts quite a figure now, but he can hardly be said to be happy. He never knows how soon the female will demand heavier presents, such as Roman coins and gold collar buttons. It seems probable that one day the courtship of the Empidae will fall down, as man's occasionally does, of its own weight.

The bowerbird is another creature that spends so much time courting the female that he never gets any work done. If all the male bowerbirds became nervous wrecks within the next ten or fifteen years, it would not surprise me. The female bowerbird insists that a playground be built for her with a specially constructed bower at the entrance. This bower is much more elaborate than an ordinary nest and is harder to build; it costs a lot more, too. The female will not come to the playground until the male has filled it up with a great many gifts: silvery leaves, red leaves, rose petals, shells, beads, berries, bones, dice, buttons, cigar bands, Christmas seals, and the Lord knows what else. When the female finally condescends to visit the playground, she is in a coy and silly mood and has to be chased in and out of the bower and up and down the playground before she will quit giggling and stand still long enough even to shake hands. The male bird is, of course, pretty well done in before the chase starts, because he has worn himself out hunting for eye-glass lenses and begonia blossoms. I imagine that many a bower-bird, after chasing a female for two or three hours, says the hell with it and goes home to bed. Next day, of course, he telephones someone else and the same trying ritual is gone through with again. A male bowerbird is as exhausted as a night-club habitué before he is out of his twenties.

The male fiddler crab has a somewhat easier time, but it can hardly be said that he is sitting pretty. He has one enormously large and powerful claw, usually brilliantly colored, and you might sup-pose that all he had to do was reach out and grab some passing cutie. The very earliest fiddler crabs may have tried this, but, if so, they got slapped for their pains. A female fiddler crab will not tol-erate any caveman stuff; she never has and she doesn't intend to start now. To attract a female, a fiddler crab has to stand on tiptoe and brandish his claw in the air. If any female in the neighborhood is interested—and you'd be surprised how many are not—she comes over and engages him in light badinage, for which he is not in the mood. As many as a hundred females may pass the time of day with him and go on about their business. By nightfall of an average courting day, a fiddler crab who has been standing on tiptoe for eight or ten hours waving a heavy claw in the air is in pretty sad shape. As in the case of the males of all species, however, he gets out of bed next morning, dashes some water on his face, and tries again.

The next time you encounter a male web-spinning spider, stop and reflect that he is too busy worrying about his love life to have any desire to bite you. Male web-spinning spiders have a tougher life than any other males in the animal kingdom. This is because the female web-spinning spiders have very poor eyesight. If a male lands on a female's web, she kills him before he has time to lay down his cane and gloves, mistaking him for a fly or a bumblebee who has tumbled into her trap. Before the species figured out what to do about this, millions of males were murdered by ladies they called on. It is the nature of spiders to perform a little dance in front of the female, but before a male spinner could get near enough for the female to see who he was and what he was up to, she would lash out at him with a flat-iron or a pair of garden shears. One night, nobody knows when, a very bright male spinner lay awake worrying about calling on a lady who had been killing suitors right and left. It came to him that this business of dancing as a love display wasn't getting anybody anywhere except the grave. He de-cided to go in for web-twitching, or strand-vibrating. The next day he tried it on one of the nearsighted girls. Instead of dropping in on her suddenly, he stayed outside the web and began monkeying with one of its strands. He twitched it up and down and in and out with such a lilting rhythm that the female was charmed. The serenade worked beautifully; the female let him live. The *Britannica*'s spider-watchers, however, report that this system is not always successful. Once in a while, even now, a female will fire three bullets into a suitor or run him through with a kitchen knife. She keeps threatening him from the moment he strikes the first low notes on the outside strings, but usually by the time he has got up to the high notes played around the center of the web, he is going to town and she spares his life.

Even the butterfly, as handsome a fellow as he is, can't always   7
win a mate merely by fluttering around and showing off. Many butterflies have to have scent scales on their wings. Hepialus carries a powder puff in a perfumed pouch. He throws perfume at the ladies when they pass. The male tree cricket, Oecanthus, goes Hepialus one better by carrying a tiny bottle of wine with him and giving drinks to such doxies as he has designs on. One of the male snails throws darts to entertain the girls. So it goes, through the long list of animals, from the bristle worm and his rudimentary dance steps to man and his gift of diamonds and sapphires. The golden-eye drake raises a jet of water with his feet as he flies over a lake; Hepialus has his powder puff, Oecanthus his wine bottle, man his etchings. It is a bright and melancholy story, the age-old desire of the male for the female, the age-old desire of the female to be amused and entertained. Of all the creatures on earth, the only males who could be figured as putting any irony into their courtship are the grebes and certain other diving birds. Every now and then a courting grebe slips quietly down to the bottom of a lake and then, with a mighty "Whoosh!," pops out suddenly a few feet from his girl friend, splashing water all over her. She seems to be persuaded that this is a purely loving display, but I like to think that the grebe always has a faint hope of drowning her or scaring her to death.

I will close this investigation into the mournful burdens of the   8
male with the *Britannica*'s story about a certain Argus pheasant. It appears that the Argus displays himself in front of a female who stands perfectly still without moving a feather. . . . The male Argus the *Britannica* tells about was confined in a cage with a female of another species, a female who kept moving around, emptying ash-trays and fussing with lampshades all the time the male was showing off his talents. Finally, in disgust, he stalked away and began displaying in front of his water trough. He reminds me of a certain

male (Homo sapiens) of my acquaintance who one night after dinner asked his wife to put down her detective magazine so that he could read a poem of which he was very fond. She sat quietly enough until he was well into the middle of the thing, intoning with great ardor and intensity. Then suddenly there came a sharp, disconcerting *slap!* It turned out that all during the male's display, the female had been intent on a circling mosquito and had finally trapped it between the palms of her hands. The male in this case did not stalk away and display in front of a water trough; he went over to Tim's and had a flock of drinks and recited the poem to the fellas. I am sure thay all told bitter stories of their own about how their displays had been interrupted by females. I am also sure that they all ended up singing "Honey, Honey, Bless Your Heart."

COMPREHENSION

1. What does Thurber say is one of the more astonishing things in the scheme of life?

2. What is a "love display"?

3. Why would Thurber not be surprised if all the male bowerbirds became nervous wrecks?

4. Why do male web-spinning spiders have a more difficult time than other males in the animal kingdom?

5. What is the meaning of Thurber's anecdote about the Argus pheasant (paragraph 8)?

PURPOSE AND AUDIENCE

1. Where does Thurber state his thesis? Why does he place it where he does?

2. What is Thurber's purpose? Is he poking fun at animals or at something else?

3. How does Thurber expect his audience to react to his essay? Is his purpose to entertain? Does he have a more serious purpose? Explain.

4. Choose several words that help Thurber convey his attitude toward his subject. How do these words help him establish his attitude?

STYLE AND STRUCTURE

1. How does Thurber set the stage for the examples he presents? What is his source for the examples in the essay?

2. Why does Thurber compare courtship through the ages to a complicated musical comedy?

3. In what way does Thurber relate each new example to the other examples he presents?

4. How does Thurber establish that each of the examples he presents relates to human beings as well as animals?

5. What figures of speech does Thurber use in his essay? What function do they serve? (See Description, pp. 78–79, for a review of figures of speech.)

WRITING WORKSHOP

1. Write an essay in which you give examples of ways men try to arouse the interest of women. Or, if you wish, consider how women attempt to interest men.

2. Write an exemplification essay defending or criticizing Thurber's impressions of courtship. How fair or unfair is his portrayal of male-female relationships?

5

Process

WHAT IS PROCESS?

A process essay explains the steps or stages in doing something. As we mentioned in chapter 2, process is closely related to narrative since both present events in chronological order. Unlike a narrative that tells a story, however, a process essay details a particular series of events that produce the same outcome whenever duplicated. Because these events form a sequence, often with a fixed order, clarity is extremely important in process writing. Whether your reader is actually to perform the process or simply to understand how it takes place, your paper must make clear the exact order of the individual steps as well as their relationships to each other and to the process as a whole. Therefore, not only must there be clear, logical transitions between the steps in a process, but the steps must be presented in *strict* chronological order—that is, in the order of performance. Unlike narratives, then, process essays do not use flashbacks or otherwise experiment with time order.

Instructions and Process Explanations

The two basic kinds of process writing fulfill different purposes. Instructions tell how to do something, and explanations tell how something is or was done. Instructions have many practical uses. A recipe, a handout about using your library's card catalog, or an operating manual for your car or your stereo are all written in the form of instructions. So are directions for finding your house or for driving to the beach. Instructions usually use the present tense and, like commands, the imperative mood: "Disconnect the system, and check the . . ." Occasionally, instructions are written in the future tense and the second person (*you*), speaking directly to readers about their anticipated actions: "Next, you should turn the knob and adjust the . . ." Thus, both tense and mood suit the purpose of instructions, enabling the readers to follow along and perform the process themselves.

On the other hand, the purpose of a process explanation is to help the readers understand the steps of a procedure although they may not duplicate that process themselves. Thus, explanation essays can examine anything from how silkworms spin their cocoons to how Michelangelo and Leonardo painted their masterpieces on plaster walls and ceilings. A process explanation may employ the first person (*I, we*) or the third (*he, she, it, they*), the past tense or the present. Since its readers need to understand, not perform, the process, the explanation does not use the second person (*you*) or the imperative mood characteristic of instructions. The style of a process explanation will vary with the writer's purpose and the regularity with which the process is or was performed. The chart below suggests some of the options available to you.

	First Person	*Third Person*
Present	"After I pin the pattern to the fabric, I cut it out with a sharp pair of scissors." (habitual process performed by the writer)	"After the photographer places the chemicals in the tray . . ." (habitual process performed by someone other than the writer)
Past	"After I pinned the pattern to the fabric . . ." (process performed in the past by the writer)	"When the mixture was cool, he added . . ." (process performed in the past by someone other than the writer)

Uses of Process Essays

Both instructions and process explanations are used in academic writing, and either can occur as the structural pattern for a part of a paper or for an entire piece of writing. For example, in a biology term paper on genetic engineering, you might devote a short section to an explanation of the process of amniocentesis; in an editorial on the negative side of fraternity life, you might decide to summarize briefly the process of pledging. On the other hand, an entire paper can be organized around a process pattern. In a political science paper you might explain the usual process by which Congress or the Supreme Court acts; in an English essay, you might trace the developmental steps through which a fictional character reached new insight; on a finance midterm, you might review the procedure for approving a commercial loan.

Process writing sometimes is used to persuade and at other times is used simply to present information. Thus, if its purpose is persuasive, a process paper may have a strong thesis like "Applying for public assistance is a needlessly complex process that discourages many potential recipients" or "The process of slaughtering baby seals is inhumane and sadistic." An informative process essay, on the other hand, may simply have a unifying idea like "Making lasagne consists of five basic steps" or "An appendectomy is a relatively routine surgical procedure."

STRUCTURING A PROCESS ESSAY

Like most other essays, a full-length process essay usually consists of three main sections. The introduction names the process and indicates why, and under what circumstances, it is performed. This section may also include information about materials or preliminary preparations. It may view the process as a whole, perhaps even listing its major stages. If the paper has a thesis, it too is stated in the introduction. Many process essays, however, have at their core nothing more debatable than "Typing your own blood is an easy procedure." Still, every process essay should have a clear unifying idea that gives readers a sense of what the process is and why it is performed. This unifying idea organizes the paper so it holds the readers' interest more effectively than an essay without a clear purpose.

To develop the thesis or the unifying idea, each paragraph in the body of the essay treats one major stage of the procedure. Each stage may group several steps, depending on the nature and complexity of the process. These steps are presented in chronological order, interrupted only for essential definitions and advice. Every step must be included and must appear in its proper place. Throughout the body of a process essay, transitional words and phrases are necessary so that each step, each stage, and each paragraph lead logically to the next. Transitions like *after this, next, then,* and *when you have finished* establish sequential and chronological relationships that help the reader follow the process. Particular words, however, should not be repeated so often that they become boring.

A short process essay without a thesis may not need a conclusion. If a paper has a thesis, however, the conclusion may restate it. The conclusion may also briefly review the procedure's major stages. Such an ending is especially useful if the paper has outlined a technical process which may seem complicated to the lay reader or if the procedure has been very long or complex. Finally, the conclusion may summarize the results of the process or explain its significance.

Designing a thorough, coherent process essay is not easy. It requires that you have a clear purpose before you begin and that you constantly consider your reader's needs. When necessary, you must explain the reasons for performing the steps, describe unfamiliar materials or equipment, define uncommon terms, and warn the reader about possible snags during the process. Sometimes you may even need to include illustrations. Besides complete information, your reader needs a clear and consistent discussion without ambiguities or surprising shifts. Thus, you should avoid unnecessary changes in tense, person, voice, and mood. Similarly, you should include appropriate articles (*a, an,* and *the*) so that your discussion moves smoothly like an essay, not abruptly like a cookbook. Careful attention to your essay's consistency as well as its overall structure will ensure that your reader understands your process explanations and instructions.

When planning a process essay that gives instructions, be sure to include only the necessary steps. If you tell readers to do things that they do not really have to do, you waste their time and effort, and you also give them more chances to make mistakes. You should also mentally test all the steps in sequence to be sure that the process will really work as you explain it. Check carefully for omitted steps or incorrect information.

For a process essay that gives an explanation you should be certain to picture the process accurately. You should distinguish between what usually or always happens and what rarely happens, between necessary steps and accidental ones. If you are writing from firsthand observation, test your explanation after writing it by observing the process again, if you possibly can. This can help you avoid omissions or mistakes.

Let's suppose you were taking a midterm in a course in childhood and adolescent behavior. One essay question calls for a process explanation: "Trace the stages that children go through in acquiring language." Before writing your essay, you quickly brainstorm and formulate the following thesis statement: "Although individual cases may differ, most children acquire language in a predictable series of stages." You then plan your essay, an extended account of the process by which children learn language, and develop the following outline.

¶1 Introduction—including thesis and outline of stages.

¶2 First stage, two to twelve months: prelinguistic behavior including "babbling" and appropriate responses to nonverbal cues.

¶3 Second stage, toward the end of the first year: single words as commands or requests; infant catalogs his or her environment.

¶4 Third stage, beginning of second year: expressive jargon, a flow of sounds that imitates adult speech; real words along with jargon.

¶5 Fourth and final stage, middle of second year to beginning of third: child begins combining real words into two-word phrases and then longer strings; missing parts of speech appear and foundations of language are established.

¶6 Conclusion and summary.

This essay, when completed, will show clearly not only what the stages of the process are but how they relate to each other. It also will support its thesis that children learn language not at random but by a well-defined process.

The following student essays, Scott Blackman's set of instructions for typing your own blood and Hilary Barshai's explanation of what people go through when they diet, illustrate the two types of process essays.

TYPING YOUR OWN BLOOD

Introduction   Typing your own blood is often used   1
as an introductory laboratory exercise.
Even if you do not wish to learn your
Unifying idea   blood type, the exercise is useful because it familiarizes you with some
simple laboratory techniques, illustrates the use of basic equipment, and
prepares you to follow the stages of an
orderly scientific procedure.

Materials   In order to type your own blood, you   2
need the following equipment: alcohol-
soaked cotton balls; a sterile lancet;
a small test tube containing 1 ml. of
saline solution; anti-A, anti-B, and

anti—Rh serums with individual eye
droppers; two microscope slides; a
grease pencil; a Pasteur pipette; three
applicator sticks; and a warm fluorescent light or other low—heat source.

**First stage
of process**

With the grease pencil, label one   3
slide Rh, and place this slide under
the low—heat source. Divide your cool
slide into two equal portions, labeling
one side A and the other B. Apply one
drop of anti—A serum to slide A, one
drop of anti—B to slide B, and one drop
of anti—Rh to the warm Rh slide.

**Second stage
of process**

Use an alcohol—soaked cotton ball to   4
swab your middle or ring finger, and
allow the excess alcohol to evaporate.
After opening the sterile lancet, prick
the sterile finger once, approximately
one—quarter inch beyond the end of the
fingernail. Now, collect several drops
of blood in the test tube containing
the saline solution, and mix the solution. In the meantime, hold another
sterile cotton ball over the cut to allow the blood to clot.

**Third stage
of process**

Next, using the Pasteur pipette,   5
transfer one drop of the saline solution containing the blood to each of
the anti—A, anti—B, and anti—Rh serums,
using a separate applicator stick to
mix each. After two or three minutes,
clumping may have appeared in one or
all of the areas. A—clumping denotes A—
type blood, B—clumping indicates B—type

blood, A— and B—clumping signifies AB
blood, and no clumping denotes O blood.
Rh—clumping means that your blood is Rh
positive; the absence of Rh—clumping
indicates that you have Rh—negative
blood.

Conclusion By following the simple steps out— 6
lined above, you will learn much that
will be of practical value in your fu—
ture scientific explorations. As an
added bonus, you will also learn your
blood type.

Points for Special Attention

Structure. Scott Blackman's instructions are so clear that they would make sense without the introductory and concluding paragraphs. Although the paper would then lack a clear statement of the unifying idea, it would still be a good example of process writing—a chronological presentation of a set of steps to be performed, preceded by a precise list of necessary materials. The introduction and conclusion introduce and reinforce the reasons why the process is being carried out.

Purpose and Style. This set of instructions, written by Scott for an introductory course in animal biology, has two purposes. It serves as a review exercise for the student author, and it provides other students with all the information they need to duplicate the process. Because it presents instructions rather than an extended explanation of a process, it is written in the second person and in the present tense, with the verbs in the form of commands. These commands, however, are not choppy or abrupt because the instructions include smooth transitions as well as appropriate articles and pronouns.

Precision. Scott's instructions are very detailed: for example, "approximately one-quarter inch beyond the end of the fingernail." This detail is based on physiological knowledge about where the cut will produce just enough blood for the test yet do little damage and heal quickly. His advice about using different applicator sticks to avoid inadvertently mixing blood samples shows that he has thought about mistakes his readers might make. A different writer might have explained the reasons for such specific instructions, but considering his audience, Scott didn't think it was necessary.

In contrast to "Typing Your Own Blood," the next essay is a process explanation.

DIETING, DIETING, DIETING

Introduction   Unlike in many European countries,   1
fat just never caught on in the United
States as I always hoped it would. I
used to sit around and think, maybe
this is the year for the Obese Olym-
pics, or the Pillsbury eat-off, or for
Bert Parks's warbling, "There she is,
Miss North, South, and Central Ameri-
cas." But it never happened. Today's
Americans are too diet-conscious. They
exercise. They count calories. They attend diet seminars. Their entire conversation is centered on how wonderful
it feels to starve. But for some people, including me, dieting isn't so
Thesis   easy; in fact, trying to lose weight
can be a slow and sometimes frustrating
process.

First step   The first, and perhaps the most dif-   2
in process   ficult step for potential dieters, is
accepting the fact that they are over-
weight. Being overweight is a condition
in which a person has more weight than
the body needs. The question is, how do
people tell that they are overweight?
Sometimes this realization is triggered
by just a little thing, like seeing a
fifty-dollar bill on the sidewalk and

not being able to pick it up, or accus-
ing the car wash of shrinking the seat
belts.

Second step
in process

Once would-be dieters recognize and   3
accept that they are overweight, their
next problem is deciding which diet to
follow. This step consists primarily of
eliminating fad diets. Each diet that
has swept the country during the past
decade promises dieters more food than
they can eat and almost instant results. Some of the most popular diets
are the pill-assisted diet, the high-
protein diet, the water diet, the fat-
picture-on-the-refrigerator-door diet,
and the cottage-cheese diet.

The weight pill has become the "in"   4
way to lose weight; however, this
weight loss is only temporary, and many
people end up fat again. Moreover, the
pills can have side effects, such as
causing anxiety and speeding up the
heart rate. The obvious disadvantage of
the high-protein diet is that it encourages an imbalance of essential food
groups. (Too much of one thing is just
as bad as too little.) The water diet,
otherwise known as the Stillman diet,
calls for lots of lean meat, eight
glasses of water daily, and a bathroom.
Another diet requires dieters to tape
pictures of themselves at their heavi-
est to the refrigerator door. This
strategy is supposed to discourage

binges, and for some it works to a certain extent. But after a short period of time, most dieters fall right back into their old eating habits. The last diet, the cottage-cheese diet, is frequently tried but with little success. All the cottage cheese does is increase a person's desire for tastier food. So much for wonder diets.

Third step in process

The next stage, regression, comes after trying these diets and failing. At this point, most people go back to their old habits, but not without a twinge of guilt. Suddenly, frustrated dieters find themselves ordering spaghetti with meat balls, broccoli covered with cheese sauce, garlic bread dripping with butter—and a diet soda. This relapse may solve the guilt complex but not the weight problem. The only surefire way of dieting successfully is the nutritional approach. The last stage in the weight-loss process begins only when dieters accept that they have to change their eating habits permanently. 5

Fourth step in process

Now dieters learn to eat properly, selecting a balanced diet from among the four food groups: dairy, bread and cereal, fruit and vegetable, and protein. At the same time, dieters may learn to count calories and may begin a program of regular exercise. This program helps burn off excess calories and 6

```
                helps keep the body in functioning
                shape. Only when dieters have perma-
                nently modified their eating habits and
                begun to eat sensibly can the actual
                weight loss begin.
Conclusion      With all these points in mind, I          7
                tackled my weight problem and won, but
                there was a time when I derived some
                comfort from the knowledge that one out
                of every three Americans is overweight.
                I never saw the "one." Everywhere I
                went, I was flanked by the two chart-
                perfect women. I was surrounded by peo-
                ple with lean and hungry looks. But I
                survived. I learned to resist self-de-
                lusion, temptation, and fad diets, and
                to be thin without starving.
```

Points for Special Attention

Structure.   Hilary Barshai's paper, written for an English composition class, is an informal overview of a process rather than a complex analysis. Hilary begins by placing her topic in the context of personal experience, widens her focus to consider Americans' attitudes toward dieting, and concludes her first paragraph with her thesis. In subsequent paragraphs, she presents the various stages in the process of trying to lose weight, signaling the start of each new step with an appropriate topic sentence ("The first . . . step"; "Once would-be dieters recognize and accept . . ."; "The next stage, regression . . ."; "Now dieters learn to eat properly . . ."). In her last paragraph, she again narrows her focus to her personal experience.

Purpose and Style.   In her essay, Hilary sets out to show her readers how difficult it is to lose weight. While she uses the first person and the past tense in her opening and closing paragraphs, the body of her process explanation employs the third person and the present tense (to designate a habitual process). Because she is *not* writing instructions that will enable a reader to duplicate the process, Hilary does not use commands. Throughout the paper, her smooth transitions help the audience to follow the process easily, even in paragraph 4, where she develops the second step (eliminating fad diets) by defining four of them. Probably the most striking stylistic device here is Hilary's use of humor as she explains how discouraging trying to lose weight can be.

The following selections illustrate how varied the purposes of process essays can be. All, however, provide orderly and clear explanations so that readers can follow the process easily.

HOW DICTIONARIES
ARE MADE

S. I. Hayakawa

Samuel Icheye Hayakawa was born in 1906 in Vancouver, British Columbia, and was educated at the University of Manitoba, McGill University, and the University of Wisconsin, from which he received his Ph.D. He has taught English at the University of Wisconsin, the University of Chicago, and San Francisco State University, serving as president of the latter between 1969 and 1972. Best known as a semanticist, he is the author of such influential books about language as Language in Action *(1939),* Language in Thought and Action *(1949; revised 1964), and* Symbol, Status and Personality *(1963). He has contributed to periodicals such as the* New Republic, Harper's, *and the* Sewanee Review, *and he also edits the periodical* ETC: A Review of General Semantics. *Most recently he has been a U.S. senator from California. Here, in writing about the process of compiling a dictionary, Hayakawa also says a good deal about what a dictionary is for and what it can tell us.*

It is widely believed that every word has a correct meaning, that we learn these meanings principally from teachers and grammarians (except that most of the time we don't bother to, so that we ordinarily speak "sloppy English"), and that dictionaries and grammars are the supreme authority in matters of meaning and usage. Few people ask by what authority the writers of dictionaries and grammars say what they say. I once got into a dispute with an Englishwoman over the pronunciation of a word and offered to look it up in the dictionary. The Englishwoman said firmly, "What for? I am English. I was born and brought up in England. The way I speak *is* English." Such self-assurance about one's own language is not uncommon among the English. In the United States, however, anyone who is willing to quarrel with the dictionary is regarded as either eccentric or mad.

Let us see how dictionaries are made and how the editors arrive at definitions. What follows applies, incidentally, only to those dictionary offices where first-hand, original research goes on—not those in which editors simply copy existing dictionaries. The task of writing a dictionary begins with reading vast amounts of the literature of the period or subject that the dictionary is to cover. As the editors read, they copy on cards every interesting or rare word, every unusual or peculiar occurrence of a common word, a large number of common words in their ordinary uses, and also the sentences in which each of these words appears, thus:

> pail
> The dairy *pails* bring home increase of milk
>
> Keats, *Endymion*
> I, 44–45

That is to say, the context of each word is collected, along with the word itself. For a really big job of dictionary-writing, such as the *Oxford English Dictionary* (usually bound in about twenty-five volumes), millions of such cards are collected, and the task of editing occupies decades. As the cards are collected, they are alphabetized and sorted. When the sorting is completed, there will be for each word anywhere from two or three to several hundred illustrative quotations, each on its card.   3

To define a word, then, the dictionary-editor places before him the stack of cards illustrating that word; each of the cards represents an actual use of the word by a writer of some literary or historical importance. He reads the cards carefully, discards some, rereads the rest, and divides up the stack according to what he thinks are the several senses of the word. Finally, he writes his definitions, following the hard-and-fast rule that each definition *must* be based on what the quotations in front of him reveal about the meaning of the word. The editor cannot be influenced by what *he* thinks a given word *ought* to mean. He must work according to the cards or not at all.   4

The writing of a dictionary, therefore, is not a task of setting up authoritative statements about the "true meanings" of words, but a task of *recording*, to the best of one's ability, what various words *have meant* to authors in the distant or immediate past. *The writer of a dictionary is a historian, not a lawgiver.* If, for example, we had been writing a dictionary in 1890, or even as late as 1919, we could have said that the word "broadcast" means "to scatter" (seed, for example), but we could not have decreed that from 1921 on, the most common meaning of the word should become "to disseminate audible messages, etc., by radio transmission." To regard the dictionary as an "authority," therefore, is to credit the dictionary-writer with gifts of prophecy which neither he nor anyone else possesses. In choosing our words when we speak or write, we can be *guided* by the historical record afforded us by the dictionary, but we cannot be *bound* by it,   5 because new situations, new experiences, new inventions, new feelings are always compelling us to give new uses to old words. Looking under a "hood," we should ordinarily have found, five hundred years ago, a monk; today, we find a motorcar engine.[1]

COMPREHENSION

1. What are the major stages of the process Hayakawa outlines?

2. How does Hayakawa say the meaning of the word *broadcast* has changed? How can you account for this change in meaning? What other words can you think of whose meanings have changed?

3. What does Hayakawa mean, in paragraph 5, when he says, *"The writer of a dictionary is a historian, not a lawgiver"*?

PURPOSE AND AUDIENCE

1. What kind of audience do you think Hayakawa is addressing here? How can you tell?

2. Hayakawa writes his process explanation in order to correct a common misconception about how dictionaries are made. What is this misconception, and how does he correct it in his thesis?

3. Why do you think Hayakawa decided to write this as a process explanation rather than as a set of instructions?

4. In paragraph 5, why do you think Hayakawa has placed the words *true meanings* in quotation marks?

5. In this brief essay, Hayakawa is writing to inform, to persuade, and to entertain. In what ways does he achieve each of these goals?

STYLE AND STRUCTURE

1. What constitutes the actual process explanation in this essay? What else does Hayakawa include? Why?

---

[1]*Webster's Third New International Dictionary* lists the word "hood" also as a shortened form of "hoodlum."

The time that elapsed between *Webster's Second Edition* (1934) and the *Third* (1961) indicates the enormous amount of reading and labor entailed in the preparation of a really thorough dictionary of a language as rapidly changing and as rich in vocabulary as English.

2. Although many process explanations are written in the past tense, this is written in the present. What do you think is the reason for this?

3. Why does Hayakawa present a visual illustration of one of the steps in the process he describes?

WRITING WORKSHOP

1. In this selection, Hayakawa has simplified a complex task. Write a process essay which simplifies this same task even further, aiming at an audience of schoolchildren. Be sure to use many examples and detailed explanations.

2. Write a process essay of explaining how you went about putting together a collection, a scrapbook, or an album of some kind. Be sure your essay makes clear why you collected or compiled your materials.

MY FIRST CONK

Malcolm X

Malcolm X was born Malcolm Little in Omaha, Nebraska, in 1925, and was assassinated in 1964 by a member of a rival religious group. During his lifetime, Malcolm X was everything from a numbers runner to a Pullman porter to a disciple of Elijah Muhammad, leader of the Black Muslims. The Autobiography of Malcolm X, from which this excerpt is taken, relates his rise from poverty to national prominence as a lecturer and religious leader. The autobiography is unusual not only in its frankness and vividness, but also in how it was written: it was dictated to Alex Haley, later the auther of Roots. *"My First Conk" explains a ritual procedure that was part of Malcolm X's young manhood and also reflects his adult view of the process. The selection begins as an autobiographical narrative, goes on to explain a process, and ends on a strongly persuasive note.*

Shorty soon decided that my hair was finally long enough to be 1
conked. He had promised to school me in how to beat the barber-
shops' three- and four-dollar price by making up congolene, and
then conking ourselves.

I took the little list of ingredients he had printed out for me, and 2
went to a grocery store, where I got a can of Red Devil lye, two
eggs, and two medium-sized white potatoes. Then at a drugstore
near the poolroom, I asked for a large jar of vaseline, a large bar of
soap, a large-toothed comb and a fine-toothed comb, one of those
rubber hoses with a metal spray-head, a rubber apron and a pair of
gloves.

"Going to lay on that first conk?" the drugstore man asked me. I 3
proudly told him, grinning, "Right!"

Shorty paid six dollars a week for a room in his cousin's shabby 4
apartment. His cousin wasn't at home. "It's like the pad's mine, he
spends so much time with his woman," Shorty said. "Now, you watch
me—"

He peeled the potatoes and thin-sliced them into a quart-sized 5
Mason fruit jar, then started stirring them with a wooden spoon as
he gradually poured in a little over half the can of lye. "Never use
a metal spoon; the lye will turn it black," he told me.

A jelly-like, starchy-looking glop resulted from the lye and po- 6
tatoes, and Shorty broke in the two eggs, stirring real fast—his own
conk and dark face bent down close. The congolene turned pale-
yellowish. "Feel the jar," Shorty said. I cupped my hand against the
outside, and snatched it away. "Damn right, it's hot, that's the lye,"
he said. "So you know it's going to burn when I comb it in—it burns
bad. But the longer you can stand it, the straighter the hair."

He made me sit down, and he tied the string of the new rubber 7
apron tightly around my neck, and combed up my bush of hair.
Then, from the big vaseline jar, he took a handful and massaged it
hard all through my hair and into the scalp. He also thickly vase-
lined my neck, ears and forehead. "When I get to washing out your
head, be sure to tell me anywhere you feel any little stinging,"
Shorty warned me, washing his hands, then pulling on the rubber
gloves, and tying on his own rubber apron. "You always got to remember that any congolene left in burns a sore into your head."

The congolene just felt warm when Shorty started combing it in. 8
But then my head caught fire.

I gritted my teeth and tried to pull the sides of the kitchen table 9
together. The comb felt as if it was raking my skin off.

My eyes watered, my nose was running. I couldn't stand it any 10
longer; I bolted to the washbasin. I was cursing Shorty with every
name I could think of when he got the spray going and started soap-
lathering my head.

He lathered and spray-rinsed, lathered and spray-rinsed, maybe 11
ten or twelve times, each time gradually closing the hot-water fau-
cet, until the rinse was cold, and that helped some.

"You feel any stinging spots?" 12

"No," I managed to say. My knees were trembling. 13

"Sit back down, then. I think we got it all out okay." 14

The flame came back as Shorty, with a thick towel, started drying 15
my head, rubbing hard. *"Easy, man, easy!"* I kept shouting.

"The first time's always worst. You get used to it better before 16
long. You took it real good, homeboy. You got a good conk."

When Shorty let me stand up and see in the mirror, my hair 17
hung down in limp, damp strings. My scalp still flamed, but not as
badly; I could bear it. He draped the towel around my shoulders,
over my rubber apron, and began again vaselining my hair.

I could feel him combing, straight back, first the big comb, then 18
the fine-tooth one.

Then, he was using a razor, very delicately, on the back of my 19
neck. Then, finally, shaping the sideburns.

My first view in the mirror blotted out the hurting. I'd seen some   20
pretty conks, but when it's the first time, on your *own* head, the
transformation, after the lifetime of kinks, is staggering.

The mirror reflected Shorty behind me. We both were grinning   21
and sweating. And on top of my head was this thick, smooth sheen
of shining red hair—real red—as straight as any white man's.

How ridiculous I was! Stupid enough to stand there simply lost   22
in admiration of my hair now looking "white," reflected in the mirror in Shorty's room. I vowed that I'd never again be without a conk,
and I never was for many years.

This was my first really big step toward self-degradation: when   23
I endured all of that pain, literally burning my flesh to have it look
like a white man's hair. I had joined that multitude of Negro men
and women in America who are brainwashed into believing that
the black people are "inferior"—and white people "superior"—that
they will even violate and mutilate their God-created bodies to try
to look "pretty" by white standards.

Look around today, in every small town and big city, from two-   24
bit catfish and soda-pop joints into the "integrated" lobby of the
Waldorf-Astoria, and you'll see conks on black men. And you'll see
black women wearing these green and pink and purple and red and
platinum-blonde wigs. They're all more ridiculous than a slapstick
comedy. It makes you wonder if the Negro has completely lost his
sense of identity, lost touch with himself.

You'll see the conk worn by many, many so-called "upper class"   25
Negroes, and, as much as I hate to say it about them, on all too
many Negro entertainers. One of the reasons that I've especially
admired some of them, like Lionel Hampton and Sidney Poitier,
among others, is that they have kept their natural hair and fought
to the top. I admire any Negro man who has never had himself
conked, or who has had the sense to get rid of it—as I finally did.

I don't know which kind of self-defacing conk is the greater shame—   26
the one you'll see on the heads of the black so-called "middle class"
and "upper class," who ought to know better, or the one you'll see
on the heads of the poorest, most downtrodden, ignorant black men.
I mean the legal-minimum-wage ghetto-dwelling kind of Negro, as
I was when I got my first one. It's generally among these poor fools
that you'll see a black kerchief over the man's head, like Aunt Je-
mima; he's trying to make his conk last longer, between trips to the
barbershop. Only for special occasions is this kerchief-protected conk
exposed—to show off how "sharp" and "hip" its owner is. The ironic
thing is that I have never heard any woman, white or black, express

any admiration for a conk. Of course, any white woman with a black man isn't thinking about his hair. But I don't see how on earth a black woman with any race pride could walk down the street with any black man wearing a conk—the emblem of his shame that he is black.

To my own shame, when I say all of this I'm talking first of all   27
about myself—because you can't show me any Negro who ever conked more faithfully than I did. I'm speaking from personal experience when I say of any black man who conks today, or any white-wigged black woman, that if they gave the brains in their heads just half as much attention as they do their hair, they would be a thousand times better off.

COMPREHENSION

1. What exactly is a conk? Why did Malcolm X want to get his hair conked? What did a conk symbolize to him at first? What did it symbolize at the time he wrote about it?

2. List the materials Shorty asked Malcolm X to buy. Is the purpose of each explained? If so, where?

3. Outline the major stages in the procedure Malcolm X describes. Are they in chronological order? Which, if any, are out of place?

PURPOSE AND AUDIENCE

1. Why does Malcolm X write this selection as a process explanation instead of a set of instructions?

2. This process explanation has a definite thesis that makes its purpose clear. What is this thesis?

3. *The Autobiography of Malcolm X* was published in 1964, when many blacks got their hair straightened regularly. Is the thesis of the selection still appropriate today?

4. Why does Malcolm X include so many references to the pain and discomfort he endured as part of the process?

5. What is the relationship between Malcolm X's personal narrative and the universal statement he makes about conking in this selection?

STYLE AND STRUCTURE

1. Identify some of the transitional words Malcolm X uses to move from step to step.

2. Only about half of this selection is devoted to the process explanation. Where does the process begin? Where does it end?

3. How does the use of dialogue strengthen the process explanation? How does it strengthen Malcolm X's thesis?

WRITING WORKSHOP

1. Write a process explanation of an unpleasant experience you have often gone through in order to conform to others' standards of physical beauty. (You might consider such procedures as shaving or getting a permanent wave.)

2. Rewrite Malcolm X's process explanation as he might have written it when he still thought of conking as a desirable process, worth all the trouble. Include all his steps, but change his thesis and slant your writing to make conking sound painless and worthwhile.

FALLING FOR APPLES

Noel Perrin

Noel Perrin, former head of the English department at Dartmouth College, was born in 1927. He has contributed essays to The New Yorker *and other periodicals and is the author of* Vermont: In All Weathers *(1973),* First Person Rural *(1978), and* Second Person Rural *(1980), "Falling for Apples" comes from* Second Person Rural, *subtitled* More Essays of a Sometime Farmer, *which includes entertaining essays on splitting wood, planting trees, and turning lambs into lamb chops and lamburgers, as well as observations on cows, grass, maple syrup, and other staples of country life. In "Falling for Apples" Perrin tells from personal experience how to make apple cider.*

The number of children who eagerly help around a farm is rather small. Willing helpers do exist, but many more of them are five years old than fifteen. In fact, there seems to be a general law that says as long as a kid is too little to help effectively, he or she is dying to. Then, just as they reach the age when they really could drive a fence post or empty a sap bucket without spilling half of it, they lose interest. Now it's cars they want to drive, or else they want to stay in the house and listen for four straight hours to The Who. That sort of thing.

There is one exception to this rule. Almost no kid that I have ever met outgrows an interest in cidering. In consequence, cider making remains a family time on our farm, even though it's been years since any daughter trudged along a fencerow with me, dragging a new post too heavy for her to carry, or begged for lessons in chainsawing.

It's not too hard to figure out why. In the first place, cidering gives the child instant gratification. There's no immediate reward for weeding a garden (unless the parents break down and offer cash), still less for loading a couple of hundred hay bales in the barn. But the minute you've ground and pressed the first bushel of apples, you can break out the glasses and start drinking. Good stuff, too. Cider has a wonderful fresh sweetness as it runs from the press.

In the second place, making cider on a small scale is simple enough so that even fairly young children—say, a pair of nine-year-olds—

can do the whole operation by themselves. Yet it's also picturesque enough to tempt people of any age. When my old college roommate was up last fall—and we've been out of college a long time—he and his wife did four pressings in the course of the weekend. They only quit then because I ran out of apples.

Finally, cider making appeals to a deep human instinct. It's the same one that makes a housewife feel so good when she takes a bunch of leftovers and produces a memorable casserole. At no cost, and using what would otherwise be wasted, she has created something. In fact, she has just about reversed entropy.   5

Cidering is like that. You take apples that have been lying on the ground for a week, apples with blotches and cankers and bad spots, apples that would make a supermarket manager turn pale if you merely brought them in the store, and out of this unpromising material you produce not one but two delicious drinks. Sweet cider now. Hard cider later.   6

The first step is to have a press. At the turn of the century, almost every farm family did. They ordered them from the Sears or Montgomery Ward catalogue as routinely as one might now order a toaster. Then about 1930 little presses ceased to be made. Pasteurized apple juice had joined the list of American food-processing triumphs. It had no particular flavor (still hasn't), but it would keep almost indefinitely. Even more appealing, it was totally sterile. That was the era when the proudest boast that, let's say, a bakery could make was that its bread was untouched by human hands. Was touched only by stainless-steel beaters and stainless-steel wrapping machines.   7

Eras end, though, and the human hand came back into favor. One result: in the 1970s home cider presses returned to the market. They have not yet returned to the Sears catalogue, but they are readily available. I know of two companies in Vermont that make them, another in East Aurora, New York, and one out in Washington state. If there isn't someone making them in Michigan or Wisconsin, there soon will be. Prices range from about 175 to 250 dollars.   8

Then you get a couple of bushels of apples. There *may* be people in the country who buy cider apples, but I don't know any of them. Old apple trees are too common. I get mine by the simple process of picking up windfalls in a derelict orchard that came with our place. I am not choosy. Anything that doesn't actually squish goes in the basket.   9

With two kids to help, collecting takes maybe twenty minutes. Kids tend to be less interested in gathering the apples than in run-   10 ning the press, but a quiet threat works wonders. Kids also worry about worms sometimes, as they scoop apples from the ground— apples that may be wet with dew, spiked with stubble, surrounded by hungry wasps. Occasionally I have countered with a short lecture on how much safer our unsprayed apples are than the shiny, worm- less, but heavily sprayed apples one finds in stores. But usually I just say that I have yet to see a worm in our cider press. That's true, too. Whether it's because there has never been one, or whether it's because in the excitement and bustle of grinding you just wouldn't notice one little worm, I don't dare to say.

As soon as you get back with the apples, it's time to make cider. 11 Presses come in two sizes: one-bushel and a-third-of-a-bushel. We have tried both. If I lived in a suburb and had to buy apples, I would use the very efficient third-of-a-bushel press and make just under a gallon at a time. Living where I do, I use the bigger press and make two gallons per pressing, occasionally a little more.

The process has two parts. First you set your pressing tub under 12 the grinder, line it with a pressing cloth, and start grinding. Or, better, your children do. One feeds apples into the hopper, the other turns the crank. If there are three children present, the third can hold the wooden hopper plate, and thus keep the apples from bounc- ing around. If there are four, the fourth can spell off on cranking. Five or more is too many, and any surplus over four is best made into a separate crew for the second pressing. I once had two three- child crews present, plus a seventh child whom my wife appointed the official timer. We did two pressings and had $4\frac{1}{4}$ gallons of cider in 43 minutes and 12 seconds. (Who won? The second crew, by more than a minute. Each crew had one of our practiced daughters on it, but the second also had the advantage of watching the first.)

As soon as the apples are ground, you put the big pressing plate 13 on and start to turn the press down. If it's a child crew, and adult meddling is nevertheless tolerated, it's desirable to have the kids turn the press in order of their age, starting with the youngest: at the end it takes a fair amount of strength (though it's not beyond two nine-year-olds working together), and a little kid coming after a big one may fail to produce a single drop.

The pressing is where all the thrills come. As the plate begins to 14 move down and compact the ground apples, you hear a kind of sigh- ing, bubbling noise. Then a trickle of cider begins to run out. Within five or ten seconds the trickle turns into a stream, and the stream into a ciderfall. Even kids who've done it a dozen times look down in awe at what their labor has wrought.

A couple of minutes later the press is down as far as it will go, 15
and the container you remembered to put below the spout is full of
rich, brown cider. Someone has broken out the glasses, and everybody is having a drink.

This pleasure goes on and on. In an average year we start making 16
cider the second week of September, and we continue until early
November. We make all we can drink ourselves, and quite a lot to
give away. We have supplied whole church suppers. One year the
girls sold about ten gallons to the village store, which made them
some pocket money they were prouder of than any they ever earned
by baby-sitting. Best of all, there are two months each year when
all of us are running the farm together, just like a pioneer family.

COMPREHENSION

1. What three reasons does Perrin give for cidering's appeal to people of
   all ages?

2. Why has cidering gradually become less and less common? Why is it
   experiencing a small revival now?

3. What are some of the advantages Perrin feels his family gains from
   cidering?

4. List the essential steps in the process of cidering.

5. Why is this essay titled "Falling for Apples"?

PURPOSE AND AUDIENCE

1. Is Perrin addressing an audience of country folk or city dwellers? How
   do you know?

2. At times, Perrin's purpose seems to be to educate his readers. Point to
   specific examples.

3. Paraphrase Perrin's thesis.

STYLE AND STRUCTURE

1. In what paragraph does the actual process of cidering begin? Where does
   it end?

2. What is the function of paragraphs 1 through 6?

3. Why does Perrin devote so much attention to the children's roles and
   attitudes?

4. Does Perrin structure this essay as a set of instructions or a process explanation? Explain. What might have influenced his choice?

5. What transitional words and phrases does Perrin use to signal the start of each new step?

WRITING WORKSHOP

1. Write a set of instructions telling how to perform a physical activity or chore you are familiar with. In your thesis, try to convince your audience of the benefits the process has for them.

2. Rewrite your instructions (see the question above) as a process explanation.

THE MAKER'S EYE: REVISING YOUR OWN MANUSCRIPTS

Donald M. Murray

In this essay, originally published in The Writer, *Donald Murray argues for the importance of the revision process to the writer. Murray, who was born in 1917 and now teaches at the University of New Hampshire, has been a Pulitzer Prize–winning journalist and an editor of* Time *magazine. He has also written various works of fiction, nonfiction, and poetry, as well as a textbook,* A Writer Teaches Writing. *As he presents the stages in the revision process, Murray illustrates their usefulness to any writer and offers his own views and those of other professional authors.*

When students complete a first draft, they consider the job of 1
writing done—and their teachers too often agree. When professional writers complete a first draft, they usually feel that they are at the start of the writing process. When a draft is completed, the job of writing can begin.

That difference in attitude is the difference between amateur and 2
professional, inexperience and experience, journeyman and craftsman. Peter F. Drucker, the prolific business writer, calls his first draft "the zero draft"—after that he can start counting. Most writers share the feeling that the first draft, and all of those which follow, are opportunities to discover what they have to say and how best they can say it.

To produce a progression of drafts, each of which says more and 3
says it more clearly, the writer has to develop a special kind of reading skill. In school we are taught to decode what appears on the page as finished writing. Writers, however, face a different category of possibility and responsibility when they read their own drafts. To them the words on the page are never finished. Each can be changed and rearranged, can set off a chain reaction of confusion or clarified meaning. This is a different kind of reading, which is possibly more difficult and certainly more exciting.

Writers must learn to be their own best enemy. They must accept 4
the criticism of others and be suspicious of it; they must accept the praise of others and be even more suspicious of it. Writers cannot depend on others. They must detach themselves from their own

pages so that they can apply both their caring and their craft to their own work.

Such detachment is not easy. Science fiction writer Ray Bradbury   5
supposedly puts each manuscript away for a year to the day and then rereads it as a stranger. Not many writers have the discipline or the time to do this. We must read when our judgment may be at its worst, when we are close to the euphoric moment of creation.

Then the writer, counsels novelist Nancy Hale, "should be critical   6
of everything that seems to him most delightful in his style. He should excise what he most admires, because he wouldn't thus admire it if he weren't . . . in a sense protecting it from criticism." John Ciardi, the poet, adds, "The last act of the writing must be to become one's own reader. It is, I suppose, a schizophrenic process, to begin passionately and to end critically, to begin hot and to end cold; and, more important, to be passion-hot and critic-cold at the same time."

Most people think that the principal problem is that writers are   7
too proud of what they have written. Actually, a greater problem for most professional writers is one shared by the majority of students. They are overly critical, think everything is dreadful, tear up page after page, never complete a draft, see the task as hopeless.

The writer must learn to read critically but constructively, to cut   8
what is bad, to reveal what is good. Eleanor Estes, the children's book author, explains: "The writer must survey his work critically, coolly, as though he were a stranger to it. He must be willing to prune, expertly and hard-heartedly. At the end of each revision, a manuscript may look . . . worked over, torn apart, pinned together, added to, deleted from, words changed and words changed back. Yet the book must maintain its original freshness and spontaneity."

Most readers underestimate the amount of rewriting it usually   9
takes to produce spontaneous reading. This is a great disadvantage to the student writer, who sees only a finished product and never watches the craftsman who takes the necessary step back, studies the work carefully, returns to the task, steps back, returns, steps back, again and again. Anthony Burgess, one of the most prolific writers in the English-speaking world, admits, "I might revise a page twenty times." Roald Dahl, the popular children's writer, states, "By the time I'm nearing the end of a story, the first part will have been reread and altered and corrected at least 150 times. . . . Good writing is essentially rewriting. I am positive of this."

Rewriting isn't virtuous. It isn't something that ought to be done.   10
It is simply something that most writers find they have to do to

discover what they have to say and how to say it. It is a condition of the writer's life.

There are, however, a few writers who do little formal rewriting, 11 primarily because they have the capacity and experience to create and review a large number of invisible drafts in their minds before they approach the page. And some writers slowly produce finished pages, performing all the tasks of revision simultaneously, page by page, rather than draft by draft. But it is still possible to see the sequence followed by most writers most of the time in rereading their own work.

Most writers scan their drafts first, reading as quickly as possible 12 to catch the larger problems of subject and form, then move in closer and closer as they read and write, reread and rewrite.

The first thing writers look for in their drafts is *information*. They 13 know that a good piece of writing is built from specific, accurate, and interesting information. The writer must have an abundance of information from which to construct a readable piece of writing.

Next writers look for *meaning* in the information. The specifics 14 must build to a pattern of significance. Each piece of specific information must carry the reader toward meaning.

Writers reading their own drafts are aware of *audience*. They put 15 themselves in the reader's situation and make sure that they deliver information which a reader wants to know or needs to know in a manner which is easily digested. Writers try to be sure that they anticipate and answer the questions a critical reader will ask when reading the piece of writing.

Writers make sure that the *form* is appropriate to the subject and 16 the audience. Form, or genre, is the vehicle which carries meaning to the reader, but form cannot be selected until the writer has adequate information to discover its significance and an audience which needs or wants that meaning.

Once writers are sure the form is appropriate, they must then 17 look at the *structure,* the order of what they have written. Good writing is built on a solid framework of logic, argument, narrative, or motivation which runs through the entire piece of writing and holds it together. This is the time when many writers find it most effective to outline as a way of visualizing the hidden spine by which the piece of writing is supported.

The element on which writers may spend a majority of their time 18 is *development*. Each section of a piece of writing must be adequately developed. It must give readers enough information so that they are satisfied. How much information is enough? That's as dif-

ficult as asking how much garlic belongs in a salad. It must be done
to taste, but most beginning writers underdevelop, underestimating
the reader's hunger for information.

As writers solve development problems, they often have to con-   19
sider questions of *dimension*. There must be a pleasing and effective
proportion among all the parts of the piece of writing. There is a
continual process of subtracting and adding to keep the piece of
writing in balance.

Finally, writers have to listen to their own voices. *Voice* is the   20
force which drives a piece of writing forward. It is an expression of
the writer's authority and concern. It is what is between the words
on the page, what glues the piece of writing together. A good piece
of writing is always marked by a consistent, individual voice.

As writers read and reread, write and rewrite, they move closer   21
and closer to the page until they are doing line-by-line editing.
Writers read their own pages with infinite care. Each sentence, each
line, each clause, each phrase, each word, each mark of punctuation,
each section of white space between the type has to contribute to
the clarification of meaning.

Slowly the writer moves from word to word, looking through lan-   22
guage to see the subject. As a word is changed, cut, or added, as a
construction is rearranged, all the words used before that moment
and all those that follow that moment must be considered and reconsidered.

Writers often read aloud at this stage of the editing process, mut-   23
tering or whispering to themselves, calling on the ear's experience
with language. Does this sound right—or that? Writers edit, shift-
ing back and forth from eye to page to ear to page. I find I must do
this careful editing in short runs, no more than fifteen or twenty
minutes at a stretch, or I become too kind with myself. I begin to
see what I hope is on the page, not what actually is on the page.

This sounds tedious if you haven't done it, but actually it is fun.   24
Making something right is immensely satisfying, for writers begin
to learn what they are writing about by writing. Language leads
them to meaning, and there is the joy of discovery, of understanding,
of making meaning clear as the writer employs the technical skills
of language.

Words have double meanings, even triple and quadruple mean-   25
ings. Each word has its own potential for connotation and denotation. And when writers rub one word against the other, they are
often rewarded with a sudden insight, an unexpected clarification.

The maker's eye moves back and forth from word to phrase to   26
sentence to paragraph to sentence to phrase to word. The maker's

eye sees the need for variety and balance, for a firmer structure, for a more appropriate form. It peers into the interior of the paragraph, looking for coherence, unity, and emphasis, which make meaning clear.

I learned something about this process when my first bifocals 27 were prescribed. I had ordered a larger section of the reading portion of the glass because of my work, but even so, I could not contain my eyes within this new limit of vision. And I still find myself taking off my glasses and bending my nose towards the page, for my eyes unconsciously flick back and forth across the page, back to another page, forward to still another, as I try to see each evolving line in relation to every other line.

When does this process end? Most writers agree with the great 28 Russian writer Tolstoy, who said, "I scarcely ever reread my published writings, if by chance I come across a page, it always strikes me: all this must be rewritten; this is how I should have written it."

The maker's eye is never satisfied, for each word has the potential 29 to ignite new meaning. This article has been twice written all the way through the writing process, and it was published four years ago. Now it is to be republished in a book. The editors make a few small suggestions, and then I read it with my maker's eye. Now it has been re-edited, re-revised, re-read, re-re-edited, for each piece of writing to the writer is full of potential and alternatives.

A piece of writing is never finished. It is delivered to a deadline, 30 torn out of the typewriter on demand, sent off with a sense of accomplishment and shame and pride and frustration. If only there were a couple more days, time for just another run at it, perhaps then . . .

COMPREHENSION

1. What difference does Murray identify between how student and professional writers view a first draft? How does he account for this difference? What problem do both share?

2. What special kind of reading skill does Murray say the writer has to develop? Why?

3. How do the professional writers Murray quotes lend support to his thesis?

4. How do professional writers consider audience, form, structure, development, and voice as they revise?

5. Why does the process of revision never actually end?

PURPOSE AND AUDIENCE

1. This essay has an explicitly stated thesis. What is it? Where does it appear?

2. Is Murray's purpose primarily to inform or to persuade? Where does he serve each of these purposes?

3. This essay was written for professional writers, not college students. How does this audience explain the author's decision to write an explanation instead of a set of instructions?

STYLE AND STRUCTURE

1. Murray does not introduce the first step in his process until paragraph 12. Why not?

2. Paragraph 20 begins with the word *finally,* signaling that the last stage in the revision process is being introduced. Where does the discussion of this stage end?

3. Murray occasionally uses analogy to make the writing process concrete and familiar. Identify some of these figures of speech.

4. Murray occasionally speaks to the reader in the first person. Locate these first-person comments, and explain how they affect you.

5. Why does Murray end his essay in the middle of a sentence?

WRITING WORKSHOP

1. How do you revise your writing? Write an essay in which you explain the steps you take, noting why this process does or does not work for you.

2. Write a set of instructions in which you attempt to convince a younger student of the importance of revision.

THE EMBALMING
OF MR. JONES

Jessica Mitford

Jessica Mitford was born in England in 1917 and grew up with her four sisters in a protected, wealthy environment. Her sheltered upbringing contrasts sharply with her later involvement in politics and investigative journalism after becoming an American citizen. Mitford turned her ironic wit on her eccentric family in her auto- biographical Daughters and Rebels *(1960), on left-wing politics in* A Fine Old Conflict *(1977), on the prison system in* Kind and Usual Punishment *(1973), and on the mortuary business in* The American Way of Death *(1963), from which this excerpt is taken. A scathing criticism of the funeral industry, this book sharpened public scru- tiny of the way funerals are handled and also prompted many angry responses from morticians. In "The Embalming of Mr. Jones," Mit- ford painstakingly and ironically describes the dual process of em- balming and restoring a cadaver. Notice as you read how Mitford's meticulous use of detail supports her thesis.*

Embalming is indeed a most extraordinary procedure, and one 1
must wonder at the docility of Americans who each year pay hundreds of millions of dollars for its perpetuation, blissfully ignorant of what it is all about, what is done, how it is done. Not one in ten thousand has any idea of what actually takes place. Books on the subject are extremely hard to come by. They are not to be found in most li- braries or bookshops.

In an era when huge television audiences watch surgical oper- 2
ations in the comfort of their living rooms, when, thanks to the animated cartoon, the geography of the digestive system has become familiar territory even to the nursery school set, in a land where the satisfaction of curiosity about almost all matters is a national pastime, the secrecy surrounding embalming can, surely, hardly be attributed to the inherent gruesomeness of the subject. Custom in this regard has within this century suffered a complete reversal. In the early days of American embalming, when it was performed in the home of the deceased, it was almost mandatory for some relative to stay by the embalmer's side and witness the procedure. Today, family members who might wish to be in attendance would cer- tainly be dissuaded by the funeral director. All others, except ap- prentices, are excluded by law from the preparation room.

A close look at what does actually take place may explain in large ₃ measure the undertaker's intractable reticence concerning a procedure that has become his major *raison d'être*. Is it possible he fears that public information about embalming might lead patrons to wonder if they really want this service? If the funeral men are loath to discuss the subject outside the trade, the reader may, understandably, be equally loath to go on reading at this point. For those who have the stomach for it, let us part the formaldehyde curtain. . . .

The body is first laid out in the undertaker's morgue—or rather, ₄ Mr. Jones is reposing in the preparation room—to be readied to bid the world farewell.

The preparation room in any of the better funeral establishments ₅ has the tiled and sterile look of a surgery, and indeed the embalmer–restorative artist who does his chores there is beginning to adopt the term "dermasurgeon" (appropriately corrupted by some mortician-writers as "demisurgeon") to describe his calling. His equipment, consisting of scalpels, scissors, augers, forceps, clamps, needles, pumps, tubes, bowls and basins, is crudely imitative of the surgeon's as is his technique, acquired in a nine- or twelve-month post-high-school course in an embalming school. He is supplied by an advanced chemical industry with a bewildering array of fluids, sprays, pastes, oils, powders, creams, to fix or soften tissue, shrink or distend it as needed, dry it here, restore the moisture there. There are cosmetics, waxes and paints to fill and cover features, even plaster of Paris to replace entire limbs. There are ingenious aids to prop and stabilize the cadaver: a Vari-Pose Head Rest, the Edwards Arm and Hand Positioner, the Repose Block (to support the shoulders during the embalming), and the Throop Foot Positioner, which resembles an old-fashioned stocks.

Mr. John H. Eckels, president of the Eckels College of Mortuary ₆ Science, thus describes the first part of the embalming procedure: "In the hands of a skilled practitioner, this work may be done in a comparatively short time and without mutilating the body other than by slight incision—so slight that it scarcely would cause serious inconvenience if made upon a living person. It is necessary to remove all the blood, and doing this not only helps in the disinfecting, but removes the principal cause of disfigurements due to discoloration."

Another textbook discusses the all-important time element: "The ₇ earlier this is done, the better, for every hour that elapses between death and embalming will add to the problems and complications encountered. . . ." Just how soon should one get going on the embalming? The author tells us, "On the basis of such scanty information made available to this profession through its rudimentary and haphazard system of technical research, we must conclude that the best results are to be obtained if the subject is embalmed before life is completely extinct—that is, before cellular death has occurred. In the average case, this would mean within an hour after somatic death." For those who feel that there is something a little rudimentary, not to say haphazard, about this advice, a comforting thought is offered by another writer. Speaking of fears entertained in early days of premature burial, he points out, "One of the effects of embalming by chemical injection, however, has been to dispel fears of live burial." How true; once the blood is removed, chances of live burial are indeed remote.

To return to Mr. Jones, the blood is drained out through the veins 8 and replaced by embalming fluid pumped in through the arteries. As noted in *The Principles and Practices of Embalming*, "every operator has a favorite injection and drainage point—a fact which becomes a handicap only if he fails or refuses to forsake his favorites when conditions demand it." Typical favorites are the carotid artery, femoral artery, jugular vein, subclavian vein. There are various choices of embalming fluid. If Flextone is used, it will produce a "mild, flexible rigidity. The skin retains a velvety softness, the tissues are rubbery and pliable. Ideal for women and children." It may be blended with B. and G. Products Company's Lyf-Lyk tint, which is guaranteed to reproduce "nature's own skin texture . . . the velvety appearance of living tissue." Suntone comes in three separate tints: Suntan; Special Cosmetic Tint, a pink shade "especially indicated for young female subjects"; and Regular Cosmetic Tint, moderately pink.

About three to six gallons of a dyed and perfumed solution of 9 formaldehyde, glycerin, borax, phenol, alcohol and water is soon circulating through Mr. Jones, whose mouth has been sewn together with a "needle directed upward between the upper lip and gum and brought out through the left nostril," with the corners raised slightly "for a more pleasant expression." If he should be buck-toothed, his teeth are cleaned with Bon Ami and coated with colorless nail polish. His eyes, meanwhile, are closed with flesh-tinted eye caps and eye cement.

The next step is to have at Mr. Jones with a thing called a trocar. 10 This is a long, hollow needle attached to a tube. It is jabbed into the abdomen, poked around the entrails and chest cavity, the contents of which are pumped out and replaced with "cavity fluid." This is done, and the hole in the abdomen sewed up, Mr. Jones's face is heavily creamed (to protect the skin from burns which may be caused by leakage of the chemicals), and he is covered with a sheet and left unmolested for a while. But not for long—there is more, much more, in store for him. He has been embalmed, but not yet restored, and the best time to start restorative work is eight to ten hours after embalming, when the tissues have become firm and dry.

The object of all this attention to the corpse, it must be remembered, is to make it presentable for viewing in an attitude of healthy repose. "Our customs require the presentation of our dead in the semblance of normality . . . unmarred by the ravages of illness, disease or mutilation," says Mr. J. Sheridan Mayer in his *Restorative Art.* This is rather a large order since few people die in the full bloom of health, unravaged by illness and unmarked by some disfigurement. The funeral industry is equal to the challenge: "In some cases the gruesome appearance of a mutilated or disease-ridden subject may be quite discouraging. The task of restoration may seem impossible and shake the confidence of the embalmer. This is the time for intestinal fortitude and determination. Once the formative work is begun and affected tissues are cleaned or removed, all doubts of success vanish. It is surprising and gratifying to discover the results which may be obtained."

The embalmer, having allowed an appropriate interval to elapse, returns to the attack, but now he brings into play the skill and equipment of sculptor and cosmetician. Is a hand missing? Costing one in plaster of Paris is a simple matter. "For replacement purposes, only a cast of the back of the hand is necessary; this is within the ability of the average operator and is quite adequate." If a lip or two, a nose or an ear should be missing, the embalmer has at hand a variety of restorative waxes with which to model replacements. Pores and skin texture are simulated by stippling with a little brush, and over this cosmetics are laid on. Head off? Decapitation cases are rather routinely handled. Ragged edges are trimmed, and head joined to torso with a series of splints, wires and sutures. It is a good idea to have a little something at the neck—a scarf or high collar—when time for viewing comes. Swollen mouth? Cut out tissue as needed from inside the lips. If too much is removed, the surface contour can easily be restored by padding with cotton. Swollen necks and cheeks are reduced by removing tissue through vertical incisions made down each side of the neck. "When the deceased is casketed, the pillow will hide the suture incisions . . . as an extra precaution against leakage, the suture may be painted with liquid sealer."

The opposite condition is more likely to be present itself—that of emaciation. His hypodermic syringe now loaded with massage cream, the embalmer seeks out and fills the hollowed and sunken areas by injection. In this procedure the backs of the hands and fingers and the under-chin area should not be neglected.

Positioning the lips is a problem that recurrently challenges the   14
ingenuity of the embalmer. Closed too tightly, they tend to give a stern, even disapproving expression. Ideally, embalmers feel, the lips should give the impression of being ever so slightly parted, the upper lip protruding slightly for a more youthful appearance. This takes some engineering, however, as the lips tend to drift apart. Lip drift can sometimes be remedied by pushing one or two straight pins through the inner margin of the lower lip and then inserting them between the two front upper teeth. If Mr. Jones happens to have no teeth, the pins can just as easily be anchored in his Armstrong Face Former and Denture Replacer. Another method to maintain lip closure is to dislocate the lower jaw, which is then held in its new position by a wire run through holes which have been drilled through the upper jaws at the midline. As the French are fond of saying, *il faut souffrir pour être belle.**

If Mr. Jones has died of jaundice, the embalming fluid will very   15
likely turn him green. Does this deter the embalmer? Not if he has intestinal fortitude. Masking pastes and cosmetics are heavily laid on, burial garments and casket interiors are color-correlated with particular care, and Jones is displayed beneath rose-colored lights. Friends will say, "How *well* he looks." Death by carbon monoxide, on the other hand, can be rather a good thing from the embalmer's viewpoint: "One advantage is the fact that this type of discoloration is an exaggerated form of a natural pink coloration." This is nice because the healthy glow is already present and needs but little attention.

The patching and filling completed, Mr. Jones is now shaved,   16
washed and dressed. Cream-based cosmetic, available in pink, flesh, suntan, brunette and blonde, is applied to his hands and face, his hair is shampooed and combed (and, in the case of Mrs. Jones, set), his hands manicured. For the horny-handed son of toil special care must be taken; cream should be applied to remove ingrained grime, and the nails cleaned. "If he were not in the habit of having them manicured in life, trimming and shaping is advised for better appearance—never questioned by kin."

Jones is now ready for casketing (this is the present participle of   17
the verb "to casket"). In this operation his right shoulder should be depressed slightly "to turn the body a bit to the right and soften the

*EDS. NOTE—It is necessary to suffer in order to be beautiful.

appearance of lying flat on the back." Positioning the hands is a matter of importance, and special rubber positioning blocks may be used. The hands should be cupped slightly for a more lifelike, relaxed appearance. Proper placement of the body requires a delicate sense of balance. It should lie as high as possible in the casket, yet not so high that the lid, when lowered, will hit the nose. On the other hand, we are cautioned, placing the body too low "creates the impression that the body is in a box."

Jones is next wheeled into the appointed slumber room where a few last touches may be added—his favorite pipe placed in his hand or, if he was a great reader, a book propped into position. (In the case of little Master Jones a Teddy bear may be clutched.) Here he will hold open house for a few days, visiting hours 10 A.M. to 9 P.M.   18

COMPREHENSION

1. How, according to Mitford, has the public's knowledge of embalming changed? How does she explain this change?

2. To what other professionals does Mitford liken the embalmer? Are these analogies flattering or critical? Explain.

3. What are the major stages of the process of embalming and restoration?

PURPOSE AND AUDIENCE

1. Mitford has a very definite purpose here; she has written this piece to convince her audience of something. What is her thesis?

2. Does Mitford expect her audience to agree with her thesis? How can you tell?

3. In her most recent book, Mitford refers to herself as a muckraker, one who informs the public of misconduct. Does she achieve this status here? Cite specific examples.

4. Why do you suppose Mitford names the cadaver Mr. Jones?

STYLE AND STRUCTURE

1. Identify the stylistic features that distinguish this process explanation from a set of instructions.

2. In this selection, as in most process essays, a list of necessary materials precedes the procedure. What additional details does Mitford include in her list in paragraph 5? How do these additions affect the reader?

3. Throughout this essay, Mitford uses extensive detail to convey her attitude without directly stating it. Give some examples of this technique.

4. Go through the essay and locate the author's remarks about the language of embalming. How are these comments about euphemisms, newly coined words, and other aspects of the language consistent with Mitford's thesis?

5. Throughout the essay, Mitford quotes a series of experts. How does she use their remarks to support her thesis?

6. What phrases signal Mitford's transitions between stages?

WRITING WORKSHOP

1. Rewrite this process explanation as a set of instructions for undertakers, condensing it so that your essay is about five hundred words long. Unlike Mitford, keep your essay objective; organize it around a unifying idea rather than an arguable thesis statement.

2. In the role of a funeral director, write a letter to Mitford in which you take issue with her essay. Explain the practice of embalming as necessary and practical. Design your process explanation, unlike Mitford's, to defend the practice.

3. Write an explanation of a process which you personally find disgusting— or delightful. Make your attitude clear in your thesis statement and your choice of words.

6

Cause and Effect

WHAT IS CAUSE AND EFFECT?

Cause and effect, like narration, links situations and events together in time since causes must always precede effects. But causality involves more than sequence: it explains why something happened—or is happening—and it can predict what probably will happen.

To determine whether true causality exists you must establish two criteria: *necessary cause* and *sufficient cause*. A necessary cause is an event that usually makes the same effect happen, and without which the effect cannot happen. For example, if you turn the key in the ignition, your car will usually start; if you don't turn the key, the car won't start. A sufficient cause is an event that is enough in itself to make the effect happen. Turning your ignition key, while necessary to start your car, is not sufficient by itself, for you must also press down on the accelerator.

Thus cause-and-effect relationships can be complex and subtle. Sometimes many different causes, perhaps none sufficient or necessary in itself, can be responsible for one effect. A couple about to divorce might cite money problems, religious differences, and a poor sex life as causes leading up to their decision to separate.

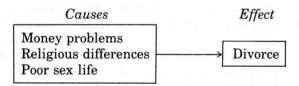

Similarly, many different effects can be produced by one cause. A hurricane, for instance, can cause property damage, injuries, and deaths.

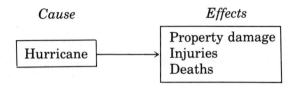

Cause   *Effects*

Hurricane ⟶ Property damage / Injuries / Deaths

As you examine situations that seem suited to cause-and-effect analysis, you will discover that most complex situations have numerous causes producing many different effects.

Predicting the future can also depend on understanding cause and effect. You can begin by looking for situations in the past that are like those in the present. Suppose, for example, that on a warm day the air is heavy and sticky, and you see a line of dark clouds moving toward you from the west, signaling that a cold front is on the way. In the past these conditions have usually caused rain, and so you grab your umbrella on the way out the door. You will not always be right, because similar situations may be just different enough to have different effects. But your chances of being right will be better if you understand cause and effect and if you apply it carefully.

Whenever you read a cause-and-effect explanation, take a few moments to think about it. Is the alleged cause necessary and sufficient? Consider this example. For nearly twenty years, the college board scores of high school seniors declined steadily. This decline began soon after television became popular, and so many people concluded that the two events were connected by cause and effect. The idea is plausible, since children did seem to be reading less in order to watch television more and since reading comprehension is one of the chief skills the tests evaluate.

But television watching was surely not a sufficient cause, and it may not even have been a necessary one. The lower scores almost certainly had several causes. During the same period, many schools moved away from required courses and deemphasized traditional subjects and skills, such as reading. Adults were reading less than they used to, and perhaps they were not encouraging their children to read. Without these other important causes, television watching might have had little—or no—effect on the test scores. Furthermore, during the 1960s and 1970s, many colleges changed their policies and admitted students who previously would not have qualified. These new admission standards may have encouraged students to take the tests who would have skipped them in earlier years. If so, the scores may have been lower because they measured the top third of high school seniors rather than the top fifth. Thus the reason for the lower scores is not clear. Perhaps television was the cause after all, but right now nobody knows for sure. In such a case, it is easy—too easy—to claim a cause-and-effect relationship without the evidence to support it.

Just as the lower scores may have had many causes, television watching may have had many effects. For instance, it may have made those same students better observers and listeners, even if they did less well on the standardized written tests. It may have given them a national or even international outlook, instead of a narrow interest in local affairs. In other words, even if watching television may have limited people in some ways, it may have broadened them in others. Is the trade-off a fair one? Perhaps, or perhaps not. But this is a very different kind of issue than the simple cause-and-effect explanation with which this discussion began.

To give your readers a complete analysis, you should try to consider all causes and effects, not just the most obvious ones or the first ones you think of. Let's look at another example. Suppose a professional basketball team, recently stocked with the best players money can buy, has had a miserable season. Since the individual players are talented and since they were successful under other coaches, fans blame the current coach for the team's losing streak and want him fired. But can the coach alone be responsible? Maybe the inability of the players to mesh well as a team is responsible for the losing streak. Maybe some of the players are suffering from injuries, personal problems, or heavy drug use. Or maybe the fans themselves are somehow to blame, for the drop in attendance at games may have affected the team's morale. Clearly, other factors besides the new coach could have caused the losing streak. Indeed, the suspected cause of the team's decline—the coach—may actually have saved the team from total collapse by keeping the players from quarreling with each other. In writing about such a situation, you must carefully identify these complex causes and effects so that your explanation is clear and logical.

Main and Contributory Causes

When you have identified several causes of an effect, often all are necessary, but one is more important than the others. That one is the *main cause,* and the others are *contributory causes*. Sometimes the main cause is obvious, but often it is not, as these examples show.

During the winter of 1977–78, an abnormally large amount of snow accumulated on the roof of the Civic Center Auditorium in Hartford, Connecticut, and the roof fell in. The newspapers reported that the weight of the snow had caused the collapse, and they were partly right. Other buildings, however, had not been flattened by the snow, so the main cause had to lie elsewhere. Insurance investigators eventually decided that the design of the roof, not the weight of the snow, was the main cause of the disaster.

In the spring of 1968, Martin Luther King, Jr., was shot and killed. During the next few nights, civil disturbances broke out in New York City, Washington, D.C., and many other cities. The media quickly identified the assassination of Dr. King as the cause. While anger over Dr. King's death surely contributed to the unrest, the main cause probably was not just the assassination itself but the racial hatred the assassination symbolized.

This diagram outlines the cause-and-effect relationships in the two situations summarized above.

Effect	Main Cause	Contributory Cause
Roof collapse	Roof design	Weight of snow
Civil disturbances	Racism	King's death

This distinction between the main or most important cause and the contributory or less important cause is useful for planning a cause-and-effect paper. When you can identify the main cause, you can emphasize it in your paper and play down the less important causes. If you properly weight each factor in your essay, your readers will more easily understand the logic of the relationships you are examining.

Immediate and Remote Causes

Another helpful way to think of causes is to classify them as *immediate* or *remote*. An *immediate cause* closely precedes an effect and thus is relatively easy to recognize as a cause. A *remote cause* is less obvious because it takes place further in the past, and perhaps farther away as well.

For examples, let's look again at the Hartford roof collapse and the civil disturbances following the death of Martin Luther King, Jr. Most people agreed that the snow was the immediate, or most obvious, cause of the roof collapse. But further study by insurance investigators considered the remote causes not so readily perceived. The design of the roof was the most important remote, or less immediately evident, cause of the collapse. In addition, perhaps the materials used in the roof's construction were partly to blame. Maybe maintenance crews had not done their jobs properly, or necessary repairs had not been made. Besides the snow, any or all of these less apparent but possibly critical factors might have contributed to the disaster. If you were the insurance investigator reporting on the causes of this event, you would want to assess all possible contributing factors rather than just the most obvious. If you did not consider the remote as well as the immediate causes, you might reach an oversimplified or false conclusion.

Similarly, although the media cited the assassination of Dr. King as the cause of the unrest, it soon became apparent that his death had been the immediate precipitating cause of these disturbances but that other frustrations and disappointments of life in the inner cities had been important remote causes. Even today, people may still disagree over whether the immediate or the remote causes were the main causes of the unrest. Still, if you were a city official writing a report about these disturbances, your failure to perceive the underlying remote causes might lead you to make inappropriate recommendations on how to avoid such demonstrations in the future.

This diagram outlines the cause-and-effect relationships in the two situations summarized above.

Effect	Immediate Cause	Possible Remote Causes
Roof collapse	Weight of snow	Roof design Roof materials Improper maintenance Repairs not made
Civil disturbances	King's death	Tensions of inner-city life, including unemployment, crime, poor health care, and poverty

In both situations, the remote causes are extremely important; to overlook them would be to produce an oversimplified and illogical analysis. In fact, often these remote causes may form a sequence called a causal chain.

The Causal Chain

Sometimes an effect can also be a cause. This is true in a causal chain, where A causes B, B causes C, C causes D, and so on.

$$
\begin{array}{l}
\text{A} \\
\text{Cause} \longrightarrow \text{B} \\
\qquad \text{Effect} \\
\qquad (\text{Cause}) \longrightarrow \text{C} \\
\qquad\qquad \text{Effect} \\
\qquad\qquad (\text{Cause}) \longrightarrow \text{D} \\
\qquad\qquad\qquad \text{Effect} \\
\qquad\qquad\qquad (\text{Cause}) \longrightarrow \text{E} \\
\qquad\qquad\qquad\qquad \text{Effect}
\end{array}
$$

If your analysis of a situation reveals a causal chain, this discovery can be useful in your writing. The very operation of a causal chain suggests an organizational pattern for a paper. In addition, following the chain automatically keeps you from discussing links out of their logical order.

Here is a simple example of a causal chain: A judge wakes up one morning in a bad mood because his bed is lumpy and his arthritis is acting up. In court that morning, he gives a first offender an unusually stiff sentence. The convict, bitter at his punishment, sets his mattress on fire, and the fumes kill several of his fellow inmates. The wife of one of these inmates becomes mentally ill as a result of her husband's death, and her two children are placed in foster homes when she is institutionalized.

The causal chain, in which the result of one action is the cause of another, has led the judge's restless night to cause two children to be deprived of their parents. Leaving out any link in the chain, or putting any link in improper order, destroys the logic and continuity of the chain. The causal chain is common in academic subjects from economics to physics; perhaps the best example is a nuclear reaction. Here, each link in the chain must be sufficient and necessary to cause the next link.

Post Hoc Reasoning

When developing a cause-and-effect paper, you must be certain that your conclusions are logical. Simply because event A precedes event B, you must not assume that event A has caused event B.

This illogical assumption, called *post hoc* reasoning, equates a chronological sequence with causality. When you fall into this trap, you are really mistaking coincidence for causality—assuming, for instance, that you failed an exam because a black cat crossed your path the day before.

Another recent event illustrates the power of *post hoc* reasoning. During the summer of 1976, the American Legion decided to hold its annual convention in Philadelphia, choosing that city because it had enough hotel rooms and because it was the headquarters for the United States bicentennial celebration. Subsequently, 180 legionnaires who had attended the convention came down with a mysterious viruslike infection, dubbed "Legionnaire's disease," and 29 died as a result. Investigators noted that virtually all of those who became ill had been staying at the Bellevue Stratford hotel. Adverse publicity caused business at the hotel to decline drastically, and in 1977 the hotel closed. Soon afterward it was sold.

This account suggests certain obvious cause-and-effect relationships:

Effect	*Cause*
Convention held in Philadelphia	Hotel rooms available Bicentennial city
Deaths	"Legionnaire's disease"
Hotel closed and sold	Bad publicity

Other cause-and-effect relationships may also exist. (For instance, the cause of the disease might be a virus.) This chart, however, represents the only relationships actually confirmed by the information in the paragraph. But what actually caused the bad publicity? It wasn't just that people who had stayed in the hotel died; rather, it was that the public assumed a cause-and-effect relationship before one was proved to exist. Although scientists have now discovered a valid cause-and-effect relationship between the Bellevue Stratford and Legionnaire's disease (bacteria responsible for the disease were found in the hotel's air-conditioning system), it was neither logical nor fair to *assume* that such a relationship existed before other possible causes had been eliminated and before clear, strong evidence was found to support the connection.

When you revise a cause-and-effect paper, make sure you have not confused words like *because, therefore,* and *consequently*—words that show a causal relationship—with words like *subsequently, later,* and *afterward*—words that show a chronological relationship. When you use a word like *because,* you are signaling your reader that you are telling *why* something happened; when you use a word like *later* you are only showing what did happen and when.

Being able to perceive and analyze cause-and-effect relationships; to distinguish causes from effects and recognize causal chains; and to sort out immediate from remote, main from contributory, and logical from illogical causes are all skills that will help you write. Understanding the nature of the cause-and-effect relationship will help you to decide when to use this pattern to structure a paper or a report.

STRUCTURING A CAUSE-AND-EFFECT ESSAY

After you have thought about the cause-and-effect relationships of your topic, you are ready to plan your paper. You have two basic options: to find causes or to predict effects. (Sometimes, of course, you may do both in one essay.) Often, your assigned topic will tell you which of these options to use. Here are a few likely topics for cause-and-effect treatment:

To find causes
: Discuss the causes of World War I. (history exam)

: Discuss the factors that contribute to the declining population of state mental hospitals. (social work paper)

To predict effects
: Outline the probable positive effects of moving elementary school children from a highly structured classroom to a relatively open classroom. (education paper)

: Assess the economic implications of national health insurance. (economics exam)

It is certainly possible to plan a cause-and-effect essay around a unifying idea rather than an arguable thesis. For instance, on an economics exam, your response to "Discuss the major effects of the Vietnam War on the United States economy" could be a straightforward presentation of factual information, an attempt to inform your readers rather than persuade them. Like nearly every paper or exam you write in college, however, your answer is more likely to take a position in a thesis statement and then defend that position. In fact, cause-and-effect analysis often requires judging and weighting factors, and your assessment of the relative significance of causes or effects may generate a thesis. Thus, when you plan your essay, you will want to formulate your thesis statement as you settle on the specific causes or effects you will discuss. This thesis statement should tell your readers three things: the points you will consider, the position you will take, and whether you will be finding causes or predicting effects. Your thesis may also indicate explicitly or implicitly the cause or effect you consider to be most important and the order in which you will treat your points.

You have several options when it comes to sequencing your causes or effects. One strategy, of course, is chronology—you can present causes or effects in the order in which they occurred. Another option is to introduce the main cause first and then to bring in the contributory causes—or to do just the opposite. Still another possibility is to begin by disposing of any events and circumstances that were *not* causes and then to explain what the real causes were. This is especially effective if you feel your readers are likely to jump to *post hoc* conclusions. Finally, you can begin with the most obvious causes or effects, those most likely to be familiar to your reader, and then move on to more subtle factors and your analysis and conclusion.

Finding Causes

Let's suppose you are planning the social-work paper mentioned above. ("Discuss the factors that contribute to the declining population of state mental hospitals.") Your assignment specifies an effect—the declining population of state mental hospitals—and asks you to discuss possible causes. Some causes might be:

- An increasing acceptance of mental illness in our society
- Prohibitive costs of in-patient care
- Increasing numbers of mental-health professionals, thus facilitating treatment outside the hospital

Many health professionals, however, feel that the most important factor is the development and use of psychotropic drugs, like thorazine, that have an altering effect on the mind. To emphasize this cause in your paper, you could construct the following thesis statement:

Less impor- **tant causes** **Effect** **Most impor-** **tant cause**	Although society's increasing acceptance of the mentally ill, the high cost of in-patient care, and the rise in the number of health professionals have all been influential in reducing the population of state mental hospitals, the most important cause of this reduction is the development and use of psychotropic drugs.

This thesis statement fully prepares your readers for your essay. It identifies the causes you will consider, and it also reveals your position—your assessment of the relative significance of these causes. It states the less important causes first and indicates their secondary importance by *although*. Similarly, in the body of your essay the least important causes would be considered first so that the essay could gradually build up to the most convincing material, the information that is likely to have the greatest impact on the reader. An outline for your paper might look like this:

¶1   Introduction—including thesis that identifies the effect and its causes
¶2   First cause: Increased acceptance of the mentally ill
¶3   Second cause: High cost of in-patient care
¶4   Third cause: Rise in the number of health professionals
¶5   Fourth cause: Development and use of psychotropic drugs (the most important cause)
¶6   Conclusion and summary

Predicting Effects

Let's suppose you were planning the education paper mentioned earlier. ("Outline the probable positive effects of moving elementary school children from a highly structured classroom to a relatively open classroom.") You would use a procedure similar to the one above to predict effects rather than find causes. After brainstorming and deciding which specific points to discuss, you might formulate this thesis statement:

Cause **Effects**	Moving children from a highly structured classroom to a relatively open one is likely to encourage more independent play, more flexibility in forming friendship groups, and ultimately more creativity.

This thesis statement clearly spells out your position by telling the reader the three main points your essay will consider; it also specifies that these points are effects of the open classroom. After introducing the cause, your essay would treat these three effects in the order in which they are presented in the thesis statement, building up to the most important point. An outline of your paper might look like this:

¶1 Introduction—including thesis that identifies the cause and its effects
¶2 First effect: More independent play
¶3 Second effect: More flexible friendship groups
¶4 Third effect: More creativity (the most important effect)
¶5 Conclusion and summary

Sometimes you will be asked to discuss *both* causes and effects. The following take-home midterm, written for a history class, analyzes some of the causes and effects of the Irish potato famine that occurred between 1847 and 1849. Notice how the writer, Evelyn Pellicane, concentrates on causes but also discusses briefly the effects of this tragedy, just as the exam question directs.

Question: The 1840s was a volatile decade in Europe. Choose one social, political, or economic event that occurred during those years, analyze its causes, and briefly note how the event influenced later developments in European history.

THE IRISH FAMINE, 1845–1849

Thesis   The Irish famine, which brought hard-   1
ship and tragedy to Ireland during the
1840s, was caused and prolonged by four
basic factors: the failure of the potato crop, the landlord–tenant system,
errors in government policy, and the
long–standing prejudice of the British
toward Ireland.

First cause   The immediate cause of the famine was   2
the failure of the potato crop. In
1845, potato disease struck the crop,
and potatoes rotted in the ground. The
1846 crop also failed, and before long
people were eating weeds. The 1847 crop

was healthy, but there weren't enough potatoes to go around, and in 1848 the blight struck again, leading to more and more evictions of tenants by land-lords.

Second cause   The tenants' position on the land had 3 never been very secure. Most had no leases and could be turned out by their landlords at any time. If a tenant owed rent, he was evicted—or, worse, put in prison, leaving his family to starve. The threat of prison caused many ten-ants to leave their land; those who could leave Ireland did so, sometimes with money provided by their landlords. Some landlords did try to take care of their tenants, but most did not. Many were absentee landlords who spent their rent money abroad.

Third cause   Government policy errors, while not 4 an immediate cause of the famine, played an important role in creating an unstable economy and perpetuating star-vation. In 1846, the government decided not to continue selling corn, as it had during the first year of the famine, claiming that low-cost purchases of corn by Ireland had paralyzed British trade by interfering with free enter-prise. Thus, 1846 saw a starving popu-lation, angry demonstrations, and panic; even those with money were un-able to buy food. Still the government insisted that, if it sent food to Ire-

land, prices would rise in the rest of
the United Kingdom and that this would
be unfair to hardworking English and
Scots. As a result, no food was sent.
Throughout the years of the famine, the
British government aggravated an already grave situation: they did nothing
to improve agricultural operations, to
help people adjust to another crop, to
distribute seeds, or to reorder the
landlord-tenant system which made the
tenants' position so insecure.

Fourth cause   At the root of this poor government   5
policy was the long-standing British
prejudice against the Irish. Hostility
between the two countries went back
some six hundred years, and the British
were simply not about to inconvenience
themselves to save the Irish. When the
Irish so desperately needed grain to
replace the damaged potatoes, it was
clear that grain had to be imported
from England. However, this meant that
the Corn Laws, which had been enacted
to keep the price of British corn high
by taxing imported grain, had to be re-
pealed. The British were unwilling to
repeal the Corn Laws. Even when they
did supply corn meal, they made no attempt to explain to the Irish how to
cook this unfamiliar food. Moreover,
the British government was determined
to make Ireland pay for its own poor,
and so it forced the collection of

taxes. Since many landlords just did
not have the tax money, they were
forced to evict their tenants. The
British government's callous and indifferent treatment of the Irish has been
called genocide.

Effects   As a result of this devastating fa-   6
mine, the population of Ireland was re-
duced from about nine million to about
six and one-half million. During the
famine years, men roamed the streets
looking for work, begging when they
found none. Epidemics of "famine fever"
and dysentery reduced the population
drastically. The most important historical result of the famine, however, was
the massive emigration to the United
States, Canada, and Great Britain of
poor, unskilled people who had to
struggle to fit into a skilled economy
and who brought with them a deep-seated
hatred of the British. (This same
hatred remained strong in Ireland it-
self--so strong that at the time of
World War II, Ireland, then independent, remained neutral rather than coming to England's aid.) Irish immigrants
faced slums, fever epidemics, jobless-
ness, and hostility--even anti-Catholic
and anti-Irish riots--in Boston, New
York, London, Glasgow, and Quebec. In
Ireland itself, poverty and discontent
continued, and by 1848 those emigrating
from Ireland included a more highly

skilled class of farmer, the ones Ireland needed to recover and to survive.

Conclusion (restatement of thesis)   The Irish famine, one of the great   7
tragedies of the nineteenth century,
was a natural disaster compounded by
the insensitivity of the British government and the archaic agricultural
system of Ireland. While the deaths
that resulted depleted Ireland's resources even more, the men and women
who emigrated to other countries permanently enriched those nations.

Points for Special Attention

Structure.   This is a relatively long essay; if it were not so clearly organized, it would be difficult to follow. Because the essay is to focus primarily on causes, Evelyn first introduces the effect—the famine itself—and then considers its causes. After she has examined the causes, she moves on to the results of the famine, with the most important one last. In this essay, then, the famine is first treated as an effect and then, toward the end, as a cause. In fact, it is the central link in a causal chain. Evelyn devotes one paragraph to her introduction and one to each cause; she sums up the effects or results in a separate paragraph and devotes the final paragraph to her conclusion. (Depending on a given paper's length and complexity, of course, more—or less—than one paragraph may be devoted to each cause or effect.) An outline for her paper might have looked like this:

¶1   Introduction—including thesis
¶2   First cause: Failure of the potato crop
¶3   Second cause: The landlord-tenant system
¶4   Third cause: Errors in government policy
¶5   Fourth cause: British prejudice
¶6   Results of the famine
¶7   Conclusion

Since the author of this paper feels that all the causes are very important and that they interconnect, they are not presented strictly in order of increasing importance. Instead, she begins with the immediate cause of the famine—the failure of the potato crop—and then digs more deeply until she arrives at the most remote cause, British prejudice. This immediate cause is also the main cause, as the other situations had existed all along.

Transitions.   The cause-and-effect relationships in this essay are both subtle and complex; Evelyn considers a series of interconnected relationships and a number of causal chains. Throughout the essay, many words suggest cause-and-effect connections: *so, therefore, because, as a result, since, led to, brought about, caused,* and the like. These are the most effective transitions for such an essay.

Answering an Exam Question.   Before planning and writing her answer, Evelyn carefully studied the exam question. She noted that it asks for both causes and effects but that its wording directs her to spend more time on causes ("analyze") than on effects ("briefly note"). Consequently, she divides her discussion in accord with these directions and is careful to indicate *explicitly* which are the causes ("government policy . . . played an important role") and which are the results ("The most important historical result . . .").

The author of this essay has obviously been influenced by outside sources; the ideas in the essay are not completely her own. Because this is an exam, however, and because the instructor is aware that the student has based her essay on class notes and assigned readings, she does not have to acknowledge her sources.

All the selections that follow focus on cause-and-effect relationships. Some selections stress causes; others emphasize effects. As these essays illustrate, the cause-and-effect pattern is so versatile that it may be used to examine topics as dissimilar as anthropology, sports, and Mickey Mouse.

THE TELEPHONE

John Brooks

*The cause-and-effect pattern of development is frequently employed
by writers who consider important historical changes. Since technology has transformed our lives, it is only natural for us to spec-
ulate about the nature and scope of these changes. In this brief
excerpt from his book* Telephone: The First Hundred Years, *John
Brooks considers the effects, both positive and negative, of the telephone on our lives.*

What has the telephone done to us, or for us, in the hundred   1
years of its existence? A few effects suggest themselves at once. It
has saved lives by getting rapid word of illness, injury, or famine
from remote places. By joining with the elevator to make possible
the multistory residence or office building, it has made possible—
for better or worse—the modern city. By bringing about a quantum
leap in the speed and ease with which information moves from place
to place, it has greatly accelerated the rate of scientific and tech-
nological change and growth in industry. Beyond doubt it has crip-
pled if not killed the ancient art of letter writing. It has made living
alone possible for persons with normal social impulses; by so doing,
it has played a role in one of the greatest social changes of this
century, the breakup of the multigenerational household. It has
made the waging of war chillingly more efficient than formerly.
Perhaps (though not provably) it has prevented wars that might
have arisen out of international misunderstanding caused by written communication. Or perhaps—again not provably—by magni-
fying and extending irrational personal conflicts based on voice contact, it has caused wars. Certainly it has extended the scope of
human conflicts, since it impartially disseminates the useful knowledge of scientists and the babble of bores, the affection of the affectionate and the malice of the malicious.

But the question remains unanswered. The obvious effects just   2
cited seem inadequate, mechanistic; they only scratch the surface.
Perhaps the crucial effects are evanescent and unmeasurable. Use
of the telephone involves personal risk because it involves exposure;
for some, to be "hung up on" is among the worst of fears; others
dream of a ringing telephone and wake up with a pounding heart.

The telephone's actual ring—more, perhaps, than any other sound in our daily lives—evokes hope, relief, fear, anxiety, joy, according to our expectations. The telephone is our nerve-end to society.

In some ways it is in itself a thing of paradox. In one sense a 3 metaphor for the times it helped create, in another sense the telephone is their polar opposite. It is small and gentle—relying on low voltages and miniature parts—in times of hugeness and violence. It is basically simple in times of complexity. It is so nearly human, recreating voices so faithfully that friends or lovers need not identify themselves by name even when talking across oceans, that to ask its effects on human life may seem hardly more fruitful than to ask the effect of the hand or the foot. The Canadian philosopher Marshall McLuhan—one of the few who have addressed themselves to these questions—was perhaps not far from the mark when he spoke of the telephone as creating "a kind of extra-sensory perception."

COMPREHENSION

1. What are some of the positive effects of the telephone that Brooks mentions? What are some negative results?

2. Brooks suggests other crucial effects the telephone may possibly have had. What are they? Can you think of any others?

3. How does using the telephone involve "personal risk"?

4. What emotions does Brooks say the telephone's ring may evoke?

5. A paradox is a seeming contradiction that is somehow true. How is the telephone "a thing of paradox"?

PURPOSE AND AUDIENCE

1. In one sentence, state the essay's thesis. Why doesn't Brooks include such a thesis statement?

2. This excerpt appears at the beginning of a complete book about the telephone. What does this location suggest about the author's probable purpose in writing these paragraphs? How well do you think he has achieved this purpose?

3. Brooks uses the first-person plural *us* in this essay instead of speaking either just about himself or about people in general. Why do you think he does this?

STYLE AND STRUCTURE

1. The essay begins with a question. Would a direct statement be more effective as an introduction? Explain.

2. How does the phrasing of the opening question prepare us to accept Brooks's thesis?

3. How does the first sentence in paragraph 2 serve as a transition between paragraphs?

4. Identify the phrases in this essay that explicitly point to cause-and-effect connections.

5. Brooks ends his brief introduction to the effects of the telephone with a quotation. Do you think this is an effective conclusion? Explain.

WRITING WORKSHOP

1. Consider a machine that has had a significant effect on your life, such as the television, the duplicating machine, the pocket calculator, the radio, the typewriter, or the electric light. Write an essay beginning with a first sentence modeled on this essay's opening: "What has ——— done to us, or for us, in the ——— years of its existence?"

2. Write an essay about the effects of the telephone for an audience of school children. You may include some of Brooks's points, but you will have to simplify his explanations considerably.

WHO KILLED THE BOG MEN
OF DENMARK? AND WHY?

Maurice Shadbolt

*Mystery stories and archaeological explorations both seek to unearth
causes which can explain perplexing situations. This selection combines archaeology and mystery to determine why a group of men
died some two thousand years ago. To explain this puzzle, Maurice
Shadbolt examines the direct and indirect causes of the deaths of
the ancient bog men of Denmark.*

Every year in the Danish town of Silkeborg, thousands of visitors 1
file past the face of a murder victim. No one will ever know his
name. It is enough to know that 2000 years ago he was as human
as ourselves. That face has moved men and women to poetry, and
to tears.

Last summer I journeyed to the lake-girt Danish town and, peer- 2
ing at that face behind glass in a modest museum, I felt awe—for
his every wrinkle and whisker tell a vivid and terrible tale from
Denmark's distant past. The rope which choked off the man's breath
is still around his neck. Yet it is a perplexingly peaceful face, in-
scrutable, one to haunt the imagination.

This strangest of ancient murder mysteries began 27 years ago, 3
on May 8, 1950, when two brothers, Emil and Viggo Højgaard, were
digging peat in Tollund Fen, near Silkeborg. Their spring sowing
finished, the brothers were storing up the umber-brown peat for
their kitchen range, and for warmth in the winter to come. It was
a peaceful task on a sunny morning. Snipe called from the aspens
and firs fringing the dank bowl of the fen, where only heather and
coarse grass grew. Then, at the depth of nine feet, their spades
suddenly struck something.

They were gazing, with fright and fascination, at a face under- 4
foot. The corpse was naked but for a skin cap, resting on its side as
if asleep, arms and legs bent. The face was gentle, with eyes closed
and lips lightly pursed. There was stubble on the chin. The bewil-
dered brothers called the Silkeborg police.

Quick to the scene, the police did not recognize the man as anyone 5
listed missing. Shrewdly guessing the brothers might have blun-
dered into a black hole in Europe's past, the police called in arche-
ologists.

Enter Prof. Peter Glob, a distinguished scholar from nearby Aar- 6
hus University, who carefully dislodged a lump of peat from beside
the dead man's head. A rope made of two twisted hide thongs en-
circled his neck. He had been strangled or hanged. But when, and
by whom? Glob ordered a box to be built about the corpse and the
peat in which it lay, so nothing might be disturbed.

Next day, the box, weighing nearly a ton, was manhandled out 7
of the bog onto a horse-drawn cart, on its way for examination at
Copenhagen's National Museum. One of Glob's helpers collapsed
and died with the huge effort. It seemed a dark omen, as if some
old god were claiming a modern man in place of a man from the
past.

Bog bodies were nothing new—since records have been kept, 8
Denmark's bogs have surrendered no fewer than 400—and the preservative qualities of the humic acid in peat have long been known.
But not until the 19th century did scientists and historians begin
to glimpse the finds and understand that the bodies belonged to
remote, murky recesses of European prehistory. None survived long:
the corpses were either buried again or crumbled quickly with exposure to light and air.

When peat-digging was revived during and after World War II, 9
bodies were unearthed in abundance—first in 1942 at Store Arden,
then in 1946, 1947 and 1948 at Borre Fen. Artifacts found beside
them positively identified them as people of Denmark's Early Iron
Age, from 400 B.C. to A.D. 400. None, then, was less than 1500 years
old, and some were probably much older. The first of the Borre Fen
finds—a full-grown male—was to prove especially significant: Borre
Fen man, too, had died violently, with a noose about his neck, strangled or hanged. And his last meal had consisted of grain.

Peter Glob, alongside his artist father (a portraitist and distin- 10
guished amateur archeologist), had been digging into Denmark's
dim past since he was a mere eight years old. For him, the Tollund
man, who had by far the best-preserved head to survive from an-
tiquity, was a supreme challenge. Since 1936, Glob had been living
imaginatively with the pagan hunters and farmers of 2000 years
ago, fossicking among their corroded artifacts, foraging among the
foundations of their simple villages; he knew their habits, the rhythms
of their lives. Suddenly, here was a man of that very time. "Majesty
and gentleness," he recalls, "seemed to stamp his features as they
did when he was alive." What was this enigmatic face trying to tell
him?

Glob was intrigued by the fact that so many of the people found 11
in bogs had died violently: strangled or hanged, throats slit, heads

battered. Perhaps they had been travelers set upon by brigands, or executed criminals. But there might be a different explanation. These murder victims all belonged to the Danish Iron Age. If they were to be explained away as victims of robber bands, there should be a much greater spread in time—into other ages. Nor would executed criminals all have had so many common traits.

Glob considered the body with care. X rays of Tollund man's [12] vertebrae, taken to determine whether he had been strangled or hanged, produced inconclusive results. The condition of the wisdom teeth suggested a man well over 20 years old. An autopsy revealed that the heart, lungs and liver were well preserved; most important, the alimentary canal was undisturbed, containing the dead man's last meal—a 2000-year-old gruel of hand-milled grains and seeds: barley, linseed, flaxseed, knotgrass, among others. Knowledge of prehistoric agriculture made it possible to determine that the man had lived in the first 200 years A.D. The mixture of grains and seeds suggested a meal prepared in winter or early spring.

Since Iron Age men were not vegetarians, why were there no [13] traces of meat? Glob also marveled that the man's hands and feet were soft; he appeared to have done little or no heavy labor in his lifetime. Possibly, then, he was high-ranking in Iron Age society.

Then, on April 26, 1952, peat-digging villagers from Grauballe, [14] 11 miles east of Tollund, turned up a second spectacularly well-preserved body, and again Glob was fast to the scene. Unmistakably another murder victim, this discovery was, unlike Tollund man, far from serene. The man's throat had been slashed savagely from ear to ear. His face was twisted with terror, and his lips were parted with a centuries-silenced cry of pain.

Glob swiftly removed the body—still imbedded in a great block [15] of peat—for preservation and study. Carbon-dating of body tissue proved Grauballe man to be about 1650 years old, a contemporary of Constantine the Great. Grauballe man was in extraordinary condition; his fingerprints and footprints came up clearly. Tallish and dark-haired, Grauballe man, like Tollund man, had never done any heavy manual work. He had been slain in his late 30s. Another similarity came to light when Grauballe man's last meal was analyzed: it had been eaten immediately before death and, like Tollund man's, like Borre Fen man's too, it was a gruel of grains and seeds, a meal of winter, or early spring. All three had perished in a similar season.

Who had killed these men of the bogs? Why in winter, or early [16] spring? Why should they—apparently—have led privileged lives? And why the same kind of meals before their sudden ends?

The bodies had told Glob all they could. Now he turned to one of 17 his favorite sources—the Roman historian Tacitus. Nearly 2000 years ago Tacitus recorded the oral traditions of Germanic tribes who inhabited northwest Europe. Tacitus' account of these wild, brave and generous blue-eyed people often shed light into dark corners of Denmark's past. Glob found these lines: "At a time laid down in the distant past, all peoples that are related by blood meet in a sacred wood. Here they celebrate their barbarous rites with a human sacrifice."

Elsewhere, Tacitus wrote: "These people are distinguished by a 18 common worship of Nerthus, or Mother Earth. They believe that she interests herself in human affairs." Tacitus confirmed early spring as a time among the Germanic tribes for offerings and human sacrifice. They were asking the goddess to hasten the coming of spring, and the summer harvest. Men chosen for sacrifice might well have been given a symbolic meal, made up of plant seeds, before being consecrated through death to the goddess—thus explaining the absence of meat. The sacrificial men, with their delicate features, neat hands and feet, might have been persons of high rank chosen by lot for sacrifice, or priests, ritually married to Nerthus.

Tacitus supplied another essential clue: the symbol of Nerthus, 19 he recorded, was a twisted metal "torque," or neck ring, worn by the living to honor the goddess. The leather nooses about the necks of Tollund man and the body from Borre Fen and some earlier bodies were replicas of those neck rings. Glob concluded that it was Nerthus—Mother Earth herself—who had preserved her victims perfectly in her peaty bosom long after those who had fed them into the bogs were dust.

Peter Glob was satisfied. He had found the killer and identified 20 the victims. The centuries-old mystery of Denmark's bog bodies was no more.

COMPREHENSION

1. Identify at least one *result* of each of the following: the Højgaard brothers discover a body; the box containing the body is moved; the humic acid in peat has preservative qualities; peat-digging is revived after World War II.

2. Identify at least one *cause* of each of the following: the man's hands and feet are soft; his last meal was grain; he died a violent death; he wears a rope around his neck.

3. From what different sources do the clues about the bog man's murder come?

PURPOSE AND AUDIENCE

1. This essay originally appeared in *The Reader's Digest,* a magazine that prints selections likely to interest a wide general audience. In what ways does this selection qualify?

2. This essay has no arguable thesis. What, then, is the author's purpose in writing the essay?

STYLE AND STRUCTURE

1. In what ways is the structure of this essay similar to that of a modern mystery story? Identify the detective, the clues, and the background research. How is this essay different from a mystery story?

2. Are the style and structure of this essay different from those of a newspaper account? If so, how?

3. The author begins in the first person as if to make himself a part of the story he is relating. Do you think his brief appearance adds to or detracts from the essay's effectiveness? Why?

4. The author begins in the present tense and then uses flashbacks. How would the impact of the essay change if the author had used strict chronological order?

5. Several quotations appear in this essay. Are these direct quotations more convincing than the author's paraphrases would be? Why or why not?

WRITING WORKSHOP

1. Write a biographical sketch of the man the Højgaard brothers discovered, establishing the causes of his death.

2. Write an editorial for the Silkeborg daily newspaper in which you discuss the benefits and drawbacks for the town of the bog man's discovery.

3. Write an essay unraveling a mystery in your own life; for instance, explain the causes of a friend's strange actions or the reasons your family settled where it did years (or generations) ago.

WHO KILLED BENNY PARET?

Norman Cousins

Born in 1912 in New Jersey, and educated at Columbia University, Norman Cousins has had a varied career as a journalist and author. He was editor of the Saturday Review *from 1940 to 1978 and has published numerous books, notably the best-selling* Anatomy of an Illness *(1979) about his struggle with a near-fatal condition. Other works include* Who Speaks for Man? *(1953),* Talks with Nehru *(1951), and* Dr. Schweitzer of Lambarene *(1960). In the 1962 essay "Who Killed Benny Paret?" Cousins investigates the causes of Paret's death. In answering the question posed by his essay's title, Cousins takes a strong stand against violence in sports.*

Sometime about 1935 or 1936 I had an interview with Mike Jacobs, the prize-fight promoter. I was a fledgling reporter at that time; my beat was education but during the vacation season I found myself on varied assignments, all the way from ship news to sports reporting. In this way I found myself sitting opposite the most powerful figure in the boxing world.

There was nothing spectacular in Mr. Jacobs' manner or appearance; but when he spoke about prize fights, he was no longer a bland little man but a colossus who sounded the way Napoleon must have sounded when he reviewed a battle. You knew you were listening to Number One. His saying something made it true.

We discussed what to him was the only important element in successful promoting—how to please the crowd. So far as he was concerned, there was no mystery to it. You put killers in the ring and the people filled your arena. You hire boxing artists—men who are adroit at feinting, parrying, weaving, jabbing, and dancing, but who don't pack dynamite in their fists—and you wind up counting your empty seats. So you searched for the killers and sluggers and maulers—fellows who could hit with the force of a baseball bat.

I asked Mr. Jacobs if he was speaking literally when he said people came out to see the killer.

"They don't come out to see a tea party," he said evenly. "They come out to see the knockout. They come out to see a man hurt. If they think anything else, they're kidding themselves."

Recently, a young man by the name of Benny Paret was killed 6
in the ring. The killing was seen by millions; it was on television.
In the twelfth round, he was hit hard in the head several times,
went down, was counted out, and never came out of the coma.

The Paret fight produced a flurry of investigations. Governor 7
Rockefeller was shocked by what happened and appointed a committee to assess the responsibility. The New York State Boxing
Commission decided to find out what was wrong. The District Attorney's office expressed its concern. One question that was solemnly studied in all three probes concerned the action of the referee.
Did he act in time to stop the fight? Another question had to do
with the role of the examining doctors who certified the physical
fitness of the fighters before the bout. Still another question involved Mr. Paret's manager; did he rush his boy into the fight without adequate time to recuperate from the previous one?

In short, the investigators looked into every possible cause except 8
the real one. Benny Paret was killed because the human fist delivers
enough impact, when directed against the head, to produce a massive hemorrhage in the brain. The human brain is the most delicate
and complex mechanism in all creation. It has a lacework of millions
of highly fragile nerve connections. Nature attempts to protect this
exquisitely intricate machinery by encasing it in a hard shell. For-
tunately, the shell is thick enough to withstand a great deal of
pounding. Nature, however, can protect man against everything
except man himself. Not every blow to the head will kill a man—
but there is always the risk of concussion and damage to the brain.
A prize fighter may be able to survive even repeated brain concus-
sions and go on fighting, but the damage to his brain may be permanent.

In any event, it is futile to investigate the referee's role and seek 9
to determine whether he should have intervened to stop the fight
earlier. That is not where the primary responsibility lies. The primary responsibility lies with the people who pay to see a man hurt.
The referee who stops a fight too soon from the crowd's viewpoint
can expect to be booed. The crowd wants the knockout; it wants to
see a man stretched out on the canvas. This is the supreme moment
in boxing. It is nonsense to talk about prize fighting as a test of
boxing skills. No crowd was ever brought to its feet screaming and
cheering at the sight of two men beautifully dodging and weaving
out of each other's jabs. The time the crowd comes alive is when a
man is hit hard over the heart or the head, when his mouthpiece
flies out, when the blood squirts out of his nose or eyes, when he

wobbles under the attack and his pursuer continues to smash at him with pole-axe impact.

Don't blame it on the referee. Don't even blame it on the fight 10
managers. Put the blame where it belongs—on the prevailing mores that regard prize fighting as a perfectly proper enterprise and vehicle of entertainment. No one doubts that many people enjoy prize fighting and will miss it if it should be thrown out. And that is precisely the point.

COMPREHENSION

1. Why, according to Mike Jacobs, do people come to see a prizefight? Does Cousins agree with him?

2. What were the official responses to Paret's death?

3. What was the immediate cause of Paret's death? What remote causes did the investigators consider? What, according to Cousins, is the main cause? (That is, where does the "primary responsibility" lie?)

4. Why does Cousins feel that "it is futile to investigate the referee's role"?

5. Cousins ends his essay with "And that is precisely the point." What is the "point" to which he refers?

PURPOSE AND AUDIENCE

1. This persuasive essay has a strong thesis. What is it?

2. This essay appeared on May 5, 1962, a month after Paret died. What do you suppose its impact was on its audience? Is the impact the same today, or has it changed?

3. Why does Cousins present information about Mike Jacobs in the first two paragraphs?

4. At whom is this essay aimed—boxing enthusiasts, sports writers, or a general audience? What led you to your conclusion?

5. Does Cousins expect his audience to agree with his thesis? How does he try to win their sympathy for his position?

STYLE AND STRUCTURE

1. The essay begins with a brief narrative describing a meeting between Cousins and Mike Jacobs. Where does this narrative introduction end?

2. Once Paret's death is mentioned and the persuasive portion of the essay begins, the introductory narrative never resumes. Why not? Do you think this weakens the essay? Explain.

3. Sort out the complex cause-and-effect relationships discussed in paragraph 9.

4. Look at the last two sentences in paragraph 9. How does the contrast between them advance the essay's thesis?

5. What strategy does Cousins use in his conclusion? Is it effective? Explain.

WRITING WORKSHOP

1. Write a cause-and-effect essay examining how the demands of the public affect a professional sport. (You might examine violence in hockey or football, for example, or the ways in which an individual player cultivates an image for the fans.)

2. Write a cause-and-effect essay about a time when you did something you felt was dishonest or unwise in response to peer pressure. Be sure to identify the causes for your actions.

A BIOLOGICAL HOMAGE
TO MICKEY MOUSE

Stephen Jay Gould

Stephen Jay Gould was born in 1941 and teaches biology, geology, and the history of science at Harvard University. This essay from his book The Panda's Thumb *(1980) continues the "reflections in natural history" he began with* Ever Since Darwin *(1977). Both books are collections of essays first published in* Natural History *magazine. Reflecting on subjects as diverse as Piltdown man, the grouping and naming of species, the migration of the sea turtle, and the intelligence of dinosaurs, Gould's essays are consistently lively and eclectic. Many of them bear directly or indirectly on the theory of evolution, as does this essay, in which Gould considers the evolution of Mickey Mouse.*

. . . Mickey Mouse turned a respectable fifty last year. To mark the occasion, many theaters replayed his debut performance in *Steamboat Willie* (1928). The original Mickey was a rambunctious, even slightly sadistic fellow. In a remarkable sequence, exploiting the exciting new development of sound, Mickey and Minnie pummel, squeeze, and twist the animals on board to produce a rousing chorus of "Turkey in the Straw." They honk a duck with a tight embrace, crank a goat's tail, tweak a pig's nipples, bang a cow's teeth as a stand-in xylophone, and play bagpipe on her udder.

Christopher Finch, in his semiofficial pictorial history of Disney's work, comments: "The Mickey Mouse who hit the movie houses in the late twenties was not quite the well-behaved character most of us are familiar with today. He was mischievous, to say the least, and even displayed a streak of cruelty." But Mickey soon cleaned up his act, leaving to gossip and speculation only his unresolved relationship with Minnie and the status of Morty and Ferdie. Finch continues: "Mickey . . . had become virtually a national symbol, and as such he was expected to behave properly at all times. If he occasionally stepped out of line, any number of letters would arrive at the Studio from citizens and organizations who felt that the nation's moral well-being was in their hands. . . . Eventually he would be pressured into the role of straight man."

As Mickey's personality softened, his appearance changed. Many Disney fans are aware of this transformation through time, but few

Mickey's evolution during 50 years (left to right). As Mickey became increasingly well behaved over the years, his appearance became more youthful. Measurements of three stages in his development revealed a larger relative head size, larger eyes, and an enlarged cranium—all traits of juvenility. © Walt Disney Productions

(I suspect) have recognized the coordinating theme behind all the alterations—in fact, I am not sure that the Disney artists themselves explicitly realized what they were doing, since the changes appeared in such a halting and piecemeal fashion. In short, the blander and inoffensive Mickey became progressively more juvenile in appearance. (Since Mickey's chronological age never altered—like most cartoon characters he stands impervious to the ravages of time—this change in appearance at a constant age is a true evolutionary transformation. Progressive juvenilization as an evolutionary phenomenon is called neoteny. More on this later.)

The characteristic changes of form during human growth have inspired a substantial biological literature. Since the head-end of an embryo differentiates first and grows more rapidly in utero* than the foot-end (an antero-posterior gradient, in technical language), a newborn child possesses a relatively large head attached to a medium-sized body with diminutive legs and feet. This gradient is reversed through growth as legs and feet overtake the front end. Heads continue to grow but so much more slowly than the rest of the body that relative head size decreases.

*EDS. NOTE—In the womb.

In addition, a suite of changes pervades the head itself during human growth. The brain grows very slowly after age three, and the bulbous cranium of a young child gives way to the more slanted, lower-browed configuration of adulthood. The eyes scarcely grow at all and relative eye size declines precipitously. But the jaw gets bigger and bigger. Children, compared with adults, have larger heads and eyes, smaller jaws, a more prominent, bulging cranium, and smaller, pudgier legs and feet. Adult heads are altogether more apish, I'm sorry to say.

Mickey, however, has traveled this ontogenetic pathway in reverse during his fifty years among us. He has assumed an ever more childlike appearance as the ratty character of *Steamboat Willie* became the cute and inoffensive host to a magic kingdom. By 1940, the former tweaker of pig's nipples gets a kick in the ass for insubordination (as the *Sorcerer's Apprentice* in *Fantasia*). By 1953, his last cartoon, he has gone fishing and cannot even subdue a squirting clam.

The Disney artists transformed Mickey in clever silence, often using suggestive devices that mimic nature's own changes by different routes. To give him the shorter and pudgier legs of youth, they lowered his pants line and covered his spindly legs with a baggy outfit. (His arms and legs also thickened substantially—and acquired joints for a floppier appearance.) His head grew relatively larger and its features more youthful. The length of Mickey's snout has not altered, but decreasing protrusion is more subtly suggested by a pronounced thickening. Mickey's eye has grown in two modes: first, by a major, discontinuous evolutionary shift as the entire eye of ancestral Mickey became the pupil of his descendants, and second, by gradual increase thereafter.

Mickey's improvement in cranial bulging followed an interesting 8 path since his evolution has always been constrained by the unaltered convention of representing his head as a circle with appended ears and an oblong snout. The circle's form could not be altered to provide a bulging cranium directly. Instead, Mickey's ears moved back, increasing the distance between nose and ears, and giving him a rounded, rather than a sloping, forehead.

You may, indeed, now ask what an at least marginally respect- 9 able scientist has been doing with a mouse like that. In part, fiddling around and having fun, of course. (I still prefer *Pinocchio* to *Citizen Kane*.) But I do have a serious point . . . to make. We must . . . ask why Disney chose to change his most famous character so gradually and persistently in the same direction? National symbols are not altered capriciously and market researchers (for the doll industry in particular) have spent a good deal of time and practical effort learning what features appeal to people as cute and friendly. Biologists also have spent a great deal of time studying a similar subject in a wide range of animals.

In one of his most famous articles, Konrad Lorenz argues that 10 humans use the characteristic differences in form between babies and adults as important behavioral cues. He believes that features of juvenility trigger "innate releasing mechanisms" for affection and nurturing in adult humans. When we see a living creature with babyish features, we feel an automatic surge of disarming tenderness. The adaptive value of this response can scarcely be questioned, for we must nurture our babies. Lorenz, by the way, lists among his releasers the very features of babyhood that Disney affixed progressively to Mickey: "a relatively large head, predominance of the brain capsule, large and low-lying eyes, bulging cheek region, short and thick extremities, a springy elastic consistency, and clumsy movements. . . ."

Lorenz emphasizes the power that juvenile features hold over us, 11 and the abstract quality of their influence, by pointing out that we judge other animals by the same criteria—although the judgment may be utterly inappropriate in an evolutionary context. We are, in short, fooled by an evolved response to our own babies, and we transfer our reaction to the same set of features in other animals.

Many animals, for reasons having nothing to do with the inspi- 12 ration of affection in humans, possess some features also shared by human babies but not by human adults—large eyes and a bulging forehead with retreating chin, in particular. We are drawn to them,

Humans feel affection for animals with juvenile features: large eyes, bulging craniums, retreating chins (left column). Small-eyed, long-snouted animals (right column) do not elicit the same response. From *Studies in Animal and Human Behavior,* vol. II, by Konrad Lorenz, 1971. Methuen & Co. Ltd.

we cultivate them as pets, we stop and admire them in the wild—while we reject their small-eyed, long-snouted relatives who might make more affectionate companions or objects of admiration. Lorenz points out that the German names of many animals with features mimicking human babies end in the diminutive suffix *chen,* even though the animals are often larger than close relatives without such features—*Rotkehlchen* (robin), *Eichhörnchen* (squirrel), and *Kaninchen* (rabbit), for example.

In a fascinating section, Lorenz then enlarges upon our capacity for biologically inappropriate response to other animals, or even to inanimate objects that mimic human features. "The most amazing objects can acquire remarkable, highly specific emotional values by 'experiential attachment' of human properties. . . . Steeply rising, somewhat overhanging cliff faces or dark storm-clouds piling up have the same, immediate display value as a human being who is standing at full height and leaning slightly forwards"—that is, threatening.

We cannot help regarding a camel as aloof and unfriendly be- 14
cause it mimics, quite unwittingly and for other reasons, the "gesture of haughty rejection" common to so many human cultures. In
this gesture, we raise our heads, placing our nose above our eyes.
We then half-close our eyes and blow out through our nose—the
"harumph" of the stereotyped upperclass Englishman or his well-
trained servant. "All this," Lorenz argues quite cogently, "symbol-
izes resistance against all sensory modalities emanating from the
disdained counterpart." But the poor camel cannot help carrying its
nose above its elongate eyes, with mouth drawn down. As Lorenz
reminds us, if you wish to know whether a camel will eat out of
your hand or spit, look at its ears, not the rest of its face.

In his important book *Expression of the Emotions in Man and* 15
Animals, published in 1872, Charles Darwin traced the evolutionary basis of many common gestures to originally adaptive actions
in animals later internalized as symbols in humans. Thus, he ar-
gued for evolutionary continuity of emotion, not only of form. We
snarl and raise our upper lip in fierce anger—to expose our nonexistent fighting canine tooth. Our gesture of disgust repeats the
facial actions associated with the highly adaptive act of vomiting
in necessary circumstances. Darwin concluded, much to the distress
of many Victorian contemporaries: "With mankind some expressions, such as the bristling of the hair under the influence of extreme terror, or the uncovering of the teeth under that of furious
rage, can hardly be understood, except on the belief that man once
existed in a much lower and animal-like condition."

In any case, the abstract features of human childhood elicit pow- 16
erful emotional responses in us, even when they occur in other animals. I submit that Mickey Mouse's evolutionary road down the
course of his own growth in reverse reflects the unconscious discovery of this biological principle by Disney and his artists. In fact, the
emotional status of most Disney characters rests on the same set of
distinctions. To this extent, the magic kingdom trades on a biological illusion—our ability to abstract and our propensity to transfer
inappropriately to other animals the fitting responses we make to
changing form in the growth of our own bodies.

COMPREHENSION

1. What specific differences does Gould identify between the Mickey Mouse
   of *Steamboat Willie* and the Mickey Mouse of today?

2. What, according to Gould, do the evolutionary changes in Mickey Mouse
   signify?

3. What effects should these changes have had on the way Mickey's fans perceived him?

4. How do the changes in Mickey compare with the changes observed in human development?

5. Why, according to Gould's interpretation of Lorenz, are humans more drawn to some animals than to others?

PURPOSE AND AUDIENCE

1. How do you know Gould is writing for a general audience rather than for scientists?

2. In paragraph 9, Gould offers two explanations of why his essay focuses on Mickey Mouse. How does his serious purpose relate to his not-so-serious one?

3. What is Gould's thesis?

4. Why does Gould present Lorenz's theories?

5. Gould alternately tries to entertain, persuade, and inform his readers. Identify paragraphs that serve each purpose.

STYLE AND STRUCTURE

1. Is this essay's primary focus on finding causes, predicting effects, or both? Explain.

2. Identify the specific passages in this selection that make causal connections.

3. Although his subject matter is scientific, Gould's verbal asides occasionally give his essay a playful tone. Give some examples of Gould's playful comments on his subject matter.

4. Consider Gould's use of language. What does he gain by juxtaposing words like *cranium, ontogenetic,* and *neoteny* with words like *pudgier, ratty,* and *fiddling around*?

5. Gould frequently uses *I* and *we* in this selection. Where—and why—does he do this?

WRITING WORKSHOP

1. If you have access to photos of yourself as you grew up, choose half a dozen taken at key periods in your life. Using Gould's discussion as a guide, describe the changes in your appearance. Do you think the changes affected people who knew you?

2. Consider the cartoon or comic strip character you liked best when you were a child and the one you prefer today. Write an essay in which you consider how the changes in your perceptions and values have affected your tastes in cartoon characters.

THE FATE OF THE EARTH

Jonathan Schell

Born in 1943, Jonathan Schell currently writes for The New Yorker
*where this essay first appeared in a series of articles later collected
in* The Fate of the Earth *(1982). In the book, Schell considers the
effects of nuclear holocaust upon the earth's people and institutions,
including the possible extinction of mankind. Schell's book, and this
excerpt from it, are meant to awaken readers and warn them of the
threat that nuclear weapons pose to the world. Through grim, thorough detail and a dispassionate tone, "The Fate of the Earth" describes the effects of a hydrogen bomb dropped on New York City.*

What happened at Hiroshima was less than a millionth part of   1
a holocaust at present levels of world nuclear armament. The more
than millionfold difference amounts to more than a difference in
magnitude; it is also a difference in kind. The authors of "Hiroshima
and Nagasaki"* observe that "an atomic bomb's massive destruction
and indiscriminate slaughter involves the sweeping breakdown of
all order and existence—in a word, the collapse of society itself,"
and that therefore "the essence of atomic destruction lies in the
totality of its impact on man and society." This is true also of a
holocaust, of course, except that the totalities in question are now
not single cities but nations, ecosystems, and the earth's ecosphere.
Yet with the exception of fallout, which was relatively light at Hiroshima and Nagasaki (because both the bombs were air-burst), the
immediate devastation caused by today's bombs would be of a sort
similar to the devastation in those cities. The immediate effects of
a twenty-megaton bomb are not different in kind from those of a
twelve-and-a-half-kiloton bomb; they are only more extensive. . . .
In bursts of both weapons, for instance, there is a radius within
which the thermal pulse can ignite newspapers: for the twelve-and-
a-half-kiloton weapon, it is a little over two miles; for the twenty-
megaton weapon, it is twenty-five miles. (Since there is no inherent
limit on the size of a nuclear weapon, these figures can be increased
indefinitely, subject only to the limitations imposed by the technical
capacities of the bomb builder—and of the earth's capacity to absorb

*EDS. NOTE—A comprehensive study, carried out by a group of distinguished
Japanese scientists, of the consequences of the bombing of those two cities.

the blast. The Soviet Union, which has shown a liking for sheer size in so many of its undertakings, once detonated a sixty-megaton bomb.) Therefore, while the total effect of a holocaust is qualitatively different from the total effect of a single bomb, the experience of individual people in a holocaust would be, in the short term (and again excepting the presence of lethal fallout wherever the bombs were ground-burst), very much like the experience of individual people in Hiroshima. The Hiroshima people's experience, accordingly, is of much more than historical interest. It is a picture of what our whole world is always poised to become—a backdrop of scarcely imaginable horror lying just behind the surface of our normal life, and capable of breaking through into that normal life at any second. Whether we choose to think about it or not, it is an omnipresent, inescapable truth about our lives today that at every single moment each one of us may suddenly become the deranged mother looking for her burned child; the professor with the ball of rice in his hand whose wife has just told him "Run away, dear!" and died in the fires; Mr. Fukai running back into the firestorm; the naked man standing on the blasted plain that was his city, holding his eyeball in his hand; or, more likely, one of millions of corpses. For whatever our "modest hopes" as human beings may be, every one of them can be nullified by a nuclear holocaust.

One way to begin to grasp the destructive power of present-day nuclear weapons is to describe the consequences of the detonation of a one-megaton bomb, which possesses eighty times the explosive power of the Hiroshima bomb, on a large city, such as New York. Burst some eighty-five hundred feet above the Empire State Building, a one-megaton bomb would gut or flatten almost every building between Battery Park and 125th Street, or within a radius of four and four-tenths miles, or in an area of sixty-one square miles, and would heavily damage buildings between the northern tip of Staten Island and the George Washington Bridge, or within a radius of about eight miles, or in an area of about two hundred square miles. A conventional explosive delivers a swift shock, like a slap, to whatever it hits, but the blast wave of a sizable nuclear weapon endures for several seconds and "can surround and destroy whole buildings" (Glasstone). People, of course, would be picked up and hurled away from the blast along with the rest of the debris. Within the sixty-one square miles, the walls, roofs, and floors of any buildings that had not been flattened would be collapsed, and the people and furniture inside would be swept down onto the street. (Technically, this zone would be hit by various overpressures of at least five pounds per square inch. Overpressure is defined as the pressure in excess of normal atmospheric pressure.) As far away as ten miles from ground zero, pieces of glass and other sharp objects would be hurled about by the blast wave at lethal velocities. In Hiroshima, where buildings were low and, outside the center of the city, were often constructed of light materials, injuries from falling buildings were often minor. But in New York, where the buildings are tall and are constructed of heavy materials, the physical collapse of the city would certainly kill millions of people. The streets of New York are narrow ravines running between the high walls of the city's buildings. In a nuclear attack, the walls would fall and the ravines would fill up. The people in the buildings would fall to the street with the debris of the buildings, and the people in the street would be crushed by this avalanche of people and buildings. At a distance of two miles or so from ground zero, winds would reach four hundred miles an hour, and another two miles away they would reach a hundred and eighty miles an hour. Meanwhile, the fireball would be growing, until it was more than a mile wide, and rocketing upward, to a height of over six miles. For ten seconds, it would broil the city below. Anyone caught in the open within nine miles of ground zero would receive third-degree burns and would probably be killed; closer to the explosion, people would be charred and killed instantly. From Greenwich Village up to Central Park, the heat would be great enough to melt metal and glass. Readily inflammable materials, such as newspapers and dry leaves, would ignite in all five boroughs (though in only a small part of Staten Island) and west to the Passaic River, in New Jersey, within a radius of about nine and a half miles from ground zero, thereby creating an area of more than two hundred and eighty square miles in which mass fires were likely to break out.

If it were possible (as it would not be) for someone to stand at Fifth Avenue and Seventy-second Street (about two miles from ground zero) without being instantly killed, he would see the following sequence of events. A dazzling white light from the fireball would illumine the scene, continuing for perhaps thirty seconds. Simultaneously, searing heat would ignite everything flammable and start to melt windows, cars, buses, lampposts, and everything else made of metal or glass. People in the street would immediately catch fire, and would shortly be reduced to heavily charred corpses. About five seconds after the light appeared, the blast wave would strike, laden with the debris of a now nonexistent midtown. Some buildings might be crushed, as though a giant fist had squeezed them on all sides, and others might be picked up off their foundations and whirled uptown with the other debris. On the far side of Central Park, the

West Side skyline would fall from south to north. The four-hundred-mile-an-hour wind would blow from south to north, die down after a few seconds, and then blow in the reverse direction with diminished intensity. While these things were happening, the fireball would be burning in the sky for the ten seconds of the thermal pulse. Soon huge, thick clouds of dust and smoke would envelop the scene, and as the mushroom cloud rushed overhead (it would have a diameter of about twelve miles) the light from the sun would be blotted out, and day would turn to night. Within minutes, fires, ignited both by the thermal pulse and by broken gas mains, tanks of gas and oil, and the like, would begin to spread in the darkness, and a strong, steady wind would begin to blow in the direction of the blast. As at Hiroshima, a whirlwind might be produced, which would sweep through the ruins, and radioactive rain, generated under the meteorological conditions created by the blast, might fall. Before long, the individual fires would coalesce into a mass fire, which, depending largely on the winds, would become either a conflagration or a firestorm. In a conflagration, prevailing winds spread a wall of fire as far as there is any combustible material to sustain it; in a firestorm, a vertical updraft caused by the fire itself sucks the surrounding air in toward a central point, and the fires therefore converge in a single fire of extreme heat. A mass fire of either kind renders shelters useless by burning up all the oxygen in the air and creating toxic gases, so that anyone inside the shelters is asphyxiated, and also by heating the ground to such high temperatures that the shelters turn, in effect, into ovens, cremating the people inside them. In Dresden, several days after the firestorm raised there by Allied conventional bombing, the interiors of some bomb shelters were still so hot that when they were opened the inrushing air caused the contents to burst into flame. Only those who had fled their shelters when the bombing started had any chance of surviving. (It is difficult to predict in a particular situation which form the fires will take. In actual experience, Hiroshima suffered a firestorm and Nagasaki suffered a conflagration.)

In this vast theatre of physical effects, all the scenes of agony and death that took place at Hiroshima would again take place, but now involving millions of people rather than hundreds of thousands. Like the people of Hiroshima, the people of New York would be burned, battered, crushed, and irradiated in every conceivable way. The city and its people would be mingled in a smoldering heap. And then, as the fires started, the survivors (most of whom would be on the periphery of the explosion) would be driven to abandon to the flames those family members and other people who were unable to flee, or else to die with them. Before long, while the ruins burned, the processions of injured, mute people would begin their slow progress out of the outskirts of the devastated zone. However, this time a much smaller proportion of the population than at Hiroshima would have a chance of escaping. In general, as the size of the area of devastation increases, the possibilities for escape decrease. When the devastated area is relatively small, as it was at Hiroshima, people who are not incapacitated will have a good chance of escaping to safety before the fires coalesce into a mass fire. But when the devastated area is great, as it would be after the detonation of a megaton bomb, and fires are springing up at a distance of nine and a half miles from ground zero, and when what used to be the streets are piled high with burning rubble, and the day (if the attack occurs in the daytime) has grown impenetrably dark, there is little chance that anyone who is not on the very edge of the devastated area will be able to make his way to safety. In New York, most people would die wherever the blast found them, or not very far from there.

If instead of being burst in the air the bomb were burst on or near the ground in the vicinity of the Empire State Building, the overpressure would be very much greater near the center of the blast area but the range hit by a minimum of five pounds per square inch of overpressure would be less. The range of the thermal pulse would be about the same as that of the air burst. The fireball would be almost two miles across, and would engulf midtown Manhattan from Greenwich Village nearly to Central Park. Very little is known about what would happen to a city that was inside a fireball, but one would expect a good deal of what was there to be first pulverized and then melted or vaporized. Any human beings in the area would be reduced to smoke and ashes; they would simply disappear. A crater roughly three blocks in diameter and two hundred feet deep would open up. In addition, heavy radioactive fallout would be created as dust and debris from the city rose with the mushroom cloud and then fell back to the ground. Fallout would begin to drop almost immediately, contaminating the ground beneath the cloud with levels of radiation many times lethal doses, and quickly killing anyone who might have survived the blast wave and the thermal pulse and might now be attempting an escape; it is difficult to believe that there would be appreciable survival of the people of the city after a megaton ground burst. And for the next twenty-four hours or so more fallout would descend downwind from the blast, in a plume whose direction and length would depend on the speed and the direction of the wind that happened to be blowing at the time of the attack. If the wind was blowing at fifteen miles an hour, fallout of lethal intensity would descend in a plume about a hundred and fifty miles long and as much as fifteen miles wide. Fallout that was sublethal but could still cause serious illness would extend another hundred and fifty miles downwind. Exposure to radioactivity in human beings is measured in units called rems—an acronym for "roentgen equivalent in man." The roentgen is a standard measurement of gamma- and X-ray radiation, and the expression "equivalent in man" indicates that an adjustment has been made to take into account the differences in the degree of biological damage that is caused by radiation of different types. Many of the kinds of harm done to human beings by radiation—for example, the incidence of cancer and of genetic damage—depend on the dose accumulated over many years; but radiation sickness, capable of causing death, results from an "acute" dose, received in a period of anything from a few seconds to several days. Because almost ninety per cent of the so-called "infinite-time dose" of radiation from fallout—that is, the dose from a given quantity of fallout that one would receive if one lived for many thousands of years—is emitted in the first week, the one-week accumulated dose is often used as a convenient measure for calculating the immediate harm from fallout. Doses in the thousands of rems, which could be expected throughout the city, would attack the central nervous system and would bring about death within a few hours. Doses of around a thousand rems, which would be delivered some tens of miles downwind from the blast, would kill within two weeks everyone who was exposed to them. Doses of around five hundred rems, which would be delivered as far as a hundred and fifty miles downwind (given a wind speed of fifteen miles per hour), would kill half of all exposed able-bodied young adults. At this level of exposure, radiation sickness proceeds in the three stages observed at Hiroshima. The plume of lethal fallout could descend, depending on the direction of the wind, on other parts of New York State and parts of New Jersey, Pennsylvania, Delaware, Maryland, Connecticut, Massachusetts, Rhode Island, Vermont, and New Hampshire, killing additional millions of people. The circumstances in heavily contaminated areas, in which millions of people were all declining together, over a period of weeks, toward painful deaths, are ones that, like so many of the consequences of nuclear explosions, have never been experienced.

A description of the effects of a one-megaton bomb on New York City gives some notion of the meaning in human terms of a megaton of nuclear explosive power, but a weapon that is more likely to be used against New York is the twenty-megaton bomb, which has one thousand six hundred times the yield of the Hiroshima bomb. The

Soviet Union is estimated to have at least a hundred and thirteen twenty-megaton bombs in its nuclear arsenal, carried by Bear intercontinental bombers. In addition, some of the Soviet SS–18 missiles are capable of carrying bombs of this size, although the actual yields are not known. Since the explosive power of the twenty-megaton bombs greatly exceeds the amount necessary to destroy most military targets, it is reasonable to suppose that they are meant for use against large cities. If a twenty-megaton bomb were air-burst over the Empire State Building at an altitude of thirty thousand feet, the zone gutted or flattened by the blast wave would have a radius of twelve miles and an area of more than four hundred and fifty square miles, reaching from the middle of Staten Island to the northern edge of the Bronx, the eastern edge of Queens, and well into New Jersey, and the zone of heavy damage from the blast wave (the zone hit by a minimum of two pounds of overpressure per square inch) would have a radius of twenty-one and a half miles, or an area of one thousand four hundred and fifty square miles, reaching to the southernmost tip of Staten Island, north as far as southern Rockland County, east into Nassau County, and west to Morris County, New Jersey. The fireball would be about four and a half miles in diameter and would radiate the thermal pulse for some twenty seconds. People caught in the open twenty-three miles away from ground zero, in Long Island, New Jersey, and southern New York State, would be burned to death. People hundreds of miles away who looked at the burst would be temporarily blinded and would risk permanent eye injury. (After the test of a fifteen-megaton bomb on Bikini Atoll, in the South Pacific, in March of 1954, small animals were found to have suffered retinal burns at a distance of three hundred and forty-five miles.) The mushroom cloud would be seventy miles in diameter. New York City and its suburbs would be transformed into a lifeless, flat, scorched desert in a few seconds.

If a twenty-megaton bomb were ground-burst on the Empire State Building, the range of severe blast damage would, as with the one-megaton ground blast, be reduced, but the fireball, which would be almost six miles in diameter, would cover Manhattan from Wall Street to northern Central Park and also parts of New Jersey, Brooklyn, and Queens, and everyone within it would be instantly killed, with most of them physically disappearing. Fallout would again be generated, this time covering thousands of square miles with lethal intensities of radiation. A fair portion of New York City and its incinerated population, now radioactive dust, would have risen into the mushroom cloud and would now be descending on the surrounding territory. On one of the few occasions when local fallout was generated by a test explosion in the multi-megaton range, the fifteen-megaton bomb tested on Bikini Atoll, which was exploded seven feet above the surface of a coral reef, "caused substantial contamination over an area of more than seven thousand square miles," according to Glasstone. If, as seems likely, a twenty-megaton bomb ground-burst on New York would produce at least a comparable amount of fallout, and if the wind carried the fallout onto populated areas, then this one bomb would probably doom upward of twenty million people, or almost ten per cent of the population of the United States.

COMPREHENSION

1. What differences does Schell cite between the bombing of Hiroshima and the possible future holocaust he describes? What similarities does he acknowledge?

2. What is the first effect Schell considers? Why does he discuss it first?

3. What effect does Schell focus on in paragraph 3?

4. In paragraph 4, why does Schell maintain that so few people would escape after the blast?

5. What variation on his theme does Schell introduce in paragraph 5? What effects of this new scenario does he consider?

6. What additional possibility is the subject of paragraph 6? Why does Schell feel this possibility is a likely one?

7. According to Schell's essay, what could be the ultimate outcome of a twenty-megaton bomb ground-burst on New York?

PURPOSE AND AUDIENCE

1. Schell's purpose is persuasive, yet he is also presenting factual information. How does the detailed information he presents advance his persuasive purpose?

2. How does Schell ensure that a general audience will be able to understand his points and remain interested in his essay? Consider his use of definition, parenthetical clarification, and analogy.

3. What is Schell's purpose in opening this essay with vivid details from the experience at Hiroshima?

4. What is Schell's thesis? Where is this thesis explicitly stated?

STYLE AND STRUCTURE

1. What tense does Schell use for most of his verbs? Why?

2. This essay has extremely long paragraphs. Why didn't Schell break them up into shorter ones?

3. What is the effect of the parenthetical "as it would not be" at the beginning of paragraph 3?

4. Does Schell's indefinite language, such as "If instead," "Very little is known," and "one would expect" in paragraph 5, weaken his argument? Why or why not?

5. How does Schell gradually intensify his argument as he moves from paragraph 5 to paragraph 6 to paragraph 7?

6. How does Schell's style suit his essay? Why does he avoid the sensational style his subject matter might seem to call for?

WRITING WORKSHOP

1. Consider the impact this essay has had on you or your friends. Write an essay in which you try to predict effects of Schell's work on readers, considering how his ideas might change people's assumptions or plans.

2. Using Schell's information (and being sure to acknowledge it), write a letter to the President of the United States. By outlining the probable effects of the bomb, try to convince the President to support nuclear disarmament. Or, use the same information to convince the President that the U.S. must continue to develop new and stronger atomic weapons to defend itself.

7

Comparison and Contrast

WHAT IS COMPARISON AND CONTRAST?

Imagine two wedding photographs, one of your grandparents and the other of your parents. Individually each photograph reveals a great deal of information. Each couple has just celebrated a happy occasion, and each is surrounded by friends and family. The styles of dress show that the first picture was taken during the 1930s and the second in the late 1950s. But place these two photographs side by side, and you can gain insights that you could not get by looking at each picture separately. Now, your view of both pictures and your awareness of their similarities and differences enable you to make a statement about more than the individuals who posed for these pictures. Despite the fact that these two pictures were taken at very different times—one before World War II during a time of international uncertainty and economic depression and the other at a time of peace and prosperity—both couples smile at the camera a little self-consciously and seem to look optimistically toward the future. There are, as these pictures assert, human values that war and the economy cannot overshadow.

We arrived at this conclusion by using a method of thinking called comparison and contrast. A *comparison* shows how two or more similar things are alike, and a *contrast* shows how they are different. Because the two naturally go together, more often than not you will use *comparison and contrast* to consider both similarities and differences. A special form of comparison, called *analogy,* looks for similarities between two essentially different things. By comparing ants and people, for instance, an author can use an analogy to make a suggestive point about workers on an assembly line or a crowd filing into a sports stadium.

Throughout our lives we are bombarded with countless bits of information from newspapers, television, radio, and personal experience: the police strike in Memphis; city workers walk out in Philadelphia; the Senate debates government spending; a tax revolt succeeds in California. The list is endless. Yet somehow we must make sense of the jumbled facts and figures that surround us. One way we have of understanding information like this is to put it side by side with other data and then to compare and contrast. Do the police in Memphis have the same complaints as the city workers in Philadelphia? What are the differences between the two situations? Is the national debate on spending akin to the California debate on taxes? How do they differ? We make similar distinctions every day about matters that directly affect us. When we make personal decisions, we consider alternatives, asking ourselves whether one option seems better than another. Should I buy a car with manual or automatic transmission? What are the advantages and disadvantages of each? Should I major in history or business? What job opportunities will each major offer me? Should I register as a Democrat or a Republican, or should I join a smaller political party? What are the positions of each on government spending, welfare, and taxes?

Because this way of thinking is central to our understanding of the world, comparison and contrast is often required in papers and on essay examinations:

> Compare and contrast the attitudes toward science and technology expressed in Stanislaw Lem's *Solaris* and Isaac Asimov's *I, Robot.* (English)
>
> What are the similarities and differences between mitosis and meiosis? (biology)
>
> Discuss the relative advantages and disadvantages of establishing a partnership and incorporating. (business law)
>
> Discuss the advantages and disadvantages of heterogeneous pupil grouping. (education)

Uses of Comparison and Contrast

You aren't likely to sit down and say to yourself, "I think I'll write a comparison-and-contrast essay today. Now what shall I write about?" Usually you will use comparison and contrast because you have been told to or because you decide it suits your topic. In the examples above, for instance, the instructors have phrased their questions to tell students how to treat the material. When you read the questions, certain key words and phrases—*compare and contrast, similarities and differences, advantages and disadvantages*—indicate that you should use a comparison-and-contrast pattern to organize your essay. Sometimes you may not even need such key phrases. Consider the question, "Which of the two Adamses, John and Samuel, had the greatest influence on the timing and course of the American Revolution?" The word *which* is enough to point to a contrast.

Comparison and contrast have other uses too. When you make an evaluation, for instance, you are employing comparison and contrast in a special context. If you, as a student in hospital management, were asked to evaluate two health delivery systems, you could begin by looking up the standards used by experts in their evaluations, compare each system's performance with those standards, and then contrast the systems with each other, concluding perhaps that both systems met minimum standards but that one was more cost-efficient than the other. Or if you were evaluating this year's new cars for a consumer newsletter, you might establish some criteria—gas economy, handling, comfort, sturdiness, style—and compare the cars with respect to each criterion. If different cars were best in each, your readers could then decide which features mattered most.

Thesis Statement

You decide to write a comparison-and-contrast essay, then, because you want to show how certain things are essentially the same or different. Your purpose in writing a comparison-and-contrast essay may be informational or judgmental. An informational essay simply presents two or more items side by side to illustrate their similarities or differences. It does not judge the relative merits of the items and often does not contain a thesis statement (although it always has a unifying idea). An essay in which you make judgments, on the other hand, always has a thesis. This thesis establishes the significance of the comparison or contrast and takes an arguable position on the relative merits of the items discussed. In a college paper that uses a comparison-and-contrast pattern, a thesis statement almost always strengthens the writing by clarifying its purpose.

As in other essays, your thesis statement should tell your readers what to expect in your essay. It should mention not only the subjects to be compared and contrasted but also the point the comparison is to make. In addition, your thesis should indicate whether you will concentrate on similarities or differences or whether you will balance the two. The very structure of your thesis sentence can help to show the focus of your essay. As the following sentences illustrate, a thesis statement can emphasize the central concern of the essay by stating it in the main, rather than the subordinate, clause of the sentence:

> Even though doctors and nurses perform distinctly different tasks at a hospital, their functions overlap in their contacts with patients.

> Although Melville's *Moby Dick* and London's *The Sea Wolf* are both about the sea, the major characters, minor characters, and themes of *Moby Dick* establish its greater complexity.

The structure of the first sentence emphasizes similarities, and the structure of the second highlights differences. Moreover, both sentences establish the things to be compared or contrasted as well as the significance or purpose of the juxtaposition.

Basis of Comparison

Before you can compare or contrast two things, you must determine what elements they have in common. For example, although cats and dogs are very different pets, both can learn from their owners. Cats and dogs may be taught different behaviors in different ways, but these differences can be analyzed because both animals share a common element, that of being trainable. Without a common element, there would be no basis for analysis—that is, no basis of comparison.

In addition to being shared by both subjects, a basis of comparison should lead you, and thus your reader, beyond the obvious. For instance, at first the idea of a comparison-and-contrast essay based on an analogy between bees and people might seem absurd. After all, these two creatures differ in species, physical structure, and intelligence. Their differences are so obvious that an essay based on them would be pointless. But, with further analysis, you might decide there are quite a few similarities between the two. Both are social animals that live in complex social structures, and both have tasks to perform and roles to fulfill in their societies. Thus, you would focus your essay on the common elements that seem most provocative—social structures and roles—rather than those elements that lead nowhere—species, physical structure, and intelligence. If you tried to compare bees and Volkswagens or humans and golf tees, however, you would run into trouble. Although some points of comparison could be found, they would be trivial. Why bother to point out that both bees and Volkswagens travel great distances or that both people and tees are needed to play golf? Neither statement establishes a meaningful basis for comparison.

When two subjects are very similar, it is the contrast that is worth writing about. And when two subjects are not very much alike, you should find enlightening similarities. In either case, after you brainstorm to generate ideas, you should think about each point to decide whether it is significant or not. To test each comparison and contrast, ask yourself: Does the comparison lead readers beyond the obvious? Is there a meaningful basis for the comparison? Does it support my thesis? Does it serve my writing purpose?

Selecting Points for Discussion

Your next step is to select those points that have a bearing on your thesis. You do this by determining the emphasis of your thesis, whether it emphasizes similarities, differences, or both, and what the major point of your paper is. If your purpose for comparing two types of house plants is to explain which is easier to raise than the other, you would contrast points having to do with plant care, not those that focus exclusively on plant biology.

When you compare and contrast, make sure that you treat the same common elements for each subject you discuss. For instance, if you were going to compare and contrast two novels, you might consider the following elements in both works.

Novel A	*Novel B*
Major characters	Major characters
Minor characters	Minor characters
Themes	Themes

A frequent error that you should avoid is to discuss different elements for each subject. Doing this obscures any basis of comparison that might exist. The two novels, for example, could not be meaningfully compared or contrasted if you discussed elements such as these:

Novel A	*Novel B*
Major characters	Plot
Minor characters	Author's life
Themes	Symbols

STRUCTURING A COMPARISON-AND-CONTRAST ESSAY

After you have formulated your thesis statement, established your basis of comparison, and selected your points for discussion, you are ready to organize your paper. Like every other type of essay examined in this book, a comparison-and-contrast essay has an introduction, several body paragraphs, and a conclusion. Within the body of your paper, there are two basic comparison-and-contrast patterns you can follow: you can discuss each subject separately, devoting one or more paragraphs to subject A and then the same number to subject B; or you can discuss one common element in each section, making your points about subject A and subject B in turn. As you might expect, both organizational patterns have advantages and disadvantages that you should consider before you use them.

Subject-by-Subject Comparison

When you make a subject-by-subject comparison, you essentially write a separate essay about each subject, but you organize these miniature essays in parallel. In discussing each subject, you use the *same basis of comparison* to select your points, and you arrange these points in the same order. Usually you present points in order of increasing significance to hold your readers' interest:

¶1 Introduction—thesis: Even though doctors and nurses perform distinctly different tasks at a hospital, their functions overlap in their contacts with patients.

¶2 Doctor's functions:
Teaching patients
Assessing patients
Dispensing medication

¶3 Nurse's functions:
Teaching patients
Assessing patients
Dispensing medication

¶4 Conclusion

Subject-by-subject comparison is usually used only for short papers. In longer papers, where many points are made about each subject, this organizational pattern puts too many demands upon your readers, requiring them to remember all your points throughout your paper. In addition, because of the size of each section, your paper may sound like two separate essays weakly connected by a transitional phrase. Instead, for longer or more complex papers, it is best to discuss each point of comparison for both subjects together, making your comparisons as you go along.

Point-by-Point Comparison

When you use a point-by-point comparison, your paper is organized differently. Paragraph by paragraph, you first make a point about one subject, then follow it with a comparable point about the other. This alternating pattern continues throughout the body of your essay, until all your comparisons or contrasts have been made. The following outline illustrates a point-by-point comparison:

¶1   Introduction—thesis: Although Melville's *Moby Dick* and London's *The Sea Wolf* are both about the sea, *Moby Dick* is a more complex work than *The Sea Wolf*.

¶2–3 Minor characters:
      The Sea Wolf
      Moby Dick

¶4–5 Major characters:
      The Sea Wolf
      Moby Dick

¶6–7 Themes:
      The Sea Wolf
      Moby Dick

¶8   Conclusion

This arrangement enables the writer to widen his discussion from minor characters to themes. As he does so, he establishes the relative complexity of each work and proves his thesis.

Point-by-point comparison works best for long papers because your readers can follow the comparisons or contrasts more easily as they go along. Readers do not have to wait several paragraphs to find out the differences between *Moby Dick* and *The Sea Wolf,* or to remember on page six what you said on page three. Nevertheless, it is easy to fall into a pattern of monotonous, back-and-forth sentences when writing point-by-point comparison. To avoid this, try to vary your sentence length and structure as you move from point to point.

In college you will often need to write comparison-and-contrast essays on midterm and final examinations. The following question, from a science-fiction final examination, is typical of the kind you will encounter:

> *Question:* Choose any two of the books you have read this semester, and discuss how their views of the future differ. Account if you can for the differences you uncover.

Here is an answer to this question by a student, Jane Czerak:

Introduction

When science fiction discusses an- 1
other world, it is actually discussing
our world, and when science fiction
discusses the future, it is actually
discussing the present. Both Robert
Heinlein's *Starship Troopers* and John
Brunner's *Stand on Zanzibar* are near-
future science fiction—supposedly set
fifty years from the time they were
written. Although these books are alike

Thesis (emphasizing differences)

in some ways, they differ in other ways
that reflect the moods of the times in
which they were written.

First subject (view of the future)

Starship Troopers takes place in a 2
world that is substantially different
from ours. Earth is the center of an
empire that encompasses several of the
outer planets. Space exploration has
led to the colonization of a number of
worlds and the inevitable alien encounter. Earth is locked in mortal combat
with buglike aliens who are bent on ap-
propriating the living space that people on earth need to survive. The re-

sult of this struggle is that the
military has assumed great power. In
order to obtain citizenship, a person
must first serve in the armed forces.
The vote is achieved only by those who
have fought the bugs and survived.

**First subject
(reflection of
the past)**   In many ways, *Starship Troopers* re-   3
flects the times in which it was writ-
ten. The 1950s was a decade in which
the United States still had faith in
military power and in its ability to
police the world. Despite the example
of Korea, America viewed its atomic arsenal as an umbrella that would protect
it from harm. The world of *Starship
Troopers* is one which faces an alien
challenge. War is seen as an inevitable
result of man's expansion, and only
through struggle can man establish his
right to survive. In this light, the
bugs can be seen as symbols of all that
threatened the United States throughout
the 1950s.

**Second
subject (view
of the future)**   The world of *Stand on Zanzibar* is   4
very much like ours today. The story
takes place in the near future, and the
first half of the book is set in New
York City. Many of the problems that
beset New York today are still present
in the future, but they are even more
severe. Because of overpopulation, living space is at a premium, and people
can afford apartments only by sharing
the expense with others. Corporations

have assumed great power and virtually
run the government. Every facet of life
seems to be permeated by television and
advertising. People are encouraged to
buy as much as they can whenever they
can—this in spite of the fact that
earth's resources seem to be declining
at an alarming rate. In order to try to
cope with this suicidal way of life,
most states have passed laws strictly
limiting people's right to bear children.

**Second
subject
(reflection of
the past)**

Stand on Zanzibar was published in   5
1968 and very accurately expresses the
mood of those times. Possibly because
of the joint effects of the war in
Vietnam and the Johnson presidency,
Americans were examining their personal
and national goals. The population explosion, ecology, and corporate power
became topics of great interest. Brunner takes these problems and examines
what would happen if Americans continued their present course of action. The
result is the world of *Stand on Zanzibar* where the United States consumes
most of the earth's resources and continually searches our overextended
planet for more.

Conclusion

Although *Starship Troopers* and *Stand*   6
on Zanzibar were written only nine
years apart, they differ greatly in
concept. Great changes took place in
the United States between 1959 and

1968, and these books reflect the
shifts in priorities and consciousness
that occurred. Using the near future as
settings for their works, Heinlein and
Brunner create interesting and subtle

Restatement
of thesis

works which nonetheless are as different as the volatile times in which they
were written.

Points for Special Attention

Structure.   Jane Czerak chose to answer her examination question by using a subject-by-subject comparison. Although her discussion is somewhat involved, she actually makes only two major points
about both books: that they treat the future in different ways and
that this treatment reflects the times in which they were written.
Because readers can easily keep these ideas in mind, a subject-by-
subject discussion was a good strategy for Jane to use. Of course,
she could have used a point-by-point discussion and written an equally
good paper. Often the choice is a matter of personal preference—a
different writer might simply have liked point-by-point better. Because Jane was writing a final exam and time was limited, she chose
the strategy that enabled her to organize her essay most quickly
and easily.

Transition.   Any comparison-and-contrast essay needs transition so that it flows smoothly. Without adequate transition, a point-
by-point comparison can produce a series of choppy paragraphs, and
a subject-by-subject comparison can read like two separate essays.
In addition to connecting the sections of an essay, transitional words
and phrases like the following, when used properly, can highlight
similarities and differences for your reader:

on the one hand . . . on the other hand . . .
even though
on the contrary
in spite of
although
despite
unlike
both

like
likewise
similarly

Jane could have used these phrases more often than she does, particularly when she shifts from the first subject in her discussion to the second. By adding a transitional phrase, such as *on the other hand,* she not only could have emphasized the differences between the two books she is discussing but also could have improved the transition between the two sections of her paper.

without transition:	The world of *Stand on Zanzibar* is very much like ours today.
with transition:	On the other hand, the world of *Stand on Zanzibar* is very much like ours today.

Topic Sentences.   A topic sentence presents the main idea of a paragraph; often it appears as the paragraph's first sentence. Like transitional phrases, topic sentences guide your reader through your paper. When reading a comparison-and-contrast essay, a reader can easily become lost in a jumble of points, especially if the paper is long and complex. Direct, clearly stated topic sentences act as guideposts, alerting your reader to the comparisons and contrasts you are making. Jane's topic sentences are straightforward and reinforce her major points about each book. And, as in any good comparison-and-contrast essay, each of the points discussed in part one of her paper is also discussed in part two. Notice how her topic sentences reinforce this balance:

Starship Troopers takes place in a world that is substantially different from ours.	The world of *Stand on Zanzibar* is very much like ours today.
In many ways, *Starship Troopers* reflects the times in which it was written.	*Stand on Zanzibar* was published in 1968 and very accurately expresses the mood of those times.

The selections that follow illustrate both point-by-point and subject-by-subject comparison. Moreover, each uses transitional elements and topic sentences to enhance clarity and to achieve balance between categories. Although the reading selections vary greatly in organization, length, and complexity, each is primarily concerned with the similarities and differences between its subjects.

FROM SONG TO SOUND: BING AND ELVIS

Russell Baker

Russell Baker was born in 1925 in Virginia. After graduating from Johns Hopkins University he worked as a reporter for the Baltimore Sun *and the* New York Times. *He has contributed to a number of magazines including* Ladies' Home Journal, McCall's, Saturday Evening Post, *and* Sports Illustrated. *He writes a syndicated column, "The Observer," that often treats contemporary social and political issues in a humorous or satirical manner. He won the Pulitzer Prize in 1979 for distinguished commentary. His books include* Poor Russell's Almanac *(1972),* The Upside Down Man *(1977), and* So This Is Depravity *(1980). "From Song to Sound" appeared in "The Observer." In this essay Baker compares two eras as well as the two performers who represented them.*

The grieving for Elvis Presley and the commercial exploitation   1
of his death were still not ended when we heard of Bing Crosby's
death the other day. Here is a generational puzzle. Those of an age
to mourn Elvis must marvel that their elders could really have
cared about Bing, just as the Crosby generation a few weeks ago
wondered what all the to-do was about when Elvis died.

Each man was a mass culture hero to his generation, but it tells   2
us something of the difference between generations that each man's
admirers would be hard-pressed to understand why the other could
mean very much to his devotees.

There were similarities that ought to tell us something. Both   3
came from obscurity to national recognition while quite young and
became very rich. Both lacked formal music education and went on
to movie careers despite lack of acting skills. Both developed distinctive musical styles which were originally scorned by critics and
subsequently studied as pioneer developments in the art of popular
song.

In short, each man's career followed the mythic rags-to-triumph   4
pattern in which adversity is conquered, detractors are given their
comeuppance and estates, fancy cars and world tours become the
reward of perseverance. Traditionally this was supposed to be the
history of the American business striver, but in our era of committee
capitalism it occurs most often in the mass entertainment field, and

so we look less and less to the board room for our heroes and more and more to the microphone.

Both Crosby and Presley were creations of the microphone. It made it possible for people with frail voices not only to be heard beyond the third row but also to caress millions. Crosby was among the first to understand that the microphone made it possible to sing to multitudes by singing to a single person in a small room.

Presley cuddled his microphone like a lover. With Crosby the microphone was usually concealed, but Presley brought it out on stage, detached it from its fitting, stroked it, pressed it to his mouth. It was a surrogate for his listener, and he made love to it unashamedly.

The difference between Presley and Crosby, however, reflected generational differences which spoke of changing values in American life. Crosby's music was soothing; Presley's was disturbing. It is too easy to be glib about this, to say that Crosby was singing to, first, Depression America, and, then, to wartime America, and that his audiences had all the disturbance they could handle in their daily lives without buying more at the record shop and movie theater.

Crosby's fans talk about how "relaxed" he was, how "natural," how "casual and easy going." By the time Presley began causing sensations, the entire country had become relaxed, casual and easy going, and its younger people seemed to be tired of it, for Elvis's act was anything but soothing and scarcely what a parent of that placid age would have called "natural" for a young man.

Elvis was unseemly, loud, gaudy, sexual—that gyrating pelvis!— in short, disturbing. He not only disturbed parents who thought music by Crosby was soothing but also reminded their young that they were full of the turmoil of youth and an appetite for excitement. At a time when the country had a population coming of age with no memory of troubled times, Presley spoke to a yearning for disturbance.

It probably helped that Elvis's music made Mom and Dad climb the wall. In any case, people who admired Elvis never talk about how relaxed and easy going he made them feel. They are more likely to tell you he introduced them to something new and exciting.

To explain each man in terms of changes in economic and political life probably oversimplifies the matter. Something in the culture was also changing. Crosby's music, for example, paid great attention to the importance of lyrics. The "message" of the song was as essential to the audience as the tune. The words were usually inane and witless, but Crosby—like Sinatra a little later—made them vital. People remembered them, sang them. Words still had meaning.

Although many of Presley's songs were highly lyrical, in most it wasn't the words that moved audiences; it was the "sound." Rock 'n' roll, of which he was the great popularizer, was a "sound" event. Song stopped being song and turned into "sound," at least until the Beatles came along and solved the problem of making words sing to the new beat.   12

Thus a group like the Rolling Stones, whose lyrics are often elaborate, seems to the Crosby-tuned ear to be shouting only gibberish, a sort of accompanying background noise in a "sound" experience. The Crosby generation has trouble hearing rock because it makes the mistake of trying to understand the words. The Presley generation has trouble with Crosby because it finds the sound unstimulating and cannot be touched by the inanity of the words. The mutual deafness may be a measure of how far we have come from really troubled times and of how deeply we have come to mistrust the value of words.   13

COMPREHENSION

1. List the similarities between Crosby and Presley that Baker considers.

2. List the differences Baker notes between the two men.

3. How does Baker account for the differences?

4. What, according to Baker's essay, is the difference between *song* and *sound*?

5. What are some nonmusical examples of the "mutual deafness" Baker mentions in his final paragraph?

PURPOSE AND AUDIENCE

1. This column was printed in newspapers all over the country shortly after Bing Crosby died. How does its subject matter make it particularly appropriate for this diverse audience?

2. What is the essay's thesis?

3. At times, Baker seems to be guilty of making unsupported generalizations. (For example, he assumes that his readers, like him, have "come to mistrust the value of words.") How do you suppose he expected his audience to react to such assumptions?

STYLE AND STRUCTURE

1. Baker considers both similarities and differences. Why does he deal with similarities first? What sentence signals his move from similarities to differences?

2. Which of the two patterns of organization (subject-by-subject or point-by-point) does Baker use here? Why? Could he have used the other pattern? Why or why not?

3. Paragraphs in this essay are relatively short because their length was determined by narrow newspaper columns. If you were typing this essay on standard paper, would you combine any paragraphs or make any other changes in paragraphing? If so, where?

4. Can you tell by the essay's language whether Baker is a fan of Presley or Crosby or both? If so, how?

5. Baker uses the microphone to illustrate *both* similarities and differences. Could another symbol—the radio or phonograph, for instance—have been used as effectively? Why or why not?

WRITING WORKSHOP

1. Choose any two musicians or groups, and analyze their similarities and differences as performers.

2. Compare and contrast the lyrics of a Bing Crosby song with one sung by Elvis Presley.

3. Write an article for an Elvis Presley fan magazine in which you compare and contrast him with Bing Crosby. Use Baker's facts, but slant them to show Presley in a much more favorable light. If you can, supply additional information to supplement Baker's account.

4. Find newsmagazine accounts of Presley's and Crosby's funerals, and write an essay comparing and contrasting them.

GRANT AND LEE:
A STUDY IN CONTRASTS

Bruce Catton

Bruce Catton was born in 1899 and died in 1978. A recognized authority on the Civil War, he won the Pulitzer Prize for history and the National Book Award. Catton has edited American Heritage *and served as the Director of Information for the United States Department of Commerce. Among his books are* Mr. Lincoln's Army *(1951),* Terrible Swift Sword *(1963), and* Gettysburg: The Final Fury *(1974). "Grant and Lee: A Study in Contrasts," which first appeared in a collection of historical essays entitled* The American Story, *is tightly organized and has explicit topic sentences and transitions. Further, this essay identifies not only differences but also important similarities between the two opposing generals.*

When Ulysses S. Grant and Robert E. Lee met in the parlor of a   1
modest house at Appomattox Court House, Virginia, on April 9, 1865, to work out the terms for the surrender of Lee's Army of Northern Virginia, a great chapter in American life came to a close, and a great new chapter began.

These men were bringing the Civil War to its virtual finish. To   2
be sure, other armies had yet to surrender, and for a few days the fugitive Confederate government would struggle desperately and vainly, trying to find some way to go on living now that its chief support was gone. But in effect it was all over when Grant and Lee signed the papers. And the little room where they wrote out the terms was the scene of one of the poignant, dramatic contrasts in American history.

They were two strong men, these oddly different generals, and   3
they represented the strengths of two conflicting currents that, through them, had come into final collision.

Back of Robert E. Lee was the notion that the old aristocratic   4
concept might somehow survive and be dominant in American life.

Lee was tidewater Virginia, and in his background were family,   5
culture, and tradition . . . the age of chivalry transplanted to a New World which was making its own legends and its own myths. He embodied a way of life that had come down through the age of knighthood and the English country squire. America was a land that was beginning all over again, dedicated to nothing much more

255

complicated than the rather hazy belief that all men had equal rights and should have an equal chance in the world. In such a land Lee stood for the feeling that it was somehow of advantage to human society to have a pronounced inequality in the social structure. There should be a leisure class, backed by ownership of land; in turn, society itself should be keyed to the land as the chief source of wealth and influence. It would bring forth (according to this ideal) a class of men with a strong sense of obligation to the community; men who lived not to gain advantage for themselves, but to meet the solemn obligations which had been laid on them by the very fact that they were privileged. From them the country would get its leadership; to them it could look for the higher values—of thought, of conduct, of personal deportment—to give it strength and virtue.

Lee embodied the noblest elements of this aristocratic ideal. 6 Through him, the landed nobility justified itself. For four years, the Southern states had fought a desperate war to uphold the ideals for which Lee stood. In the end, it almost seemed as if the Confederacy fought for Lee; as if he himself was the Confederacy . . . the best thing that the way of life for which the Confederacy stood could ever have to offer. He had passed into legend before Appomattox. Thousands of tired, underfed, poorly clothed Confederate soldiers, long since past the simple enthusiasm of the early days of the struggle, somehow considered Lee the symbol of everything for which they had been willing to die. But they could not quite put this feeling into words. If the Lost Cause, sanctified by so much heroism and so many deaths, had a living justification, its justification was General Lee.

Grant, the son of a tanner on the Western frontier, was every- 7 thing Lee was not. He had come up the hard way and embodied nothing in particular except the eternal toughness and sinewy fiber of the men who grew up beyond the mountains. He was one of a body of men who owed reverence and obeisance to no one, who were self-reliant to a fault, who cared hardly anything for the past but who had a sharp eye for the future.

These frontier men were the precise opposites of the tidewater 8 aristocrats. Back of them, in the great surge that had taken people over the Alleghenies and into the opening Western country, there was a deep, implicit dissatisfaction with a past that had settled into grooves. They stood for democracy, not from any reasoned conclusion about the proper ordering of human society, but simply because they had grown up in the middle of democracy and knew how it worked. Their society might have privileges, but they would be privileges each man had won for himself. Forms and patterns meant nothing. No man was born to anything, except perhaps to a chance to show how far he could rise. Life was competition.

Yet along with this feeling had come a deep sense of belonging to a national community. The Westerner who developed a farm, opened a shop, or set up in business as a trader, could hope to prosper only as his own community prospered—and his community ran from the Atlantic to the Pacific and from Canada down to Mexico. If the land was settled, with towns and highways and accessible markets, he could better himself. He saw his fate in terms of the nation's own destiny. As its horizons expanded, so did his. He had, in other words, an acute dollars-and-cents stake in the continued growth and development of his country.

And that, perhaps, is where the contrast between Grant and Lee becomes most striking. The Virginia aristocrat, inevitably, saw himself in relation to his own region. He lived in a static society which could endure almost anything except change. Instinctively, his first loyalty would go to the locality in which that society existed. He would fight to the limit of endurance to defend it, because in defending it he was defending everything that gave his own life its deepest meaning.

The Westerner, on the other hand, would fight with an equal tenacity for the broader concept of society. He fought so because everything he lived by was tied to growth, expansion, and a constantly widening horizon. What he lived by would survive or fall with the nation itself. He could not possibly stand by unmoved in the face of an attempt to destroy the Union. He would combat it with everything he had, because he could only see it as an effort to cut the ground out from under his feet.

So Grant and Lee were in complete contrast, representing two diametrically opposed elements in American life. Grant was the modern man emerging; beyond him, ready to come on the stage, was the great age of steel and machinery, of crowded cities and a restless burgeoning vitality. Lee might have ridden down from the old age of chivalry, lance in hand, silken banner fluttering over his head. Each man was the perfect champion of his cause, drawing both his strengths and his weaknesses from the people he led.

Yet it was not all contrast, after all. Different as they were—in background, in personality, in underlying aspiration—these two great soldiers had much in common. Under everything else, they were marvelous fighters. Furthermore, their fighting qualities were really very much alike.

Each man had, to begin with, the great virtue of utter tenacity and fidelity. Grant fought his way down the Mississippi Valley in spite of acute personal discouragement and profound military handicaps. Lee hung on in the trenches at Petersburg after hope itself had died. In each man there was an indomitable quality ... the born fighter's refusal to give up as long as he can still remain on his feet and lift his two fists.

Daring and resourcefulness they had, too; the ability to think 15
faster and move faster than the enemy. These were the qualities which gave Lee the dazzling campaigns of Second Manassas and Chancellorsville and won Vicksburg for Grant.

Lastly, and perhaps greatest of all, there was the ability, at the 16
end, to turn quickly from war to peace once the fighting was over. Out of the way these two men behaved at Appomattox came the possibility of a peace of reconciliation. It was a possibility not wholly realized, in the years to come, but which did, in the end, help the two sections to become one nation again ... after a war whose bitterness might have seemed to make such a reunion wholly impossible. No part of either man's life became him more than the part he played in this brief meeting in the McLean house at Appomattox. Their behavior there put all succeeding generations of Americans in their debt. Two great Americans, Grant and Lee—very different, yet under everything very much alike. Their encounter at Appomattox was one of the great moments of American history.

COMPREHENSION

1. What took place at Appomattox Court House on April 9, 1865? Why did the meeting at Appomattox signal the closing of "a great chapter in American life"?

2. How does Robert E. Lee represent the old aristocracy?

3. How does Ulysses S. Grant represent Lee's opposite?

4. According to Catton, where is it that "the contrast between Grant and Lee becomes most striking"?

5. What similarities does Catton see between the two men?

PURPOSE AND AUDIENCE

1. Catton's purpose in contrasting Grant and Lee is to make a general statement about the differences between two currents in American history. Summarize these differences. Do you think the differences still exist today?

2. Is Catton's purpose in comparing Grant and Lee the same as his purpose in contrasting them? That is, do their similarities also make a statement about America? Explain.

3. State the essay's thesis in your own words.

4. Why do you suppose Catton provides the background for the meeting at Appomattox but presents no information about the dramatic meeting itself?

STYLE AND STRUCTURE

1. Does Catton use subject-by-subject or point-by-point comparison? Why do you think he chose the structure he did?

2. In this essay, topic sentences are extremely important and extremely helpful to the reader. Explain the functions of the following sentences: "Grant . . . was everything Lee was not" (paragraph 7); "So Grant and Lee were in complete contrast . . ." (12); "Yet it was not all contrast, after all" (13); "Lastly, and perhaps greatest of all . . ." (16).

3. Catton carefully uses transitions in his essay. Identify the transitional words or expressions that link each paragraph to the preceding one.

4. Some of Catton's paragraphs (3, 4, 15) are only one or two sentences long. Others (5, 6, 16) are much longer. How can you explain such variation in paragraph length?

5. Most of this essay is devoted to the contrast between Grant and Lee. Where are their similarities mentioned? Why does Catton do this?

WRITING WORKSHOP

1. Write a similar "study in contrasts" about two people you know well—two teachers, your parents, two relatives, two friends—or about two fictional characters you are very familiar with.

2. Write a dialogue between two people you know that reveals their contrasting attitudes toward school, work, or any other subject.

DENOTATION AND CONNOTATION

Laurence Perrine

Laurence Perrine was born in 1915 in Toronto, Canada. He graduated from Oberlin College and received his Ph.D. from Yale. Presently he is a professor of English at Southern Methodist University. Perrine is a veteran teacher and the author of a number of books, articles, and texts. His best-known work is the textbook Sound and Sense: An Introduction to Poetry, *first published in 1956 and revised regularly thereafter. "Denotation and Connotation," from* Sound and Sense, *distinguishes between the dictionary meaning of a word and the very different meanings that the same word may suggest or connote. As you read, notice how Perrine's illustrations make his comparisons easy to understand.*

A primary distinction between the practical use of language and the literary use is that in literature, especially in poetry, a *fuller* use is made of individual words. To understand this, we need to examine the composition of a word. 1

The average word has three component parts: sound, denotation, and connotation. It begins as a combination of tones and noises, uttered by the lips, tongue, and throat, for which the written word is a notation. But it differs from a musical tone or a noise in that it has a meaning attached to it. The basic part of this meaning is its DENOTATION or denotations: that is, the dictionary meaning or meanings of the word. Beyond its denotations, a word may also have connotations. The CONNOTATIONS are what it suggests beyond what it expresses: its overtones of meaning. It acquires these connotations by its past history and associations, by the way and the circumstances in which it has been used. The word *home,* for instance, by denotation means only a place where one lives, but by connotation it suggests security, love, comfort, and family. The words *childlike* and *childish* both mean "characteristic of a child," but *childlike* suggests meekness, innocence, and wide-eyed wonder, while *childish* suggests pettiness, willfulness, and temper tantrums. If we name over a series of coins: *nickel, peso, lira, shilling, sen, doubloon,* the word *doubloon,* to four out of five readers, will immediately suggest pirates, though one will find nothing about pirates in looking up its meaning in the dictionary. Pirates are part of its connotation. 2

Connotation is very important to the poet, for it is one of the ³
means by which he can concentrate or enrich his meaning—say
more in fewer words. Consider, for instance, the following short
poem:

THERE IS NO FRIGATE LIKE A BOOK

There is no frigate like a book
  To take us lands away,
Nor any coursers like a page
  Of prancing poetry:
This traverse may the poorest take
  Without oppress of toll;
How frugal is the chariot
  That bears the human soul!
Emily Dickinson (1830–1886)

In this poem Emily Dickinson is considering the power of a book ⁴
or of poetry to carry us away, to let us escape from our immediate
surroundings into a world of the imagination. To do this she has
compared literature to various means of transportation: a boat, a
team of horses, a wheeled land vehicle. But she has been careful to
choose kinds of transportation and names for them that have romantic connotations. "Frigate" suggests exploration and adventure;
"coursers," beauty, spirit, and speed; "chariot," speed and the ability
to go through the air as well as on land. (Compare "Swing Low,
Sweet Chariot" and the myth of Phaethon, who tried to drive the
chariot of Apollo, and the famous painting of Aurora with her horses,
once hung in almost every school.) How much of the meaning of the
poem comes from this selection of vehicles and words is apparent if
we try to substitute for them, say, *steamship, horses,* and *streetcar.*

Just as a word has a variety of connotations, so also it may have ⁵
more than one denotation. If we look up the word *spring* in the
dictionary, for instance, we will find that it has between twenty-
five and thirty distinguishable meanings: It may mean (1) a pounce
or leap, (2) a season of the year, (3) a natural source of water, (4) a
coiled elastic wire, etc. This variety of denotation, complicated by
additional tones of connotation, makes language confusing and difficult to use. Any person using words must be careful to define by
context precisely the meanings that he wishes. But the difference
between the writer using language to communicate information and
the poet is this: the practical writer will always attempt to confine
his words to one meaning at a time; the poet will often take advantage of the fact that the word has more than one meaning by using

it to mean more than one thing at the same time. Thus when Edith Sitwell in one of her poems writes, "This is the time of the wild spring and the mating of tigers," she uses the word *spring* to denote both a season of the year and a sudden leap and she uses *tigers* rather than *lambs* or *birds* because it has a connotation of fierceness and wildness that the other two lack.

WHEN MY LOVE SWEARS THAT SHE IS MADE OF TRUTH

When my love swears that she is made of truth,
I do believe her, though I know she lies,
That she might think me some untutored youth,
Unlearnèd in the world's false subtleties.
Thus vainly thinking that she thinks me young,   5
Although she knows my days are past the best,
Simply I credit her false-speaking tongue;
On both sides thus is simple truth supprest.
But wherefore says she not she is unjust?°   unfaithful
And wherefore say not I that I am old?   10
Oh, love's best habit is in seeming trust,
And age in love loves not to have years told:
Therefore I lie with her and she with me,
And in our faults by lies we flattered be.
William Shakespeare (1564–1616)

A frequent misconception of poetic language is that the poet seeks 6 always the most beautiful or noble-sounding words. What he really seeks are the most *meaningful* words, and these vary from one context to another. Language has many levels and varieties, and the poet may choose from them all. His words may be grandiose or humble, fanciful or matter of fact, romantic or realistic, archaic or modern, technical or everyday, monosyllabic or polysyllabic. Usually his poem will be pitched pretty much in one key. The words in Emily Dickinson's "There is no frigate like a book" and those in Thomas Hardy's "The Man He Killed" . . . are chosen from quite different areas of language, but each poet has chosen the words most meaningful for his own poetic context. Sometimes a poet may import a word from one level or area of language into a poem composed mostly of words from a different level or area. If he does this clumsily, the result will be incongruous and sloppy. If he does it skillfully, the result will be a shock of surprise and an increment of meaning for the reader. In fact, the many varieties of language open to the poet provide his richest resource. His task is one of constant exploration and discovery. He searches always for the secret affinities of words that allow them to be brought together with soft explosions of meaning. . . .

The person using language to convey information is largely indifferent to the sound of his words and is hampered by their connotations and multiple denotations. He tries to confine each word to a single exact meaning. He uses, one might say, a fraction of the word and throws the rest away. The poet, on the other hand, tries to use as much of the word as he can. He is interested in sound and uses it to reinforce meaning. . . . He is interested in connotation and uses it to enrich and convey meaning. And he may use more than one denotation.

7

The purest form of practical language is scientific language. The scientist needs a precise language for conveying information precisely. The fact that words have multiple denotations and various overtones of meaning is a hindrance to him in accomplishing his purpose. His ideal language would be a language with a one-to-one correspondence between word and meaning; that is, every word would have one meaning only, and for every meaning there would be only one word. Since ordinary language does not fulfill these conditions, he has invented one that does. A statement in his language looks something like this:

8

$$SO_2 + H_2O = H_2SO_3$$

In such a statement the symbols are entirely unambiguous; they have been stripped of all connotation and of all denotations but one. The word *sulfurous,* if it occurred in poetry, might have all kinds of connotations: fire, smoke, brimstone, hell, damnation. But H_2SO_3 means one thing and one thing only: sulfurous acid.

The ambiguity and multiplicity of meanings possessed by words are an obstacle to the scientist but a resource to the poet. Where the scientist wants singleness of meaning, the poet wants richness of meaning. Where the scientist requires and has invented a strictly one-dimensional language, in which every word is confined to one denotation, the poet needs a multidimensional language, and he creates it partly by using a multidimensional vocabulary, in which to the dimension of denotation he adds the dimensions of connotation and sound.

9

The poet, we may say, plays on a many-stringed instrument. And he sounds more than one note at a time.

10

The first problem in reading poetry, therefore, or in reading any kind of literature, is to develop a sense of language, a feeling for words. One needs to become acquainted with their shape, their color,

11

and their flavor. There are two ways of doing this: extensive use of the dictionary and extensive reading.

COMPREHENSION

1. What does Perrine say is the difference between the practical use of language and the literary use of language?

2. Define *denotation* and *connotation*.

3. Why is connotation so important to the poet?

4. Explain what Perrine means when he says "A frequent misconception of poetic language is that the poet seeks always the most beautiful or noble-sounding words."

5. Differentiate between *poetic* and *scientific* uses of language.

PURPOSE AND AUDIENCE

1. This selection is from an introductory poetry text designed for college undergraduates. How can you tell it is not from an advanced text?

2. What is the purpose for which Perrine has written this chapter? That is, do you think he means to entertain, inform, or persuade? Explain.

3. Perrine gives many examples of poetic uses of language and few examples of scientific uses. Why does he do this?

STYLE AND STRUCTURE

1. Does Perrine use a subject-by-subject or point-by-point comparison?

2. What points does Perrine make about both denotation and connotation?

3. Identify the topic sentences, and show how they emphasize the main points of the essay.

4. Why does Perrine end with a discussion of poetic and scientific uses of language?

5. Which words reveal Perrine's attitude toward poetic and scientific language?

WRITING WORKSHOP

1. In a comparison-and-contrast essay, discuss the different denotations and connotations of one of the following word pairs.

gay—homosexual   letter carrier—mailman
girl—woman   average—mediocre
lady—woman   police officer—cop
Negro—black   alcoholic—drunk
mother—parent   mentally ill—crazy

2. Find descriptions of the same event in two different newspapers. Write a comparison-and-contrast essay concentrating on the denotations and connotations of the words used in the two stories.

RUNNERS VS. SMOKERS

Joseph Epstein

Joseph Epstein was born in Chicago and educated at the University of Chicago. He currently teaches at Northwestern University and edits the American Scholar, *the journal of the Phi Beta Kappa Society. He has been a senior editor of the* Encyclopaedia Britannica *and has published articles in many periodicals including* Harpers, Commentary, New York, New York Review of Books, *and* Atlantic Monthly. *Epstein has also written three books:* Divorced in America *(1974),* Familiar Territory *(1979), and* Ambition: The Secret Passion *(1981). "Runners vs. Smokers" originally appeared in the "Life and Letters" column of the* American Scholar *and was later included in* Familiar Territory. *In this essay Epstein focuses on smokers and runners, comparing their idiosyncrasies and inconsistencies.*

The smugness of runners, their vanity, may be inherent in the very activity of running itself. Runners chalk up achievement daily, or at least on each day that they run. They have had the body out for a tune-up, a cleaning, an overhaul, whereas the rest of us haven't. Their situation is akin to that of the woman whose car is just out of the car wash or the man who has just had a shoe shine. How grubby, at such moments, everyone else's cars and shoes look! A pity, really. One would think people would have enough self-respect not to let their personal possessions get so run down. A man named Joe Henderson, a consulting editor to *Runner's World,* remarks in that magazine about not missing his daily run in nearly four years: "That's what I'm proudest of: There's something in the way I run that keeps me eager and healthy." Implicit in that sentence is the thought, "And you, Pudge, your *not* running is doubtless what keeps you logy and sickly." Reading the writings of runners, listening to them talk, one is reminded of Proust describing Albertine on her first appearance at the beach at Balbec, leading her little band of friends who all had "that mastery over their limbs which comes from perfect bodily condition and a sincere contempt for the rest of humanity."

The contempt of joggers and runners for the rest of humanity is often quite sincere, but I am not sure that it is deserved. Apart from competitive long-distance runners, who tend to be a self-enclosed and solitary lot in a lonely and grueling sport, most joggers and runners are not, at least in my experience and observation, among the best athletes. This may have to do with the fact that running has never been rated very high by serious athletes, other than as a means to an end. Often it has been used by coaches and trainers as a salubrious punishment for such misdeeds as reporting in over-weight at the beginning of a season, missing a practice, fouling up in one way or another. Few athletes who have known the pleasure of sport at a fairly high level can content themselves with running as a source of satisfaction in and of itself. Serious athletes under-stand the need to be in shape, but in shape for something quite palpable: the game that they play. Joggers and runners are people who are content merely to be in shape for its own sake.

The pleasure of jogging and running is rather like that of wearing a fur coat in Texas in August: the true joy comes in being able to take the damn thing off. And because the runner or jogger regards running and jogging as its own end, an element of puritanical fanaticism easily insinuates itself. Thus a writer on the subject named Tom Osler, who does "not wish to be numbered with those who make claims of special life-extending benefits from it [running]," turns out to have run once for twenty-four hours straight, covering a distance of 114 miles (not, surely, everybody's idea of a day well spent). Thus *Runner's World* informs female readers that it is quite all right to run pregnant, right up to the day of delivery. There are people who are now beginning to run up mountains. Soon, doubtless, races will be held in which the contestants will wear lead in their shoes, or carry snow tires in their arms, or strap their accountants on their backs. If it feels good to remove a fur coat in Texas in August, how much better it will feel to remove a fur coat, leather leggings, and a tank helmet in Yucatan.

Committed joggers and runners would dispute all this. As for the argument that others use running as a means to an end while for them it is an end in itself, this they wouldn't concede at all. Running is not merely getting in shape per se; it is, many runners would reply, getting in shape for life. "Since I started running regularly, my outlook is better, my confidence greater, my self-regard higher"— such is the kind of testimonial one finds in the letters columns of the running magazines. Besides, what is the matter with getting in shape per se? Is not good health one of those things worth pursuing as an end in itself?

It is, up to a point. The point is when the concern with good health becomes unseemly—almost, one is tempted to say, unhealthy. The most cheering thing about good health is that it allows one not to think about one's health. Think too closely about it, dwell on it too long, and, lo, it will depart. Has there ever been a less robust crowd than the customers (and usually the clerks) in health food stores— with their sallow skins, dull eyes, bony carcasses, the human equivalent of horses ready to be shipped off to the glue factory? Joggers and runners, though they look rather better, are similarly preoccupied, even obsessed, with their bodies. "I eat bread sparingly," writes Tom Osler. "In the summer, I consume large quantities of fruit juices. . . . I do not use salt at the table or at the stove. I do not use sugar, because it seems to make my skin break out in acne." In an article titled "Running Through Pregnancy" in *Runner's World,* we learn that runners "have little trouble with irregularity. Some even experience a frequency increase in bowel movements." In the pages of the same magazine Joe Henderson reports that he thinks of a running high "as the way we're supposed to feel when not constipated." If one did not know what was being talked about— running—one might feel like an eavesdropper listening in on conversations in a nursing home for the elderly.

As it turns out, many joggers and runners do seem to require a 6 certain amount of nursing, and the precise benefits of jogging and running are very much in the flux of controversy. As nearly as I can make out, internists appear to think jogging/running quite a good thing for circulation, respiration, general metabolism. Orthopedists, bone and joint men, appear to deplore it, citing its potential for injury: shin splints, stone bruises, tendonitis of the knee or ankle, spinal troubles. All physicians agree that great care must be taken, especially if one is past forty years old, when too strenuous a running program can be dangerous. To die from a heart attack while jogging seems neither a glorious nor a philosophical death. The French used to speak of dying as "stumbling into eternity," which seems to me far preferable to running toward the same destination.

While runners come from a diversity of backgrounds, there is 7 much to unite them. An article in *The Runner* puts it thus: "The enemy lines are drawn. Divergent lifestyles foster a seesaw phenomenon. One side must be put down for the other to go up: smoker versus non-smoker, vegetarian versus meat-eater, runner versus non-runner." If ever two groups were opposed, surely these two groups are runners and smokers. Running is one of the few things that cannot be done while smoking, and smoking is one of the chief things runners despise. The same article in *The Runner* notes that "a lot of runners are extremely obnoxious about that [smoking].

They're pompous. They're rude. They go and take a cigarette out of someone's hand."

Yet why, pressed to a hasty generalization, do I tend to prefer   8
the company of smokers over that of runners? The most obvious reason is that smokers are not always talking about their smoking and their bad health in the way runners, when not on crutches, tend to talk about their running and good health. Smokers as a group tend therefore to be rather less boring than runners. But the reasons, I think, go deeper.

Although Robert Coles* has not yet written a book about them,   9
smokers are today something of a persecuted minority in the United States. A friend who works in a large corporation reports to me that at least one department head there refuses to hire smokers because other people in the department stridently complain about the smoke. States and municipalities have of late held referendums—and some have put laws upon the books—outlawing smoking in public places. We may one day be headed for a new Volstead Act** prohibiting smoking. Smokers meanwhile have come to take on the hesitant manners of the persecuted. "Do you mind if I smoke?" once the most perfunctory of questions, is perfunctory no longer. "Damn right I mind, buddy!" can come shooting back in response.

"The exquisite vice," as Oscar Wilde called smoking cigarettes,   10
has become the nasty habit. Where once the cigarette was an accoutrement of elegance—think of André Malraux, Humphrey Bogart, Franklin Delano Roosevelt, all of whom could almost be said to have worn cigarettes, and worn them very well—the cigarette has now become a mark of enslavement to a shameful practice. "God gave us tobacco to quiet our passions and soothe our grief," says a character in Balzac. But no longer. Nowadays it is said that around 80 percent of all smokers would like to be able to quit.

That roughly 100,000 of the 390,000 annual deaths owed to can-   11
cer can be linked to smoking, that smoking is a great stimulus to heart attack, that it reduces sexual appetite in men, that some 37,000,000 people will shorten their lives because of smoking—none of this would most smokers dispute. As I believed it as a smoker, so do they believe it. The fact is that smoking has nothing to do with belief, or with rationality. But quitting smoking is one of the world's great small nuisances—"Quitting smoking is easy," said Mark

---

*EDS. NOTE—American sociologist who specializes in the study of minorities.

**EDS. NOTE—The constitutional amendment that prohibited the sale of alcoholic beverages.

Twain, a cigar smoker, "I have done it a thousand times"—so difficult in its way that comparing nicotine addiction with that of alcohol and heroin, while farfetched, is not altogether crazy. Having finally succeeded in stopping smoking after many abortive attempts, I now find that I have exchanged one habit for another, and spend half my waking hours with a hard candy or lozenge in my mouth. I may be one of the first men in history to die of tooth decay.

Yet smoking, and struggling to quit smoking, does give one a [12] keen sense of human imperfectibility. My attempts to quit smoking—so small and mean a thing, as I keep telling myself, to ask of so large and generous an intelligence—long ago killed off the last remaining vestiges of utopianism in me. I do not mean to imply that smoking makes anyone more intelligent. Given all that is known about smoking, it is a supremely unintelligent thing to do. Toward the end of my struggle I found myself smoking less and despising myself more. But this most pertinacious and exasperating habit teaches a healthy regard for human limitation.

Runners, on the other hand, are full of thoughts of human possibility. If one runs seven miles in the spring, perhaps by autumn [13] one can do ten miles. The pages of the running magazines revel in the mention of runners in their seventies and eighties. I have read about a new magazine calling itself *Nutrition Health Review,* which (according to an ad in the magazine *Mother Jones*) asks, "Can You Live to Be 100?" The question is rhetorical, and the answer is that, watching what you eat and imbibe, you can indeed. But why stop at 100? Why not 120, or 150, or 200?

"What!" Frederick the Great is supposed to have said to a general [14] who informed him of his troops' refusal to go into battle, "Do they expect to live forever?" Runners, like all truly self-absorbed perfectibilitarians, do seem to expect to live forever. Perhaps they do not expect to run forever—only up to the age of (say) ninety, at which point many could be got to agree to taper off. "I grow old . . . I grow old . . . / I shall wear the bottoms of my trousers rolled," says J. Alfred Prufrock. But were he a runner, he would doubtless add: "But, look, above my rolled-up trousers I wear the two-toned singlet of tricot from Sport International, which prevents chafing and whose mesh bottom prevents it from clinging, thus helping me keep dry. While below I wear the Wildcat running shoe, from Autry Industries, Inc., whose thick heel and ankle padding helps protect my Achilles tendons." Our new Prufrock shall no longer walk but now run upon the beach / no longer hear the mermaids singing, each to each / but only the pounding of blood in his ears / drowning out thoughts of death and other legitimate fears.

COMPREHENSION

1. Why are runners smug?

2. Why does Epstein feel that the contempt runners feel for the rest of society is undeserved?

3. What does Epstein mean when he says that runners use running not as a means to an end but as an end in itself?

4. Why does Epstein prefer the company of smokers to that of runners?

5. In what way do runners view life differently from smokers?

PURPOSE AND AUDIENCE

1. What is the thesis of this essay? Is it stated or implied? Why do you think the author decided to present the thesis as he did?

2. What is Epstein's purpose in writing this essay?

3. At what audience is this essay aimed? What changes might Epstein make if he were addressing an audience of smokers or an audience of runners?

STYLE AND STRUCTURE

1. What organizational pattern does this comparison-and-contrast essay follow? Why does Epstein use the pattern he does?

2. How effective is the simile comparing running to wearing a fur coat in Texas? What is Epstein trying to convey to his readers? Can you think of a more effective simile?

3. Epstein uses quotations from *Runner's World* and *The Runner*. What does he accomplish with these quotations?

4. How does Epstein make the transition between his discussions of running and smoking? Underline the sentence that links these sections.

5. Does Epstein present his subject with a serious or light tone? Explain.

WRITING WORKSHOP

1. Assume you are a runner, and write a comparison-and-contrast essay that is favorable to runners and unfavorable to smokers.

2. Write an essay in which you compare any two groups that have divergent life-styles: parents vs. children, readers vs. nonreaders, vegetarians vs. meat-eaters, drinkers vs. nondrinkers, singles vs. marrieds, and so on.

READING THE RIVER

Mark Twain

*Mark Twain (1835–1910), the pseudonym for Samuel L. Clemens,
was born in Florida, Missouri, and raised in the river town of Han-
nibal, Missouri. He left school at the age of twelve and traveled
extensively throughout the west, working as a riverboat pilot, a printer,
and a newspaper reporter. When the Civil War broke out, Twain
joined a volunteer company in the Confederate army but left after
one week to become a prospector. After the war, he began a career
as a humorist and writer, achieving great success as a lecturer.
Among his most popular works are* The Adventures of Tom Sawyer
(1876), Life on the Mississippi *(1883), and* The Adventures of
Huckleberry Finn *(1885). "Reading the River" is from* Life on the
Mississippi. *In this essay Twain illustrates one conflict he felt when
making the transition from inexperienced passenger to experienced
steamboat pilot.*

. . . The face of the water, in time, became a wonderful book—a 1
book that was a dead language to the uneducated passenger but
which told its mind to me without reserve, delivering its most cherished secrets as clearly as if it uttered them with a voice. And it
was not a book to be read once and thrown aside, for it had a new
story to tell every day. Throughout the long twelve hundred miles
there was never a page that was void of interest, never one that
you could leave unread without loss, never one that you would want
to skip, thinking you could find higher enjoyment in some other
thing. There never was so wonderful a book written by man, never
one whose interest was so absorbing, so unflagging, so sparklingly
renewed with every reperusal. The passenger who could not read it
was charmed with a peculiar sort of faint dimple on its surface (on
the rare occasions when he did not overlook it altogether) but to
the pilot that was an *italicized* passage; indeed it was more than
that, it was a legend of the largest capitals with a string of shouting
exclamation-points at the end of it, for it meant that a wreck or a
rock was buried there that could tear the life out of the strongest
vessel that ever floated. It is the faintest and simplest expression
the water ever makes, and the most hideous to a pilot's eye. In truth,
the passenger who could not read this book saw nothing but all
manner of pretty pictures in it, painted by the sun and shaded by

the clouds, whereas to the trained eye these were not pictures at all, but the grimmest and most dead-earnest of reading matter.

Now when I had mastered the language of this water, and had come to know every trifling feature that bordered the great river as familiarly as I knew the letters of the alphabet, I had made a valuable acquisition. But I had lost something, too. I had lost something which could never be restored to me while I lived. All the grace, the beauty, the poetry, had gone out of the majestic river! I still kept in mind a certain wonderful sunset which I witnessed when steamboating was new to me. A broad expanse of the river was turned to blood; in the middle distance the red hue brightened into gold, through which a solitary log came floating, black and conspicuous; in one place a long, slanting mark lay sparkling upon the water; in another the surface was broken by boiling, tumbling rings, that were as many-tinted as an opal; where the ruddy flush was faintest, was a smooth spot that was covered with graceful circles and radiating lines, ever so delicately traced; the shore on our left was densely wooded, and the somber shadow that fell from this forest was broken in one place by a long, ruffled trail that shone like silver; and high above the forest wall a clean-stemmed dead tree waved a single leafy bough that glowed like a flame in the unobstructed splendor that was flowing from the sun. There were graceful curves, reflected images, woody heights, soft distances; and over the whole scene, far and near, the dissolving lights drifted steadily, enriching it every passing moment with new marvels of coloring.

I stood like one bewitched. I drank it in, in a speechless rapture. The world was new to me, and I had never seen anything like this at home. But as I have said, a day came when I began to cease from noting the glories and the charms which the moon and the sun and the twilight wrought upon the river's face; another day came when I ceased altogether to note them. Then, if that sunset scene had been repeated, I should have looked upon it without rapture, and should have commented upon it, inwardly, after this fashion: "This sun means that we are going to have wind to-morrow; that floating log means that the river is rising, small thanks to it; that slanting mark on the water refers to a bluff reef which is going to kill somebody's steamboat one of these nights, if it keeps on stretching out like that; those tumbling 'boils' show a dissolving bar and a changing channel there; the lines and circles in the slick water over yonder are a warning that that troublesome place is shoaling up dangerously; that silver streak in the shadow of the forest is the 'break' from a new snag, and he has located himself in the very best place he could have found to fish for steamboats; that tall dead tree, with a single living branch, is not going to last long, and then how is a body ever going to get through this blind place at night without the friendly old landmark?"

No, the romance and beauty were all gone from the river. All the value any feature of it had for me now was the amount of usefulness it could furnish toward compassing the safe piloting of a steamboat. Since those days, I have pitied doctors from my heart. What does the lovely flush in a beauty's cheek mean to a doctor but a "break" that ripples above some deadly disease? Are not all her visible charms sown thick with what are to him the signs and symbols of hidden decay? Does he ever see her beauty at all, or doesn't he simply view her professionally and comment upon her unwholesome condition all to himself? And doesn't he sometimes wonder whether he has gained most or lost most by learning his trade? 4

COMPREHENSION

1. How is the Mississippi River like a book?

2. When the passenger sees a dimple in the water's surface, what does the pilot see?

3. What did Twain gain as he became a skilled pilot? What did he lose?

4. Why does Twain say, in his conclusion, that he feels sorry for doctors? What do doctors and steamboat pilots have in common?

PURPOSE AND AUDIENCE

1. What is Twain's thesis? State it in your own words.

2. Twain knows his audience is made up of passengers, not pilots. How does he make sure his readers understand the pilot's viewpoint?

3. Is Twain's purpose in describing the Mississippi to inform, to entertain, or to persuade? Explain.

STYLE AND STRUCTURE

1. How does Twain organize his comparison and contrast? Why do you think he made the choice he did?

2. In what order does Twain arrange his points of comparison? Why does he use this order?

3. In his first sentence, Twain compares the Mississippi River to a book. Trace this comparison and variations of it (that is, other references to language, punctuation, or reading) throughout the essay. Is the comparison between river and book an effective one? Explain.

4. Underline the transitional words and phrases that Twain uses in his essay. How do they highlight the arrangement of details in the essay?

WRITING WORKSHOP

1. Write a comparison-and-contrast essay in which you show how increased knowledge of an academic subject has either increased or decreased your enthusiasm for it.

2. Think of a relative or friend you knew when you were a child. Consider how your opinion of this person has changed and how it has stayed the same.

3. Find two magazine articles or newspaper stories on the same subject. Write an essay in which you point out and account for the differences in the two treatments of the subject.

8

Classification
and Division

WHAT IS CLASSIFICATION AND DIVISION?

One way we bring order to a confusing world is by sorting the things around us into categories according to the kind of things they are. On the simplest level this involves putting some kinds of things together in one place, like clothes in a particular closet, and other kinds of things elsewhere, like books in the bookcase and pots and pans in the kitchen cabinet. On a more abstract level, we pigeonhole people: he's a preppie, she's a jock, Senator Bafflegab is a liberal, Congressman Whiplash is a conservative. These are everyday examples of a way of thinking that relies on two related processes: classification and division.

Classification gets its name from the word *class,* which means a group of things that all have one or more characteristics in common—important to the things themselves, and also to your purpose in classifying. For example, *2001: A Space Odyssey, Star Wars,* and *E.T.* are all movies, all with science-fiction plots, so they can all be thought of as belonging to the class of *science-fiction movies. Science-fiction movies,* in turn, belong to a higher class, *movies,* that also includes other kinds of films: comedies, spy movies, musicals, horror movies, and so on. The higher the level to which you take your classification, the more members the class will have, but the less they will have specifically in common; a 1933 documentary on the Great Depression is a movie no less than Ingmar Bergman's symbolic drama *The Seventh Seal,* but you can say little about the content of one that will be true of the other.

Most things have several different attributes, and so they can be classified in any of several different ways. Let's take as an example a college student named Lisa. Because she is in her first year at State College, she can be classified as a freshman. But she also belongs to other classes: women, Californians, Orientals, aspiring economists, brunettes, amateur guitarists, and so on. Which class you assign her to depends on what you are thinking or writing about. Of course, if you are writing about juniors, men, Michiganders, Greeks, mathematicians-to-be, redheads, or championship figure skaters, she does not belong.

Division is essentially the opposite of classification. You start with a class and then divide it into lower classes, called subclasses, or into its individual members. For example, you might start with the class *college students* and divide it into the subclasses *undergraduates, graduate students, extension students,* and so forth. And if you needed to, you could divide these subclasses still further— say, *undergraduates* into *freshmen, sophomores, juniors,* and *seniors.* Again, there are other ways you can divide *undergraduates:* by race and culture, by majors, by sex, by home state or country, or by college attended. Which principle of division you use depends on your purpose.

There are three rules for proper division. First, all of the subclasses should result from the same principle of division. If you are dividing *undergraduates* into *freshmen, sophomores,* and the like, you cannot include the subclass *scholarship students,* for this subclass results from one principle of division—financial aid received— while the others result from another principle, amount of academic credit earned. Second, all of the subclasses should be on the same level. In the series *undergraduates, graduate students, extension students,* and *sophomores,* the last of these, *sophomores,* does not belong because it is on a lower level—that is, it is a subclass of *undergraduates.* Third, the subclasses should account for all the members of the class they belong to, with no omissions or repetitions. The series *freshmen, sophomores, juniors,* and *students on probation* is incomplete because it omits *seniors* and repetitive because *students on probation* may include some freshmen, sophomores, and juniors.

Classification and division are often used together. A writer may begin with a large class, like *programs to develop alternative energy sources.* He or she may then divide it into major subclasses, such as *solar energy programs, synthetic fuel development programs,* and so on. Finally, perhaps after doing some research, he or she will classify various programs by assigning each of them to one of the subclasses.

Uses of Classification and Division

Certain kinds of topics and questions require you to use classification, division, or both, based on the way they are worded. Suppose you are asked "What kinds of policies can be used to direct and control the national economy?" Here the word *kinds* suggests division. (Other words, such as *types,* can also serve as clues). You should begin with the class of *policies that affect nations' economies* and divide it into subclasses: *fiscal policies, monetary policies,* and so on. Then you would subdivide these again, until you reached a level of division that you thought was appropriate and manageable. Other topics can become more manageable through classification and division. Suppose you were planning a paper on Mark Twain's nonfiction prose for your English course. You might first divide the large class, *Twain's nonfiction prose,* into major subclasses—his travel books, essays, autobiographical writings, and letters. Next you would classify the individual works—that is, assign the works you plan to discuss to these subclasses, which you could then discuss one at a time.

This last example suggests another use for classification and division. By assigning Twain's nonfiction prose works to four large subclasses, you have made the best possible arrangement for comparing and contrasting similar works. In effect, you have used one pattern not only to organize your writing but also to enable you to use another, different pattern effectively. And, after dividing Twain's nonfiction prose into four subclasses, you might decide that one of those subclasses, such as *Twain's travel writings,* is large and rich enough to be worth a paper on its own. So division can be an excellent way to narrow a writing topic.

Classification and division are also useful after you have generated ideas for your writing by brainstorming. When you brainstorm, as chapter 1 explains, you first consider your larger topic, listing all the related points you can think of. Next, you *divide* your topic into logical categories and *classify* the items on your list into one category or another, perhaps narrowing, expanding, or eliminating some categories—or some points—as you go along. This picking and choosing, sorting and grouping reduces your material until it is manageable and eventually suggests your thesis and the main points of your essay.

STRUCTURING A CLASSIFICATION-AND-DIVISION ESSAY

Once you decide to use classification or division as your pattern of development, you need to plan your essay. If your topic consists of many individual items that you want to group, your main task will be to classify. If your topic consists of a large class that you want to partition, your main task will be to divide. Often you will use both processes to be certain that your analysis is complete. Regardless of your initial vantage point, your result will be the same—a system that categorizes the members of a group.

This system must be logical and consistent. Just as a clear basis of comparison determines the points in a comparison-and-contrast essay, so a principle of classification determines the system you use to categorize items in classification or division. Because every group of people, things, or ideas can be divided in many ways, your purpose in classifying determines which principle you use. When you are in line at the bookstore with only twenty dollars, the cost of different books may be your only principle of selection. As you carry your books across campus, however, weight may matter more. Finally, as you study and read, the quality of your books should be paramount. Similarly, when you organize an essay, your principle of classification is determined by your writing situation—your assignment, your purpose, your audience, and your special knowledge and interests.

When you set out to classify information, you must first decide what principle you are going to use—what quality you regard your items as having in common. Then, you should group the individual items together and assign them a collective name. For instance, in planning an essay on the relative merits of different modes of transportation, you might compile the following list:

    foot power
    bicycles
    roller skates
    skateboards
    cars
    buses
    subways
    trolleys
    trains
    airplanes
    motorcycles
    mopeds
    ocean liners

Looking over the list, you notice that some modes of transportation can be used whenever you like, while others are "public"—they have their own schedules and destinations and you have to accommodate your plans to them. Each of these two categories is a class, and you can assign each mode of transportation to one class or the other:

Class 1	*Class 2*
foot power	buses
bicycles	subways
roller skates	trolleys
skateboards	trains
cars	airplanes
motorcycles	ocean liners
mopeds	

At some point, you give each category a name; here, category 1 becomes "private transportation," and category 2 becomes "public transportation." Now you are ready to explain what distinguishes the two types of transportation or to argue in favor of one rather than the other in your essay.

You could also have approached the same writing assignment in the opposite direction, by division. If you want to write about the advantages and disadvantages of different types of transportation, you might begin by considering which categories you want to focus on. Do you want to contrast foot power and machine power? Cheap wheels and expensive ones? Land, sea, and air transport? Public and private transportation? Each of these represents a different principle of division, and each principle will generate a different thesis and a different essay. Once you select the principle you want to use to structure your essay, you can start to list different kinds of transportation and assign each to the categories that have emerged from your division. If you happened to choose "public and private transportation," you might well generate the same list above.

Once you define your principle, apply it to your topic, and by classification or division derive your categories, you should plan their discussion in your essay. Just as a comparison-and-contrast essay makes comparable points about its subjects, so your classification essay should treat all categories similarly. When you discuss comparable points for each, you ensure that your reader sees your distinctions among categories and understands your definition of each category.

Finally, arrange your categories in some logical order, preferably so that one leads to the next and the least important yields to the most important. Such an order ensures that your reader sees how the categories relate and how significant each is. Whatever this order, it should correspond with your unifying idea or support your thesis since that establishes the relative value of your categories.

Like other essays, the classification-and-division essay does not necessarily have to have a thesis. It must, however, have a unifying idea, usually an enumeration of the categories into which your subject is divided or classified. But in most academic writing, your essay needs a thesis if it is to communicate more than simple information, if it is to convince your readers that your categories are significant and that their relationships to each other and to the whole subject are logical. Listing different kinds of investments, for instance, would be pointless if you did not evaluate the strengths and weaknesses of each and then make recommendations based on your assessment. Similarly, your term paper about Twain's nonfiction would accomplish nothing if it merely classified his writings. Instead, your arrangement should communicate your view of these works to your reader, perhaps demonstrating that some types of Twain's nonfiction deserve higher public regard.

Once your thesis or unifying idea is formulated and you have established your subclasses, you should plan your classification or division papers around the same three major sections that other essays have: introduction, body, and conclusion. Your introduction should orient the reader by mentioning your topic, the principle by which your material is divided and classified, and the individual subclasses you plan to discuss. If your paper has a thesis, it, too, should be stated in the introduction. Once your readers have this information, they can easily follow your paper as it develops. In the subsequent body paragraphs, you should treat the categories one by one in the order in which your introduction presents them. Finally, your conclusion should restate your thesis, summing up the points you have made.

Classification

Let's suppose that you are preparing that term paper on Mark Twain's nonfiction works for an American literature course. You have read *Roughing It, Life on the Mississippi,* and *The Innocents Abroad.* Besides these books derived from his experiences, you have read his autobiography. This, in turn, led you to some of his correspondence and essays. You realize that the works you have studied can easily be classified as four different types of Twain's nonfiction: travel books, essays, letters, and autobiography. Your categories make sense to you as a way to organize your paper, but you know that you also need a strong thesis statement so that your paper does more than just list his nonfiction works. You decide that you want to persuade the reader to reconsider the reputations of some of these works, and you formulate this thesis: "Although the popular travel books are the best known of Mark Twain's nonfiction works, his essays, his letters, and particularly his autobiography deserve equal attention." You might diagram your classification like this:

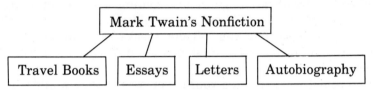

Then you might expand this classification diagram into an outline:

I. Introduction—thesis: Although the popular travel books are the best known of Mark Twain's nonfiction works, his essays, his letters, and particularly his autobiography deserve equal attention.
II. Travel books
   A. *Roughing It*
   B. *The Innocents Abroad*
   C. *Life on the Mississippi*
III. Essays
   A. "Fenimore Cooper's Literary Offenses"
   B. "How To Tell A Story"
   C. "The Awful German Language"
IV. Letters
   A. To W. D. Howells
   B. To his family
V. Autobiography
VI. Conclusion, including restatement of thesis

Since this will be a long term paper, each of the outline's divisions or subdivisions would require several paragraphs.

Once your term paper is finished, you are confident that it will be clear and persuasive despite its length because you have carefully considered each of the characteristics of an effective classification. First of all, you applied only *one* principle of classification when you grouped Twain's nonfiction works according to literary genre. Of course, you selected this system rather than another—for example, theme, subject matter, stage in his career, or contemporary critical reception—because it suited your purpose. In fact, if you had written your term paper for a political science course, you might even have examined Twain as a social critic by classifying his works according to the amount or kind of political commentary in each. Your system, however, was most appropriate for your writing situation.

Given the group of works you classified, your system was logical. If you had divided Twain's works into novels, essays, short stories, letters, and political works, for instance, you would have mixed two principles of classification, genre and content. As a result, a highly political novel like *The Gilded Age* would have fit more than one category. Likewise, had you left out essays as a subclass, for instance, you could not have classified several significant works of nonfiction.

In addition, you arranged your subclasses so they would support your thesis. Since you challenged the dominance of Twain's travel books, you discussed them briefly early in your paper. Similarly, the autobiography made your best case for the merit of the other nonfiction works and thus was most effective placed last. Of course, you could have arranged your categories in several other orders, such as shorter to longer works or least to most popular, depending on the details of your argument.

Finally, you are certain that you have treated your categories comparably. In fact, you verified this by underlining each point in your rough draft and cross-checking the order of points from category to category. You knew your case would be weakened if you inadvertently skipped style in your discussion of Twain's letters after you had included it for every other category. This omission might lead your readers to suspect either that you could not discuss this point because you had not done enough research on the letters or that you had ignored the point because the style of his letters did not measure up somehow. Your careful organization, however, prevented such questions by your reader.

Division

When you plan a paper such as the essay on Mark Twain's works, your main task is classification. For other topics, however, your main task is division. Suppose you are planning a paper on investments for your finance course. You want to discuss different kinds of investments, so you plan to use division—the process of breaking a class into categories—to analyze your topic. Based on your preliminary research, you decide to concentrate on the categories of investments usually considered by a new investor with a moderate income, namely stocks, bonds, real estate, and mutual funds:

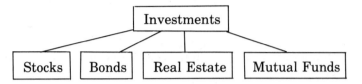

Based on this division, you formulate your thesis: "Carefully selected stocks, bonds, and real estate are all sound investments, but the beginner would be best advised to invest in mutual funds."

You realize that the body of your essay should devote a paragraph or two to each category in turn, explaining the same aspects of each kind of investment so that their relative merits are clear. If you consider stability, ease of liquidation, and potential for long-term growth for stocks, you know you should consider the same points—and no others—for bonds, real estate, and mutual funds. If you change considerations, your treatment will be unbalanced, and your readers will be confused.

If you were assigned a long paper, you might want to treat each type of investment in further detail by dividing it into smaller subclasses. In this way, you could distinguish between common and preferred stocks, municipal and corporate bonds, commercial and residential real estate, and stock and money-market mutual funds. For a short paper, however, such subdivision would not be practical. You would have only enough space to concentrate on more general distinctions between broader categories or to limit your topic to one subdivision. You might outline such a short paper on investments like this:

¶1   Introduction—thesis: Carefully selected stocks, bonds, and real estate are all sound investments, but the beginner would be best advised to invest in mutual funds.

¶2   First category: Advantages and disadvantages of stocks.

¶3   Second category: Advantages and disadvantages of bonds.

¶4   Third category: Advantages and disadvantages of real estate.

¶5   Fourth category: Advantages and disadvantages of mutual funds, emphasizing advantages.

¶6   Conclusion, including restatement of thesis.

The following student essay, written by Linda Mauro for an exam in her American government course, is structured according to the pattern of division. This essay divides a whole, the powers of the federal government, into its parts, using a principle of division taken from the Constitution.

Question: By enumerating the duties of each of the three branches of the federal government, explain the constitutional theory of separation of powers.

SEPARATION OF POWERS: HOW IT WORKS

Introduction and unifying idea
The United States Constitution divided the federal government into three branches and established a system of separation of powers so that no one branch would be too powerful. Under this system, each of the branches—legislative, executive, and judicial—has a separate function, and each acts to check and balance the workings of the others.

1

Branch 1:
The legislative branch of government includes the two houses of Congress, the Senate and the House of Representatives. The Senate has the power to remove officials from office by impeachment. Either house of Congress may introduce bills, which must be passed by both houses and approved by the president before they become law. (Bills which involve raising revenue must originate in the House.) Congress has many other powers specified by the Constitution, among them the powers to collect taxes, establish post offices, grant patents and copyrights, borrow money, regulate commerce with other

2

countries, coin money and punish coun-
terfeiting, establish naturalization
laws, raise and fund armed forces, and
declare war.

Branch 2:   The executive power of government is   3
vested in the president. The president
serves as commander in chief of the
armed forces. He has the power to make
treaties with foreign nations and to
appoint ambassadors, Supreme Court jus-
tices, cabinet members, and other officials, subject to the approval of Congress. He can also fill vacancies that
may occur in Congress due to deaths or
resignations. The Constitution also
specifies that the president give regular state-of-the-union messages. Finally, as the nation's chief executive
officer, the president serves many
ceremonial functions, receiving and
visiting heads of state and other foreign dignitaries.

Branch 3:   The most important part of the judi-   4
cial branch of government is the Su-
preme Court. The judicial branch, which
also includes the United States Superior Court and, in fact, the entire
federal court system, is empowered to
rule on all laws of the federal government. Specific examples might be suits
in which the United States is a party,
cases involving ambassadors, disputes
between two states, and cases of treason.

Conclusion   Later constitutional amendments and   5
court decisions have redefined and
reinterpreted the powers of all three
branches of government, but the principle of separation of powers remains.

Points for Special Attention

Organization.   The question itself, which asked students to explain the whole by reviewing its parts, made division the logical organizational pattern. Each of the three paragraphs in the body of the essay relates the functions of one branch of government. Linda does not feel that any one branch is more significant or powerful than any other; in fact, their relative equality is the point of the system. Therefore her body paragraphs do not follow an order of increasing importance. But they are not randomly arranged either, as their sequence reflects the cycle by which bills are passed by Congress, signed into law by the president, and reviewed by the Supreme Court. The exam question did not require such planning, but Linda evidently saw an opportunity and used it.

Parallel Treatment of Categories.   Since the three branches of government have different responsibilities, Linda could not treat identical points for each. She could not, for instance, note the influence each branch has on the armed forces or on impeachment proceedings because these items simply do not apply to all branches. She did, however, follow her principle of classification and provide comparable information—their constitutional duties—for each.

Transition Between Categories.   In each body paragraph, Linda clearly announces every new branch of government in the first sentence. Because of these topic sentences, a reader knows which branch of government will be considered in the paragraph. These sentences serve as transitions, marking the shifts from category to category. A longer essay or a less familiar classification system might require additional transitions to show the relationships among parts or between a part and the whole. Words such as *first, next, then, finally, like, unlike,* and *besides,* as well as comparatives (*more, less*) and superlatives (*most, least*), can reveal these connections.

Answering an Exam Question. As was mentioned in chapter 1, an important part of writing an essay is making sure you understand the assignment. This exam question does *not* ask the student to evaluate the system or to compare it to any other; it simply asks for an explanation. Since Linda knew that the system depends on three components—the legislative, executive, and judicial branches of government—she immediately decided to use division to structure her essay. Since the question asks for an enumeration, not an evaluation or interpretation, she did not waste time volunteering unnecessary opinions.

This more technical student paper, written by Patrick Knight for an advanced pharmacology course, uses a complex classification-and-division structure. He first divides depression into three categories in order to assess different kinds of drug therapy. He also classifies the drugs used to treat depression. Both sections provide essential information and prepare the reader to understand and accept the essay's implied thesis. Both advance the paper's purpose, warning consumers against a certain type of drug and advising that only patients suffering from certain kinds of depression use it.

TREATMENT OF DEPRESSION: A NOTE
OF CAUTION TO THE CONSUMER

Introduction   Depression is a well-recognized prob-   1
lem in American society, and most per-
sons will admit to having felt depressed at one time or another. In the
overwhelming majority of instances,
such a feeling is not indicative of any
serious disorder. Problems arise, however, when the depression becomes so
severe or prolonged as to produce a noticeable change in a person's life-
style and behavior.

Division by type of depression
Type 1   Three very general categories of   2
depression have been identified. First,
exogenous depressions are those in
which an individual reacts inordinately
to some precipitating situation, such

as the death of a loved one or a major
business failure. Exaggerated reactions, usually occurring in persons with
neurotic tendencies, may be prolonged
Type 2 and incapacitating. Next, some persons
seem to have been depressed all of their
lives, and their self—esteem is chroni-
cally rock bottom. As these individuals
find little joy in social interaction,
they generally avoid contact with other
people. Such depression is most often
seen in alcoholics, narcotic addicts,
and persons with sociopathic behavior
Type 3 patterns. In the last group, depressive
symptoms have a definite onset, but an
external precipitating factor cannot be
identified. This endogenous depression,
which occurs more frequently in the elderly, is characterized by marked apa-
thy, lack of energy, feelings of guilt
and worthlessness, early—morning awak-
ening, and decreased appetite. Each type
of depression may, under certain conditions, warrant the use of antidepressant
drugs.

Division by Drugs available for the treatment of   3
type of drug depression fall into two major cate-
Type 1 gories. The first is the tricyclic an-
tidepressants. While several drugs are
included in this category (common trade
names include Tofranil, Norpramin, Per-
tofrane, Elavil, Aventyl, Vivactil, and
Sinequan), there are no major differences in effectiveness. Side effects

are generally not severe and may include drowsiness, dryness of the mouth,
and excessive sweating.

Type 2   The other major class of antidepres-   4
sants is the monoamine oxidase inhibi-
tors (abbreviated MAO inhibitors). Two
of these drugs, isocarboxazid (Marplan)
and phenelzine (Nardil), are chemically
related. The other one, tranylcypromine
(Parnate), is chemically distinct.
These drugs are less consistently effective and more potentially toxic than
the tricyclics. Some of the side effects of the MAO inhibitors include
agitation, hallucinations, a severe
hepatitislike reaction, and high blood
pressure.

The blood-pressure-elevating effect   5
is probably the basis for considerable
sentiment against the MAO inhibitors,
and rightfully so. These drugs may in-
teract with many of the ingredients in
nonprescription cold products to produce a dangerous elevation of blood
pressure. Additionally, the depressed
person should not take an MAO inhibitor
simultaneously with a tricyclic. Mania
and convulsions may result if these two
drugs are combined.

One of the greatest dangers associ-   6
ated with the MAO inhibitors revolves
around the effects of certain foods.
Common food products—especially aged
cheeses but also sour cream, chianti,

sherry, beer, pickled herring, chocolate, yeast, broad beans, canned figs, raisins, chicken livers, and meat prepared with tenderizers—contain a chemical (tyramine) which may react with the MAO inhibitor to produce a severe attack of high blood pressure usually accompanied by a splitting headache and, possibly, confusion. Brain hemorrhage has even been reported in some cases, but usually these individuals already had some previous defect in the blood vessels of the brain.

While all of the MAO inhibitors 7 should be used with caution because of their potential to produce dangerous rises in blood pressure in association with certain foods, tranylcypromine has most frequently been implicated in these reactions. Indeed, the potential hazard of this drug can be great, especially if the user is not hospitalized and cannot therefore be closely watched by skilled medical personnel. In 1964 the safety of tranylcypromine was so severely questioned that it was removed from the market by the Food and Drug Administration. Now the drug has returned, with the warning that its use should be limited to hospitalized or closely supervised patients who have not responded to other antidepressant therapy.

Conclusion   If you do not fall into one of the   8
categories stated above and your physi-
cian has prescribed tranylcypromine
(Parnate), it would be best to discuss
with him or her your concern about this
drug. If your physician is unaware of
the potential dangers of tranylcypromine, ask him or her to consult with
your pharmacist. This professional will
be able to provide complete information
about the effects of tranylcypromine
taken with certain foods and medica-
tions.

Points for Special Attention

Parallel Treatment of Categories.   This essay discusses kinds
of depression and kinds of drugs used to treat depression. Each
category is clearly described and mutually exclusive; no category of
depression or of drug is omitted. Each is also treated equally. Each
kind of depression, for example, is described in terms of its causes,
its symptoms, and the kinds of people likely to suffer from it; each
discussion includes all these points and no others. Similarly, both
kinds of drugs are considered only in terms of the chemical similarities among the drugs in each category and the side effects associated with each group.

Structure.   Patrick Knight's essay illustrates how useful the
classification-and-division pattern can be as part of an essay. His
essay's structure may be outlined like this:

¶1   Introduction
¶2   Categories of depression
¶3   First type of drug used to treat depression (tricyclic anti-
       depressants)
¶4   Second type of drug used to treat depression (MAO inhibi-
       tors)
¶5   Side effects of MAO inhibitors in general
¶6   Side effects of MAO inhibitors in combination with certain
       foods

Purpose and Audience.   Although most of Patrick's paper concentrates on the negative side effects of the MAO inhibitors, both of the classifications that introduce the essay have important functions. The essay's purpose is to warn certain categories of people about certain kinds of drugs. Ultimately, the paper focuses on one subclass of MAO inhibitor, tranylcypromine. Here, classification is the means by which Patrick narrows his subject from depression, to treatment of depression, to treatment of depression with any of the MAO inhibitors, and finally to treatment of depression with tranylcypromine.

Patrick's thesis, that MAO inhibitors can be dangerous, is not explicitly stated until the last paragraph, but he communicates throughout his paper the warning that although severe depression can be treated with drugs, MAO inhibitors should be used with caution because of their potentially dangerous side effects.

Each of the essays that follow uses classification and/or division as its pattern of development. In some cases, the pattern is used to explain ideas; in others, it is used to persuade the reader of something.

FRIENDS, GOOD FRIENDS—
AND SUCH GOOD FRIENDS

Judith Viorst

Judith Viorst was born in Newark, New Jersey, and now lives in Washington, D.C. Poet, journalist, and award-winning author of children's books, she is also a contributing editor of Redbook *magazine, for which she writes a regular column. Her 1968 book of light verse,* It's Hard to Be Hip over Thirty and Other Tragedies of Married Life, *was a best-seller and brought her a large audience. This essay, which was originally a* Redbook *column, is an informal but thoughtful attempt to gain and share a deeper understanding of the purposes different friends serve in our lives.*

Women are friends, I once would have said, when they totally   1
love and support and trust each other, and bare to each other the
secrets of their souls, and run—no questions asked—to help each
other, and tell harsh truths to each other (no, you can't wear that
dress unless you lose ten pounds first) when harsh truths must be
told.

Women are friends, I once would have said, when they share the   2
same affection for Ingmar Bergman, plus train rides, cats, warm
rain, charades, Camus, and hate with equal ardor Newark and
Brussels sprouts and Lawrence Welk and camping.

In other words, I once would have said that a friend is a friend   3
all the way, but now I believe that's a narrow point of view. For the
friendships I have and the friendships I see are conducted at many
levels of intensity, serve many different functions, meet different
needs and range from those as all-the-way as the friendship of the
soul sisters mentioned above to that of the most nonchalant and
casual playmates.

Consider these varieties of friendship: 4

1. Convenience friends. These are the women with whom, if our   5
paths weren't crossing all the time, we'd have no particular reason
to be friends: a next-door neighbor, a woman in our car pool, the
mother of one of our children's closest friends or maybe some mommy
with whom we serve juice and cookies each week at the Glenwood
Co-op Nursery.

Convenience friends are convenient indeed. They'll lend us their   6
cups and silverware for a party. They'll drive our kids to soccer

when we're sick. They'll take us to pick up our car when we need a lift to the garage. They'll even take our cats when we go on vacation. As we will for them.

But we don't, with convenience friends, ever come too close or 7
tell too much; we maintain our public face and emotional distance. "Which means," says Elaine, "that I'll talk about being overweight but not about being depressed. Which means I'll admit being mad but not blind with rage. Which means that I might say that we're pinched this month but never that I'm worried sick over money."

But which doesn't mean that there isn't sufficient value to be 8
found in these friendships of mutual aid, in convenience friends.

2. Special-interest friends. These friendships aren't intimate, and 9
they needn't involve kids or silverware or cats. Their value lies in some interest jointly shared. And so we may have an office friend or a yoga friend or a tennis friend or a friend from the Women's Democratic Club.

"I've got one woman friend," says Joyce, "who likes, as I do, to 10
take psychology courses. Which makes it nice for me—and nice for her. It's fun to go with someone you know and it's fun to discuss what you've learned, driving back from the classes." And for the most part, she says, that's all they discuss.

"I'd say that what we're doing is *doing* together, not being to- 11
gether," Suzanne says of her Tuesday-doubles friends. "It's mainly a tennis relationship, but we play together well. And I guess we all need to have a couple of playmates."

I agree. 12

My playmate is a shopping friend, a woman of marvelous taste, 13
a woman who knows exactly *where* to buy *what,* and furthermore is a woman who always knows beyond a doubt what one ought to be buying. I don't have the time to keep up with what's new in eyeshadow, hemlines and shoes and whether the smock look is in or finished already. But since (oh, shame!) I care a lot about eyeshadow, hemlines and shoes, and since I don't *want* to wear smocks if the smock look is finished, I'm very glad to have a shopping friend.

3. Historical friends. We all have a friend who knew us when . . . 14
maybe way back in Miss Meltzer's second grade, when our family lived in that three-room flat in Brooklyn, when our dad was out of work for seven months, when our brother Allie got in that fight where they had to call the police, when our sister married the endodontist from Yonkers and when, the morning after we lost our virginity, she was the first, the only, friend we told.

The years have gone by and we've gone separate ways and we've 15
little in common now, but we're still an intimate part of each other's past. And so whenever we go to Detroit we always go to visit this

friend of our girlhood. Who knows how we looked before our teeth were straightened. Who knows how we talked before our voice got un-Brooklyned. Who knows what we ate before we learned about artichokes. And who, by her presence, puts us in touch with an earlier part of ourselves, a part of ourself it's important never to lose.

"What this friend means to me and what I mean to her," says 16 Grace, "is having a sister without sibling rivalry. We know the texture of each other's lives. She remembers my grandmother's cabbage soup. I remember the way her uncle played the piano. There's simply no other friend who remembers those things."

4. Crossroads friends. Like historical friends, our crossroads friends 17 are important for *what was*—for the friendship we shared at a crucial, now past, time of life. A time, perhaps, when we roomed in college together; or worked as eager young singles in the Big City together; or went together, as my friend Elizabeth and I did, through pregnancy, birth and that scary first year of new motherhood.

Crossroads friends forge powerful links, links strong enough to 18 endure with not much more contact than once-a-year letters at Christmas. And out of respect for those crossroads years, for those dramas and dreams we once shared, we will always be friends.

5. Cross-generational friends. Historical friends and crossroads 19 friends seem to maintain a special kind of intimacy—dormant but always ready to be revived—and though we may rarely meet, whenever we do connect, it's personal and intense. Another kind of intimacy exists in the friendships that form across generations in what one woman calls her daughter-mother and her mother-daughter relationships.

Evelyn's friend is her mother's age—"but I share so much more 20 than I ever could with my mother"—a woman she talks to of music, of books and of life. "What I get from her is the benefit of her experience. What she gets—and enjoys—from me is a youthful perspective. It's a pleasure for both of us."

I have in my own life a precious friend, a woman of 65 who has 21 lived very hard, who is wise, who listens well; who has been where I am and can help me understand it; and who represents not only an ultimate ideal mother to me but also the person I'd like to be when I grow up.

In our daughter role we tend to do more than our share of self- 22 revelation; in our mother role we tend to receive what's revealed. It's another kind of pleasure—playing wise mother to a questing younger person. It's another very lovely kind of friendship.

6. Part-of-a-couple friends. Some of the women we call our friends 23 we never see alone—we see them as part of a couple at couples' parties. And though we share interests in many things and respect

each other's views, we aren't moved to deepen the relationship. Whatever the reason, a lack of time or—and this is more likely—a lack of chemistry, our friendship remains in the context of a group. But the fact that our feeling on seeing each other is always, "I'm *so* glad she's here" and the fact that we spend half the evening talking together says that this too, in its own way, counts as a friendship.

(Other part-of-a-couple friends are the friends that came with the 24
marriage, and some of these are friends we could live without. But sometimes, alas, she married our husband's best friend; and sometimes, alas, she *is* our husband's best friend. And so we find ourself dealing with her, somewhat against our will, in a spirit of what I'll call *reluctant* friendship.)

7. Men who are friends. I wanted to write just of women friends, 25
but the women I've talked to won't let me—they say I must mention man-woman friendships too. For those friendships can be just as close and as dear as those that we form with women. Listen to Lucy's description of one such friendship:

"We've found we have things to talk about that are different from 26
what he talks about with my husband and different from what I talk about with his wife. So sometimes we call on the phone or meet for lunch. There are similar intellectual interests—we always pass on to each other the books that we love—but there's also something tender and caring too."

In a couple of crises, Lucy says, "he offered himself, for talking 27
and for helping. And when someone died in his family he wanted me there. The sexual, flirty part of our friendship is very small, but *some*—just enough to make it fun and different." She thinks—and I agree—that the sexual part, though small, is always *some,* is always there when a man and a woman are friends.

It's only in the past few years that I've made friends with men, 28
in the sense of a friendship that's *mine,* not just part of two couples. And achieving with them the ease and the trust I've found with women friends has value indeed. Under the dryer at home last week, putting on mascara and rouge, I comfortably sat and talked with a fellow named Peter. Peter, I finally decided, could handle the shock of me minus mascara under the dryer. Because we care for each other. Because we're friends.

8. There are medium friends, and pretty good friends, and very 29
good friends indeed, and these friendships are defined by their level of intimacy. And what we'll reveal at each of these levels of intimacy is calibrated with care. We might tell a medium friend, for example, that yesterday we had a fight with our husband. And we might tell a pretty good friend that this fight with our husband made us so

mad that we slept on the couch. And we might tell a very good friend that the reason we got so mad in that fight that we slept on the couch had something to do with that girl who works in his office. But it's only to our very best friends that we're willing to tell all, to tell what's going on with that girl in his office.

The best of friends, I still believe, totally love and support and trust each other, and bare to each other the secrets of their souls, and run—no questions asked—to help each other, and tell harsh truths to each other when they must be told.　30

But we needn't agree about everything (only 12-year-old girl friends agree about *everything*) to tolerate each other's point of view. To accept without judgment. To give and to take without ever keeping score. And to *be* there, as I am for them and as they are for me, to comfort our sorrows, to celebrate our joys.　31

COMPREHENSION

1. In her first three paragraphs, Viorst refutes her own previously held assumptions about friends. What are these assumptions? With what is she replacing them?

2. What does Viorst mean when she says that with convenience friends we keep "our public face and emotional distance"?

3. What does Viorst mean in paragraph 24 by "a reluctant friendship"?

4. What distinguishes medium, pretty good, and best friends?

PURPOSE AND AUDIENCE

1. Viorst wrote this article for an audience she knows and understands well. Does she expect this audience to be in agreement with her? How can you tell?

2. Does this article have a thesis? If so, what is it?

3. This essay, although it was written by a woman and is aimed at an audience of women, presents stereotypes about the female sex. Identify some of these stereotypes, and note any that some women might object to.

4. In paragraph 28, why does Viorst say, "It's only in the past few years that I've made friends with men"?

STYLE AND STRUCTURE

1. Why do you think Viorst selected division and classification as her es-

say's pattern of development? Could she have expressed the same ideas in an essay structured according to a different pattern? Explain.

2. Throughout the essay Viorst refers to many of her own friends by name and even quotes them. Why do you think she does this?

3. Although Viorst begins the essay in the first person singular (*I, my*), later she alternates between the first person singular and the first person plural (*we, our*). How do you account for this?

4. Although this is a classification essay, Viorst also uses narrative and definition. Where does she use each?

5. As is often the case, classification in this essay involves comparison and contrast. Explain.

6. Many times Viorst repeats a word or phrase to emphasize a point, to show a relationship between two pieces of information, or to act as a transition. An example is "I once would have said" in paragraphs 2 and 3. Find other examples of such repetition, and explain in each case why it is used.

7. Where does Viorst introduce the actual classification? Where does she complete her classification and begin her conclusion?

WRITING WORKSHOP

1. Classify your own friends (male or female) in a similar essay. You may borrow Viorst's categories or devise your own.

2. If you have one good friend who serves many purposes for you, apply several of Viorst's categories to your friend. In a brief division and classification essay, show how your friend is many different things to you.

SEX BIAS IN TEXTBOOKS

Lenore J. Weitzman and Diane Rizzo

Although male and female roles have changed in nearly every area of our lives, corresponding changes have not always occurred in the depiction of those roles in books written for children. Lenore J. Weitzman and Diane Rizzo find this particularly disturbing because of the profound influence these books have on their readers. Notice how the authors analyze statistical data to draw conclusions and how they organize those data into categories.

Textbooks have always been a cornerstone of our education sys- 1
tem. Although the main function of textbooks is to convey specific information, textbooks also provide the child with ethical and moral values. Thus, at the same time that a child is learning history or math, he or she is also learning what is good, desirable, just.

This second type of information—which sociologists refer to as 2
the "latent content" of textbooks—provides standards for how men, women, boys, and girls should act. This latent content was the focus of research we carried on for the last three years. During that time, we have analyzed the latent content of the most widely used text-book series in the United States in each of five subject areas: science, arithmetic, reading, spelling, and social studies. (A grant from the Rockefeller Family Fund supported the research.) Through com-puter analysis, we obtained data on the sex, age, racial distribution, and activities of the textbook characters by grade level and subject area.

This article will summarize the ways in which the two sexes are 3
portrayed and the type of behavior encouraged for each.

Sex Distribution. Since women comprise 51 percent of the U.S. 4
population, one might expect half the people in textbook illustra-tions to be females. However, males overwhelmingly predominate in all series: Females are only 31 percent of the total, while males are 69 percent. Of over 8,000 pictures analyzed, more than 5,500 are of males. Girl students using these books are likely to feel ex-cluded.

Sex Differences by Grade Level. The percentage of females 5

301

varies by grade level. In all series combined, females comprise a third of the illustrations at the second grade level, but only a fifth of the total on the sixth grade level. In other words, by the sixth grade, there are four pictures of males for every picture of a female. This contrast is vividly illustrated in the accompanying figure. Thus, as the textbooks increase in sophistication, women become less numerous and, by implication, less significant as role models.

This decline in female role models makes it harder for a girl student to identify with the textbook characters and thus may make it harder for her to assimilate the lesson. Covertly, she is being told that she, a female, is less important as the textbook world shifts to the world of adults—to the world of men.   6

This declining representation of females is particularly striking in some of the series. For example, in the second grade spelling series, 43 percent of the illustrations are of females, but in the sixth grade series, the percentage has declined to a mere 15 percent.   7

Sex Differences in Activities. The pictures of children show three striking differences between the boys and girls. First, boys are portrayed as active, skillful, and adventuresome; girls are typically shown as passive—as watching and waiting for boys.   8

Second, while boys are depicted as intelligent and as mastering work-related skills, girls are shown engaging in domestic activities or in grooming themselves, trying on clothes, and shopping. Third, girls are depicted as affectionate, nurturing, and emotional, but boys almost never embrace or cry. Thus, the young boy is taught that to be manly he must control his emotions. In the same way that girls are constrained by images which stereotype them as pretty   9

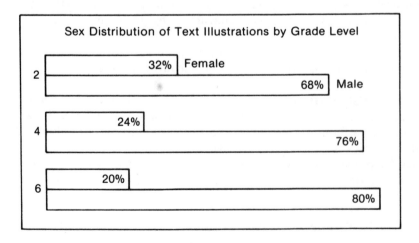

Sex Distribution of Text Illustrations by Grade Level

and passive, boys are constrained by images which stereotype them as strong and unemotional. The textbooks thereby encourage both sexes to limit their development.

Adult men and women in textbooks are even more sex-stereo- 10 typed. While only a few women are shown outside the home, men are portrayed in over 150 occupational roles. A young boy is told he can be anything from a laborer to a doctor. He is encouraged to imagine himself in a wide variety of roles and both to dream about and plan his occupational future.

In contrast, the future for young girls seems preordained: Almost 11 all adult women in textbooks are housewives. In reality, however, 9 out of 10 women in our society will work at some point in their lives. By ignoring women workers, the textbooks fail to provide the necessary occupational role models for girls and thus unnecessarily restrict future horizons.

Sex Differences in Subject Areas. There are systematic dif- 12 ferences in the treatment that girls and women receive in different subject areas. The percentage of females in illustrations varies from a high of 33 percent in social studies to a low of 26 percent in science. These subject differences are important in understanding why children like certain subjects and want to major in them—or why, in contrast, they feel unwelcome because of the covert messages they receive.

In science, the most male-oriented series, 74 percent of the pictures 13 are of males. The science texts seem to imply that the world of science is a masculine domain. When boys are shown, they are actively involved in experiment—looking through microscopes and pouring chemicals. In contrast, when girls are shown, they observe the boys' experiments. The epitome of the male prototype in science is the astronaut. But only boys are pictured as astronauts and, in the text, only boys are told to imagine that they can explore the moon.

In mathematics textbooks, many problems are based on sex-ster- 14 eotyped roles, with men earning money and women dividing pies. Further, despite the Equal Pay Act of 1963, we found math problems in which girls were paid less than boys for the same work. (It would be hard to imagine a textbook publisher allowing an example in which a black child is paid less than a white child.)

In the reading series, story titles provide a good indicator of the 15 relative importance of males and females. Boys predominate in every grade. The series examined had 102 stories about boys and only 35 about girls.

Even the female heroines reinforce traditional female roles. For 16 example, Kirsten, the heroine of a third grade story, wins over the girls who have rejected her by making Danish cookies and having the most popular booth at the school fair. The moral in this story is that girls can succeed by cooking and serving. But Kirsten slights herself and the very skill that had earned her favor when she says, "It's easy; even I can do it, and you know how stupid I am." Thus, even when girls succeed, they tend to deprecate themselves. In contrast, boys show a great deal of confidence and pride.

Both the reading and spelling series demonstrate a surprising amount of antagonism and hostility toward females. In the spelling series, female characters are yelled at and pushed around. In the reading series, they are shown as stupid and clumsy three times as frequently as males. 17

In social studies, the best series studied, women were often skillful and important. Here, mothers play a crucial role in passing on their cultural tradition to their daughters. Although we applaud these positive pictures of women, it should be noted that mothers in the series teach only their daughters, not their sons. Similarly, fathers teach only sons. Thus, traditional sex roles are perpetuated. Today, boys need to learn to manage in the home and to be parents, and girls need to learn about vocations and the outdoors. Textbooks could expand rather than contract children's potential. 18

Although this series has the largest percentage of females in pictures, still 2 out of 3 are pictures of males. Women are in the section on the home but are absent from the sections on history, government, and society. 19

After studying these textbooks for three years, one cannot help but conclude that children are being warped by the latent messages in them. We urge teachers to examine the textbooks they use and to check the ways in which sex roles are stereotyped. Only teachers can change the impact that these books will have on our young people and on the next generation of adults. Teachers can tell their girl students about the world and the real options they have in it. Teachers can encourage them to dream and can help them plan. 20

What is sorely lacking in textbooks and thus desperately needed in the classroom is a new image of adult women and a wide range of adult role models for young girls. Girls—and boys too—should learn about the history of women in this country, about suffrage and the current women's liberation movement, and about female heroines of our country and the world. What a difference it would make if young girls could point to adult women with pride and feel that they themselves have an exciting life ahead. 21

While we must all create pressure to change the textbooks, in   22
the meantime, it is up to teachers to counteract the latent messages
in them and to create positive images of adult women in the minds
of students.

COMPREHENSION

1. What information are the authors classifying in this essay?

2. How does the percentage of females in textbook illustrations vary according to grade level?

3. What are the three differences between illustrations of boys and girls in activities?

4. How do the social studies texts differ from the others Weitzman and Rizzo examined?

5. What recommendations do the authors make at the end of the essay? Can you make these recommendations more specific than they do?

PURPOSE AND AUDIENCE

1. This essay is written to convince. What is its thesis? Where is this position stated?

2. This article appeared in 1975 in a journal aimed at teachers. Would it also be appropriate for a P.T.A. periodical? For a magazine whose readers are primarily homemakers? Explain.

STYLE AND STRUCTURE

1. The first two paragraphs of this essay contain an unusual amount of information for an introduction to a brief essay. Is all the information necessary? Why or why not?

2. What is the function of the essay's brief third paragraph? Is it necessary? Should it have been developed further? Explain.

3. When the authors consider sex differences by grade level, they use a bar graph as an illustration. Do you find the graph helpful or intrusive? Why?

4. Would you find the section on sex differences in activities more helpful if some actual textbook pictures had been included, or do you consider the section convincing as it is? Explain.

5. The section developed in paragraphs 12 through 19 has several subdivisions. On what basis are these subdivisions made?

WRITING WORKSHOP

1. Write an essay in which you classify your own textbooks according to a principle of your choice. You might classify them according to level of difficulty, subject matter, format, approach, attitude toward the reader, or whatever. Be sure to specify the features of each category you set up and establish categories that support a thesis.

2. Think about some of the books you liked when you were a child. Write a short classification essay examining the different roles assigned in them to women (or to men).

FOUR WAYS OF READING

Donald Hall

Born in Connecticut in 1928, Donald Hall now lives and writes on a farm in New Hampshire. He is an eclectic and prolific writer, having published several volumes of poetry, works of literary criticism, and books about sports. In addition, he has taught writing at the University of Michigan, written books about writing (including college texts), and edited several anthologies of poetry. In this essay, which originally appeared in the New York Times, *Hall identifies four different ways in which readers approach a text, thus questioning the assumption that reading is a single activity.*

Everywhere one meets the idea that reading is an activity desirable in itself. It is understandable that publishers and librarians—and even writers—should promote this assumption, but it is strange that the idea should have general currency. People surround the idea of reading with piety, and do not take into account the purpose of reading or the value of what is being read. Teachers and parents praise the child who reads, and praise themselves, whether the text be *The Reader's Digest* or *Moby Dick*. The advent of TV has increased the false values ascribed to reading, since TV provides a vulgar alternative. But this piety is silly; and most reading is no more cultural nor intellectual nor imaginative than shooting pool or watching *What's My Line*. 1

It is worth asking how the act of reading became something to value in itself, as opposed for instance to the act of conversation or the act of taking a walk. Mass literacy is a recent phenomenon, and I suggest that the aura which decorates reading is a relic of the importance of reading to our great-great-grandparents. Literacy used to be a mark of social distinction, separating a small portion of humanity from the rest. The farm laborer who was ambitious for his children did not daydream that they would become schoolteachers or doctors; he daydreamed that they would learn to read, and that a world would therefore open up to them in which they did not have to labor in the fields fourteen hours a day for six days a week in order to buy salt and cotton. On the next rank of society, ample time for reading meant that the reader was free from the necessity to spend most of his waking hours making a living of any kind. . . . 2

Reading is an inactivity, and therefore a badge of social class. Of course, these reasons for the piety attached to reading are never acknowledged. They show themselves in the shape of our attitudes toward books; reading gives off an air of gentility.

It seems to me possible to name four kinds of reading, each with 3 a characteristic manner and purpose. The first is reading for information—reading to learn about a trade, or politics, or how to accomplish something. We read a newspaper this way, or most textbooks, or directions on how to assemble a bicycle. With most of this sort of material, the reader can learn to scan the page quickly, coming up with what he needs and ignoring what is irrelevant to him, like the rhythm of the sentence, or the play of metaphor. Courses in speed reading can help us read for this purpose, training the eye to jump quickly across the page. If we read *The New York Times* with the attention we should give a novel or a poem, we will have time for nothing else, and our mind will be cluttered with clichés and dead metaphor. Quick eye-reading is a necessity to anyone who wants to keep up with what's happening, or learn much of what has happened in the past. The amount of reflection, which interrupts and slows down the reading, depends on the material.

But it is not the same activity as reading literature. There ought 4 to be another word. If we read a work of literature properly, we read slowly, and we hear all the words. If our lips do not actually move, it's only laziness. The muscles in our throats move, and come together when we see the word "squeeze." We hear the sounds so accurately that if a syllable is missing in a line of poetry we hear the lack, though we may not know what we are lacking. In prose we accept the rhythms, and hear the adjacent sounds. We also register a track of feeling through the metaphors and associations of words. Careless writing prevents this sort of attention, and becomes offensive. But the great writers reward this attention. Only by the full exercise of our powers to receive language can we absorb their intelligence and their imagination. This kind of reading goes through the ear—though the eye takes in the print, and decodes it into sound— to the throat and the understanding, and it can never be quick. It is slow and sensual, a deep pleasure that begins with touch and ends with the sort of comprehension that we associate with dream.

Too many intellectuals read in order to reduce images to abstractions. With a philosopher one reads slowly, as if it were literature, but much time must be spent with the eyes turned away from the pages, reflecting on the text. To read literature this way is to turn it into something it is not—to concepts clothed in character, or philosophy sugar-coated. It think that most literary intellectuals read this way, including the brighter Professors of English, with the result that they miss literature completely, and concern themselves with a minor discipline called the history of ideas. I remember a course in Chaucer at my University in which the final exam largely required the identification of a hundred or more fragments of Chaucer, none as long as a line. If you liked poetry, and read Chaucer through a couple of times slowly, you found yourself knowing them all. If you were a literary intellectual, well-informed about the great chain of being, chances are you had a difficult time. To read literature is to be intimately involved with the words on the page, and never to think of them as the embodiments of ideas which can be expressed in other terms. On the other hand, intellectual writing—closer to mathematics on a continuum that has at its opposite pole lyric poetry—requires intellectual reading, which is slow because it is reflective and because the reader must pause to evaluate concepts.

But most of the reading which is praised for itself is neither   6
literary nor intellectual. It is narcotic. Novels, stories and biographies—historical sagas, monthly regurgitations of book clubs, four- and five-thousand word daydreams of the magazines—these are the opium of the suburbs. The drug is not harmful except to the addict himself, and is no more injurious to him than Johnny Carson or a bridge club, but it is nothing to be proud of. This reading is the automated daydream, the mild trip of the housewife and the tired businessman, interested not in experience and feeling but in turning off the possibilities of experience and feeling. Great literature, if we read it well, opens us up to the world, and makes us more sensitive to it, as if we acquired eyes that could see through things and ears that could hear smaller sounds. But by narcotic reading, one can reduce great literature to the level of *The Valley of the Dolls*. One can read *Anna Karenina* passively and inattentively, and float down the river of lethargy as if one were reading a confession magazine: "I Spurned My Husband for a Count."

I think that everyone reads for narcosis occasionally, and perhaps   7
most consistently in late adolescence, when great readers are born. I remember reading to shut the world out, away at a school where I did not want to be; I invented a word to name my disease: "bibliolepsy," on the analogy of narcolepsy. But after a while the books became a window on the world, and not a screen against it. This change doesn't always happen. I think that late adolescent narcotic reading accounts for some of the badness of English departments. As a college student, the boy loves reading and majors in English because he would be reading anyway. Deciding on a career, he takes

up English teaching for the same reason. Then in graduate school he is trained to be a scholar, which is painful and irrelevant, and finds he must write papers and publish them to be a Professor—and at about this time he no longer requires reading for narcosis, and he is left with nothing but a Ph.D. and the prospect of fifty years of teaching literature; and he does not even like literature.

Narcotic reading survives the impact of television, because this type of reading has even less reality than melodrama; that is, the reader is in control: once the characters reach into the reader's feelings, he is able to stop reading, or glance away, or superimpose his own daydream. The trouble with television is that it writes its own script. Literature is often valued precisely because of its distance from the tangible. Some readers prefer looking into the text of a play to seeing it performed. Reading a play, it is possible to stage it oneself by an imaginative act; but it is also possible to remove it from real people. Here is Virginia Woolf, who was lavish in her praise of the act of reading, talking about reading a play rather than seeing it: "Certainly there is a good deal to be said for reading *Twelfth Night* in the book if the book can be read in a garden, with no sound but the thud of an apple falling to the earth, or of the wind ruffling the branches of the trees." She sets her own stage; the play is called *Virginia Woolf Reads Twelfth Night in a Garden.* Piety moves into narcissism, and the high metaphors of Shakespeare's lines dwindle into the flowers of an English garden; actors in ruffles wither, while the wind ruffles branches.

8

COMPREHENSION

1. What four kinds of reading does Hall identify?

2. Why, according to Hall, is reading almost universally valued as "an activity desirable in itself"?

3. What is the primary difference between reading for information and reading literature?

4. What is narcotic reading? What are some positive aspects of narcotic reading? What are some of its negative points?

5. What does Hall mean when he says, "I think that late adolescent narcotic reading accounts for some of the badness of English departments" (paragraph 7)?

PURPOSE AND AUDIENCE

1. Hall identifies four categories of reading in order to support his thesis. What is his thesis, and how does his system of classification support it?

2. This essay originally appeared in the *New York Times*. What concessions does Hall—literary critic, poet, professor of writing—make to his general audience?

STYLE AND STRUCTURE

1. Is Hall's essay an example of division or classification? Explain.

2. According to what two principles does Hall set up his categories? What information does he consider for every category?

3. How does Hall signal transitions between categories? Identify the specific words and phrases he uses.

4. Does Hall introduce his categories in random order, or is there some logic to their organization? Explain.

5. Why does Hall write more about the last category than about any of the other three?

6. Why does Hall choose a quote by Virginia Woolf to close his essay? Which of his points does it support?

WRITING WORKSHOP

1. Consider the kinds of reading you do. Devise your own categories and write an essay in which you assess the relative merits of each kind of reading.

2. Make a list of your dozen favorite books. Classify these books into categories based on subject matter, the period of your life they played a part in, or any other principle you like. Write an essay in which you convey to your audience the importance of each kind of book.

THE TECHNOLOGY
OF MEDICINE

Lewis Thomas

"The Technology of Medicine" is an excerpt from Lives of a Cell
*(1974), a collection of columns by Lewis Thomas which originally
appeared in the* New England Journal of Medicine. *In "The Technology of Medicine" Thomas discusses the relative cost and effectiveness of three different levels of medical treatment. (For biographical information about Lewis Thomas, see page 142.)*

Technology assessment has become a routine exercise for the sci- 1
entific enterprises on which the country is obliged to spend vast
sums for its needs. Brainy committees are continually evaluating
the effectiveness and cost of doing various things in space, defense,
energy, transportation, and the like, to give advice about prudent
investments for the future.

Somehow medicine, for all the $80-odd billion that it is said to 2
cost the nation, has not yet come in for much of this analytical
treatment. It seems taken for granted that the technology of medicine simply exists, take it or leave it, and the only major technol-
ogic problem which policy-makers are interested in is how to deliver
today's kind of health care, with equity, to all the people.

When, as is bound to happen sooner or later, the analysts get 3
around to the technology of medicine itself, they will have to face
the problem of measuring the relative cost and effectiveness of all
the things that are done in the management of disease. They make
their living at this kind of thing, and I wish them well, but I imagine
they will have a bewildering time. For one thing, our methods of
managing disease are constantly changing—partly under the influence of new bits of information brought in from all corners of biologic science. At the same time, a great many things are done that
are not so closely related to science, some not related at all.

In fact, there are three quite different levels of technology in 4
medicine, so unlike each other as to seem altogether different undertakings. Practitioners of medicine and the analysts will be in
trouble if they are not kept separate.

1. First of all, there is a large body of what might be termed 5
"nontechnology," impossible to measure in terms of its capacity to
alter either the natural course of disease or its eventual outcome.

A great deal of money is spent on this. It is valued highly by the professionals as well as the patients. It consists of what is sometimes called "supportive therapy." It tides patients over through diseases that are not, by and large, understood. It is what is meant by the phrases "caring for" and "standing by." It is indispensable. It is not, however, a technology in any real sense, since it does not involve measures directed at the underlying mechanism of disease.

It includes the large part of any good doctor's time that is taken   6
up with simply providing reassurance, explaining to patients who fear that they have contracted one or another lethal disease that they are, in fact, quite healthy.

It is what physicians used to be engaged in at the bedside of   7
patients with diphtheria, meningitis, poliomyelitis, lobar pneumonia, and all the rest of the infectious diseases that have since come under control.

It is what physicians must now do for patients with intractable   8
cancer, severe rheumatoid arthritis, multiple sclerosis, stroke, and advanced cirrhosis. One can think of at least twenty major diseases that require this kind of supportive medical care because of the absence of an effective technology. I would include a large amount of what is called mental disease, and most varieties of cancer, in this category.

The cost of this nontechnology is very high, and getting higher   9
all the time. It requires not only a great deal of time but also very hard effort and skill on the part of physicians; only the very best of doctors are good at coping with this kind of defeat. It also involves long periods of hospitalization, lots of nursing, lots of involvement of nonmedical professionals in and out of the hospital. It represents, in short, a substantial segment of today's expenditures for health.

2. At the next level up is a kind of technology best termed "half-   10
way technology." This represents the kinds of things that must be done after the fact, in efforts to compensate for the incapacitating effects of certain diseases whose course one is unable to do very much about. It is a technology designed to make up for disease, or to postpone death.

The outstanding examples in recent years are the transplanta-   11
tions of hearts, kidneys, livers, and other organs, and the equally spectacular inventions of artificial organs. In the public mind, this kind of technology has come to seem like the equivalent of the high technologies of the physical sciences. The media tend to present each new procedure as though it represented a breakthrough and therapeutic triumph, instead of the makeshift that it really is.

In fact, this level of technology is, by its nature, at the same time   12
highly sophisticated and profoundly primitive. It is the kind of thing
that one must continue to do until there is a genuine understanding
of the mechanisms involved in disease. In chronic glomeruloneph-
ritis, for example, a much clearer insight will be needed into the
events leading to the destruction of glomeruli by the immunologic
reactants that now appear to govern this disease, before one will
know how to intervene intelligently to prevent the process, or turn
it around. But when this level of understanding has been reached,
the technology of kidney replacement will not be much needed and
should no longer pose the huge problems of logistics, cost, and ethics
that it poses today.

An extremely complex and costly technology for the management   13
of coronary heart disease has evolved—involving specialized am-
bulances and hospital units, all kinds of electronic gadgetry, and
whole platoons of new professional personnel—to deal with the end
results of coronary thrombosis. Almost everything offered today for
the treatment of heart disease is at this level of technology, with
the transplanted and artificial hearts as ultimate examples. When
enough has been learned to know what really goes wrong in heart
disease, one ought to be in a position to figure out ways to prevent
or reverse the process, and when this happens the current elaborate
technology will probably be set to one side.

Much of what is done in the treatment of cancer, by surgery,   14
irradiation, and chemotherapy, represents halfway technology, in
the sense that these measures are directed at the existence of already established cancer cells, but not at the mechanisms by which
cells become neoplastic.

It is a characteristic of this kind of technology that it costs an   15
enormous amount of money and requires a continuing expansion of
hospital facilities. There is no end to the need for new, highly trained
people to run the enterprise. And there is really no way out of this,
at the present state of knowledge. If the installation of specialized
coronary-care units can result in the extension of life for only a few
patients with coronary disease (and there is no question that this
technology is effective in a few cases), it seems to me an inevitable
fact of life that as many of these as can be will be put together, and
as much money as can be found will be spent. I do not see that
anyone has much choice in this. The only thing that can move medicine away from this level of technology is new information, and the
only imaginable source of this information is research.

3. The third type of technology is the kind that is so effective   16
that it seems to attract the least public notice; it has come to be

taken for granted. This is the genuinely decisive technology of modern medicine, exemplified best by modern methods for immunization against diphtheria, pertussis, and the childhood virus diseases, and the contemporary use of antibiotics and chemotherapy for bacterial infections. The capacity to deal effectively with syphilis and tuberculosis represents a milestone in human endeavor, even though full use of this potential has not yet been made. And there are, of course, other examples: the treatment of endocrinologic disorders with appropriate hormones, the prevention of hemolytic disease of the newborn, the treatment and prevention of various nutritional disorders, and perhaps just around the corner the management of Parkinsonism and sickle-cell anemia. There are other examples, and everyone will have his favorite candidates for the list, but the truth is that there are nothing like as many as the public has been led to believe.

The point to be made about this kind of technology—the real high technology of medicine—is that it comes as the result of a genuine understanding of disease mechanisms, and when it becomes available, it is relatively inexpensive, and relatively easy to deliver. 17

Offhand, I cannot think of any important human disease for which medicine possesses the outright capacity to prevent or cure where the cost of the technology is itself a major problem. The price is never as high as the cost of managing the same diseases during the earlier stages of no-technology or halfway technology. If a case of typhoid fever had to be managed today by the best methods of 1935, it would run to a staggering expense. At, say, around fifty days of hospitalization, requiring the most demanding kind of nursing care, with the obsessive concern for details of diet that characterized the therapy of that time, with daily laboratory monitoring, and, on occasion, surgical intervention for abdominal catastrophe, I should think $10,000 would be a conservative estimate for the illness, as contrasted with today's cost of a bottle of chloramphenicol and a day or two of fever. The halfway technology that was evolving for poliomyelitis in the early 1950s, just before the emergence of the basic research that made the vaccine possible, provides another illustration of the point. Do you remember Sister Kenny, and the cost of those institutes for rehabilitation, with all those ceremonially applied hot fomentations, and the debates about whether the affected limbs should be totally immobilized or kept in passive motion as frequently as possible, and the masses of statistically tormented data mobilized to support one view or the other? It is the cost of that kind of technology, and its relative effectiveness, that must be compared with the cost and effectiveness of the vaccine. 18

Pulmonary tuberculosis had similar episodes in its history. There   19
was a sudden enthusiasm for the surgical removal of infected lung
tissue in the early 1950s, and elaborate plans were being made for
new and expensive installations for major pulmonary surgery in
tuberculosis hospitals, and then INH and streptomycin came along
and the hospitals themselves were closed up.

It is when physicians are bogged down by their incomplete tech-   20
nologies, by the innumerable things they are obliged to do in medicine when they lack a clear understanding of disease mechanisms,
that the deficiencies of the health-care system are most conspicuous.
If I were a policy-maker, interested in saving money for health care
over the long haul, I would regard it as an act of high prudence to
give high priority to a lot more basic research in biologic science.
This is the only way to get the full mileage that biology owes to the
science of medicine, even though it seems, as used to be said in the
days when the phrase still had some meaning, like asking for the
moon.

COMPREHENSION

1. Why, according to Thomas, hasn't the technology of medicine been subject to the same careful evaluation as other kinds of technology?

2. Why does Thomas expect that analyzing the technology of medicine will
   be difficult?

3. What three categories of technology does Thomas identify? Give several
   examples of each.

4. Why does Thomas say his second category is "at the same time highly
   sophisticated and profoundly primitive"?

5. How can medicine move away from the second level of technology?

6. Why does Thomas consider this third category "the real high technology
   of medicine"? What are its advantages over the other two categories?

7. Does the last line of the essay suggest that Thomas considers his recommendations achievable or out of reach? Explain.

PURPOSE AND AUDIENCE

1. In this essay, Thomas divides the technology of medicine into three categories in order to make a point about their relative merits. What is
   that point?

2. What is Thomas's thesis? Where is it located?

3. Although Thomas's major concern is the quality of medicine, this essay frequently mentions the cost of health care. How is this emphasis likely to affect the lay audience the essay is addressed to?

STYLE AND STRUCTURE

1. Thomas sets his three categories of technology apart with numbers; in addition, what transitional elements does he use to distinguish his categories? Why do you think he uses both words and numbers?

2. Is Thomas's essay structured around classification or division? Explain.

3. What principle of classification has Thomas used in creating his categories?

4. Is Thomas's treatment of his three categories parallel? What information does he present for all three?

5. What factors determine the order in which Thomas presents his categories?

6. How does Thomas signal the end of his formal classification and division and the beginning of his recommendations about the future of medicine? Is this transition enough to let the reader know that the essay is taking a different direction? Explain.

WRITING WORKSHOP

1. What different kinds of medical care have you received? Try to set up three or four categories on any basis you like, and write an essay in which you reach a conclusion about which kind of experience was most satisfactory.

2. Classify another kind of technology—the technology of games. What levels of technology exist? What are their relative merits? What conclusions can you draw?

REPORTS, INFERENCES, JUDGMENTS

S. I. Hayakawa

The well-known semanticist S. I. Hayakawa has a great interest in words and their meanings. He believes that seemingly minor differences in meaning sometimes can be tremendously important; for this reason, we must choose our words carefully. Here, Hayakawa distinguishes three words which are frequently confused and thus classifies statements into three distinct types. He makes the differences among his categories clear with many vivid examples and precise definitions. (For biographical information about S. I. Hayakawa, see page 165.)

For the purposes of the interchange of information, the basic symbolic act is the *report* of what we have seen, heard, or felt: "There is a ditch on each side of the road." "You can get those at Smith's Hardware Store for $2.75." "There aren't any fish on that side of the lake, but there are on this side." Then there are reports of reports: "The longest waterfall in the world is Victoria Falls in Rhodesia." "The Battle of Hastings took place in 1066." "The papers say that there was a smash-up on Highway 41 near Evansville." Reports adhere to the following rules: first, they are *capable of verification;* second, they *exclude,* as far as possible, *inferences* and *judgments.* (These terms will be defined later.)

VERIFIABILITY

Reports are verifiable. We may not always be able to verify them ourselves, since we cannot track down the evidence for every piece of history we know, nor can we all go to Evansville to see the remains of the smash-up before they are cleared away. But if we are roughly agreed upon the names of things, upon what constitutes a "foot," or "yard," "bushel," "kilogram," "meter," and so on, and upon how to measure time, there is relatively little danger of our misunderstanding each other. Even in a world such as we have today, in which everybody seems to be quarreling with everybody else, *we still to a surprising degree trust each other's reports.* We ask directions of total strangers when we are traveling. We follow directions on road signs without being suspicious of the people who put them up. We read books of information about science, mathematics, automotive engineering, travel, geography, the history of costume, and other such factual matters, and we usually assume that the author is doing his best to tell us as truly as he can what he knows. And we are safe in so assuming most of the time. With the interest given today to the discussion of biased newspapers, propagandists, and the general untrustworthiness of many of the communications we receive, we are likely to forget that we still have an enormous amount of reliable information available and that deliberate misinformation, except in warfare, is still more the exception than the rule. The desire for self-preservation that compelled men to evolve means for the exchange of information also compels them to regard the giving of false information as profoundly reprehensible.

At its highest development, the language of reports is the language of science. By "highest development" we mean greatest general usefulness. Presbyterian and Catholic, workingman and capitalist, East German and West German *agree* on the meanings of such symbols as *2 × 2 = 4, 100° C, HNO₃, 3:35* A.M., *1940* A.D., *1,000 kilowatts, Quercus agrifolia,* and so on. But how, it may be asked, can there be agreement about even this much among people who disagree about political philosophies, ethical ideas, religious beliefs, and the survival of my business versus the survival of yours? The answer is that circumstances *compel men to agree,* whether they wish to or not. If, for example, there were a dozen different religious sects in the United States, each insisting on its own way of naming the time of the day and the days of the year, the mere necessity of having a dozen different calendars, a dozen different kinds of watches, and a dozen sets of schedules for business hours, trains, and television programs, to say nothing of the effort that would be required for translating terms from one nomenclature to another, would make life as we know it impossible.[1]

---

[1]According to information supplied by the Association of American Railroads, "Before 1883 there were nearly 100 different time zones in the United States. It wasn't until November 18 of that year that . . . a system of standard time was adopted here and in Canada. Before then there was nothing but local or 'solar' time. . . . The Pennsylvania Railroad in the East used Philadelphia time, which was five minutes slower than New York time and five minutes faster than Baltimore time. The Baltimore & Ohio used Baltimore time for trains running out of Baltimore, Columbus time for Ohio, Vincennes (Indiana) time for those going out of Cincinnati. . . . When it was noon in Chicago, it was 12:31 in Pittsburgh, 12:24 in Cleveland, 12:17 in Toledo, 12:13 in Cincinnati, 12:09 in Louisville, 12:07 in Indianapolis, 11:50 in St. Louis, 11:48 in Dubuque, 11:39 in St. Paul, and 11:27 in Omaha. There were 27 local time zones in Michigan alone. . . . A person traveling from Eastport, Maine, to San Francisco, if he wanted always to have the right railroad time and get off at the right place, had to twist the hands of his watch 20 times en route." Chicago *Daily News* (September 29, 1948).

The language of reports, then, including the more accurate re- 4
ports of science, is "map" language, and because it gives us reasonably accurate representations of the "territory," it enables us to get
work done. Such language may often be dull reading: one does not
usually read logarithmic tables or telephone directories for entertainment. But we could not get along without it. There are num-
berless occasions in the talking and writing we do in everyday life
that *require that we state things in such a way that everybody will
be able to understand and agree with our formulation.*

INFERENCES

. . . An inference, as we shall use the term, is a *statement about* 5
the unknown made on the basis of the known. We may *infer* from
the material and cut of a woman's clothes her wealth or social position; we may *infer* from the character of the ruins the origin of
the fire that destroyed the building; we may *infer* from a man's
calloused hands the nature of his occupation; we may *infer* from a
senator's vote on an armaments bill his attitude toward Russia; we
may *infer* from the structure of the land the path of a prehistoric
glacier; we may *infer* from a halo on an unexposed photographic
plate its past proximity to radioactive materials; we may *infer* from
the sound of an engine the condition of its connecting rods. Inferences may be carefully or carelessly made. They may be made on
the basis of a broad background of previous experience with the
subject matter or with no experience at all. For example, the inferences a good mechanic can make about the internal condition of a
motor by listening to it are often startlingly accurate, while the
inferences made by an amateur (if he tries to make any) may be
entirely wrong. But the common characteristic of inferences is that
they are statements about matters which are not directly known,
made on the basis of what has been observed.[2]

The avoidance of inferences . . . requires that we make no guesses 6
as to what is going on in other people's minds. When we say, "He
was angry," we are not reporting; we are making an inference from
such observable facts as the following: "He pounded his fist on the

[2]The behaviorist school of psychology tries to avoid inferences about what is going
on in other people's minds by describing only external behavior. A famous joke about
behaviorism goes: Two behaviorists meet on the street. The first says, "You're fine.
How am I?"

table; he swore; he threw the telephone directory at his stenographer." In this particular example, the inference appears to be safe; nevertheless, it is important to remember, especially for the purposes of training oneself, that it is an inference. Such expressions as "He thought a lot of himself," "He was scared of girls," "He has an inferiority complex," made on the basis of casual observation, and "What Russia really wants to do is to establish a communist world dictatorship," made on the basis of casual reading, are highly inferential. We should keep in mind their inferential character and . . . should substitute for them such statements as "He rarely spoke to subordinates in the plant," "I saw him at a party, and he never danced except when one of the girls asked him to," "He wouldn't apply for the scholarship, although I believe he could have won it easily," and "The Russian delegation to the United Nations has asked for A, B, and C. Last year they voted against M and N and voted for X and Y. On the basis of facts such as these, the newspaper I read makes the inference that what Russia really wants is to establish a communist world dictatorship. I agree."

Even when we exercise every caution to avoid inferences and to 7
report only what we see and experience, we all remain prone to error, since the making of inferences is a quick, almost automatic process. We may watch a car weaving as it goes down the road and say, "Look at that *drunken driver*," although what we see is only the *irregular motion of the car*. I once saw a man leave a dollar at a lunch counter and hurry out. Just as I was wondering why anyone should leave so generous a tip in so modest an establishment, the waitress came, picked up the dollar, put it in the cash register as she punched up ninety cents, and put a dime in her pocket. In other words, my description to myself of the event, "a dollar tip," turned out to be not a report but an inference.

All this is not to say that we should never make inferences. The 8
inability to make inferences is itself a sign of mental disorder. For example, the speech therapist Laura L. Lee writes, "The aphasic [brain-damaged] adult with whom I worked had great difficulty in making inferences about a picture I showed her. She could tell me what was happening at the moment in the picture, but could not tell me what might have happened just before the picture or just afterwards."[3] Hence the question is not whether or not we make inferences; the question is whether or not we are aware of the inferences we make.

[3]"Brain Damage and the Process of Abstracting: A Problem in Language Learning," *ETC.: A Review of General Semantics*, XVI (1959), 154–62.

Report	Can be verified or disproved
Inference	A statement about the unknown made on the basis of the known
Judgment	An expression of the writer's approval or disapproval

JUDGMENTS

... By judgments, we shall mean *all expressions of the writer's* 9
*approval or disapproval of the occurrences, persons, or objects he is
describing.* For example, a report cannot say, "It was a wonderful
car," but must say something like this: "It has been driven 50,000
miles and has never required any repairs." Again, statements such
as "Jack lied to us" must be suppressed in favor of the more verifiable statement, "Jack told us he didn't have the keys to his car
with him. However, when he pulled a handkerchief out of his pocket
a few minutes later, a bunch of car keys fell out." Also a report may
not say, "The senator was stubborn, defiant, and uncooperative," or
"The senator courageously stood by his principles"; it must say instead, "The senator's vote was the only one against the bill."

Many people regard statements such as the following as state- 10
ments of "fact': "Jack *lied* to us," "Jerry is a *thief*," "Tommy is *clever*."
As ordinarily employed, however, the word "lied" involves first an
inference (that Jack knew otherwise and deliberately misstated the
facts) and second a judgment (that the speaker disapproves of what
he has inferred that Jack did). In the other two instances, we may
substitute such expressions as, "Jerry was convicted of theft and
served two years at Waupun," and "Tommy plays the violin, leads
his class in school, and is captain of the debating team." After all,
to say of a man that he is a "thief" is to say in effect, "He has stolen
and will steal again"—which is more of a prediction than a report.
Even to say, "He has stolen," is to make an inference (and simultaneously to pass a judgment) on an act about which there may be
difference of opinion among those who have examined the evidence
upon which the conviction was obtained. But to say that he was
"convicted of theft" is to make a statement capable of being agreed
upon through verification in court and prison records.

Scientific verifiability rests upon the external observation of facts, 11
not upon the heaping up of judgments. If one person says, "Peter is
a deadbeat," and another says, "I think so too," the statement has
not been verified. In court cases, considerable trouble is sometimes
caused by witnesses who cannot distinguish their judgments from

the facts upon which those judgments are based. Cross-examinations under these circumstances go something like this:

> WITNESS: That dirty double-crosser Jacobs ratted on me.
> DEFENSE ATTORNEY: Your honor, I object.
> JUDGE: Objection sustained. (Witness's remark is stricken from the record.) Now, try to tell the court exactly what happened.
> WITNESS: He double-crossed me, the dirty, lying rat!
> DEFENSE ATTORNEY: Your honor, I object!
> JUDGE: Objection sustained. (Witness's remark is again stricken from the record.) Will the witness try to stick to the facts.
> WITNESS: But I'm telling you the facts, your honor. He did double-cross me.

This can continue indefinitely unless the cross-examiner exercises some ingenuity in order to get at the facts behind the judgment. To the witness it is a "fact" that he was "double-crossed." Often patient questioning is required before the factual bases of the judgment are revealed.

Many words, of course, simultaneously convey a report and a   12
judgment on the fact reported. . . . For the purposes of a report as here defined, these should be avoided. Instead of "sneaked in," one might say "entered quietly"; instead of "politician," "congressman" or "alderman" or "candidate for office"; instead of "bureaucrat," "public official"; instead of "tramp," "homeless unemployed"; instead of "dictatorial set-up," "centralized authority"; instead of "crackpot," "holder of nonconformist views." A newspaper reporter, for example, is not permitted to write, "A crowd of suckers came to listen to Senator Smith last evening in that rickety firetrap and ex-dive that disfigures the south edge of town." Instead he says, "Between 75 and 100 people heard an address last evening by Senator Smith at the Evergreen Gardens near the South Side city limits."

COMPREHENSION

1. What is the basic difference between reports on the one hand and inferences and judgments on the other?

2. What everyday examples of reports does Hayakawa mention?

3. Why, according to Hayakawa, couldn't we get along without reports?

4. Define *inference* and *judgment,* and give two of your own examples of each.

5. Why do you think Hayakawa considers the distinction between reports, inferences, and judgments so important?

PURPOSE AND AUDIENCE

1. Is the primary purpose of Hayakawa's essay to entertain, to inform, or to persuade? Explain.

2. Does this essay have an explicitly stated thesis? If so, where is it?

3. Why does Hayakawa use *we* rather than *I* or *one* throughout the essay?

STYLE AND STRUCTURE

1. After Hayakawa defines *inference* in paragraph 5, he follows with a sentence that presents a series of examples. How does the structure of that sentence clarify his definition?

2. This essay specifically exemplifies each kind of statement the author examines. Why is such evidence particularly important in an essay on this subject?

3. What is the purpose of the hypothetical conversation in paragraph 11? Does it effectively serve this purpose?

4. Why does Hayakawa include additional information in footnotes instead of integrating it into the body of his essay? Is all the footnoted information necessary?

WRITING WORKSHOP

1. Select a fairly long newspaper story on a topic that interests you. Classify its information as reports, inferences, and judgments. Then write a classification-and-division essay about what you discover.

2. Study a picture in a newspaper or magazine carefully. Decide which of your observations about it are facts, which are inferences, and which are judgments. Write a classification-and-division paper explaining your decisions.

9

Definition

WHAT IS DEFINITION?

Any time you take an exam you are likely to encounter questions that require definitions. You might be asked to define *behaviorism,* tell what a *cell* is, explain the meaning of the literary term *naturalism,* include a clear, comprehensive definition of *mitosis* in your answer, or define *authority.* Such exam questions can't always be answered in one or two sentences. They call for definitions that might require several paragraphs.

Most people think of definition in terms of dictionaries—explaining what a word means. That's certainly one thing a definition does. But the term has much wider application. It also includes explaining what something, or even someone, *is*—that is, its essential nature. A definition answers the question, "What is _____?" Sometimes the answer can be given in a sentence. At other times it requires a paragraph, an essay, or even a whole book. These latter are often called *extended definitions.*

Such extended definitions are useful for many academic assignments besides exams. A thoughtful definition can clarify precise scientific terms as well as more general concepts from any course. Definitions can explain abstractions like *freedom* or controversial terms like *right to life* or slang terms whose meanings may vary from locale to locale or change as time passes. In some situations, a specific definition can be essential because a term has more than one meaning, because you are using it in an uncommon way, or because you suspect the term is unfamiliar to your readers.

Although the extended-definition essays considered in this section are long, many of them also contain shorter definitions like those in the dictionary. Furthermore, papers often incorporate brief definitions of terms to clarify points or establish basic information that equips the reader to follow the rest of the discussion. Whether it appears in another kind of essay or acts as a center for an extended definition, the dictionary or brief formal definition establishes the essential meaning of a term.

Formal or Dictionary Definitions

Thumb through any dictionary, and you will see pages of words followed by definitions. These definitions all follow a standard three-part structure: first the term to be defined, then the general class it is a part of, and finally the qualities that differentiate it from the other terms in the same class.

Term	Class	Differentiation
Behaviorism	is a theory	that regards the objective facts of a subject's actions as the only valid basis for psychological study.
A cell	is a unit of protoplasm	with a nucleus, cytoplasm, and an enclosing membrane.
Naturalism	is a literary movement	whose original adherents believed that writers should treat life with scientific objectivity.
Mitosis	is the process	of nuclear division of cells, consisting of prophase, metaphase, anaphase, and telophase.
Authority	is the power	to command and require obedience.

Ordinarily it is not necessary or desirable to supply readers with a dictionary definition of each term you use. They generally will either know what a word means or easily be able to look it up. Sometimes, however, it is essential to define your terms—for example, when a word has several meanings, each of which might fit your context, or when you want to use a word in a special way. Occasionally a brief formal definition may be part of a longer definition essay; there it can introduce the extended definition or even help to establish the essay's unifying idea or thesis. All definitions, regardless of length and context, include the term, its class, and its distinguishing qualities—the three components that pinpoint what something is and what it is not.

Extended or Essay-Length Definitions

An extended definition includes the basic parts of a formal definition—the term, its class, and its distinguishing characteristics. Beyond these essentials, an extended definition does not follow a set pattern. Instead, it adapts whatever techniques best suit the term being defined and the writing situation. In fact, any of the essay patterns explored in this book can be used to structure a definition essay. Usually, you can select an appropriate pattern after considering the term or subject you wish to define as well as your purpose and writing situation. Sometimes, as you brainstorm, jotting down your ideas about the term or subject, a pattern will naturally suggest itself. At other times, working out the term's formal definition will suggest distinctions or illustrations around which a pattern can grow. For example, the formal definitions of the five terms discussed earlier might be extended using different patterns of development.

Exemplification.   To explain what behaviorism is, you could give examples. Carefully chosen cases exemplifying behaviorist assumptions and methods could show how this theory of psychology applies in different situations. Through these examples your reader could see exactly how behaviorism works and what it can and can't account for. Often, giving examples can be the clearest way to explain something unusual, especially when it is unfamiliar to your readers. If you were defining dreams as the symbolic representations of mental states, those words might convey little to readers who did not know much about psychology. But a few examples could help you make your point. Many students have dreams about taking exams—perhaps dreaming that they remember nothing about the course, or indeed never took it, or that they are writing their answers with vanishing ink. You might explain the nature of dreams by interpreting these particular dreams, which may symbolize anxiety about a particular course or school in general.

Description.   You can explain the nature of something by describing it. The concept of a cell would be difficult to grasp from the formal definition given above. Your readers would understand the cell more clearly if you were to explain what it looks like, possibly with the aid of a diagram or two. Concentrating on the cell membrane, cytoplasm, and nucleus, you could detail each structure's appearance and function. With these clear descriptions, your reader would be equipped to visualize the whole cell and understand its workings. Of course, there is more to description than the visual. You would define Italian cooking by describing the taste and smell, as well as the appearance, of spaghetti and veal parmigiana just as you would define a disease partly by describing how its symptoms feel to a patient.

Comparison and Contrast. An extended definition of *naturalism* could employ a comparison-and-contrast structure. Naturalism is one of several major movements in American literature, and its literary aims could be contrasted with those of other literary movements like romanticism or realism. Or you could compare and contrast the plots and characters of several naturalistic works with those of romantic or realistic works. When defining something unfamiliar, you can compare it to something similar but more familiar to your readers. For example, your readers may never have heard of the Chinese dish called sweet and sour cabbage, but you can help them understand it by saying that it tastes like cole slaw. You may also define an object by contrasting it with something very much unlike it, especially if the two otherwise have a lot in common. One way to explain the British sport of Rugby football is by contrasting it with American football, which is less flowing and more violent.

Process. An extended definition of *mitosis* should be organized as a process analysis since mitosis is a process. You could explain the four stages of mitosis, making sure that you point out the transition from one phase to another. By tracing the process from stage to stage for the reader, you could be certain that this type of cell division is clearly defined. Similarly some objects must be defined in terms of what they do. A computer is a machine that *does* what other computers do, not something that *looks* like other computers, and so an extended definition of a computer would probably include a process analysis.

Classification. Finally, you could define *authority* using classification and division. Based on Max Weber's model, you could divide the class *authority* into subclasses such as: traditional authority, charismatic authority, and legal-bureaucratic authority. Then, through parallel discussions explaining how each type of authority is legitimized, you could clarify this very broad term for your reader. In both extended and formal definitions, classification can be very useful. By saying what class an object belongs to, you are explaining what kind of thing it is. For instance, monetarism is an economic theory; *The Adventures of Huckleberry Finn* is a novel; emphysema is a disease. And by dividing that class into subclasses, you can be more specific. Emphysema is not merely a disease, it is a disease of the lungs, which classifies it with tuberculosis but not with appendicitis.

Each of these patterns of development helps define by emphasizing a central, essential characteristic of the subject. Naturally, other options are also available. Cause and effect or narration can be used to structure definition papers, as can any combination of patterns. Additionally, a few techniques are unique to definition:

- You can define a term by using *synonyms*
- You can define a term by using *negation* (telling what it is *not*)
- You can define a term by using *enumeration* (listing its characteristics)

Although your definitions and definition essays may take many forms, you should be certain that they are clear and that they actually define. You should be sure you provide a true definition, not just a descriptive statement such as "Happiness is a pizza and a sixpack." Likewise, repetition is not definition, so don't include the term you are defining in your definition. Explaining that "abstract art is a school of artists whose works are abstract" clarifies nothing for your reader. Finally, define as precisely as possible. Name the class of the term you are defining, stating, for example, that "mitosis is a process" rather than "mitosis is when a cell divides." Further, define this class as narrowly and as accurately as possible. Be specific when you differentiate your term from other members of its narrowed class. Only careful attention to the language and structure of your definition can ensure that your meaning will be clear to your reader.

STRUCTURING A DEFINITION ESSAY

Like any other paper, a definition essay should have an introduction with a thesis, a body, and a conclusion. Although a dictionary definition is not arguable, an extended definition can be. It may show the term being defined in a special light determined by your attitude toward the subject, by your purpose in defining the term, and by your audience. Thus, your extended-definition paper about literary naturalism could argue that this movement was a logical outgrowth of nineteenth-century science and industry. And your essay defining the cell could maintain that the complexities of this unit of protoplasm probably will never be fully understood. Such a thesis provides a center for a definition essay and makes it more than just a catalog of facts.

Let's suppose that you are assigned a short paper in your introductory psychology course. You decide to examine *behaviorism*. First, you have to recognize that your topic entails a definition. If the topic can be summed up in a form such as this—"A is B"; "The true nature of A is B"; "A means B"—then it's a definition. If you are only defining a word, that will probably not call for extended definition. For example, you can define *behaviorism* as a *word* in a sentence, or possibly two. But to explain the meaning of the *concept* of behaviorism, and its position in the history and current knowledge of psychiatry, calls for much more extended writing. You must go beyond the dictionary into the world.

Second, you have to decide what kinds of explanation are most suitable for your topic and your intended audience. If you are trying to define *behaviorism* for readers who know very little about psychology, you might use comparisons that relate behaviorism to your readers' experiences, such as how they were brought up by their parents and how they trained their pets. You might use examples, but the examples would relate not to psychological experiments or clinical treatment but to experiences in everyday life. If, on the other hand, you direct your paper to your psychology instructor, that reader obviously already knows what behaviorism is, and your purpose is to show that you know too. One way to show that you understand a theory is to compare it with other theories that claim to explain human behavior. Another is to give examples of how it works in practice. You might also choose to give some of the background and history of the theory. In a term paper you might even include all of these patterns. After considering your paper's scope and audience, you decide that since behaviorism is still somewhat controversial, your best strategy is to supplement a formal definition with examples showing how behaviorist assumptions and methods are applied in specific situations, drawing on your class notes and your textbook. These examples will support your thesis that behaviorism is a valid approach for treating certain psychological dysfunctions. In combination, your examples will define *behaviorism* as it is understood today.

An outline for your essay might look like this:

¶1 Introduction—thesis: For modern psychologists, behaviorism has evolved into a valid approach for treating a wide variety of psychological dysfunctions.

¶2 Background: An introductory definition of behaviorism, including its origins and evolution

¶3 First example: The use of behaviorism to help psychotics function in an institutional setting

¶4 Second example: The use of behaviorism to treat neurotic behavior such as chronic anxiety, a phobia, or a pattern of destructive acts

¶5 Third example: The use of behaviorism to treat normal but antisocial or undesirable behavior such as heavy smoking or overeating

¶6 Conclusion—restatement of thesis

Notice how the three examples in this paper define behaviorism with the complexity, the detail, and the breadth that a formal definition could not duplicate. It is more like a textbook explanation—and in fact, textbook explanations are often written as extended definitions.

The following student essay, written by Pat Good for an art history course, defines a controversial artistic movement. Using information from her class notes, Pat presents the thesis that dadaism was not a short-lived eccentric fad but a significant creative movement.

THE DADA SPIRIT

Introduction
Formal definition
The dada movement is defined in *Webster's New Collegiate Dictionary* as "a movement in art and literature based on deliberate irrationality and negation of traditional artistic values." In fact, the word *dada* is often assumed to be synonymous with antiart and nihil-

Negation
Thesis
ism. This assumption ignores both that one of the purposes of this movement, like any other such movement, was to produce art and also that there was a very positive side to its seemingly negative form of expression.

Background   One characteristic of any new move-   2
ment in art or literature is reaction
against forms which have been established in the past. These forms are
questioned and explored, and, when
found to be no longer adequate, they
are replaced with something new. The
Contrast   major difference between dada and earlier artistic movements was that the
dadaists were more extreme. Their often
outrageous shock tactics were aimed not
only at existing art forms but at the
values of the bourgeoisie, who thought
good art was synonymous with good
taste. But simply to call dada the "negation of traditional artistic values,"
as some critics do, ignores the creative force behind this movement.

Comparison   Like any other artistic movement, the   3
dada movement was intent more on keep-
ing the creative force alive than on
destroying anything. It just happened
Contrast   that the dadaists believed that to acquire a set form, a trademark, or any
identifiable characteristics was a sign
that the creative impulse was dying.
They felt that, in order for their art
to be constantly alive, it had to be
constantly changing. This constant flux
caused much contradiction within the
movement itself. But these contradic-
tions were themselves part of the movement. The ideas of two artists could be
totally dissimilar and even contradic-

tory, but if these ideas were personal and disconnected from any preconceived values, then they were dada. Thus, the importance of dada was not in any method or form but in the direct and individual statement.

Example   Up until the time of the movement,   4 much art had been based on some type of representation. Marcel Duchamp was one who refuted this principle and some of his own past work by inventing the ready—made. The ready—made was an object, often commercially made, which he extracted directly from his environment and elevated to the position of art. He simply took a bottle rack and called it "A Bottle Rack." He reversed the usual order of the procedure, and, instead of making his work of art imitative, he made the thing itself the work of art. The irony and rebelliousness of Duchamp's acts contain the spirit of dada. But the ready—made could not be called a typical example of dada because there really could be no typical example. After Duchamp made the ready-made, no one else could make another one. Each artist had to invent his own vital form of expression.

Conclusion (restatement of thesis)   Often the dada movement is seen by   5 critics only as something which set out to destroy existing art forms and social values without offering other forms or values to replace them. This

view ignores the fact that the aspira-
tions of the dadaists were some of the
most idealistic ever. They wanted to
assert the independent spirit and the
freedom of the artist. That they remained as unstructured as possible in
trying to do this should not be passed
off as simply "deliberate irrationality
and the negation of traditional artistic values." After all, the ground they
cleared made it possible for future
artists to confront the twentieth century, perceiving it in new ways and
representing it in new forms.

Points for Special Attention

Topic and Thesis. *Dada* is a term that is perfectly suited to
an extended definition. It cannot be defined adequately with a syn-
onym because there really is no equivalent term. Besides, *dada* is
a term unfamiliar to many, and so a paper that defines it is likely
to interest a reader. Pat Good's thesis is that despite the conventional view, dada was a positive, valuable artistic movement. This
gives an argumentative slant to her paper and increases its interest.

Formal Definition. This essay begins somewhat convention-
ally with a dictionary excerpt which provides a clear, three-part
definition. This can be a dreary opening and can even be misleading
if the dictionary is seen simply as an authority. But Pat, acknowl-
edging the inadequacy of that definition, proceeds to do something
less conventional: she refutes the commonly held assumption that
dada is an antiart movement. In doing so, she more fully defines
the term, enlarging the formal definition she gives at the beginning.

Development. Pat uses familiar techniques to compose her extended definition of *dada*. She begins her definition with negation,
stating what dada is not; she then presents some necessary background about art movements, comparing and contrasting dada with
other movements to make some distinctions that are critical to her

definition. Next, she explains the rationale behind dada, telling what the movement really stands for. In the fourth paragraph she offers an extended example of dada, Duchamp's ready-made. Each of these techniques contributes to the effectiveness of her definition.

No one pattern is more appropriate than another for a definition paper. In fact, combining several patterns may most effectively define the significant aspects of your term. Your choice of pattern should evolve naturally from your knowledge of your material, your purpose, and the needs of your audience. The essays that follow employ exemplification, comparison and contrast, narration, and other methods of developing extended definitions.

THE ASTONISHING TALMUD

Leo Rosten

*Born in Poland in 1908 and educated in the United States and
England, Rosten has worked as an English teacher, a writer for
Look magazine, and a Hollywood script writer. His books include*
The Education of H*Y*M*A*N K*A*P*L*A*N *(1937), based on
his humorous experiences teaching English to European immigrants during the Depression;* Captain Newman, M.D., *which was
made into a movie starring Gregory Peck; and* The Joys of Yiddish,
*a celebration of the language and culture of European Jews. In this
essay, using various patterns of development and sprinkling numerous quotations throughout, Rosten defines a term with which
many of his readers may be unfamiliar.*

Ask your most learned friends where the following sagacities   1
originated:

"All's well that ends well." (Shakespeare, of course.)   2

"A man betrays his character through three things: his tipping,   3
his tippling and his temper." (Oscar Wilde? Or was it Voltaire?)

"Give every man the benefit of the doubt." (Cicero? Oliver Wen-   4
dell Holmes?)

"A dream uninterpreted is like a letter unopened." (Surely Sig-   5
mund Freud?)

It may surprise you to learn that each of these aphorisms comes   6
from the Talmud.[1] And I am willing to wager that 95 percent of our
best-educated Americans cannot tell you what is meant by the "Talmud"—though it is one of the main sources for what we know about
Judaism in the pre-Christian era, and the reservoir from which all
of Judaism, Christianity and Islam drew their basic moral code,
many of their articles of faith, and the foundations of their theology.

Examples? Take these flashing insights into the enduring areas   7
of human concern, all in the Talmud:

Ethics: "What is hateful to you, never do to a fellow man: that is   8
the whole Law—all the rest is commentary."

Adam: "Why did God create only one man? So that thereafter no   9
one could say, 'My ancestors were nobler than yours,' or that virtue

---

[1]The Talmudic sages left many writings not included in the Talmud itself but
later compiled to form a group of volumes called the "Midrash." In this article, I use
the "Talmud" in its broader sense to include the Midrash.

and vice are inherited, or that some races are better than others. ... And to teach us that whoever destroys a single life is as guilty as though he had destroyed the entire world; and that whoever saves one life earns as much merit as if he had saved the whole world."

Women: "The Lord did not create woman from man's head, so that he can command her; nor from man's foot, so that she would be his slave. God made Eve from Adam's side so that woman will always be nearest man's heart. ... Be careful not to make a woman weep: God counts her tears." 10

Children: "Never threaten a child: either punish him or forgive him. ... If you must strike a child, use a string." 11

Law: "For capital crimes, a majority of one judge may acquit, but only a majority of two can convict. ... Judges who sentence a man to death may not eat or drink for the next 24 hours." 12

Truth: "If you add to the truth, you subtract from it." 13

Conduct: "When the wise get angry, they lose their wisdom. ... Better embarrassment in this world than shame in the world to come." 14

Worry: "Don't worry too much about tomorrow: who knows what may befall you today?" 15

Now I must apologize. Have I given you the impression that the Talmud is a fascinating succession of noble ideas and scintillating epigrams? Alas, not so. The ideas *are* majestic, the reasoning is subtle and sublime, the aphorisms are superb. But they are buried in a text that is ensnarled in archaic technicalities, pedantic digressions, quaint superstitions, exasperating *pilpul* (hair-splitting) and obsessiveness about matters which today seem as irrelevant as the size of Nebuchadnezzar's tonsils. The analyses remind me of medieval arguments over the number of angels who can sit on the point of a needle. 16

But we must not forget that the problems with which the great Talmudists—rabbis and philosophers, judges and scholars—wrestled were anything but remote or absurd to *them.* They were trying to clarify what God meant by every word, phrase, metaphor, injunction or prohibition in the Pentateuch, or Torah (Genesis, Exodus, Leviticus, Numbers, Deuteronomy). To the Hebrew sages, their work was sanctified and imperative. 17

They were not trying to produce a work of art. They were hammering out a code of faith, laws and ethics—binding on their leaders no less than on their children—about the intricacies of religion: rituals of worship; obligations of marriage; conditions under which obedience to, or rebellion against, alien rulers must be observed; 18

circumstances under which ransom must be paid (women took precedence over men) or apostates ostracized; obligatory kindness due orphans and widows, animals or slaves—in short, the sacred responsibilities of men and women to God, to each other and to the community. Thus the Talmud may be described as a combination of all the papal bulls, the American Constitution, the Napoleonic Code, and the collected reasonings and decisions of our Supreme Court. We shall see how many scholars and centuries it took to complete so monumental a task.

The Talmud is not, as many think, the Torah, the first five books of the Old Testament, which ancient Hebrews called "the Books of Moses" or "the Law of Moses." The Talmud is a massive compilation of 63 massektoth ("little books"). These are transcripts of symposiums that went on, by some estimates, for 1200 years—from the fifth century before the Christian era to the eighth century A.D. More than 2000 scholar-rabbi-sages conducted these debates, which were held in the great academies of the Holy Land and of Babylon. To these centers of scholarship came the most brilliant and erudite sages, and the most complex correspondence from rabbis and rabbinical courts in other parts of the world. Each land produced its own Talmud, but it is the Babylonian work we call *the* Talmud. It is more than three times as long and has been preserved in toto: the century-earlier Jerusalem Talmud was not. 19

The Talmud is meant to be studied, not merely read. It is an almanac, a casebook, a reference encyclopedia. (An English-language translation runs to 35 volumes.) While it revolves around the commanding questions about the human condition, the debates and commentaries (and the omnibus commentaries *upon* commentaries) also concern the less lofty, ranging from adultery to agriculture (how should Egyptian beans be planted?); from admonitions about personal hygiene to the treatment of wizards; from Satan to pedagogy ("No more than 25 children shall be in a class"); from the merciful slaughter of livestock to rules governing mourning and penance; from every variety of sin to that salvation promised by the appearance of the Messiah. No topic is absent; the most majestic wisdom accompanies the most mundane preoccupations. 20

But if there is one theme in the tumultuous pages of the Talmud, I think it is this: Every Jew must devote himself to endless acts of compassion. For as the Talmud observes, "The Torah begins with acts of loving and ends with kindness; it begins with God clothing Adam and Eve, and ends with God burying Moses. . . . The beginning and end of the Torah is performing acts of loving-kindness." 21

I have always cherished this passage: "When my time comes to die," said the frog, "I shall go down to the sea, there to be swallowed by one of its creatures. For in that way, even my death will be an act of kindness." [22]

The Talmud was for centuries known to the Christian world only in random and garbled extracts. It was damned and outlawed and torn to shreds or cast into flames—in Paris, Rome, Toledo, Constantinople—by churchmen and emperors, from Justinian down to the Nazis and other fanatics in our midst. [23]

Still, the Talmud was constantly studied and discussed by every male Jew (and aristocratic females), as it is today by "practicing" Jews in every land on earth. Tremendous importance and *mitzvahs* (good deeds) have always been associated with reading a portion of the Torah or Talmud every day, especially on the Sabbath. To do so was and is to earn a "portion of bliss" in the world to come. [24]

In Jerusalem and in Córdoba, Bombay, Kobe, Khartoum or Kiev, wherever Jews landed after the Diaspora (dispersion after the banishments from their Holy Land), the little shops, marketplaces, country fairs contained the spectacle of merchants, cobblers, laborers, draymen, bakers and barbers poring over the *Pirke Aboth* (Ethics of the Fathers), the most beloved Talmud section. [25]

Down the centuries Jewish communities rang with the impassioned disputes of those exploring the grandeur of God's message and the complexities of Biblical exegesis. "Learning is achieved only in the company of others," says the Talmud. In 1887, the small town of Kroze, Poland (now Kražiai, Lithuania), sheltered but 200 Jewish families; yet these families formed nine permanent study groups, employed ten male and two female teachers and could boast two full-time bookbinders and repairers. It is no wonder that Mohammed called the Jews "the People of the Book." [26]

The Talmud is celebrated as a treasury of parables, fables and anecdotes of great insight and power. They are not meant to entertain, please note. They are vehicles for instruction, arresting ways of driving home a moral. I give you my favorite: [27]

"In a harbor, two ships sailed: one setting forth on a voyage, the other coming home to port. Everyone cheered the ship going out, but the ship sailing in was scarcely noticed. To this, a wise man said: 'Do not rejoice over a ship setting out to sea, for you cannot know what terrible storms it may encounter, and what fearful dangers it may have to endure. Rejoice rather over the ship that has safely reached port and brings its passengers home in peace.' [28]

"And this is the way of the world: When a child is born, all rejoice; when someone dies, all weep. We should do the opposite. For no one [29] can tell what trials and travails await a newborn child; but when a mortal dies in peace, we should rejoice, for he has completed a long journey, and there is no greater boon than to leave this world with the imperishable crown of a good name."

COMPREHENSION

1. Does a formal definition of the Talmud appear anywhere in the essay? If so, where? If not, provide one.

2. How does the Talmud reflect the laws, rituals, and ethics of Judaism? Give specific examples.

3. What, according to Rosten, is the Talmud's major theme? What passage does he offer as an illustration of this theme? What other topics does the Talmud deal with?

4. What does Rosten think is the real purpose of the Talmud's parables?

PURPOSE AND AUDIENCE

1. This essay was written for *The Reader's Digest*. Do you think its tone is appropriate for this general-interest magazine, which is widely read by Christians as well as Jews? Why or why not?

2. Does this essay include an explicit thesis? If so, where? If not, suggest a thesis for the essay.

3. Where is Rosten trying to entertain? To inform? To persuade? Which of these do you think is his primary purpose? Explain.

STYLE AND STRUCTURE

1. Why do you think Rosten begins his essay with a series of quotations? How does the use of quotations throughout his article strengthen his definition?

2. What patterns of development does Rosten use to define the Talmud? What other patterns might he have used?

3. Why does the title call the Talmud "astonishing"? Do you think this claim is supported in the essay? Explain.

4. Find in the essay examples of the following techniques characteristic of definition: definition by negation, explanation of the term's origins, and definition by analogy.

5. What technique does Rosten use to define briefly words or phrases he

thinks his audience may be unfamiliar with? Are there additional words or phrases you think he should have defined? Which ones? Look them up in a dictionary, and write brief definitions for them similar to Rosten's.

6. Rosten concludes with his favorite anecdote. Is this anecdote an effective conclusion? Why or why not?

WRITING WORKSHOP

1. Choose a significant document or ritual that is part of your own religious or cultural heritage. Define it, using any pattern or combination of patterns you choose, but include a formal definition somewhere in your essay. Assume your readers are not familiar with the term you are defining.

2. With Rosten's article as source material, write a simple definition of the Talmud, using a series of examples to structure your essay. Imagine that your audience is a group of Jewish school children.

DYSLEXIA

Eileen Simpson

This selection, an excerpt from Reversals: A Personal Account of
Victory over Dyslexia, *defines a developmental disorder that afflicts
some twenty-three million Americans—and has afflicted noted figures like Hans Christian Andersen, W. B. Yeats, Thomas Edison,
and Woodrow Wilson. Eileen Simpson, now a psychotherapist and
the author of short stories, a novel, and the recently published* Poets
in their Youth, *struggled all her life with her handicap and was
able to overcome it by gaining an understanding of what dyslexia
is. Here she presents a working definition for her readers, comparing the examples she selects with her own experience as a child.*

Dyslexia (from the Greek, *dys,* faulty, + *lexis,* speech, cognate   1
with the Latin *legere,* to read), developmental or specific dyslexia
as it's technically called, the disorder I suffered from, is the inability
of otherwise normal children to read. Children whose intelligence
is below average, whose vision or hearing is defective, who have not
had proper schooling, or who are too emotionally disturbed or brain-
damaged to profit from it belong in other diagnostic categories. They,
too, may be unable to learn to read, but they cannot properly be
called dyslexics.

For more than seventy years the essential nature of the affliction   2
has been hotly disputed by psychologists, neurologists, and educa-
tors. It is generally agreed, however, that it is the result of a neuro-
physiological flaw in the brain's ability to process language. It is
probably inherited, although some experts are reluctant to say this
because they fear people will equate "inherited" with "untreatable."
Treatable it certainly is: not a disease to be cured, but a malfunction
that requires retraining.

Reading is the most complex skill a child entering school is asked   3
to develop. What makes it complex, in part, is that letters are less
constant than objects. A car seen from a distance, close to, from
above, or below, or in a mirror still looks like a car even though the
optical image changes. The letters of the alphabet are more whim-
sical. Take the letter *b.* Turned upside down it becomes a *p.* Looked
at in a mirror, it becomes a *d.* Capitalized, it becomes something
quite different, a *B.* The *M* upside down is a *W.* The *E* flipped over
becomes <u>Ǝ</u>. This reversed *E* is familiar to mothers of normal chil-

342

dren who have just begun to go to school. The earliest examples of art work they bring home often have I LOV☰ YOU written on them.

Dyslexics differ from other children in that they read, spell, and   4 write letters upside down and turned around far more frequently and for a much longer time. In what seems like a capricious manner, they also add letters, syllables, and words, or, just as capriciously, delete them. With palindromic words (was–saw, on–no), it is the order of the letters rather than the orientation they change. The new word makes sense, but not the sense intended. Then there are other words where the changed order—"sorty" for story—does not make sense at all.

The inability to recognize that g, *g*, and G are the same letter,   5 the inability to maintain the orientation of the letters, to retain the order in which they appear, and to follow a line of text without jumping above or below it—all the results of the flaw—can make of an orderly page of words a dish of alphabet soup.

Also essential for reading is the ability to store words in memory   6 and to retrieve them. This very particular kind of memory dyslexics lack. So, too, do they lack the ability to hear what the eye sees, and to see what they hear. If the eye sees "off," the ear must hear "off" and not "of," or "for." If the ear hears "saw," the eye must see that it looks like "saw" on the page and not "was." Lacking these skills, a sentence or paragraph becomes a coded message to which the dyslexic can't find the key.

It is only a slight exaggeration to say that those who learned to   7 read without difficulty can best understand the labor reading is for a dyslexic by turning a page of text upside down and trying to decipher it.

While the literature is replete with illustrations of the way these   8 children write and spell, there are surprisingly few examples of how they read. One, used for propaganda purposes to alert the public to the vulnerability of dyslexics in a literate society, is a sign warning that behind it are guard dogs trained to kill. The dyslexic reads:

Wurring
Guard God
Patoly

for

Warning
Guard Dog
Patrol

and, of course, remains ignorant of the danger.

Looking for a more commonplace example, and hoping to recap- 9
ture the way I must have read in fourth grade, I recently observed
dyslexic children at the Educational Therapy Clinic in Princeton,
through the courtesy of Elizabeth Travers, the director. The first
child I saw, eight-year-old Anna (whose red hair and brown eyes
reminded me of myself at that age), had just come to the Clinic and
was learning the alphabet. Given the story of "Little Red Riding
Hood," which is at the second grade level, she began confidently
enough, repeating the title from memory, then came to a dead stop.
With much coaxing throughout, she read as follows:

Grandma you a top. Grandma [looks over at picture of Red Riding
Hood]. Red Riding Hood [long pause, presses index finger into the
paper. Looks at me for help. I urge: Go ahead] the a [puts head close
to the page, nose almost touching] on Grandma

for

Once upon a time there was a little girl who had a red coat with a
red hood. Etc.

"Grandma" was obviously a memory from having heard the story 10
read aloud. Had I needed a reminder of how maddening my silences
must have been to Miss Henderson, and how much patience is required to teach these children, Anna, who took almost ten minutes
to read these few lines, furnished it. The main difference between
Anna and me at that age is that Anna clearly felt no need to invent.
She was perplexed, but not anxious, and seemed to have infinite
tolerance for her long silences.

Toby, a nine-year-old boy with superior intelligence, had a year 11
of tutoring behind him and could have managed "Little Red Riding
Hood" with ease. His text was taken from the *Reader's Digest's
Reading Skill Builder,* Grade IV. He read:

A kangaroo likes as if he had but truck together warm. His saw neck
and head do not . . . [Here Toby sighed with fatigue] seem to feel
happy back. They and tried and so every a tiger likes Moses and
shoots from lonesome day and shouts and long shore animals. And
each farm play with five friends . . .

He broke off with the complaint, "This is too hard. Do I have to 12
read any more?"

His text was: 13

A kangaroo looks as if he had been put together wrong. His small neck and head do not seem to fit with his heavy back legs and thick tail. Soft eyes, a twinkly little nose and short front legs seem strange on such a large strong animal. And each front paw has five fingers, like a man's hand.

An English expert gives the following bizarre example of an adult 14 dyslexic's performance:

An the bee-what in the tel mother of the biothodoodoo to the majoram or that emidrate eni eni Krastrei, mestriet to Ketra lotombreidi to ra from treido as that.

His text, taken from a college catalogue the examiner happened to have close at hand, was:

It shall be in the power of the college to examine or not every licentiate, previous to his admission to the fellowship, as they shall think fit.

That evening when I read aloud to Auntie for the first time, I 15 probably began as Toby did, my memory of the classroom lesson keeping me close to the text. When memory ran out, and Auntie did not correct my errors, I began to invent. When she still didn't stop me, I may well have begun to improvise in the manner of this patient—anything to keep going and keep up the myth that I was reading—until Auntie brought the "gibberish" to a halt.

COMPREHENSION

1. In one sentence, define *dyslexia*.
2. How are dyslexics different from normal children who are just learning to read and write?
3. What essential skills for reading do dyslexics lack?
4. Why did Simpson visit the Educational Therapy Clinic?
5. How is Anna's behavior different from the behavior of Simpson as a child? How can you account for this difference?
6. Why did Simpson, like other dyslexics, resort to "improvising" when she read aloud?

PURPOSE AND AUDIENCE

1. In paragraph 2, Simpson suggests her purpose in defining *dyslexia*. What is this purpose?

2. Does this essay have a thesis? If so, what is it? If not, why not?

3. Does Simpson expect her audience to be familiar with dyslexia? How can you tell?

STYLE AND STRUCTURE

1. In paragraph 1, Simpson uses formal definition and negation. Locate an example of each technique.

2. In the body of her essay, Simpson develops her definition with examples, description, and comparison and contrast. Find examples of each technique.

3. In presenting examples of the reading performances of dyslexics, Simpson begins with an eight-year-old child, moves to a nine-year-old child with superior intelligence, and concludes with an adult. Why does she organize her examples in this manner?

4. Simpson concludes her essay with a personal note. Is this an effective conclusion? Why or why not?

WRITING WORKSHOP

1. Write an essay in which you define a handicap you have or a handicap you are familiar with through the experiences of a friend or family member. Use examples and any other appropriate techniques to develop your definition.

2. Use what you now know about dyslexia to write an essay in which you define a similar handicap by comparing and contrasting it with dyslexia.

3. Even without a handicap, you have probably found some task or skill very difficult to master, though others found it easy. Name and define the "condition" which hindered your learning, using whatever techniques are appropriate for your definition.

EUPHEMISM

Neil Postman

Born in 1931 and currently Professor of Media Ecology at New York University, Neil Postman is widely known for his essays and books advocating radical education reform. In addition to contributing to periodicals like the Atlantic *and* The Nation, *Postman is the author of* Television and the Teaching of English *(1961); coauthor of* Linguistics: A Revolution in Teaching *(1966) and* Teaching as a Subversive Activity *(1969); and author of* Crazy Talk, Stupid Talk: How We Defeat Ourselves by the Way We Talk and What to Do About It *(1976), in which "Euphemism" appeared. Here he discusses the value of using euphemisms in speaking and writing, considering the political as well as the linguistic implications.*

A euphemism is commonly defined as an auspicious or exalted term (like "sanitation engineer") that is used in place of a more down-to-earth term (like "garbage man"). People who are partial to euphemisms stand accused of being "phony" or of trying to hide what it is they are really talking about. And there is no doubt that in some situations the accusation is entirely proper. For example, one of the more detestable euphemisms I have come across in recent years is the term "Operation Sunshine," which is the name the U.S. Government gave to some experiments it conducted with the hydrogen bomb in the South Pacific. It is obvious that the government, in choosing this name, was trying to expunge the hideous imagery that the bomb evokes and in so doing committed, as I see it, an immoral act. This sort of process—giving pretty names to essentially ugly realities—is what has given euphemizing such a bad name. And people like George Orwell have done valuable work for all of us in calling attention to how the process works. But there is another side to euphemizing that is worth mentioning, and a few words here in its defense will not be amiss.

To begin with, we must keep in mind that things do not have "real" names, although many people believe that they do. A garbage man is not "really" a "garbage man," any more than he is really a "sanitation engineer." And a pig is not called a "pig" because it is so dirty, nor a shrimp a "shrimp" because it is so small. There are

things, and then there are the names of things, and it is considered
a fundamental error in all branches of semantics to assume that a
name and a thing are one and the same. It is true, of course, that
a name is usually so firmly associated with the thing it denotes that
it is extremely difficult to separate one from the other. That is why,
for example, advertising is so effective. Perfumes are not given names
like "Bronx Odor," and an automobile will never be called "The
Lumbering Elephant." Shakespeare was only half right in saying
that a rose by any other name would smell as sweet. What we call
things affects how we will perceive them. It is not only harder to
sell someone a "horse mackerel" sandwich than a "tuna fish" sandwich, but even though they are the "same" thing, we are likely to
enjoy the taste of tuna more than that of the horse mackerel. It
would appear that human beings almost naturally come to *identify*
names with things, which is one of our more fascinating illusions.
But there is some substance to this illusion. For if you change the
names of things, you change how people will regard them, and that
is as good as changing the nature of the thing itself.

Now, all sorts of scoundrels know this perfectly well and can   3
make us love almost anything by getting us to transfer the charm
of a name to whatever worthless thing they are promoting. But at
the same time and in the same vein, euphemizing is a perfectly
intelligent method of generating new and useful ways of perceiving
things. The man who wants us to call him a "sanitation engineer"
instead of a "garbage man" is hoping we will treat him with more
respect than we presently do. He wants us to see that he is of some
importance to our society. His euphemism is laughable only if we
think that he is not deserving of such notice or respect. The teacher
who prefers us to use the term "culturally different children" instead of "slum children" is euphemizing, all right, but is doing it to
encourage us to see aspects of a situation that might otherwise not
be attended to.

The point I am making is that there is nothing in the process of   4
euphemizing itself that is contemptible. Euphemizing is contemptible when a name makes us see something that is not true or diverts
our attention from something that is. The hydrogen bomb kills.
There is nothing else that it does. And when you experiment with
it, you are trying to find out how widely and well it kills. Therefore,
to call such an experiment "Operation Sunshine" is to suggest a
purpose for the bomb that simply does not exist. But to call "slum
children" "culturally different" is something else. It calls attention,
for example, to legitimate reasons why such children might feel
alienated from what goes on in school.

I grant that sometimes such euphemizing does not have the in-   5
tended effect. It is possible for a teacher to use the term "culturally
different" but still be controlled by the term "slum children" (which
the teacher may believe is their "real" name). "Old people" may be
called "senior citizens," and nothing might change. And "lunatic
asylums" may still be filthy, primitive prisons though they are called
"mental institutions." Nonetheless, euphemizing may be regarded
as one of our more important intellectual resources for creating new
perspectives on a subject. The *attempt* to rename "old people" "senior
citizens" was obviously motivated by a desire to give them a political identity, which they not only warrant but which may yet have
important consequences. In fact, the fate of euphemisms is very
hard to predict. A new and seemingly silly name may replace an
old one (let us say, "chairperson" for "chairman") and for years no
one will think or act any differently because of it. And then, gradually, as people begin to assume that "chairperson" is the "real"
and proper name (or "senior citizen" or "tuna fish" or "sanitation
engineer"), their attitudes begin to shift, and they will approach
things in a slightly different frame of mind. There is a danger, of
course, in supposing that a new name can change attitudes quickly
or always. There must be some authentic tendency or drift in the
culture to lend support to the change, or the name will remain
incongruous and may even appear ridiculous. To call a teacher a
"facilitator" would be such an example. To eliminate the distinction
between "boys" and "girls" by calling them "childpersons" would be
another.

But to suppose that such changes never "amount to anything" is   6
to underestimate the power of names. I have been astounded not
only by how rapidly the name "blacks" has replaced "Negroes" (a
kind of euphemizing in reverse) but also by how significantly perceptions and attitudes have shifted as an accompaniment to the
change.

The key idea here is that euphemisms are a means through which   7
a culture may alter its imagery and by so doing subtly change its
style, its priorities, and its values. I reject categorically the idea
that people who use "earthy" language are speaking more directly
or with more authenticity than people who employ euphemisms.
Saying that someone is "dead" is not to speak more plainly or honestly than saying he has "passed away." It is, rather, to suggest a
different conception of what the event means. To ask where the
"shithouse" is, is no more to the point than to ask where the "rest-
room" is. But in the difference between the two words, there is
expressed a vast difference in one's attitude toward privacy and

propriety. What I am saying is that the process of euphemizing has no moral content. The moral dimensions are supplied by what the words in question express, what they want us to value and to see. A nation that calls experiments with bombs "Operation Sunshine" is very frightening. On the other hand, a people who call "garbage men" "sanitation engineers" can't be all bad.

COMPREHENSION

1. What is a euphemism? Give examples.

2. What, according to Postman, "has given euphemizing such a bad name"?

3. In paragraph 2, what misconception does Postman set out to correct? Why?

4. What does Postman see as the value of euphemizing? What are its potential dangers?

5. What does Postman mean in paragraph 6 when he refers to the shift from "Negroes" to "blacks" as "a kind of euphemizing in reverse"?

PURPOSE AND AUDIENCE

1. What is Postman's purpose in writing this essay, besides just defining *euphemism*? What is his thesis?

2. What attitude does Postman assume his audience already has about euphemizing? How do you know this?

3. In paragraph 1, Postman introduces the "detestable" euphemism "Operation Sunshine"; he brings it up again in paragraphs 4 and 7. What effect does the repetition of this term have on the reader? Does this effect in any way counter the essay's purpose? Why or why not?

STYLE AND STRUCTURE

1. What technique does Postman rely most heavily upon in developing his definition?

2. Where does Postman define *euphemism* through its effects?

3. Most of Postman's paragraphs are of similar length; paragraph 6, however, is much shorter. What might account for this?

4. What information in the conclusion echoes the essay's introduction? Is this repetition an effective closing technique? Explain.

WRITING WORKSHOP

1. Write an essay in which you define *euphemism* by presenting examples. Begin by listing all the euphemisms you can; then classify them into related groups. In your thesis, make a point about the kinds of words people euphemize.

2. Write a definition essay whose purpose is to convince your readers of the potential dangers of euphemizing. Use examples to support your thesis.

THE MODERN COWBOY

John R. Erickson

John R. Erickson, born in 1943, spent two years working as a cowboy on an Oklahoma ranch. He has published three books: Through Time and the Valley *(1978),* Panhandle Cowboy *(1980) and* The Modern Cowboy *(1981), from whose first chapter this selection is excerpted. Elsewhere in the book Erickson, a Texan, goes into detail about the work, play, and family life of the cowboy; the tools of his trade; the modern cattle business; and the cowboy's future. In this selection Erickson sets out to clear up the public's misconceptions about the cowboy by providing an accurate, up-to-date definition.*

I have met the American cowboy on ranches in the Texas and Oklahoma Panhandles. I have ridden with him and worked beside him. I have eaten lunch with him on the ground and drunk water from his cup. I am tempted to describe him as I have seen him described in several books: "Merely folks, just a plain everyday bowlegged human." It is a marvelous description, and very quotable. However, the temptation to use it merely points out the degree to which, on the subject of cowboys, we have come to rely on books and observations of the past. The fact is—and I rather hate to admit this—that I have known only one bowlegged cowboy, and I think he was born that way. Legend tells us that cowboys are supposed to have legs warped by long days in the saddle, and maybe fifty years ago they did. Today they don't. We can begin our description of the modern cowboy with the observation that, at least on one point of anatomy, he ain't what he used to be.

The cowboy I know is a workingman. He is defined by his work, which should not be confused with the term "job." Cowboy work is more than a job; it is a life-style and a medium of expression. Remove the cowboy from his working environment and you have someone else, someone who resembles a cowboy in outward appearance but who, to one degree or another, is an imposter. Standing on a street corner, the cowboy is just an ordinary human. But out in the pasture, when he's a-horseback and holds a rope in his hands, he assumes the qualities that have made him a legend.

The fact that the cowboy is defined by his work has made him a difficult subject to study. To see him at his best, you almost have to work with him day after day, and to understand what he does in his work, you almost have to possess a fundamental knowledge of the skills of his profession. Perhaps the people who are in the best position to observe and discuss the working cowboy are the men who work with him every day—other cowboys. Unfortunately, most cowboys don't write, and most writers don't work on ranches.

The cowboy does not own property. Owners of ranchland go by   4
various titles, among them rancher, cattleman, and stockman. The rancher owns the land, manages the operation, and makes decisions about buying and selling. Of course you can find instances where the two roles overlap. Some ranchers work beside their cowboys, and some cowboys are permitted to make management decisions, and in small ranching operations family members function in both capacities. But as a general rule it is safe to say that ranchers and cowboys are not the same breed. The term *cowboy,* as I use it, means a workingman who has mastered the skills needed in working around cattle, while the term *rancher* implies ownership and management.

In the cow lot or on a roundup crew the social differences between   5
rancher and cowboy don't mean much, but elsewhere they are clearly defined. Ranchers are often prominent leaders in the community; cowboys are not. Ranchers often sit on governing boards of businesses, churches, and schools; cowboys do not. Ranchers are frequently the subject of articles in livestock journals, while the cowboys are rarely mentioned. The rancher and his wife may belong to the country club, but the cowboy and his wife won't. The rancher has his circle of friends, the cowboy has his, and they do not often overlap.

There is one difference between them that goes right to the heart   6
of the matter: the rancher can take the day off or go into town whenever he wishes, but the cowboy can't. The cowboy's life is tied to the rhythms and patterns of animals: a cow that must be milked twice a day, chickens that must be turned out in the morning and shut up at night, horses that must be fed and watered, pregnant heifers that must be watched, and, in winter, cows that must be fed seven days a week. The rancher and the cowboy may dress alike, talk alike, and even think alike, but at six o'clock in the evening, one goes down to the milking barn while the other attends a meeting in town.

The cowboy is a workingman, yet he has little in common with   7
the urban blue-collar worker. In the first place, as we have already observed, cowboy work is not just a job, with established work days, certain hours, and guaranteed holidays. Since he lives where he works, and since he deals with animals instead of machines, the

cowboy is never really off work. He is on call 24 hours a day, 7 days a week, 365 days a year. The work is not always hard, but as a friend once observed to me, "It's damned sure steady." A calving heifer, a prairie fire, a sick horse may have him up at any hour of the day or night, and in this business there is no such thing as time-and-a-half for overtime.

In the second place, cowboys, unlike urban blue-collar workers, 8 do not belong to a union, and they probably never will. The cowboy life attracts a special type of individual, one who can shift for himself and endure isolation, and one who thrives on physical hardship, a certain amount of danger, and low wages. These are not the qualities of a joiner, but of a loner. You might even go so far as to say that there is a little bit of outlaw in most of them—not that they are dishonest or deceitful, but rather that they are incorrigible, like a spirited horse that is never quite broke and gentle, even though he may take the bit and saddle. Some cowboys stay in the profession simply because they don't fit anywhere else. They tried other jobs and couldn't adapt, or they went into business for themselves and failed. They returned to cowboying because it was in their bones and blood.

This stubborn, independent quality of the cowboy has fascinated 9 the American public and has contributed to his status as a myth and a legend. We like to think of ourselves as a free and independent people, ready at any moment to tell the boss, the mayor, or the president himself to go straight to hell. Of course this is more a dream than a reality. Most of us are indentured to mortgage payments and car payments and live in terror of an IRS audit. Perhaps the cowboy, riding his horse across an endless prairie, has become a symbol of what we used to be—or at least what we *think* we used to be—and of what we would be if we could. He doesn't have to punch a time clock, drive through snarls of traffic every morning and afternoon, shave or wear a tie to work, or participate in hollow rituals in order to gain advancement. When he gets tired of the scenery, or if the boss crowds him too close, he packs his few possessions in a pickup and horse trailer and moves on to another ranch. In the American cowboy we find qualities we deeply admire—simplicity, independence, physical strength, courage, peace of mind, and self-respect—but which, to one degree or another, we have surrendered in order to gain something else. These qualities have made the cowboy the most powerful mythical character in our folklore, and one which reaches to the very core of our identity as a people.

The typical cowboy, if we may speak of such an animal, does not 10 carry a pistol, strum a guitar, or burst into song at the end of the day. He has never rescued a maiden in distress or cleaned the outlaws out of a saloon. He can ride a bucking horse, but he can also get piled. He can rope a calf in the pasture, but he can also burn three loops before he makes the catch. In his working environment, he is dressed in blue jeans, a long-sleeved shirt, boots, western hat, and a vest. He looks good in these clothes, like an animal in its skin. In his work he moves with ease and grace, and sitting astride his horse he exudes confidence and authority. We are tempted to say that he is handsome, even though he might lack the physical endowments that we usually associate with that term.

But take him off his horse, throw him into a bathtub, scrub him down, put him in a set of "good" clothes, and send him to town, and we will meet an entirely different man. All at once he becomes graceless and awkward. He isn't wearing his work hat and we see that he is getting bald, or if he has a good head of hair, it looks as though he has plastered it with lard and run a rake through it. His eyes, which outside are naturally set into a squint, seem puffy in the fluorescent light, and they do not sparkle. His "good" clothes are appalling, and we can hardly keep from laughing at him.

The mythology and legend of the Cowboy begin in this humble human vessel. But the working cowboy is neither a myth nor a legend. He is an ordinary mortal. If we stopped at this point, we would have performed the ritual known as debunking, wherein a notable figure is taken like a buck deer, strung up, skinned and gutted, and held up naked for all to see. But I'm not setting out to debunk the cowboy. If he sometimes falls short of our expectations, he will surpass them when we see him at his best. And he is at his best when he is at his work. Ultimately, the cowboy *is* what he *does*.

So what is a cowboy? Is he a heroic figure or just a common laborer? It's hard to say. I've seen both sides, and I think it would be a mistake to place too much emphasis on one side or the other. If we view him only as a symbol and a mythical figure, then we lose contact with his humanness and fall into the kind of sentimentality that allows some observers to ignore the poverty, the loneliness, the exploitation of cowboys, and to gloss over the darker side of the cattle industry with little homilies about the "honor" of being a cowboy. But neither do we want to strip him down to enzymes and electrons or to present him as just another human fop doomed to mediocrity and failure, for this view would deny that he can rise above himself through displays of skill, strength, and courage. And that would be false.

If the cowboy is a hero, then we will want to know the price he pays for this honor. If he is a common man, then we will want to know why he has fascinated our people for a hundred years. For the moment let us content ourselves with this definition: The cowboy is a common laborer with heroic tendencies and a sense of humor.

COMPREHENSION

1. Why does Erickson say, in paragraph 3, "The fact that the cowboy is defined by his work has made him a difficult subject to study"?

2. How does Erickson distinguish between cowboys and ranchers? What does he consider the most striking difference?

3. How do cowboys differ from urban blue-collar workers?

4. According to Erickson, why does the American public see the cowboy as a mythical or legendary figure?

5. How does the actual cowboy differ from the average American's image of him?

6. In Erickson's opinion, is the modern cowboy a heroic figure, a common laborer, or both? Explain.

PURPOSE AND AUDIENCE

1. What does Erickson hope to convey to his readers through the personal testimony he offers in paragraph 1?

2. In defining the modern cowboy, telling what the cowboy is and what he is not, Erickson effectively conveys his thesis. What is this thesis?

3. Erickson bases some of his points on what he sees as his audience's view of the cowboy. What preconceptions does he assume his audience has?

4. Would this essay have been more effective if Erickson had discussed specific cowboy heroes with whom his readers might be familiar? Explain. Why do you think he does not?

STYLE AND STRUCTURE

1. In his introduction, noting that he has only known one bowlegged cowboy, Erickson says the cowboy "ain't what he used to be." Where else does he support this point?

2. Where does Erickson develop his definition by using negation? By describing? By comparing and contrasting? By enumerating the cowboy's characteristics?

3. Where does Erickson present a formal definition?

4. Why does Erickson discuss what he calls "the cowboy I know" before he introduces the cowboy of myth and legend?

WRITING WORKSHOP

1. Using one example or several different ones, define the cowboy as he is represented in popular films.

2. Write an essay in which you define another kind of American hero.

NEW SUPERSTITIONS
FOR OLD

Margaret Mead

The noted anthropologist Margaret Mead was born in 1901 in Philadelphia and died in 1978. Regarded as an expert on family structure, she taught anthropology at Columbia University, from which she received a Ph.D. in 1929, and served as Curator of Ethnology at the American Museum of Natural History between 1964 and 1969. As a writer, she is perhaps best known for her anthropological studies Coming of Age in Samoa *(1928) and* Growing Up in New Guinea *(1930); she was the author or coauthor of some forty other books, including the autobiographical* Blackberry Winter *(1972). In her many publications and in her lectures, Mead explored social and ethical issues of the past and present. In "New Superstitions for Old" she tackles a characteristically complex topic: superstition.*

Once in a while there is a day when everything seems to run 1 smoothly and even the riskiest venture comes out exactly right. You exclaim, "This is my lucky day!" Then as an afterthought you say, "Knock on wood!" Of course, you do not really believe that knocking on wood will ward off danger. Still, boasting about your own good luck gives you a slightly uneasy feeling—and you carry out the little protective ritual. If someone challenged you at that moment, you would probably say, "Oh, that's nothing. Just an old superstition."

But when you come to think about it, what is superstition? 2

In the contemporary world most people treat old folk beliefs as 3 superstitions—the belief, for instance, that there are lucky and unlucky days or numbers, that future events can be read from omens, that there are protective charms or that what happens can be influenced by casting spells. We have excluded magic from our current world view, for we know that natural events have natural causes.

In a religious context, where truths cannot be demonstrated, we 4 accept them as a matter of faith. Superstitions, however, belong to the category of beliefs, practices and ways of thinking that have been discarded because they are inconsistent with scientific knowledge. It is easy to say that other people are superstitious because they believe what we regard to be untrue. "Superstition" used in that sense is a derogatory term for the beliefs of other people that we do not share. But there is more to it than that. For superstitions lead a kind of half life in a twilight world where, sometimes, we partly suspend our disbelief and act as if magic worked.

Actually, almost every day, even in the most sophisticated home, something is likely to happen that evokes the memory of some old folk belief. The salt spills. A knife falls to the floor. Your nose tickles. Then perhaps, with a slightly embarrassed smile, the person who spilled the salt tosses a pinch over his left shoulder. Or someone recites the old rhyme, "Knife falls, gentleman calls." Or as you rub your nose you think, That means a letter. I wonder who's writing? No one takes these small responses very seriously or gives them more than a passing thought. Sometimes people will preface one of these ritual acts—walking around instead of under a ladder or hastily closing an umbrella that has been opened inside a house—with such remarks as "I remember my great-aunt used to . . ." or "Germans used to say you ought not . . ." And then, having placed the belief at some distance away in time or space, they carry out the ritual.

Everyone also remembers a few of the observances of childhood—wishing on the first star; looking at the new moon over the right shoulder; avoiding the cracks in the sidewalk on the way to school while chanting, "Step on a crack, break your mother's back"; wishing on white horses, on loads of hay, on covered bridges, on red cars; saying quickly, "Bread-and-butter" when a post or a tree separated you from the friend you were walking with. The adult may not actually recite the formula "Star light, star bright . . ." and may not quite turn to look at the new moon, but his mood is tempered by a little of the old thrill that came when the observance was still freighted with magic.

Superstition can also be used with another meaning. When I discuss the religious beliefs of other peoples, especially primitive peoples, I am often asked, "Do they really have a religion, or is it all just superstition?" The point of contrast here is not between a scientific and a magical view of the world but between the clear, theologically defensible religious beliefs of members of civilized societies and what we regard as the false and childish views of the heathen who "bow down to wood and stone." Within the civilized religions, however, where membership includes believers who are educated and urbane and others who are ignorant and simple, one always finds traditions and practices that the more sophisticated will dismiss offhand as "just superstition" but that guide the steps of those who live by older ways. Mostly these are very ancient beliefs, some handed on from one religion to another and carried from country to country around the world.

Very commonly, people associate superstition with the past, with   8
very old ways of thinking that have been supplanted by modern
knowledge. But new superstitions are continually coming into being
and flourishing in our society. Listening to mothers in the park in
the 1930's, one heard them say, "Now, don't you run out into the
sun, or Polio will get you." In the 1940's elderly people explained
to one another in tones of resignation, "It was the Virus that got
him down." And every year the cosmetics industry offers us new
magic—cures for baldness, lotions that will give every woman radiant skin, hair coloring that will restore to the middle-aged the
charm and romance of youth—results that are promised if we will
just follow the simple directions. Families and individuals also have
their cherished, private superstitions. You must leave by the back
door when you are going on a journey, or you must wear a green
dress when you are taking an examination. It is a kind of joke, of
course, but it makes you feel safe.

These old half-beliefs and new half-beliefs reflect the keenness of   9
our wish to have something come true or to prevent something bad
from happening. We do not always recognize new superstitions for
what they are, and we still follow the old ones because someone's
faith long ago matches our contemporary hopes and fears. In the
past people "knew" that a black cat crossing one's path was a bad
omen, and they turned back home. Today we are fearful of taking
a journey and would give anything to turn back—and then we notice
a black cat running across the road in front of us.

Child psychologists recognize the value of the toy a child holds   10
in his hand at bedtime. It is different from his thumb, with which
he can close himself in from the rest of the world, and it is different
from the real world, to which he is learning to relate himself. Psychologists call these toys—these furry animals and old, cozy baby
blankets—"transitional objects"; that is, objects that help the child
move back and forth between the exactions of everyday life and the
world of wish and dream.

Superstitions have some of the qualities of these transitional ob-   11
jects. They help people pass between the areas of life where what
happens has to be accepted without proof and the areas where se-
quences of events are explicable in terms of cause and effect, based
on knowledge. Bacteria and viruses that cause sickness have been
identified; the cause of symptoms can be diagnosed and a rational
course of treatment prescribed. Magical charms no longer are needed
to treat the sick; modern medicine has brought the whole sequence
of events into the secular world. But people often act as if this
change had not taken place. Laymen still treat germs as if they

were invisible, malign spirits, and physicians sometimes prescribe antibiotics as if they were magic substances.

Over time, more and more of life has become subject to the con- 12 trols of knowledge. However, this is never a one-way process. Scientific investigation is continually increasing our knowledge. But if we are to make good use of this knowledge, we must not only rid our minds of old, superseded beliefs and fragments of magical practice, but also recognize new superstitions for what they are. Both are generated by our wishes, our fears and our feeling of helplessness in difficult situations.

Civilized peoples are not alone in having grasped the idea of 13 superstitions—beliefs and practices that are superseded but that still may evoke the different worlds in which we live—the sacred, the secular and the scientific. They allow us to keep a private world also, where, smiling a little, we can banish danger with a gesture and summon luck with a rhyme, make the sun shine in spite of storm clouds, force the stranger to do our bidding, keep an enemy at bay and straighten the paths of those we love.

COMPREHENSION

1. What kinds of long-standing rituals does Mead consider to be superstitions? Can you think of others?

2. In what way are religion and superstition similar? How are they different?

3. Why does Mead say many superstitions have disappeared?

4. Why do we retain so many superstitions?

5. What are transitional objects? How does Mead relate them to superstitions?

PURPOSE AND AUDIENCE

1. This essay was originally published in 1966 in a magazine aimed at young mothers. In what way, if any, does Mead tailor her subject to fit her readers? How could she have increased the essay's relevance for this audience?

2. What is the thesis of Mead's essay? Where does it appear?

3. Can you determine Mead's attitude toward her subject? Does she feel that superstitions are silly or useful? Explain.

STYLE AND STRUCTURE

1. What methods of development does Mead use to expand her definition of superstition? What other methods might she have used?

2. Where, if anywhere, does Mead formally define superstition? Define it in your own words.

3. How does the extended comparison between superstitions and a child's toy advance the essay's argument?

4. Mead opens her essay by directly addressing her readers and their superstitions; she uses this device later in the essay, too. What is the effect of this technique?

WRITING WORKSHOP

1. Write an extended definition of your own idea of superstition, using a series of examples to support your thesis.

2. Write a definition of superstition in which you use one extended example, perhaps a personal experience or observation, as the basis of your paper.

3. Mead's essay distinguishes between science and superstition, but perhaps this contrast is overstated. Are there any similarities? Write an essay in which you compare the two in order to define superstition as a form of primitive or unsophisticated science (or to define science as sophisticated superstition).

10

Argumentation

WHAT IS ARGUMENTATION?

All of us like a good argument. We enjoy the confrontation of an intellectual exchange that allows us to test our ideas and see how they stand up. Long after we graduate, we remember the heated debates that took place in college classrooms or dormitories. But there is a difference between an argument and an exchange of opinions, or for that matter a bout of name-calling. Arguments follow rules designed to ensure that ideas are presented fairly and logically. Not surprisingly then, the first rules governing argumentation were formulated thousands of years ago by the ancient Greeks. They designed their rules to apply to public speaking, but as you will see in this chapter, these techniques apply to writing as well.

Argument is a reasoned, logical way of demonstrating that your position, belief, or conclusion is valid and that others are not. One purpose of argument is to persuade reasonable people to agree with your position. Another is simply to defend your position, to establish its validity even if others cannot be persuaded to agree. A third purpose of argumentation is to attack some position you believe to be misguided, untrue, or evil, without necessarily offering an alternative of your own. (You could, for example, attack the president's budget without presenting your own version.)

Although argument and persuasion are related, they are not the same. Persuasion—getting other people to change their minds—is one purpose of argument but not the only one. And although argument, the appeal to reason, is one means of persuasion, there are others: appeals to the audience's self-interest, to its moral sense, or to its emotions. You could, for instance, use all three of these appeals to argue against lowering the drinking age in your state from eighteen to sixteen years of age. Appealing to your audience's self-interest, you could point out how an increased number of accidents involving drunk drivers would cost taxpayers more money and could cost some of them their lives. You could state, if you believed it to be true, that teenage drinking is morally wrong and should not be condoned by the state. And finally, you could appeal to your audience's emotions by telling a particularly sad story about a sixteen-year-old alcoholic. All of these appeals are relevant and fair, and any of them might succeed.

Of course what appeal you choose depends partly on the results you want to achieve. It also depends on your sense of your audience. But there is an ethical question involved—the age-old question of whether and when the end justifies the means. Most people would agree that lies and threats are unacceptable means of persuasion among rational people, yet they are commonly used in international diplomacy, and nearly everyone resorts to them from time to time. But it is unquestionably true that in college, and often outside it as well, the most acceptable form of persuasion—indeed often the only acceptable form—is argument, the appeal to reason.

Choosing a Topic

In argument, as in all writing, choosing the right topic is important. It should be one that you care about, one in which you have an intellectual or emotional interest. But you should not be pigheaded. If the evidence goes against your position you should be able to change your thesis or even the subject. And you should be able, in advance, to consider your topic from other people's viewpoints so that you understand what they believe and can build a logical case that appeals to their sense of reason. If you think you cannot do this, then you should abandon your topic and pick another one that you can deal with more objectively.

Besides caring about your topic, you should be well informed about it. Opinion unsupported by evidence is not persuasive. Furthermore, you should select a limited issue, one narrow enough that it can be treated properly in the space available to you, or confine your discussion to a particular aspect of a broad issue. You should also consider your purpose—what you expect your argument to accomplish and how you wish your audience to respond. If your topic is so far-reaching that you cannot specify what you want to persuade a reader to think and to do, or so idealistic that your expectations are impossible or unreasonable, your essay will not be effective.

Taking a Stand

After you have chosen your topic, and informed yourself on it if necessary, you are ready to take your stand—to state the position you will argue in the form of a thesis:

Solar power is the best available solution to the coming energy crisis.

This thesis says that you believe there will be an energy crisis in the future, that there is more than one possible solution to the crisis, and that solar energy is a better solution than any other. In your argument you will have to support each of these three assertions logically and persuasively. Here is an opposing thesis on the same topic:

If there is to be an energy crisis, solar power is not the solution to it.

This thesis questions, by its use of the word *if*, whether there will be an energy crisis, and it states that solar power, even if it is a promising alternate source of energy, could not solve such a crisis, at least not by itself. This is a simpler position to argue, with only one assertion that requires support. That is not to say, of course, that it is more true.

Before going any further, you should examine your thesis to make sure that it is debatable. There is no point in arguing a position that everyone already agrees with or that cannot be settled through logic. It is also wise to test your own attitude toward your thesis. If you are so convinced you are right that you cannot understand or respect opposing views and the people who hold them, then you probably do not have the objectivity you will need to develop a sound and persuasive argument. Argument is demanding, and it particularly demands clear thought and a reasonably cool head. Of course you should care about your subject and feel your position is right, but the strength of your conviction does not guarantee that your argument will be strong.

Gathering Evidence

Evidence is information that supports or opposes your thesis. Irrelevant information is not evidence at all. Both fact and opinion can be evidence, but fact is verifiable independent of who says it, while opinion is personal judgment that may or may not be verifiable, depending on what facts and reasoning support it. It is a *fact*, for example, that ever since 1965 over 45,000 people a year have been killed on the nation's highways. Your *opinion* might be that the installation of automatic seatbelts on all cars could dramatically reduce this figure. If you wanted to use the fact to support your opinion, to make it into evidence, you would have to show your readers why that fact makes your opinion more likely to be true.

After deciding on a topic, you should gather as much evidence as you can. Brainstorm to think of experiences and examples that would support your thesis. If your topic is technical or demands specific knowledge, go to the library and use the card catalog, periodical indexes, and reference books to locate the information you need.

When selecting and reviewing material, remember three things. First, read selections or consider positions that represent the full range of opinions on your subject, not just one side or another. Look especially hard at those that disagree with the position you plan to take. Then you will understand your opposition and be able to refute it effectively when you write your paper. Second, keep in mind the limits of your paper. You will need fewer facts and examples for a brief essay than you will for a term paper. Finally, review all your material to see whether it connects with your thesis in such a way that you may be able to use it as evidence.

Analyzing Your Audience

Before writing any essay, you should analyze the characteristics, values, and interests of your audience. When writing an argument, however, certain questions require special attention. Once you know who your audience will be, you need to assess what beliefs or opinions they are likely to hold and whether they are friendly, neutral, or hostile to your thesis. It's probably best to assume that some of your readers, if not a majority, are at least skeptically neutral and possibly hostile. That assumption will keep you from making claims you can't support. If your position is really controversial, you should assume an informed and determined opposition is looking for holes in your argument.

Often you begin with a purpose in mind but must decide on an audience. If you want to make something happen, who has the power to do it? Whom do you have to persuade, and how would those readers respond to your efforts? Sometimes you will need to appeal to several different audiences, tailoring your persuasive method and approach to each.

Each of these considerations influences your approach to your subject. It would be relatively easy to convince college students that tuition should be lowered or instructors that salaries should be raised. You could be reasonably sure, in advance, that each group would be friendly and would agree with your position. But argument requires more than telling people what they already believe. It would be much harder to convince college students that tuition should be raised to pay for an increase in instructors' salaries or to persuade instructors to forgo raises so that tuition can remain the same. Yet these are the kinds of challenges that persuasive argument should be used to meet. Whether your readers are mildly sympathetic, neutral, or even hostile to your position, your purpose is to change their views to match your own more closely.

What kind of evidence might change a reader's mind? That depends on the reader, on the issue, and on the facts at hand. Why should a student agree to pay higher tuition? You might concede that tuition is high but point out that it has not been raised for three years, while the college's costs have kept going up. Heating and maintaining the buildings cost more and professors' salaries have failed to keep pace with the cost of living, with the result that several excellent teachers have recently left the college for higher-paid jobs. Furthermore, cuts in government funding have already caused a reduction in the number of courses offered. On the other hand, if faculty salaries have not kept up with inflation, why should a professor agree to no raise at all this year? You could say that because government cuts in funding have already reduced course offerings and because the government has also reduced funds for loans for the many students from families whose incomes average $20,000 or less, any further rise in tuition to pay for faculty salaries might cause many students to drop out—and that in turn would cost some instructors their jobs. As you can see, the evidence and reasoning you use in an argument depend to a great extent on who you want to persuade and what you know about them.

Deductive and Inductive Argument

In argument, there are two basic ways to move from your evidence to your conclusion. One is called *deductive reasoning*. It moves from a general premise or assumption to a specific conclusion, and it is what most people mean when they speak of logic. Using certain strict logical forms, deduction holds that if all the statements in the argument are true—then the conclusion must be true. The other is *inductive reasoning,* and it works quite differently. Induction proceeds from individual observations to a more general conclusion and uses no strict form. It requires only that all the relevant evidence be stated and that the conclusion fit the evidence better than any other conclusion would.

The basic form of a deductive argument is called a *syllogism.* A syllogism is a three-step argument consisting of a major premise, which is usually a general statement; a minor premise, which is a related but more specific statement; and a conclusion, which has to be drawn from those premises. For example:

Major premise:	All Olympic runners are fast.
Minor premise:	John is an Olympic runner.
Conclusion:	Therefore, John is fast.

As you can see, if each of the premises is true, then the conclusion is true—and it is the only true conclusion that you can draw. You cannot say that John is slow, because that contradicts the premises, nor can you say that John is tall, because that goes beyond the premises.

Of course this argument seems obvious, and it is much simpler than an argumentative essay would be. But a deductive argument can be powerful, and its premises can be fairly elaborate. The Declaration of Independence has at its core a deductive argument which might be summarized in this way:

Major premise:	Tyrannical rulers deserve no loyalty.
Minor premise:	King George III is a tyrannical ruler.
Conclusion:	Therefore, King George III deserves no loyalty.

The major premise is one of those truths the Declaration claims to be self-evident. Much of the Declaration consists of evidence to support the minor premise, King George's tyranny. And the conclusion, because it is drawn from those premises, has the force of irrefutable logic: the king deserves no loyalty from his American subjects, who are therefore entitled to revolt against him.

When a conclusion follows logically from the major and minor premises, then the argument is said to be *valid.* This means only that there is no error in its logic. But if the syllogism is wrong in form, the argument is not valid and the conclusion is not sound. For example:

Major premise: All dogs are animals.
Minor premise: All cats are animals.
Conclusion: Therefore, all dogs are cats.

Of course the conclusion is absurd. But how did we wind up with such a ridiculous conclusion when both premises are obviously true? The answer is that although both cats and dogs are animals, cats are not included in the major premise of the syllogism. Thus the form of the syllogism is defective, and the argument is invalid.

But even if a syllogism is valid—that is, correct in its form—its conclusion will not necessarily be *true*. For example:

Major premise: All dogs are brown.
Minor premise: My poodle Toby is a dog.
Conclusion: Therefore, Toby is brown.

As it happens, Toby is black. The conclusion is false because the major premise is false: many dogs are not brown. If Toby had actually been brown, the conclusion would have been correct, but only by chance, not by logic.

Unlike deduction, induction has no distinctive form, and its conclusions are less definitive than those of syllogisms whose forms are valid and whose premises are clearly true. Still, there is a sequence of events which is common to much inductive thinking and to some writing based on that thinking. First, usually, comes a question to be answered—or, especially in scientific work, a tentative answer to such a question, called a *hypothesis*. Then you gather all the evidence you can find that is relevant to the question and that may be important to finding the answer. Finally you draw a conclusion, often called an *inference,* that answers the question and takes the evidence into account. Here is a very simple example:

Question: How did that living-room window get broken?
Evidence: There is a baseball on the living-room floor.
              The baseball was not there this morning.
              Some children were playing baseball this
                 afternoon.
              They were playing in the vacant lot across from
                 the window.
              They stopped playing a little while ago.
              They aren't in the vacant lot now.
Conclusion: One of the kids hit or threw the ball through the
                 window. Then they all ran away.

The conclusion seems obvious. That is because it takes all of the evidence into account. But if it turned out that the children had been playing softball, not baseball, then that one additional piece of evidence would make the conclusion very doubtful—and the true answer would be much harder to infer. And just because the conclusion is believable does not necessarily make it true. Even if the children had been playing baseball, the window could have been broken in some other way. Perhaps a bird flew against it, and perhaps the baseball in the living room had been there unnoticed all day, so that the second piece of "evidence" is not true.

Since inductive arguments tend to be more complicated than this example, how can you move from the evidence you have collected to a sound conclusion? That crucial step can be a big one, and indeed it is sometimes called an "inductive leap." There are no rules for making that leap, nor does the form of induction point to any particular kind of conclusion the way deduction does. One way to infer a conclusion is to think of as many conclusions as possible, then to choose the one you think is most believable and fits the evidence best.

Considering alternate conclusions is one way to avoid misusing a hypothesis. In the example above, a hypothesis something like this might follow the question:

Hypothesis: Those children playing baseball broke the
               living-room window.

Many people stop reasoning at this point, without gathering and considering the evidence. That is often called "jumping to a conclusion," and it is well-named, because it amounts to a premature inductive leap. In induction, however, the hypothesis is merely the starting point. The rest of the inductive process continues as if the question were still to be answered—as in fact it is until all the evidence has been taken into account.

Fallacies of Argument

Fallacies are statements that may look like arguments but are not logically defensible and may actually be deceptive. When detected they can backfire and turn even a sympathetic audience against your position. Here are some of the more common fallacies that you should watch out for.

Begging the Question. The fallacy of begging the question results when a debatable premise is presented as if it were true. This tactic asks us to agree that certain points are self-evident when they are not.

Restrictions against foreign steel are dangerous because they infringe upon free trade.

Restrictions against foreign steel by nature infringe upon free trade. Whether they are dangerous or not is another matter. The statement begs the question because it assumes what it should be proving—that free trade is a good thing.

Argument from Analogy. This fallacy occurs when an argument is based on an analogy, which is a comparison of two unlike things. Although analogies can explain an abstract or unclear idea, they never prove anything.

The overcrowded conditions in some parts of our city have forced people together like rats in a cage. Like rats, they will eventually turn upon each other, fighting and killing until a balance is restored. It is therefore necessary that we vote to appropriate funds to build low-cost housing.

No evidence is offered that people behave like rats under these or any conditions. Simply because two things have some characteristics in common, it does not necessarily follow that they are alike in other respects.

Personal Attack. This fallacy tries to turn attention away from the facts of an issue by attacking the motives or character of one's opponents.

The public should not take seriously Dr. Mason's plan for upgrading county health services. He is a former alcoholic whose second wife recently divorced him.

This attack on Dr. Mason's character says nothing about the quality of his plan. Sometimes there is a connection between a person's private and public lives—for example, in a case of conflict of interest. But no evidence of such a connection is given here.

Hasty or Sweeping Generalization. This fallacy occurs when a general principle is applied mistakenly to a special case.

> Since preschool programs help children form social relationships, Amy and Fred Winkler should send their son Marc to nursery school.

Perhaps Marc would benefit from nursery school, perhaps not. Perhaps like many other children he is shy, or frail in health, or otherwise not ready for the experience. General rules, however widely they may be accepted, nearly always have exceptions, and it may just have happened that the case in point is one of those exceptions.

Either/Or Fallacy. This is an argument that assumes that there are only two alternatives when more exist.

> We must choose between life and death, between total disarmament and nuclear war. There can be no neutrality on this issue.

In fact, history suggests that these alternatives may be less likely than some form of the armed truce that has held since 1945. An argument like this misrepresents issues and forces people to choose between extremes instead of exploring more moderate possibilities.

STRUCTURING AN ARGUMENTATIVE ESSAY

An argument, like other kinds of essays, has an introduction, stating a thesis, and a conclusion. But the body of an argument has its own special structure, originating with the ancient Greeks and used, with variations, ever since. The *Declaration of Independence* more or less follows the classical design: introduction, thesis statement, outline of the argument, proof of the thesis, refutation of opposing arguments, and conclusion.

Jefferson begins the Declaration of Independence by presenting the issue that the document addresses: the obligation of the people of the American colonies to tell the world why they must separate from Great Britain. Next Jefferson states his thesis that because of the tyranny of the British king, the colonies must replace his rule with another form of government. In the body of the Declaration of Independence, he offers as evidence twenty-eight examples of injustice endured by the American colonies. Following the evidence, Jefferson anticipates possible counterarguments and rebuts them by explaining how time and time again the colonists have appealed to the British for redress, but without result. In his concluding paragraph, Jefferson restates the thesis and reinforces it one final time. He ends with a flourish: he speaks for the representatives of the states, explicitly dissolving all connections between England and America.

Not all arguments, however, follow this pattern. Your material, your thesis, your purpose, your audience, the type of argument you are writing, and the limitations of your assignment ultimately determine the strategies you use. Nevertheless, the typical argument may include: presentation of evidence; connecting the evidence with the thesis by induction or deduction; refuting opposing evidence and arguments.

Introduction: Introduce the issue.
State the thesis.
Body: Induction—offer evidence to support the thesis.
Deduction—use syllogisms to support the thesis.
State the arguments against the thesis and rebut them.
Conclusion: Sum up the argument, if it is long and complex.
Restate the thesis.
Make a forceful closing statement.

If your thesis is especially novel or controversial, rebuttal may come first. William Buckley uses this technique in his essay "Capital Punishment." For the same reason, opposing positions may even be mentioned in the introduction—provided they are discussed later in the argument.

Let's suppose that your journalism instructor has given you the following assignment: "Select a controversial topic that interests you, and write a brief editorial. Direct your editorial to readers who do not share your views, and try to convince them that your position is reasonable. Be sure to acknowledge the view your audience holds and to refute any criticisms of your argument that you can anticipate." You are especially well informed about one local issue because you have just read a series of articles on it. A citizens group has formed to lobby for a local ordinance that would authorize spending tax dollars for parochial schools in your community. Since you have also recently studied the constitutional doctrine of separation of church and state in your American history class, you know you could argue fairly and strongly against the position taken by this group.

An outline of your essay might look like this:

¶1 Introduce the issue: Should public tax revenues be spent on aid to parochial schools?
Thesis: Despite the pleas of citizen groups like Parochial School Parents United, using tax dollars to support church-affiliated schools directly violates the United States Constitution.

¶2 Evidence (deduction): Explain general principle of separation of church and state in the Constitution.

¶3 Evidence (induction): Present recent examples of court cases interpreting and applying this principle.

¶4 Evidence (deduction): Interpret how the Constitution and the court cases apply to your community's situation.

¶5 Anticipate and refute opposition: Specify and answer arguments used by Parochial School Parents United.

¶6 Conclusion: Sum up the argument, restate the thesis, and end with a strong closing statement.

The following student essay written by Marc Sidon illustrates a number of techniques discussed above.

IN DEFENSE OF VIDEO GAMES

Introduction   I am a devoted player of video games.   1
Pac Man, Zaxxon, Donkey Kong, and Tron
are just some of the machines I have
successfully challenged. These games
require skill, intelligence, and lots
of practice. That is why I was sur-
Presentation prised to learn that my playing is an
of controversy "addiction" and that the money I spend
contributes to my "mental and physical
degeneration." This is the language
that Parents Against Video Games uses
in their efforts to bar video games
from our township. Although they may
mean well and some of their criticisms
Thesis may be valid, this group ignores the
good points of video games while blaming them for a number of evils they do
not cause.

Evidence (personal example)

After reading the comments that Parents Against Video Games have made, it seems obvious to me that none of its members ever actually played a machine. If they had, they would have realized the challenge that first-class games present. Stand behind someone playing the popular game Centipede, and see the speed and accuracy of the reflexes needed to play the game well. From the top of the screen a many-segmented insect winds its way through a series of obstacles. The player, who manipulates a gun at the bottom of the screen, tries to hit the segments before they overtake and destroy him. As the game progresses the segments move faster and faster until only someone with very good reflexes can manipulate the control.

2

Evidence (personal examples)

In addition to requiring good reflexes, video games often call for a surprising amount of strategy. To the novice the game of Pac Man may look like a random series of moves with which players try to escape "ghosts" who are programmed to "eat" them. In fact there is a complex series of patterns that players must discover and follow to score well. The same holds true for Zaxxon, a game that has a three-dimension-like display with stunning graphics. The difficulty of this game is so great that the manufacturers, SEGA/Gremlin, actually distribute

3

guides to help players meet the challenges they encounter. Just a glance at these guides should be enough to convince anyone that Zaxxon demands unprecedented sophistication in strategy.

Evidence (personal examples)

Finally, and perhaps most important, 4 video games can give players hours of fun. Where else can you escape the day-to-day routine of work or school by driving a race car through a series of ever-changing landscapes or by guiding a craft through a geometric space tunnel? At their best, video games project players into a fantasy world that forces them, intellectually and physically, to become totally involved. Not even chess or pinball can confront players on so many levels at once. With the memory capacity of a full computer at its disposal, a single video game can present players with a variety of challenges, each adjusted to and responsive to player responses. The allure of this sophisticated technology must be spreading, for now it is common to see junior executives on their lunch breaks, hunched over a phosphorescent screen filled with alien invaders or gobbling heads.

Opposing arguments

If video games are so attractive, why 5 then is Parents Against Video Games opposed to them? First, they blame video games for "seducing" young people away from their studies. Second, they

claim that children become hopelessly addicted to the games and
spend all their money on them. Finally,
they say that video games emphasize
combat and do nothing to develop the
intellectual capacities of the
players.

Refutation of opposing arguments   Although there is some truth in these   6
charges, they are all sweeping
generalizations. People have always
looked for a scapegoat to blame for the
behavior of adolescents. Before video
games, comic books and then television were seen as reasons for
declining literacy. What seems certain
is that none of these factors in
themselves can take the blame for
absence rates from school, teenage
crime, or any of the other ills
associated with growing up. Certainly
some children get carried away with
video games and play them excessively,
but most deal with them intelligently.
Moreover, when compared to other forms
of entertainment, movies and rock
concerts, for instance, the price of
video games does not seem out of line.
While a number of video games do
emphasize war and shooting, others such
as Frogger and Turbo are decidedly nonviolent. In any event, the symbolic
violence on the screen is less
realistic and shocking than that on
primetime television.

Summary of argument	In an article in *Science 81,* John 7 Tierney puts video games in perspective. He says that these games actually develop a kind of "electronic literacy" that prepares children for a world run by computers. Parents Against Video
Restatement of thesis	Games should recognize this and stop condemning these computer games. Instead, they should accept the fact that video games are now a fixture in our
Concluding statement	culture. A second look might show this group that video games do have benefits and that the useful functions they perform outweigh the occasional problems that they cause.

Points for Special Attention

Choosing the Topic.   Marc Sidon chose a topic of great interest to him. In his introduction he establishes the controversial nature of his topic and shows how the stand taken by Parents Against Video Games affects him. As this paper shows, an argument does not always have to be about a burning issue. It can be about anything that you feel strongly about, as long as you take a stand on your subject.

Gathering Evidence.   Because of his involvement with his subject, Marc was able to provide enough examples from his own experience to make his point and did not have to do research in the library. This does not mean, however, that Marc did not spend a great deal of time thinking of ideas and selecting evidence. In his conclusion Marc refers to an article that puts video games in a broader perspective. He brings in this new material to sustain interest and add authority to the points he has made.

Certainly statistics, studies, and expert testimony—if they exist—would make Marc's argument more solid and less personal. But an argument from personal experience, if it is carefully thought through, can be valid too.

Refuting Opposing Arguments.   Marc spends two paragraphs stating and refuting arguments made by Parents Against Video Games. He begins this section by asking a rhetorical question and then listing the reasons Parents Against Video Games opposes arcade games. Marc counters their charges by identifying a fallacy in their argument—their sweeping generalizations—and by offering specific reasons why the generalizations may not be valid.

Audience.   Marc wrote his essay for his freshman composition class and assumed a general audience, one that would read an editorial in the local paper. He regarded his view as original and concluded that his readers, mostly adults, would be skeptical and have to be persuaded he was right. For this reason he is careful to explain the games that he refers to and to avoid slang that might not appeal to his audience. In his introduction and again in paragraph 6 Marc concedes points that he thinks are valid and, in this way, presents himself to his audience as a reasonable person. He avoids name-calling and goes into great detail to support his assertions and convince his audience that what he says is true. In doing so he outlines points that he knows will appeal to his audience, that games demand excellent reflexes and complex strategy and that they provide hours of fun.

Organization.   Marc uses several strategies discussed earlier in the chapter. He begins his essay by introducing the issue he is going to discuss, that the stand taken by Parents Against Video Games is shortsighted. His thesis is straightforward and clearly states his position on the issue: video games have a number of benefits and cannot be blamed for problems young people have. The argument itself is inductive, with general statements supported by evidence. In his fifth paragraph Marc anticipates three criticisms of his argument, and in the sixth paragraph he refutes them. Although his conclusion is rather brief, it does reinforce and support his main idea.

Though this is an inductive argument, it does not follow the inductive sequence of question-evidence-conclusion. Rather, it presents its conclusions first, then offers evidence in support. Both strategies can be effective and which you choose depends on how you wish your argument to affect your readers. The thesis-and-support structure is more commonly used because it is more emphatic, even dramatic: you stake out your position and then defend it. But the question-evidence-conclusion structure may be best when you believe

your conclusion is so radical that you need to lead up to it gradually—or so surprising, or amusing, that you want to save it for last.

The five essays that follow represent a wide range of historical
and topical perspectives. Each, however, presents a formal argument to support a controversial thesis. As you read each essay, try
to identify the characteristic strategies of the classical pattern for
argument.

THE DECLARATION
OF INDEPENDENCE

Thomas Jefferson

Thomas Jefferson was born in what is now Albemarle County, Virginia, in 1743. He attended William and Mary College and became a lawyer in 1767. He served in the Virginia House of Burgesses and became known as a leading patriot. As a result, he was named a delegate to the Continental Congress and was chosen to draft the Declaration of Independence, which was then amended by the Congress. After the Revolution, he was governor of Virginia, then a member of the Continental Congress, minister to France, secretary of state in Washington's first cabinet, vice-president to John Adams, and eventually president. During his retirement Jefferson designed and founded the University of Virginia. He died on July 4, 1826. The Declaration of Independence challenges a basic assumption of the age in which it was written—the divine right of kings. In order to accomplish his ends, Jefferson followed many of the principles of argumentative writing. Unlike many modern revolutionary manifestos, the Declaration of Independence is a model of clarity and precision that attempts to establish and support its thesis by means of irrefutable logic and reason.

When in the course of human events, it becomes necessary for 1 one people to dissolve the political bands which have connected them with another, and to assume among the powers of the earth, the separate and equal station to which the Laws of Nature and of Nature's God entitle them, a decent respect to the opinions of mankind requires that they should declare the causes which impel them to the separation.

We hold these truths to be self-evident, that all men are created 2 equal, that they are endowed by their Creator with certain unalienable rights, that among these are life, liberty and the pursuit of happiness. That to secure these rights, governments are instituted among men, deriving their just powers from the consent of the governed. That whenever any form of government becomes destructive of these ends, it is the right of the people to alter or to abolish it, and to institute new government, laying its foundation on such principles and organizing its powers in such form, as to them shall seem most likely to effect their safety and happiness.

Prudence, indeed, will dictate that governments long established should not be changed for light and transient causes; and accordingly all experience hath shown, that mankind are more disposed to suffer, while evils are sufferable, than to right themselves by abolishing the forms to which they are accustomed. But when a long train of abuses and usurpations, pursuing invariably the same object, evinces a design to reduce them under absolute despotism, it is their right, it is their duty, to throw off such government, and to provide new guards for their future security. Such has been the patient sufferance of these Colonies; and such is now the necessity which constrains them to alter their former systems of government. The history of the present King of Great Britain is a history of repeated injuries and usurpations, all having in direct object the establishment of an absolute tyranny over these States. To prove this, let facts be submitted to a candid world.

He has refused his assent to laws, the most wholesome and necessary for the public good. 3

He has forbidden his Governors to pass laws of immediate and pressing importance, unless suspended in their operation till his assent should be obtained; and when so suspended, he has utterly neglected to attend to them. 4

He has refused to pass other laws for the accommodation of large districts of people, unless those people would relinquish the right of representation in the legislature, a right inestimable to them and formidable to tyrants only. 5

He has called together legislative bodies at places unusual, uncomfortable, and distant from the depository of their public records, for the sole purpose of fatiguing them into compliance with his measures. 6

He has dissolved representative houses repeatedly, for opposing with manly firmness his invasions on the rights of the people. 7

He has refused for a long time, after such dissolutions, to cause others to be elected; whereby the legislative powers, incapable of annihilation, have returned to the people at large for their exercise; the State remaining in the meantime exposed to all the dangers of invasion from without and convulsions within. 8

He has endeavoured to prevent the population of these states; for that purpose obstructing the laws for naturalization of foreigners; refusing to pass others to encourage their migration hither, and raising the conditions of new appropriations of lands. 9

He has obstructed the administration of justice, by refusing his assent to laws for establishing judiciary powers. 10

He has made judges dependent on his will alone, for the tenure of their offices, and the amount and payment of their salaries. 11

He has erected a multitude of new offices, and sent hither swarms 12 of officers to harass our people, and eat out their substance.

He has kept among us, in times of peace, standing armies without 13 the consent of our legislatures.

He has affected to render the military independent of and supe- 14 rior to the civil power.

He has combined with others to subject us to a jurisdiction foreign 15 to our constitution, and unacknowledged by our laws; giving his assent to their acts of pretended legislation:

For quartering large bodies of armed troops among us: 16

For protecting them, by a mock trial, from punishment for any 17 murders which they should commit on the inhabitants of these States:

For cutting off our trade with all parts of the world: 18

For imposing taxes on us without our consent: 19

For depriving us in many cases of the benefits of trial by jury: 20

For transporting us beyond seas to be tried for pretended offences: 21

For abolishing the free system of English laws in a neighbouring 22 Province, establishing therein an arbitrary government, and enlarging its boundaries so as to render it at once an example and fit instrument for introducing the same absolute rule into these Colonies:

For taking away our Charters, abolishing our most valuable laws, 23 and altering fundamentally the forms of our governments:

For suspending our own legislatures, and declaring themselves 24 invested with power to legislate for us in all cases whatsoever.

He has abdicated government here, by declaring us out of his 25 protection and waging war against us.

He has plundered our seas, ravaged our coasts, burnt our towns, 26 and destroyed the lives of our people.

He is at this time transporting large armies of foreign mercen- 27 aries to complete the works of death, desolation and tyranny, already begun with circumstances of cruelty and perfidy scarcely paralleled in the most barbarous ages, and totally unworthy the head of a civilized nation.

He has constrained our fellow citizens taken captive on the high 28 seas to bear arms against their country, to become the executioners of their friends and brethren, or to fall themselves by their hands.

He has excited domestic insurrections amongst us, and has en- 29 deavoured to bring on the inhabitants of our frontiers, the merciless Indian savages, whose known rule of warfare, is an undistinguished destruction of all ages, sexes, and conditions.

In every stage of these oppressions we have petitioned for redress 30 in the most humble terms: our repeated petitions have been answered only by repeated injury. A prince whose character is thus marked by every act which may define a tyrant is unfit to be the ruler of a free people.

Nor have we been wanting in attention to our British brethren. We have warned them from time to time of attempts by their legislature to extend an unwarrantable jurisdiction over us. We have reminded them of the circumstances of our emigration and settlement here. We have appealed to their native justice and magnanimity, and we have conjured them by the ties of our common kindred to disavow these usurpations, which would inevitably interrupt our connections and correspondence. They too have been deaf to the voice of justice and of consanguinity. We must, therefore, acquiesce in the necessity, which denounces our separation, and hold them, as we hold the rest of mankind, enemies in war, in peace friends.

We, therefore, the Representatives of the United States of America, in General Congress assembled, appealing to the Supreme Judge of the world for the rectitude of our intentions, do, in the name, and by authority of the good people of these Colonies, solemnly publish and declare, That these United Colonies are, and of right ought to be, Free and Independent States; that they are absolved from all allegiance to the British Crown, and that all political connection between them and the state of Great Britain, is and ought to be totally dissolved; and that as Free and Independent States, they have full power to levy war, conclude peace, contract alliances, establish commerce, and to do all other acts and things which Independent States may of right do. And for the support of this declaration, with a firm reliance on the protection of Divine Providence, we mutually pledge to each other our lives, our fortunes, and our sacred honor.

COMPREHENSION

1. What "truths" does Jefferson assert are "self-evident"?

2. What does Jefferson say is the source from which governments derive their powers?

3. What reasons does Jefferson give to support his premise that the United States should break away from Great Britain?

4. What conclusions about the British crown does Jefferson draw from the facts he presents?

PURPOSE AND AUDIENCE

1. What is the thesis of the Declaration of Independence?

2. The Declaration of Independence was written during a period now referred to as the Age of Reason. In what ways has Jefferson tried to make his document reasonable?

3. For what audience is the document intended?

4. How does Jefferson attempt to convince his audience that he is reasonable?

5. In paragraph 31, following the list of grievances, why does Jefferson address his "British brethren"?

STYLE AND STRUCTURE

1. Construct a topic outline of the Declaration of Independence.

2. Is the Declaration of Independence an example of inductive or deductive reasoning?

3. How does Jefferson create smooth and logical transitions from one paragraph to another?

4. Why does Jefferson list all of his twenty-eight grievances?

5. Jefferson begins the last paragraph of the Declaration of Independence with "We, therefore . . ." What clues about the intent of the document do these words give?

6. What particular words does Jefferson use that are rare today?

WRITING WORKSHOP

1. Write an argumentative essay from the point of view of King George III, and try to convince the colonists that they should not break away from Great Britain. If you can, refute several of the points Jefferson lists in the Declaration.

2. Following Jefferson's example, write a declaration of independence from your school, job, family, or any other institution with which you are connected.

3. Write an essay in which you state a grievance that you share with other members of some group, and then argue for the best way to eliminate it.

OUR YOUTH SHOULD SERVE

Steven Muller

Steven Muller was born in Hamburg, Germany, in 1927. He came to the United States in 1940 and received his B.A. from the University of California and his Ph.D. from Cornell University in 1958. He has taught at Haverford College and Cornell and has been the director of the Center for International Studies at Cornell. Muller has published many articles in academic journals and has been on the board of editors of Daedalus, a journal of interdisciplinary studies. He is presently the president of Johns Hopkins University. In "Our Youth Should Serve" Muller argues strongly for the establishment of a youth corps for which high school graduates could volunteer.

Too many young men and women now leave school without a   1
well-developed sense of purpose. If they go right to work after high school, many are not properly prepared for careers. But if they enter college instead, many do not really know what to study or what to do afterward. Our society does not seem to be doing much to encourage and use the best instincts and talents of our young.

On the one hand, I see the growing problems of each year's new   2
generation of high-school graduates. After twelve years of schooling—and television—many of them want to participate actively in society; but they face either a job with a limited future or more years in educational institutions. Many are wonderfully idealistic: they have talent and energy to offer, and they seek the meaning in their lives that comes from giving of oneself to the common good. But they feel almost rejected by a society that has too few jobs to offer them and that asks nothing of them except to avoid trouble. They want to be part of a new solution; instead society perceives them as a problem. They seek a cause; but their elders preach only self-advancement. They need experience on which to base choice; yet society seems to put a premium on the earliest possible choice, based inescapably on the least experience.

NECESSARY TASKS

On the other hand, I see an American society sadly in need of   3
social services that we can afford less and less at prevailing costs

386

of labor. Some tasks are necessary but constitute no career; they should be carried out, but not as anyone's lifetime occupation. Our democracy profoundly needs public spirit, but the economy of our labor system primarily encourages self-interest. The Federal government spends billions on opportunity grants for post-secondary education, but some of us wonder about money given on the basis only of need. We ask the young to volunteer for national defense, but not for the improvement of our society. As public spirit and public services decline, so does the quality of life. So I ask myself why cannot we put it all together and ask our young people to volunteer in peacetime to serve America?

I recognize that at first mention, universal national youth service   4
may sound too much like compulsory military service or the Hitler Youth or the Komsomol. I do not believe it has to be like that at all. It need not require uniforms or camps, nor a vast new Federal bureaucracy, nor vast new public expenditures. And it should certainly not be compulsory.

A voluntary program of universal national youth service does of   5
course require compelling incentives. Two could be provided. Guaranteed job training would be one. Substantial Federal assistance toward post-secondary education would be the other. This would mean that today's complex measures of Federal aid to students would be ended, and that there would also be no need for tuition tax credits for post-secondary education. Instead, prospective students would *earn* their assistance for post-secondary education by volunteering for national service, and only those who earned assistance would receive it. Present Federal expenditures for the assistance of students in post-secondary education would be converted into a simple grant program, modeled on the post-World War II GI Bill of Rights.

VOLUNTEERS

But what, you say, would huge numbers of high-school graduates   6
do as volunteers in national service? They could be interns in public agencies, local, state and national. They could staff day-care programs, neighborhood health centers, centers to counsel and work with children; help to maintain public facilities, including highways, rail beds, waterways and airports; engage in neighborhood renewal projects, both physical and social. Some would elect military service, others the Peace Corps. Except for the latter two alternatives and others like them, they could live anywhere they pleased. They would not wear uniforms. They would be employed

and supervised by people already employed locally in public-agency careers.

Volunteers would be paid only a subsistence wage, because they   7
would receive the benefits of job training (not necessarily confined to one task) as well as assistance toward post-secondary education if they were so motivated and qualified. If cheap mass housing for some groups of volunteers were needed, supervised participants in the program could rebuild decayed dwellings in metropolitan areas.

All that might work. But perhaps an even more attractive version   8
of universal national youth service might include private industrial and commercial enterprise as well. A private employer would volunteer to select a stated number of volunteers. He would have their labor at the universally applied subsistence wage; in return he would offer guaranteed job training as well as the exact equivalent of what the Federal government would have to pay for assistance toward post-secondary education. The inclusion of volunteer private employers would greatly amplify job-training opportunities for the youth volunteers, and would greatly lessen the costs of the program in public funds.

DIRECT BENEFITS

The direct benefits of such a universal national-youth-service   9
program would be significant. Every young man and woman would face a meaningful role in society after high school. Everyone would receive job training, and the right to earn assistance toward post-secondary education. Those going on to post-secondary education would have their education interrupted by a constructive work experience. There is evidence that they would thereby become more highly motivated and successful students, particularly if their work experience related closely to subsequent vocational interests. Many participants might locate careers by means of their national-service assignments.

No union jobs need be lost, because skilled workers would be   10
needed to give job training. Many public services would be performed by cheap labor, but there would be no youth army. And the intangible, indirect benefits would be the greatest of all. Young people could regard themselves as more useful and needed. They could serve this country for a two-year period as volunteers, and *earn* job training and/or assistance toward post-secondary education. There is more self-esteem and motivation in earned than in unearned benefits. Universal national youth service may be no pan-

acea. But in my opinion the idea merits serious and imaginative consideration.

COMPREHENSION

1. What two problems is Steven Muller addressing?

2. What possible objections does Muller refute?

3. What incentives to volunteer would young people have?

4. What two versions of his plan does Muller suggest?

5. What would be the direct benefits of his plan?

PURPOSE AND AUDIENCE

1. What is Steven Muller's thesis?

2. At what audience is Muller aiming his essay?

3. How might Muller's academic position influence his audience's response to his essay?

4. Why does Muller refer to young people as *they*? Would this approach appeal to an audience of college students?

STYLE AND STRUCTURE

1. Like the other writers whose essays appear in this section, Steven Muller uses more than one pattern of development. Identify at least three different patterns in his essay.

2. Why does Muller follow his thesis with a discussion of possible objections to it?

3. Are the objections Muller offers the most obvious ones? Why or why not? Can you think of others?

4. How does Muller support his assertions?

5. In spite of his concluding statements, could Muller be criticized for offering his plan as a panacea?

WRITING WORKSHOP

1. Write an argumentative essay against Steven Muller's plan. Refute as many of his points as you can.

2. Write an argumentative essay in which you discuss your own plan for giving high school graduates the sense of purpose Muller feels they lack.

3. Write an essay arguing that you and your peers already have goals and purpose. Use concrete examples from your own experience and observations as support.

CAPITAL PUNISHMENT

William F. Buckley, Jr.

*William F. Buckley, Jr., the son of a millionaire, was born in 1925
in New York City. He attended the University of Mexico and graduated from Yale in 1950. While still an undergraduate, Buckley
wrote* God and Man at Yale *(1951), the book that first presented his
Christian and conservative principles. After graduating, he co-
authored with L. Brent Bozwell* McCarthy and His Enemies *(1954)
and in 1955 founded the conservative magazine* The National Review. *In 1965, Buckley ran as the Conservative Party candidate for
mayor of New York City, and in 1966 he began his popular television interview show* Firing Line. *Buckley currently writes a syndicated newspaper column and has a number of books to his credit.
"Capital Punishment" is from the collection of essays* Execution Eve
and Other Contemporary Ballads *(1975). In it Buckley refutes the
most popular arguments that are often made against the death
penalty.*

There is national suspense over whether capital punishment is 1
about to be abolished, and the assumption is that when it comes it
will come from the Supreme Court. Meanwhile, (a) the prestigious
State Supreme Court of California has interrupted executions, giving constitutional reasons for doing so; (b) the death wings are over-
flowing with convicted prisoners; (c) executions are a remote memory;
and—for the first time in years—(d) the opinion polls show that
there is sentiment for what amounts to the restoration of capital
punishment.

The case for abolition is popularly known. The other case less so, 2
and (without wholeheartedly endorsing it) I give it as it was given
recently to the Committee of the Judiciary of the House of Representatives by Professor Ernest van den Haag, under whose thinking
cap groweth no moss. Mr. van den Haag, a professor of social philosophy at New York University, ambushed the most popular arguments of the abolitionists, taking no prisoners.

(1) The business about the poor and the black suffering exces- 3
sively from capital punishment is no argument against capital punishment. It is an argument against the *administration* of justice,
not against the penalty. Any punishment can be unfairly or unjustly
applied. Go ahead and reform the processes by which capital pun-

ishment is inflicted, if you wish; but don't confuse maladministration with the merits of capital punishment.

(2) The argument that the death penalty is "unusual" is circular.[1] Capital punishment continues on the books of a majority of states, the people continue to sanction the concept of capital punishment, and indeed capital sentences are routinely handed down. What has made capital punishment "unusual" is that the courts and, primarily, governors have intervened in the process so as to collaborate in the frustration of the execution of the law. To argue that capital punishment is unusual, when in fact it has been made unusual by extra-legislative authority, is an argument to expedite, not eliminate, executions.

(3) Capital punishment is cruel. That is a historical judgment. But the Constitution suggests that what must be proscribed as cruel is (a) a particularly painful way of inflicting death, or (b) a particularly undeserved death; and the death penalty, as such, offends neither of these criteria and cannot therefore be regarded as objectively "cruel."

Viewed the other way, the question is whether capital punishment can be regarded as useful, and the question of deterrence arises.

(4) Those who believe that the death penalty does not intensify the disinclination to commit certain crimes need to wrestle with statistics that, in fact, it can't be proved that *any* punishment does that to any particular crime. One would rationally suppose that two years in jail would cut the commission of a crime if not exactly by 100 percent more than a penalty of one year in jail, at least that it would further discourage crime to a certain extent. The proof is unavailing. On the other hand, the statistics, although ambiguous, do not show either (a) that capital punishment net discourages; or (b) that capital punishment fails net to discourage. "The absence of proof for the additional deterrent effect of the death penalty must not be confused with the presence of proof for the absence of this effect."

The argument that most capital crimes are crimes of passion committed by irrational persons is no argument against the death penalty, because it does not reveal how many crimes might, but for the death penalty, have been committed by rational persons who are now deterred.

And the clincher. (5) Since we do not know for certain whether or not the death penalty adds deterrence, we have in effect the choice of two risks.

[1]The Eighth Amendment to the U.S. Constitution (part of the Bill of Rights) forbids "cruel and unusual" punishment.

Risk One: If we execute convicted murderers without thereby   10
deterring prospective murderers beyond the deterrence that could
have been achieved by life imprisonment, we may have vainly sac-
rificed the life of the convicted murderer.

Risk Two: If we fail to execute a convicted murderer whose exe-   11
cution might have deterred an indefinite number of prospective
murderers, our failure sacrifices an indefinite number of victims of
future murderers.

"If we had certainty, we would not have risks. We do not have   12
certainty. If we have risks—and we do—better to risk the life of the
convicted man than risk the life of an indefinite number of innocent
victims who might survive if he were executed."

COMPREHENSION

1. Why does Buckley say that he does not have to present the case for abolition of the death penalty?

2. Who is Ernest van den Haag?

3. What distinction does Buckley draw between capital punishment and the administration of justice?

4. Make a list of the arguments against capital punishment that Buckley and van den Haag refute.

5. What are the two risks that we must choose between? Which risk does Buckley prefer?

PURPOSE AND AUDIENCE

1. Where does Buckley state his thesis?

2. Why does Buckley introduce Ernest van den Haag into his essay?

3. Does Buckley see his audience as being for or against capital punishment?

4. What is Buckley's purpose in writing this essay?

STYLE AND STRUCTURE

1. Does Buckley present his argument using inductive or deductive reasoning?

2. Why does Buckley set off his points using letters and numbers?

3. What remarks does Buckley make on this very serious subject that he expects you to find humorous? What is the effect of those remarks?

4. What does Buckley gain or lose by reporting the arguments of another and not constructing an argument of his own?

5. Buckley's arguments are chiefly analytical. Would he have done better to have introduced statistical data or other evidence to support his thesis? Why or why not?

6. Buckley ends his essay with a quotation from van den Haag. Why does he end this way? Do you think the conclusion is effective?

WRITING WORKSHOP

1. Write an essay against the death penalty in which you refute some of van den Haag's arguments.

2. Write an essay in which you argue for or against the thesis "Capital punishment is cruel." In preparation for this essay, read several articles pertaining to the subject. Be sure to account for all material that you get from your sources.

THE CASE AGAINST MAN

Isaac Asimov

Isaac Asimov was born in 1920 in Russia and emigrated at the age of three. He graduated from Columbia University in 1940 with a Ph.D. in chemistry and taught at the Boston University School of Medicine. He has written hundreds of books and even more articles on various subjects. Asimov, however, is perhaps best known as a science-fiction writer. His two most famous works, the Foundation Trilogy *and* I, Robot, *have been translated into many languages and have earned him an international reputation as a master of the genre. Recently, Asimov has turned from science fiction to science writing. In "The Case Against Man," he looks into the future to predict what the situation could be like if the increasing world population is not curbed. Notice how Asimov establishes the reasonableness of his position and how he presents his controversial thesis to his audience.*

The first mistake is to think of mankind as a thing in itself. It 1 isn't. It is part of an intricate web of life. And we can't think even of life as a thing in itself. It isn't. It is part of the intricate structure of a planet bathed by energy from the Sun.

The Earth, in the nearly 5 billion years since it assumed approx- 2 imately its present form, has undergone a vast evolution. When it first came into being, it very likely lacked what we would today call an ocean and an atmosphere. These were formed by the gradual outward movement of material as the solid interior settled together.

Nor were ocean, atmosphere, and solid crust independent of each 3 other after formation. There is interaction always: evaporation, condensation, solution, weathering. Far within the solid crust there are slow, continuing changes, too, of which hot springs, volcanoes, and earthquakes are the more noticeable manifestations here on the surface.

Between 2 billion and 3 billion years ago, portions of the surface 4 water, bathed by the energetic radiation from the Sun, developed complicated compounds in organization sufficiently versatile to qualify as what we call "life." Life forms have become more complex and more various ever since.

But the life forms are as much part of the structure of the Earth 5 as any inanimate portion is. It is all an inseparable part of a whole.

If any animal is isolated totally from other forms of life, then death by starvation will surely follow. If isolated from water, death by dehydration will follow even faster. If isolated from air, whether free or dissolved in water, death by asphyxiation will follow still faster. If isolated from the Sun, animals will survive for a time, but plants would die, and if all plants died, all animals would starve.

It works in reverse, too, for the inanimate portion of Earth is   6
shaped and molded by life. The nature of the atmosphere has been changed by plant activity (which adds to the air the free oxygen it could not otherwise retain). The soil is turned by earthworms, while enormous ocean reefs are formed by coral.

The entire planet, plus solar energy, is one enormous intricately   7
interrelated system. The entire planet is a life form made up of nonliving portions and a large variety of living portions (as our own body is made up of nonliving crystals in bones and nonliving water in blood, as well as of a large variety of living portions).

In fact, we can pursue the analogy. A man is composed of 50   8
trillion cells of a variety of types, all interrelated and interdependent. Loss of some of those cells, such as those making up an entire leg, will seriously handicap all the rest of the organism: serious damage to a relatively few cells of an organ, such as the heart or kidneys, may end by killing all 50 trillion.

In the same way, on a planetary scale, the chopping down of an   9
entire forest may not threaten Earth's life in general, but it will produce serious changes in the life forms of the region and even in the nature of the water runoff and, therefore, in the details of geological structure. A serious decline in the bee population will affect the numbers of those plants that depend on bees for fertilization, then the numbers of those animals that depend on those particular bee-fertilized plants, and so on.

Or consider cell growth. Cells in those organs that suffer constant   10
wear and tear—as in the skin or in the intestinal lining—grow and multiply all life long. Other cells, not so exposed, as in nerve and muscle, do not multiply at all in the adult, under any circumstances. Still other organs, ordinarily quiescent, as liver and bone, stand ready to grow if that is necessary to replace damage. When the proper repairs are made, growth stops.

In a much looser and more flexible way, the same is true of the   11
"planet organism" (which we study in the science called ecology). If cougars grow too numerous, the deer they live on are decimated, and some cougars die of starvation, so that their "proper number" is restored. If too many cougars die, then the deer multiply with particular rapidity, and cougars multiply quickly in turn, till the

additional predators bring down the number of deer again. Barring interference from outside, the eaters and the eaten retain their proper numbers, and both are the better for it. (If the cougars are all killed off, deer would multiply to the point where they destroy the plants they live off, and more would then die of starvation than would have died of cougars.)

The neat economy of growth within an organism such as a human being is sometimes—for what reason, we know not—disrupted, and a group of cells begins growing without limit. This is the dread disease of cancer, and unless that growing group of cells is somehow stopped, the wild growth will throw all the body structure out of tune and end by killing the organism itself. 12

In ecology, the same would happen if, for some reason, one particular type of organism began to multiply without limit, killing its competitors and increasing its own food supply at the expense of that of others. That, too, could end only in the destruction of the larger system—most or all of life and even of certain aspects of the inanimate environment. 13

And this is exactly what is happening at this moment. For thousands of years, the single species Homo sapiens, to which you and I have the dubious honor of belonging, has been increasing in numbers. In the past couple of centuries, the rate of increase has itself increased explosively. 14

At the time of Julius Caesar, when Earth's human population is estimated to have been 150 million, that population was increasing at a rate such that it would double in 1,000 years if that rate remained steady. Today, with Earth's population estimated at about 4,000 million (26 times what it was in Caesar's time), it is increasing at a rate which, if steady, will cause it to double in 35 years. 15

The present rate of increase of Earth's swarming human population qualifies Homo sapiens as an ecological cancer, which will destroy the ecology just as surely as any ordinary cancer would destroy an organism. 16

The cure? Just what it is for any cancer. The cancerous growth must somehow be stopped. 17

Of course, it will be. If we do nothing at all, the growth will stop, as a cancerous growth in a man will stop if nothing is done. The man dies and the cancer dies with him. And, analogously, the ecology will die and man will die with it. 18

How can the human population explosion be stopped? By raising the deathrate, or by lowering the birthrate. There are no other alternatives. The deathrate will rise spontaneously and finally catastrophically, if we do nothing—and that within a few decades. To 19 make the birthrate fall, somehow (almost *any* how, in fact), is surely preferable, and that is therefore the first order of mankind's business today.

Failing this, mankind would stand at the bar of abstract justice   20 (for there may be no posterity to judge) as the mass murderer of life generally, his own included, and mass disrupter of the intricate planetary development that made life in its present glory possible in the first place.

Am I too pessimistic? Can we allow the present rate of population   21 increase to continue indefinitely, or at least for a good long time? Can we count on science to develop methods for cleaning up as we pollute, for replacing wasted resources with substitutes, for finding new food, new materials, more and better life for our waxing numbers?

Impossible! If the numbers continue to wax at the present rate.   22

Let us begin with a few estimates (admittedly not precise, but in   23 the rough neighborhood of the truth).

The total mass of living objects on Earth is perhaps 20 trillion   24 tons. There is usually a balance between eaters and eaten that is about 1 to 10 in favor of the eaten. There would therefore be about 10 times as much plant life (the eaten) as animal life (the eaters) on Earth. There is, in other words, just a little under 2 trillion tons of animal life on Earth.

But this is all the animal life that can exist, given the present   25 quantity of plant life. If more animal life is somehow produced, it will strip down the plant life, reduce the food supply, and then enough animals will starve to restore the balance. If one species of animal life increases in mass, it can only be because other species correspondingly decrease. For every additional pound of human flesh on Earth, a pound of some other form of flesh must disappear.

The total mass of humanity now on Earth may be estimated at   26 about 200 million tons, or one ten-thousandth the mass of all animal life. If mankind increases in numbers ten thousandfold, then Homo sapiens will be, perforce, the *only* animal species alive on Earth. It will be a world without elephants or lions, without cats or dogs, without fish or lobsters, without worms or bugs. What's more, to support the mass of human life, all the plant world must be put to service. Only plants edible to man must remain, and only those plants most concentratedly edible and with minimum waste.

At the present moment, the average density of population of the   27 Earth's land surface is about 73 people per square mile. Increase that ten thousandfold and the average density will become 730,000 people per square mile, or more than seven times the density of the workday population of Manhattan. Even if we assume that mankind will somehow spread itself into vast cities floating on the ocean surface (or resting on the ocean floor), the average density of human life at the time when the last nonhuman animal must be killed would be 310,000 people per square mile over all the world, land and sea alike, or a little better than three times the density of modern Manhattan at noon.

We have the vision, then, of high-rise apartments, higher and 28 more thickly spaced than in Manhattan at present, spreading all over the world, across all the mountains, across the Sahara Desert, across Antarctica, across all the oceans; all with their load of humanity and with no other form of animal life besides. And on the roof of all those buildings are the algae farms, with little plant cells exposed to the Sun so that they might grow rapidly and, without waste, form protein for all the mighty population of 35 trillion human beings.

Is that tolerable? Even if science produced all the energy and 29 materials mankind could want, kept them all fed with algae, all educated, all amused—is the planetary high-rise tolerable?

And if it were, can we double the population further in 35 more 30 years? And then double it again in another 35 years? Where will the food come from? What will persuade the algae to multiply faster than the light energy they absorb makes possible? What will speed up the Sun to add the energy to make it possible? And if vast supplies of fusion energy are added to supplement the Sun, how will we get rid of the equally vast supplies of heat that will be produced? And after the icecaps are melted and the oceans boiled into steam, what?

Can we bleed off the mass of humanity to other worlds? Right 31 now, the number of human beings on Earth is increasing by 80 million per year, and each year that number goes up by 1 and a fraction percent. Can we really suppose that we can send 80 million people per year to the Moon, Mars, and elsewhere, and engineer those worlds to support those people? And even so, merely remain in the same place ourselves?

No! Not the most optimistic visionary in the world could honestly 32 convince himself that space travel is the solution to our population problem, if the present rate of increase is sustained.

But when will this planetary high-rise culture come about? How 33 long will it take to increase Earth's population to that impossible point at the present doubling rate of once every 35 years? If it will take 1 million years or even 100,000, then, for goodness sake, let's not worry just yet.

Well, we don't have that kind of time. We will reach that dead 34 end in no more than 460 years.

At the rate we are going, without birth control, then even if 35 science serves us in an absolutely ideal way, we will reach the planetary high-rise with no animals but man, with no plants but algae, with no room for even one more person, by A.D. 2430.

And if science serves us in less than an ideal way (as it certainly 36 will), the end will come sooner, much sooner, and mankind will start fading long, long before he is forced to construct that building that will cover all the Earth's surface.

So if birth control *must* come by A.D. 2430 at the very latest, even 37 in an ideal world of advancing science, let it come *now*, in heaven's name, while there are still oak trees in the world and daisies and tigers and butterflies, and while there is still open land and space, and before the cancer called man proves fatal to life and the planet.

COMPREHENSION

1. What does Asimov mean when he says, "The first mistake is to think of mankind as a thing in itself"?

2. To what disease does Asimov compare unrestrained population growth? Do you think this is a good comparison? Why or why not?

3. At what rate is the human population increasing?

4. What will happen if the present rate of population growth continues?

5. How can science and technology help the earth's population? Are there limits to this help?

PURPOSE AND AUDIENCE

1. Much of this essay is devoted to proving to the audience that a problem actually exists. Do you think this is necessary? Could Asimov have made his point in another way? Explain.

2. What assumption does Asimov make about his audience?

3. Where does Asimov state his thesis? Why does he wait so long to do so?

4. Where does Asimov anticipate his audience's objection to his position?

STYLE AND STRUCTURE

1. Is this essay primarily an example of inductive or deductive reasoning?

2. At several points in his essay, Asimov asks questions. What is the function of these questions?

3. Much of the force of this essay comes from the comparisons that Asimov uses to make his points clear to his readers. List the different comparisons Asimov uses. What do they have in common?

4. Do you think Asimov could be criticized for being an alarmist? Does he gain any advantage in taking an extreme position? Explain.

5. Asimov rarely talks about "our" population problem. Instead, he talks as if he were a visitor from another planet viewing an alien species: "Earth's human population," "life forms," and "Homo sapiens." Why does he do this?

6. The conclusion of this essay is a single sentence. What does Asimov gain or lose by this tactic?

7. How do the introduction and conclusion tie the essay together?

WRITING WORKSHOP

1. Write an argumentative essay in which you defend the thesis that, although the population increase is a cause for concern, it is not as serious as Asimov suggests. Refute specific points in his essay whenever possible.

2. Write an essay in which you argue for or against birth control. Since this is a controversial issue, be careful to respond to the sensitivities of your audience.

POLITICS AND THE
ENGLISH LANGUAGE

George Orwell

"Politics and the English Language" was first published in 1946 in the London monthly Horizon. *It was reprinted in 1950 in* Shooting an Elephant and Other Essays. *In this essay, Orwell focuses on what he sees as the "decadence of our language." He argues for the upgrading of English and the elimination of the well-worn words and phrases that enable some in our society to defend the indefensible. (For biographical information on George Orwell, see page 65.)*

Most people who bother with the matter at all would admit that   1
the English language is in a bad way, but it is generally assumed
that we cannot by conscious action do anything about it. Our civilization is decadent and our language—so the argument runs—must
inevitably share in the general collapse. It follows that any struggle
against the abuse of language is a sentimental archaism, like preferring candles to electric light or hansom cabs to aeroplanes. Un-
derneath this lies the half-conscious belief that language is a natural growth and not an instrument which we shape for our own
purpose.

Now, it is clear that the decline of a language must ultimately   2
have political and economic causes: it is not due simply to the bad
influence of this or that individual writer. But an effect can become
a cause, reinforcing the original cause and producing the same effect
in an intensified form, and so on indefinitely. A man may take to
drink because he feels himself to be a failure, and then fail all the
more completely because he drinks. It is rather the same thing that
is happening to the English language. It becomes ugly and inac-
curate because our thoughts are foolish, but the slovenliness of our
language makes it easier for us to have foolish thoughts. The point
is that the process is reversible. Modern English, especially written
English, is full of bad habits which spread by imitation and which
can be avoided if one is willing to take the necessary trouble. If one
gets rid of these habits one can think more clearly, and to think
clearly is a necessary first step towards political regeneration: so
that the fight against bad English is not frivolous and is not the
exclusive concern of professional writers. I will come back to this

presently, and I hope that by that time the meaning of what I have said here will have become clearer. Meanwhile, here are five specimens of the English language as it is now habitually written.

These five passages have not been picked out because they are especially bad—I could have quoted far worse if I had chosen—but because they illustrate various of the mental vices from which we now suffer. They are a little below the average, but are fairly representative samples. I number them so that I can refer back to them when necessary: 3

"(1) I am not, indeed, sure whether it is not true to say that the Milton who once seemed not unlike a seventeenth-century Shelley had not become, out of an experience ever more bitter in each year, more alien [*sic*] to the founder of that Jesuit sect which nothing could induce him to tolerate."

Professor Harold Laski (Essay in *Freedom of Expression*).

"(2) Above all, we cannot play ducks and drakes with a native battery of idioms which prescribes such egregious collocations of vocables as the Basic *put up with* for *tolerate* or *put at a loss* for *bewilder*."

Professor Lancelot Hogben (*Interglossa*).

"(3) On the one side we have the free personality: by definition it is not neurotic, for it has neither conflict nor dream. Its desires, such as they are, are transparent, for they are just what institutional approval keeps in the forefront of consciousness; another institutional pattern would alter their number and intensity; there is little in them that is natural, irreducible, or culturally dangerous. But *on the other side,* the social bond itself is nothing but the mutual reflection of these self-secure integrities. Recall the definition of love. Is not this the very picture of a small academic? Where is there a place in this hall of mirrors for either personality or fraternity?"

Essay on psychology in *Politics* (New York).

"(4) All the 'best people' from the gentlemen's clubs, and all the frantic fascist captains, united in common hatred of Socialism and bestial horror of the rising tide of the mass revolutionary movement, have turned to acts of provocation, to foul incendiarism, to medieval legends of poisoned wells, to legalize their own destruction of proletarian organizations, and rouse the agitated petty-bourgeoisie to chauvinistic fervour on behalf of the fight against the revolutionary way out of the crisis."

Communist pamphlet.

"(5) If a new spirit *is* to be infused into this old country, there is one thorny and contentious reform which must be tackled, and that is the humanization and galvanization of the B.B.C. Timidity here will bespeak cancer and atrophy of the soul. The heart of Britain may be sound and of strong beat, for instance, but the British lion's roar at present is like that of Bottom in Shakespeare's *Midsummer Night's Dream*—as gentle as any sucking dove. A virile new Britain cannot continue indefinitely to be traduced in the eyes or rather ears, of the world by the effete languors of Langham Place, brazenly masquerading as 'standard English.' When the Voice of Britain is heard at nine o'clock, better far and infinitely less ludicrous to hear aitches honestly dropped than the present priggish, inflated, inhibited, schoolma'amish arch braying of blameless bashful mewing maidens!"

Letter in Tribune.

Each of these passages has faults of its own, but, quite apart from   4
avoidable ugliness, two qualities are common to all of them. The first is staleness of imagery: the other is lack of precision. The writer either has a meaning and cannot express it, or he inadvertently says something else, or he is almost indifferent as to whether his words mean anything or not. This mixture of vagueness and sheer incompetence is the most marked characteristic of modern English prose, and especially of any kind of political writing. As soon as certain topics are raised, the concrete melts into the abstract and no one seems to think of turns of speech that are not hackneyed: prose consists less and less of *words* chosen for the sake of their meaning, and more and more of *phrases* tacked together like the sections of a prefabricated hen-house. I list below, with notes and examples, various of the tricks by means of which the work of prose-construction is habitually dodged:

DYING METAPHORS

A newly invented metaphor assists thought by evoking a visual   5
image, while on the other hand a metaphor which is technically "dead" (e.g., *iron resolution*) has in effect reverted to being an ordinary word and can generally be used without loss of vividness. But in between these two classes there is a huge dump of worn-out metaphors which have lost all evocative power and are merely used because they save people the trouble of inventing phrases for themselves. Examples are: *Ring the changes on, take up the cudgels for, toe the line, ride roughshod over, stand shoulder to shoulder with, play into the hands of, no axe to grind, grist to the mill, fishing in troubled waters, on the order of the day, Achilles' heel, swan song, hotbed.* Many of these are used without knowledge of their meaning (what is a "rift," for instance?), and incompatible metaphors are frequently mixed, a sure sign that the writer is not interested in

what he is saying. Some metaphors now current have been twisted out of their original meaning without those who use them even being aware of the fact. For example, *toe the line* is sometimes written *tow the line*. Another example is *the hammer and the anvil*, now always used with the implication that the anvil gets the worst of it. In real life it is always the anvil that breaks the hammer, never the other way about: a writer who stopped to think what he was saying would be aware of this, and would avoid perverting the original phrase.

OPERATORS OR VERBAL FALSE LIMBS

These save the trouble of picking out appropriate verbs and nouns, and at the same time pad each sentence with extra syllables which give it an appearance of symmetry. Characteristic phrases are: *render inoperative, militate against, make contact with, be subjected to, give rise to, give grounds for, have the effect of, play a leading part (role) in, make itself felt, take effect, exhibit a tendency to, serve the purpose of, etc., etc.* The keynote is the elimination of simple verbs. Instead of being a single word, such as *break, stop, spoil, mend, kill*, a verb becomes a *phrase*, made up of a noun or adjective tacked on to some general-purpose verb such as *prove, serve, form, play, render*. In addition, the passive voice is wherever possible used in preference to the active, and noun constructions are used instead of gerunds (*by examination of* instead of *by examining*). The range of verbs is further cut down by means of the *-ize* and *de-* formation, and the banal statements are given an appearance of profundity by means of the *not un-* formation. Simple conjunctions and prepositions are replaced by such phrases as *with respect to, having regard to, the fact that, by dint of, in view of, in the interests of, on the hypothesis that;* and the ends of sentences are saved from anticlimax by such resounding commonplaces as *greatly to be desired, cannot be left out of account, a development to be expected in the near future, deserving of serious consideration, brought to a satisfactory conclusion*, and so on and so forth.

PRETENTIOUS DICTION

Words like *phenomenon, element, individual* (as noun), *objective, categorical, effective, virtual, basic, primary, promote, constitute, exhibit, exploit, utilize, eliminate, liquidate*, are used to dress up simple statements and give an air of scientific impartiality to biased judgments. Adjectives like *epoch-making, epic, historic, unforgettable*, *triumphant, age-old, inevitable, inexorable, veritable,* are used to dignify the sordid processes of international politics, while writing that aims at glorifying war usually takes on an archaic colour, its characteristic words being: *realm, throne, chariot, mailed fist, trident, sword, shield, buckler, banner, jackboot, clarion.* Foreign words and expressions such as *cul de sac, ancien régime, deus ex machina, mutatis mutandis, status quo, gleichschaltung, weltanschauung,* are used to give an air of culture and elegance. Except for the useful abbreviations *i.e., e.g.,* and *etc.,* there is no real need for any of the hundreds of foreign phrases now current in English. Bad writers, and especially scientific, political and sociological writers, are nearly always haunted by the notion that Latin or Greek words are grander than Saxon ones, and unnecessary words like *expedite, ameliorate, predict, extraneous, deracinated, clandestine, subaqueous* and hundreds of others constantly gain ground from their Anglo-Saxon opposite numbers.[1] The jargon peculiar to Marxist writing (*hyena, hangman, cannibal, petty bourgeois, these gentry, lacquey, flunkey, mad dog, White Guard,* etc.) consists largely of words and phrases translated from Russian, German or French; but the normal way of coining a new word is to use a Latin or Greek root with the appropriate affix and, where necessary, the *-ize* formation. It is often easier to make up words of this kind (*deregionalize, impermissible, extramarital, nonfragmentatory* and so forth) than to think up the English words that will cover one's meaning. The result, in general, is an increase in slovenliness and vagueness.

MEANINGLESS WORDS

In certain kinds of writing, particularly in art criticism and literary criticism, it is normal to come across long passages which are almost completely lacking in meaning.[2] Words like *romantic, plas-* 8

[1]An interesting illustration of this is the way in which the English flower names which were in use till very recently are being ousted by Greek ones, *snapdragon* becoming *antirrhinum, forget-me-not* becoming *myosotis,* etc. It is hard to see any practical reason for this change of fashion: it is probably due to an instinctive turning-away from the more homely word and a vague feeling that the Greek word is scientific.

[2]Example: "Comfort's catholicity of perception and image, strangely Whitmanesque in range, almost the exact opposite of aesthetic compulsion, continues to evoke that trembling atmospheric accumulative hinting at a cruel, an inexorably serene timelessness. . . . Wrey Gardiner scores by aiming at simple bull's-eyes with precision. Only they are not so simple, and through this contented sadness runs more than the surface bitter-sweet of resignation." (*Poetry Quarterly.*)

tic, values, human, dead, sentimental, natural, vitality, as used in art criticism, are strictly meaningless in the sense that they not only do not point to any discoverable object, but are hardly ever expected to do so by the reader. When one critic writes, "The outstanding feature of Mr. X's work is its living quality," while another writes, "The immediately striking thing about Mr. X's work is its peculiar deadness," the reader accepts this as a simple difference of opinion. If words like *black* and *white* were involved, instead of the jargon words *dead* and *living,* he would see at once that language was being used in an improper way. Many political words are similarly abused. The word *Fascism* has now no meaning except in so far as it signifies "something not desirable." The words *democracy, socialism, freedom, patriotic, realistic, justice,* have each of them several different meanings which cannot be reconciled with one another. In the case of a word like *democracy,* not only is there no agreed definition, but the attempt to make one is resisted from all sides. It is almost universally felt that when we call a country democratic we are praising it: consequently the defenders of every kind of régime claim that it is a democracy, and fear that they might have to stop using the word if it were tied down to any one meaning. Words of this kind are often used in a consciously dishonest way. That is, the person who uses them has his own private definition, but allows his hearer to think he means something quite different. Statements like *Marshal Pétain was a true patriot, The Soviet Press is the freest in the world, The Catholic Church is opposed to persecution,* are almost always made with intent to deceive. Other words used in variable meanings, in most cases more or less dishonestly, are: *class, totalitarian, science, progressive, reactionary, bourgeois, equality.*

Now that I have made this catalogue of swindles and perversions,   9 let me give another example of the kind of writing that they lead to. This time it must of its nature be an imaginary one. I am going to translate a passage of good English into modern English of the worst sort. Here is a well-known verse from *Ecclesiastes:*

> "I returned and saw under the sun, that the race is not to the swift, nor the battle to the strong, neither yet bread to the wise, nor yet riches to men of understanding, nor yet favour to men of skill; but time and chance happeneth to them all."

Here it is in modern English:

"Objective consideration of contemporary phenomena compels the conclusion that success or failure in competitive activities exhibits no tendency to be commensurate with innate capacity, but that a considerable element of the unpredictable must invariably be taken into account."

This is a parody, but not a very gross one. Exhibit (3), above, for instance, contains several patches of the same kind of English. It will be seen that I have not made a full translation. The beginning and ending of the sentence follow the original meaning fairly closely, but in the middle the concrete illustrations—race, battle, bread—dissolve into the vague phrase "success or failure in competitive activities." This had to be so, because no modern writer of the kind I am discussing—no one capable of using phrases like "objective consideration of contemporary phenomena"—would ever tabulate his thoughts in that precise and detailed way. The whole tendency of modern prose is away from concreteness. Now analyse these two sentences a little more closely. The first contains forty-nine words but only sixty syllables, and all its words are those of everyday life. The second contains thirty-eight words of ninety syllables: eighteen of its words are from Latin roots, and one from Greek. The first sentence contains six vivid images, and only one phrase ("time and chance") that could be called vague. The second contains not a single fresh, arresting phrase, and in spite of its ninety syllables it gives only a shortened version of the meaning contained in the first. Yet without a doubt it is the second kind of sentence that is gaining ground in modern English. I do not want to exaggerate. This kind of writing is not yet universal, and outcrops of simplicity will occur here and there in the worst-written page. Still, if you or I were told to write a few lines on the uncertainty of human fortunes, we should probably come much nearer to my imaginary sentence than to the one from *Ecclesiastes*.

As I have tried to show, modern writing at its worst does not consist in picking out words for the sake of their meaning and inventing images in order to make the meaning clearer. It consists in gumming together long strips of words which have already been set in order by someone else, and making the results presentable by sheer humbug. The attraction of this way of writing is that it is easy. It is easier—even quicker, once you have the habit—to say *In my opinion it is a not unjustifiable assumption that* than to say *I think*. If you use ready-made phrases, you not only don't have to hunt about for words; you also don't have to bother with the rhythms of your sentences, since these phrases are generally so arranged as to be more or less euphonious. When you are composing in a hurry—when you are dictating to a stenographer, for instance, or making a public speech—it is natural to fall into a pretentious, Latinized style. Tags like *a consideration which we should do well to bear in mind* or *a conclusion to which all of us would readily assent* will save many a sentence from coming down with a bump. By using stale metaphors, similes and idioms, you save much mental effort, at the cost of leaving your meaning vague, not only for your reader but for yourself. This is the significance of mixed metaphors. The sole aim of a metaphor is to call up a visual image. When these images clash—as in *The Fascist octopus has sung its swan song, the jackboot is thrown into the melting pot*—it can be taken as certain that the writer is not seeing a mental image of the objects he is naming; in other words he is not really thinking. Look again at the examples I gave at the beginning of this essay. Professor Laski (1) uses five negatives in fifty-three words. One of these is superfluous, making nonsense of the whole passage, and in addition there is the slip *alien* for akin, making further nonsense, and several avoidable pieces of clumsiness which increase the general vagueness. Professor Hogben (2) plays ducks and drakes with a battery which is able to write prescriptions, and, while disapproving of the everyday phrase *put up with,* is unwilling to look *egregious* up in the dictionary and see what it means. (3), if one takes an uncharitable attitude towards it, is simply meaningless: probably one could work out its intended meaning by reading the whole of the article in which it occurs. In (4), the writer knows more or less what he wants to say, but an accumulation of stale phrases chokes him like tea leaves blocking the sink. In (5), words and meaning have almost parted company. People who write in this manner usually have a general emotional meaning—they dislike one thing and want to express solidarity with another—but they are not interested in the detail of what they are saying. A scrupulous writer, in every sentence that he writes, will ask himself at least four questions, thus: What am I trying to say? What words will express it? What image or idiom will make it clearer? Is this image fresh enough to have an effect? And he will probably ask himself two more: Could I put it more shortly? Have I said anything that is avoidably ugly? But you are not obliged to go to all this trouble. You can shirk it by simply throwing your mind open and letting the ready-made phrases come crowding in. They will construct your sentences for you—even think your thoughts for you, to a certain extent—and at need they will perform the important service of partially concealing your meaning even from yourself. It is at this point that the special connection between politics and the debasement of language becomes clear.

In our time it is broadly true that political writing is bad writing. 12 Where it is not true, it will generally be found that the writer is some kind of rebel, expressing his private opinions and not a "party line." Orthodoxy, of whatever colour, seems to demand a lifeless, imitative style. The political dialects to be found in pamphlets, leading articles, manifestos, White Papers and the speeches of undersecretaries do, of course, vary from party to party, but they are all alike in that one almost never finds in them a fresh, vivid, homemade turn of speech. When one watches some tired hack on the platform mechanically repeating the familiar phrases—*bestial atrocities, iron heel, bloodstained tyranny, free peoples of the world, stand shoulder to shoulder*—one often has a curious feeling that one is not watching a live human being but some kind of dummy: a feeling which suddenly becomes stronger at moments when the light catches the speaker's spectac! and turns them into blank discs which seem to have no eyes behind them. And this is not altogether fanciful. A speaker who uses that kind of phraseology has gone some distance towards turning himself into a machine. The appropriate noises are coming out of his larynx, but his brain is not involved as it would be if he were choosing his words for himself. If the speech he is making is one that he is accustomed to make over and over again, he may be almost unconscious of what he is saying, as one is when one utters the responses in church. And this reduced state of consciousness, if not indispensable, is at any rate favourable to political conformity.

In our time, political speech and writing are largely the defence 13 of the indefensible. Things like the continuance of British rule in India, the Russian purges and deportations, the dropping of the atom bombs on Japan, can indeed be defended, but only by arguments which are too brutal for most people to face, and which do not square with the professed aims of political parties. Thus political language has to consist largely of euphemism, question-begging and sheer cloudy vagueness. Defenseless villages are bombarded from the air, the inhabitants driven out into the countryside, the cattle machine-gunned, the huts set on fire with incendiary bullets: this is called *pacification*. Millions of peasants are robbed of their farms and sent trudging along the roads with no more than they can carry: this is called *transfer of population* or *rectification of frontiers*. People are imprisoned for years without trial, or shot in the back of the neck or sent to die of scurvy in Arctic lumber camps: this is called *elimination of unreliable elements*. Such phraseology is needed if one wants to name things without calling up mental pictures of them. Consider for instance some comfortable English professor defending Russian totalitarianism. He cannot say outright, "I believe in killing off your opponents when you can get good results by doing so." Probably, therefore, he will say something like this:

"While freely conceding that the Soviet régime exhibits certain features which the humanitarian may be inclined to deplore, we must, I think, agree that a certain curtailment of the right to political opposition is an unavoidable concomitant of transitional periods, and that the rigours which the Russian people have been called upon to undergo have been amply justified in the sphere of concrete achievement." 14

The inflated style is itself a kind of euphemism. A mass of Latin words falls upon the facts like soft snow, blurring the outlines and covering up all the details. The great enemy of clear language is insincerity. When there is a gap between one's real and one's declared aims, one turns as it were instinctively to long words and exhausted idioms, like a cuttlefish squirting out ink. In our age there is no such thing as "keeping out of politics." All issues are political issues, and politics itself is a mass of lies, evasions, folly, hatred and schizophrenia. When the general atmosphere is bad, language must suffer. I should expect to find—this is a guess which I have not sufficient knowledge to verify—that the German, Russian and Italian languages have all deteriorated in the last ten or fifteen years, as a result of dictatorship. 15

But if thought corrupts language, language can also corrupt thought. A bad usage can spread by tradition and imitation, even among people who should and do know better. The debased language that I have been discussing is in some ways very convenient. Phrases like *a not unjustifiable assumption, leaves much to be desired, would serve no good purpose, a consideration which we should do well to bear in mind,* are a continuous temptation, a packet of aspirins always at one's elbow. Look back through this essay, and for certain you will find that I have again and again committed the very faults I am protesting against. By this morning's post I have received a pamphlet dealing with conditions in Germany. The author tells me that he "felt impelled" to write it. I open it at random, and here is almost the first sentence that I see: "(The Allies) have an opportunity not only of achieving a radical transformation of Germany's social and political structure in such a way as to avoid a nationalistic reaction in Germany itself, but at the same time of laying the foundations of a co-operative and unified Europe." You see, he "feels impelled" to write—feels, presumably, that he has 16 something new to say—and yet his words, like cavalry horses answering the bugle, group themselves automatically into the familiar dreary pattern. This invasion of one's mind by ready-made phrases (*lay the foundations, achieve a radical transformation*) can only be prevented if one is constantly on guard against them, and every such phrase anaesthetizes a portion of one's brain.

I said earlier that the decadence of our language is probably 17 curable. Those who deny this would argue, if they produced an argument at all, that language merely reflects existing social conditions, and that we cannot influence its development by any direct tinkering with words and constructions. So far as the general tone or spirit of a language goes, this may be true, but it is not true in detail. Silly words and expressions have often disappeared, not through any evolutionary process but owing to the conscious action of a minority. Two recent examples were *explore every avenue* and *leave no stone unturned,* which were killed by the jeers of a few journalists. There is a long list of flyblown metaphors which could similarly be got rid of if enough people would interest themselves in the job; and it should also be possible to laugh the *not un-* formation out of existence,[3] to reduce the amount of Latin and Greek in the average sentence, to drive out foreign phrases and strayed scientific words, and, in general, to make pretentiousness unfashionable. But all these are minor points. The defence of the English language implies more than this, and perhaps it is best to start by saying what it does *not* imply.

To begin with it has nothing to do with archaism, with the sal- 18 vaging of obsolete words and turns of speech, or with the setting up of a "standard English" which must never be departed from. On the contrary, it is especially concerned with the scrapping of every word or idiom which has outworn its usefulness. It has nothing to do with correct grammar and syntax, which are of no importance so long as one makes one's meaning clear, or with the avoidance of Americanisms, or with having what is called a "good prose style." On the other hand it is not concerned with fake simplicity and the attempt to make written English colloquial. Nor does it even imply in every case preferring the Saxon word to the Latin one, though it does imply using the fewest and shortest words that will cover one's meaning. What is above all needed is to let the meaning choose the word, and not the other way about. In prose, the worst thing one can do with words is to surrender to them. When you think of a

---

[3]One can cure oneself of the *not un-* formation by memorizing this sentence: *A not unblack dog was chasing a not unsmall rabbit across a not ungreen field.*

concrete object, you think wordlessly, and then, if you want to describe the thing you have been visualizing you probably hunt about till you find the exact words that seem to fit. When you think of something abstract you are more inclined to use words from the start, and unless you make a conscious effort to prevent it, the existing dialect will come rushing in and do the job for you, at the expense of blurring or even changing your meaning. Probably it is better to put off using words as long as possible and get one's meaning as clear as one can through pictures or sensations. Afterwards one can choose—not simply *accept*— the phrases that will best cover the meaning, and then switch round and decide what impression one's words are likely to make on another person. This last effort of the mind cuts out all stale or mixed images, all prefabricated phrases, needless repetitions, and humbug and vagueness generally. But one can often be in doubt about the effect of a word or a phrase, and one needs rules that one can rely on when instinct fails. I think the following rules will cover most cases:

   (i)   Never use a metaphor, simile or other figure of speech which
         you are used to seeing in print.
   (ii) Never use a long word where a short one will do.
   (iii) If it is possible to cut a word out, always cut it out.
   (iv) Never use the passive where you can use the active.
   (v)   Never use a foreign phrase, a scientific word or a jargon word
         if you can think of an everyday English equivalent.
   (vi) Break any of these rules sooner than say anything outright
         barbarous.

These rules sound elementary, and so they are, but they demand a deep change of attitude in anyone who has grown used to writing in the style now fashionable. One could keep all of them and still write bad English, but one could not write the kind of stuff that I quoted in those five specimens at the beginning of this article.

   I have not here been considering the literary use of language, but merely language as an instrument for expressing and not for concealing or preventing thought. Stuart Chase and others have come near to claiming that all abstract words are meaningless, and have used this as a pretext for advocating a kind of political quietism. Since you don't know what Fascism is, how can you struggle against Fascism? One need not swallow such absurdities as this, but one ought to recognize that the present political chaos is connected with the decay of language, and that one can probably bring about some improvement by starting at the verbal end. If you simplify your English, you are freed from the worst follies of orthodoxy.

You cannot speak any of the necessary dialects, and when you make a stupid remark its stupidity will be obvious, even to yourself. Political language—and with variations this is true of all political parties, from Conservatives to Anarchists—is designed to make lies sound truthful and murder respectable, and to give an appearance of solidity to pure wind. One cannot change this all in a moment, but one can at least change one's own habits, and from time to time one can even, if one jeers loudly enough, send some worn-out and useless phrase—some *jackboot, Achilles' heel, hotbed, melting pot, acid test, veritable inferno* or other lump of verbal refuse—into the dustbin where it belongs.

COMPREHENSION

1. According to Orwell, why must the decline of language have political and economic causes?

2. What qualities are common to the five passages that Orwell presents as examples in the beginning of his essay?

3. List the tricks by which "the work of prose-construction is habitually dodged."

4. What does Orwell mean when he says, "In our time, political speech and writing are largely the defence of the indefensible"?

5. What does Orwell say can be done about the decadence of the English language?

6. What will the effect of cleansing the language be?

PURPOSE AND AUDIENCE

1. Where does Orwell state his thesis? Why does he place it where he does?

2. Does Orwell feel that his audience is friendly, hostile, or neutral? Explain.

3. What is Orwell's purpose in writing this essay?

4. Does Orwell strengthen or weaken his argument by connecting language with the decline of civilization? Would he have done better arguing for the improvement of language for its own sake?

STYLE AND STRUCTURE

1. Orwell's introduction is actually a summary of his entire essay. Does the essay need such a beginning? Why or why not?

2. Why does Orwell place his five examples of bad prose at the beginning of his essay?

3. At points Orwell uses lists and headings. What purpose do they serve? Should he have used more of these?

4. Choose two pages of the essay and underline the transitional words and phrases that draw the argument together.

5. Topic sentences also help readers follow the argument of this essay. Underline the topic sentences that introduce major sections of the discussion.

6. Where does Orwell address the objections he feels his audience might have?

7. At what points does Orwell attempt to establish himself as a reasonable person? How successful is he?

8. How effectively does Orwell conclude his essay? Does he restate his thesis? What ideas does he want to leave his audience with?

WRITING WORKSHOP

1. Find your own examples of the kind of political writing that Orwell discusses. Write an essay in which you argue that in our day political writing can sometimes be the defense of the indefensible.

2. Write an essay in which you argue that things are not as bad as Orwell seems to think they are.

3. Write an essay in which you argue for or against the use of some of your favorite well-worn words and phrases.

LETTER FROM BIRMINGHAM JAIL

Martin Luther King, Jr.

Martin Luther King, Jr., was born in 1929 in Atlanta, Georgia, and assassinated in 1968 in Memphis, Tennessee. He graduated from Morehouse College in 1948 and received his B.D. from the Crozer Theological Seminary in Chester, Pennsylvania, in 1951. After receiving his Ph.D. in systematic philosophy from Boston University in 1954, he became pastor of the Dexler Avenue Baptist Church in Montgomery, Alabama. With his involvement in the Montgomery bus boycott (1955–56), King's prominence increased swiftly. In 1957 he was elected head of the Southern Christian Leadership Conference. During this time he developed a philosophy of nonviolent direct protest that would characterize his actions throughout the rest of his career. In 1963, King launched a campaign against segregation in Birmingham, Alabama, but he met fierce opposition from police as well as white moderates who saw him as dangerous. Arrested and jailed for eight days, King wrote his "Letter from Birmingham Jail" to white clergymen to explain his actions and to answer those who urged him to call off the demonstrations. Having much in common with the Declaration of Independence, the "Letter from Birmingham Jail" is a well-reasoned defense of demonstrations and civil disobedience.

April 16, 1963

My Dear Fellow Clergymen:

While confined here in the Birmingham city jail, I came across your recent statement calling my present activities "unwise and untimely." Seldom do I pause to answer criticism of my work and ideas. If I sought to answer all the criticisms that cross my desk, my secretaries would have little time for anything other than such correspondence in the course of the day, and I would have no time for constructive work. But since I feel that you are men of genuine good will and that your criticisms are sincerely set forth, I want to try to answer your statement in what I hope will be patient and reasonable terms.

I think I should indicate why I am here in Birmingham, since you have been influenced by the view which argues against "outsiders coming in." I have the honor of serving as president of the Southern Christian Leadership Conference, an organization oper-

416

ating in every southern state, with headquarters in Atlanta, Georgia. We have some eighty-five affiliated organizations across the South, and one of them is the Alabama Christian Movement for Human Rights. Frequently we share staff, educational, and financial resources with our affiliates. Several months ago the affiliate here in Birmingham asked us to be on call to engage in a nonviolent direct-action program if such were deemed necessary. We readily consented, and when the hour came we lived up to our promise. So I, along with several members of my staff, am here because I was invited here. I am here because I have organizational ties here.

But more basically, I am in Birmingham because injustice is   3
here. Just as the prophets of the eighth century B.C. left their villages and carried their "thus saith the Lord" far beyond the boundaries of their home towns, and just· as the Apostle Paul left his village of Tarsus and carried the gospel of Jesus Christ to the far corners of the Greco-Roman world, so am I compelled to carry the gospel of freedom beyond my own home town. Like Paul, I must constantly respond to the Macedonian call for aid.

Moreover, I am cognizant of the interrelatedness of all commu-   4
nities and states. I cannot sit idly by in Atlanta and not be concerned about what happens in Birmingham. Injustice anywhere is a threat to justice everywhere. We are caught in an inescapable network of mutuality, tied in a single garment of destiny. Whatever affects one directly, affects all indirectly. Never again can we afford to live with the narrow, provincial, "outside agitator" idea. Anyone who lives inside the United States can never be considered an outsider anywhere within its bounds.

You deplore the demonstrations taking place in Birmingham.   5
But your statement, I am sorry to say, fails to express a similar concern for the conditions that brought about the demonstrations. I am sure that none of you would want to rest content with the superficial kind of social analysis that deals merely with effects and does not grapple with underlying causes. It is unfortunate that demonstrations are taking place in Birmingham, but it is even more unfortunate that the city's white power structure left the Negro community with no alternative.

In any nonviolent campaign there are four basic steps: collection   6
of the facts to determine whether injustices exist; negotiation; self-purification; and direct action. We have gone through all these steps in Birmingham. There can be no gainsaying the fact that racial injustice engulfs this community. Birmingham is probably the most thoroughly segregated city in the United States. Its ugly record of brutality is widely known. Negroes have experienced grossly unjust

treatment in courts. There have been more unsolved bombings of Negro homes and churches in Birmingham than in any other city in the nation. These are the hard, brutal facts of the case. On the basis of these conditions, Negro leaders sought to negotiate with the city fathers. But the latter consistently refused to engage in good-faith negotiation.

Then, last September, came the opportunity to talk with leaders   7
of Birmingham's economic community. In the course of the negotiations, certain promises were made by the merchants—for example, to remove the stores' humiliating racial signs. On the basis of these promises, the Reverend Fred Shuttlesworth and the leaders of the Alabama Christian Movement for Human Rights agreed to a moratorium on all demonstrations. As the weeks and months went by, we realized that we were the victims of a broken promise. A few signs, briefly removed, returned; the others remained.

As in so many past experiences, our hopes had been blasted, and   8
the shadow of deep disappointment settled upon us. We had no alternative except to prepare for direct action, whereby we would present our very bodies as means of laying our case before the conscience of the local and the national community. Mindful of the difficulties involved, we decided to undertake a process of self-purification. We began a series of workshops on nonviolence, and we repeatedly asked ourselves: "Are you able to accept blows without retaliating?" "Are you able to endure the ordeal of jail?" We decided to schedule our direct-action program for the Easter season, realizing that except for Christmas, this is the main shopping period of the year. Knowing that a strong economic-withdrawal program would be the by-product of direct action, we felt that this would be the best time to bring pressure to bear on the merchants for the needed change.

Then it occurred to us that Birmingham's mayoral election was   9
coming up in March, and we speedily decided to postpone action until after election day. When we discovered that the Commissioner of Public Safety, Eugene "Bull" Connor, had piled up enough votes to be in the run-off, we decided again to postpone action until the day after the run-off so that the demonstrations could not be used to cloud the issues. Like many others, we waited to see Mr. Connor defeated, and to this end we endured postponement after postponement. Having aided in this community need, we felt that our direct-action program could be delayed no longer.

You may well ask, "Why direct action? Why sit-ins, marches, and   10
so forth? Isn't negotiation a better path?" You are quite right in calling for negotiation. Indeed, this is the very purpose of direct

action. Nonviolent direct action seeks to create such a crisis and foster such a tension that a community which has constantly re-fused to negotiate is forced to confront the issue. It seeks so to dram-atize the issue that it can no longer be ignored. My citing the crea-tion of tension as part of the work of the nonviolent-resister may sound rather shocking. But I must confess that I am not afraid of the word "tension." I have earnestly opposed violent tension, but there is a type of constructive, nonviolent tension which is necessary for growth. Just as Socrates felt that it was necessary to create a tension in the mind so that individuals could rise from the bondage of myths and half-truths to the unfettered realm of creative analysis and objective appraisal, so must we see the need for nonviolent gadflies to create the kind of tension in society that will help men rise from the dark depths of prejudice and racism to the majestic heights of understanding and brotherhood.

The purpose of our direct-action program is to create a situation so crisis-packed that it will inevitably open the door to negotiation. I therefore concur with you in your call for negotiation. Too long has our beloved Southland been bogged down in a tragic effort to live in monologue rather than dialogue. 11

One of the basic points in your statement is that the action that I and my associates have taken in Birmingham is untimely. Some have asked: "Why didn't you give the new city administration time to act?" The only answer that I can give to this query is that the new Birmingham administration must be prodded about as much as the outgoing one, before it will act. We are sadly mistaken if we feel that the election of Albert Boutwell as mayor will bring the millennium to Birmingham. While Mr. Boutwell is a much more gentle person than Mr. Connor, they are both segregationists, ded-icated to maintenance of the status quo. I have hoped that Mr. Boutwell will be reasonable enough to see the futility of massive resistance to desegregation. But he will not see this without pres-sure from devotees of civil rights. My friends, I must say to you that we have not made a single gain in civil rights without determined legal and nonviolent pressure. Lamentably, it is an historical fact that privileged groups seldom give up their privileges voluntarily. Individuals may see the moral light and voluntarily give up their unjust posture; but, as Reinhold Niebuhr has reminded us, groups tends to be more immoral than individuals. 12

We know through painful experience that freedom is never vol-untarily given by the oppressor; it must be demanded by the op-pressed. Frankly, I have yet to engage in a direct-action campaign that was "well timed" in the view of those who have not suffered 13 unduly from the disease of segregation. For years now I have heard the word "Wait!" It rings in the ear of every Negro with piercing familiarity. This "Wait" has almost always meant "Never." We must come to see, with one of our distinguished jurists, that "justice too long delayed is justice denied."

We have waited for more than 340 years for our constitutional and God-given rights. The nations of Asia and Africa are moving with jetlike speed toward gaining political independence, but we still creep at horse-and-buggy pace toward gaining a cup of coffee at a lunch counter. Perhaps it is easy for those who have never felt the stinging darts of segregation to say, "Wait." But when you have seen vicious mobs lynch your mothers and fathers at will and drown your sisters and brothers at whim; when you have seen hate-filled policemen curse, kick, and even kill your black brothers and sisters; when you see the vast majority of your twenty million Negro brothers smothering in an airtight cage of poverty in the midst of an affluent society; when you suddenly find your tongue twisted and your speech stammering as you seek to explain to your six-year-old daughter why she can't go to the public amusement park that has just been advertised on television, and see tears welling up in her eyes when she is told that Funtown is closed to colored children, and see ominous clouds of inferiority beginning to form in her little mental sky, and see her beginning to distort her personality by developing an unconscious bitterness toward white people; when you have to concoct an answer for a five-year-old son who is asking, "Daddy, why do white people treat colored people so mean?"; when you take a cross-country drive and find it necessary to sleep night after night in the uncomfortable corners of your automobile because no motel will accept you; when you are humiliated day in and day out by nagging signs reading "white" and "colored"; when your first name becomes "nigger," your middle name becomes "boy" (however old you are) and your last name becomes "John," and your wife and mother are never given the respected title "Mrs."; when you are harried by day and haunted by night by the fact that you are a Negro, living constantly at tiptoe stance, never quite knowing what to expect next, and are plagued with inner fears and outer resentments; when you are forever fighting a degenerating sense of "nobodiness"—then you will understand why we find it difficult to wait. There comes a time when the cup of endurance runs over, and men are no longer willing to be plunged into the abyss of despair. I hope, sirs, you can understand our legitimate and unavoidable impatience.

You express a great deal of anxiety over our willingness to break   15
laws. This is certainly a legitimate concern. Since we so diligently
urge people to obey the Supreme Court's decision of 1954 outlawing
segregation in the public schools, at first glance it may seem rather
paradoxical for us consciously to break laws. One may well ask:
"How can you advocate breaking some laws and obeying others?"
The answer lies in the fact that there are two types of laws: just
and unjust. I would be the first to advocate obeying just laws. One
has not only a legal but a moral responsibility to obey just laws.
Conversely, one has a moral responsibility to disobey unjust laws.
I would agree with St. Augustine that "an unjust law is no law at
all."

Now, what is the difference between the two? How does one de-   16
termine whether a law is just or unjust? A just law is a man-made
code that squares with the moral law or the law of God. An unjust
law is a code that is out of harmony with the moral law. To put it
in the terms of St. Thomas Aquinas: An unjust law is a human law
that is not rooted in eternal law and natural law. Any law that
uplifts human personality is just. Any law that degrades human
personality is unjust. All segregation statutes are unjust because
segregation distorts the soul and damages the personality. It gives
the segregator a false sense of superiority and the segregated a false
sense of inferiority. Segregation, to use the terminology of the Jewish philosopher Martin Buber, substitutes an "I-it" relationship for
an "I-thou" relationship and ends up relegating persons to the status of things. Hence segregation is not only politically, econom-
ically, and sociologically unsound, it is morally wrong and sinful.
Paul Tillich has said that sin is separation. Is not segregation an
existential expression of man's tragic separation, his awful es-
trangement, his terrible sinfulness? Thus it is that I can urge men
to obey the 1954 decision of the Supreme Court, for it is morally
right; and I can urge them to disobey segregation ordinances, for
they are morally wrong.

Let us consider a more concrete example of just and unjust laws.   17
An unjust law is a code that a numerical or power majority group
compels a minority group to obey but does not make binding on
itself. This is *difference* made legal. By the same token, a just law
is a code that a majority compels a minority to follow and that it is
willing to follow itself. This is *sameness* made legal.

Let me give another explanation. A law is unjust if it is inflicted   18
on a minority that, as a result of being denied the right to vote, had
no part in enacting or devising the law. Who can say that the leg-

islature of Alabama which set up that state's segregation laws was democratically elected? Throughout Alabama all sorts of devious methods are used to prevent Negroes from becoming registered voters, and there are some counties in which, even though Negroes constitute a majority of the population, not a single Negro is registered. Can any law enacted under such circumstances be considered democratically structured?

Sometimes a law is just on its face and unjust in its application. For instance, I have been arrested on a charge of parading without a permit. Now, there is nothing wrong in having an ordinance which requires a permit for a parade. But such an ordinance becomes unjust when it is used to maintain segregation and to deny citizens the First-Amendment privilege of peaceful assembly and protest. 19

I hope you are able to see the distinction I am trying to point out. In no sense do I advocate evading or defying the law, as would the rabid segregationist. That would lead to anarchy. One who breaks an unjust law must do so openly, lovingly, and with a willingness to accept the penalty. I submit that an individual who breaks a law that conscience tells him is unjust, and who willingly accepts the penalty of imprisonment in order to arouse the conscience of the community over its injustice, is in reality expressing the highest respect for law. 20

Of course, there is nothing new about this kind of civil disobedience. It was evidenced sublimely in the refusal of Shadrach, Meshach, and Abednego to obey the laws of Nebuchadnezzar, on the ground that a higher moral law was at stake. It was practiced superbly by the early Christians, who were willing to face hungry lions and the excruciating pain of chopping blocks rather than submit to certain unjust laws of the Roman Empire. To a degree, academic freedom is a reality today because Socrates practiced civil disobedience. In our own nation, the Boston Tea Party represented a massive act of civil disobedience. 21

We should never forget that everything Adolf Hitler did in Germany was "legal" and everything the Hungarian freedom fighters did in Hungary was "illegal." It was "illegal" to aid and comfort a Jew in Hitler's Germany. Even so, I am sure that, had I lived in Germany at the time, I would have aided and comforted my Jewish brothers. If today I lived in a Communist country where certain principles dear to the Christian faith are suppressed, I would openly advocate disobeying that country's anti-religious laws. 22

I must make two honest confessions to you, my Christian and Jewish brothers. First, I must confess that over the past few years I have been gravely disappointed with the white moderate. I have 23 almost reached the regrettable conclusion that the Negro's great stumbling block in his stride toward freedom is not the White Citizen's Counciler or the Ku Klux Klanner, but the white moderate, who is more devoted to "order" than to justice; who prefers a negative peace which is the absence of tension to a positive peace which is the presence of justice; who constantly says, "I agree with you in the goal you seek, but I cannot agree with your methods of direct action"; who paternalistically believes he can set the timetable for another man's freedom; who lives by a mythical concept of time and who constantly advises the Negro to wait for a "more convenient season." Shallow understanding from people of good will is more frustrating than absolute misunderstanding from people of ill will. Lukewarm acceptance is much more bewildering than outright rejection.

I had hoped that the white moderate would understand that law 24 and order exist for the purpose of establishing justice and that when they fail in this purpose they become the dangerously structured dams that block the flow of social progress. I had hoped that the white moderate would understand that the present tension in the South is a necessary phase of the transition from an obnoxious negative peace, in which the Negro passively accepted his unjust plight, to a substantive and positive peace, in which all men will respect the dignity and worth of human personality. Actually, we who engage in nonviolent direct action are not the creators of tension. We merely bring to the surface the hidden tension that is already alive. We bring it out in the open, where it can be seen and dealt with. Like a boil that can never be cured so long as it is covered up but must be opened with all its ugliness to the natural medicines of air and light, injustice must be exposed, with all the tension its exposure creates, to the light of human conscience and the air of national opinion, before it can be cured.

In your statement you assert that our actions, even though peace- 25 ful, must be condemned because they precipitate violence. But is this a logical assertion? Isn't this like condemning a robbed man because his possession of money precipitated the evil act of robbery? Isn't this like condemning Socrates because his unswerving commitment to truth and his philosophical inquiries precipitated the act by the misguided populace in which they made him drink hemlock? Isn't this like condemning Jesus because his unique God-consciousness and never-ceasing devotion to God's will precipitated the evil act of crucifixion? We must come to see that, as the federal courts have consistently affirmed, it is wrong to urge an individual to cease his efforts to gain his basic constitutional rights because the quest may precipitate violence. Society must protect the robbed and punish the robber.

I had also hoped that the white moderate would reject the myth   26 concerning time in relation to the struggle for freedom. I have just received a letter from a white brother in Texas. He writes: "All Christians know that the colored people will receive equal rights eventually, but it is possible that you are in too great a religious hurry. It has taken Christianity almost two thousand years to accomplish what it has. The teachings of Christ take time to come to earth." Such an attitude stems from a tragic misconception of time, from the strangely irrational notion that there is something in the very flow of time that will inevitably cure all ills. Actually, time itself is neutral; it can be used either destructively or constructively. More and more I feel that the people of ill will have used time much more effectively than have the people of good will. We will have to repent in this generation not merely for the hateful words and actions of the bad people, but for the appalling silence of the good people. Human progress never rolls in on wheels of inevitability; it comes through the tireless efforts of men willing to be co-workers with God, and without this hard work, time itself becomes an ally of the forces of social stagnation. We must use time creatively, in the knowledge that the time is always ripe to do right. Now is the time to make real the promise of democracy and transform our pending national elegy into a creative psalm of brotherhood. Now is the time to lift our national policy from the quicksand of racial injustice to the solid rock of human dignity.

You speak of our activity in Birmingham as extreme. At first I   27 was rather disappointed that fellow clergymen would see my nonviolent efforts as those of an extremist. I began thinking about the fact that I stand in the middle of two opposing forces in the Negro community. One is a force of complacency, made up in part of Negroes who, as a result of long years of oppression, are so drained of self-respect and a sense of "somebodiness" that they have adjusted to segregation; and in part of a few middle-class Negroes who, because of a degree of academic and economic security and because in some ways they profit by segregation, have become insensitive to the problems of the masses. The other force is one of bitterness and hatred, and it comes perilously close to advocating violence. It is expressed in the various black nationalist groups that are springing up across the nation, the largest and best-known being Elijah Muhammad's Muslim movement. Nourished by the Negro's frustration over the continued existence of racial discrimination, this movement is made up of people who have lost faith in America, who have absolutely repudiated Christianity, and who have concluded that the white man is an incorrigible "devil."

I have tried to stand between these two forces, saying that we need emulate neither the "do-nothingism" of the complacent nor the hatred and despair of the black nationalist. For there is the more excellent way of love and nonviolent protest. I am grateful to God that, through the influence of the Negro church, the way of non-violence became an integral part of our struggle.

If this philosophy had not emerged, by now many streets of the South would, I am convinced, be flowing with blood. And I am further convinced that if our white brothers dismiss as "rabble-rousers" and "outside agitators" those of us who employ nonviolent direct action, and if they refuse to support our nonviolent efforts, millions of Negroes will, out of frustration and despair, seek solace and se-curity in black-nationalist ideologies—a development that would inevitably lead to a frightening racial nightmare.

Oppressed people cannot remain oppressed forever. The yearning for freedom eventually manifests itself, and that is what has hap-pened to the American Negro. Something within has reminded him of his birthright of freedom, and something without has reminded him that it can be gained. Consciously or unconsciously, he has been caught up by the *Zeitgeist,* and with his black brothers of Africa and his brown and yellow brothers of Asia, South America, and the Caribbean, the United States Negro is moving with a sense of great urgency toward the promised land of racial justice. If one recognizes this vital urge that has engulfed the Negro community, one should readily understand why public demonstrations are taking place. The Negro has many pent-up resentments and latent frustrations, and he must release them. So let him march; let him make prayer pilgrimages to the city hall; let him go on freedom rides—and try to understand why he must do so. If his repressed emotions are not released in nonviolent ways, they will seek expression through vio-lence; this is not a threat but a fact of history. So I have not said to my people, "Get rid of your discontent." Rather, I have tried to say that this normal and healthy discontent can be channeled into the creative outlet of nonviolent direct action. And now this ap-proach is being termed extremist.

But though I was initially disappointed at being categorized as an extremist, as I continued to think about the matter I gradually gained a measure of satisfaction from the label. Was not Jesus an extremist for love: "Love your enemies, bless them that curse you, do good to them that hate you, and pray for them which despitefully use you, and persecute you." Was not Amos an extremist for justice:

"Let justice roll down like waters and righteousness like an ever-flowing stream." Was not Paul an extremist for the Christian gospel: "I bear in my body the marks of the Lord Jesus." Was not Martin Luther an extremist: "Here I stand; I cannot do otherwise, so help me God." And John Bunyan: "I will stay in jail to the end of my days before I make a butchery of my conscience." And Abraham Lincoln: "This nation cannot survive half slave and half free." And Thomas Jefferson: "We hold these truths to be self-evident, that all men are created equal. . . ." So the question is not whether we will be extremists, but what kind of extremists we will be. Will we be extremists for hate or for love? Will we be extremists for the preservation of injustice or for the extension of justice? In that dramatic scene on Calvary's hill three men were crucified. We must never forget that all three were crucified for the same crime—the crime of extremism. Two were extremists for immorality, and thus fell below their environment. The other, Jesus Christ, was an extremist for love, truth, and goodness, and thereby rose above his environment. Perhaps the South, the nation, and the world are in dire need of creative extremists.

I had hoped that the white moderate would see this need. Perhaps I was too optimistic; perhaps I expected too much. I suppose I should have realized that few members of the oppressor race can understand the deep groans and passionate yearnings of the oppressed race, and still fewer have the vision to see that injustice must be rooted out by strong, persistent, and determined action. I am thankful, however, that some of our white brothers in the South have grasped the meaning of this social revolution and committed themselves to it. They are still all too few in quantity, but they are big in quality. Some—such as Ralph McGill, Lillian Smith, Harry Golden, James McBride Dabbs, Ann Braden, and Sarah Patton Boyle—have written about our struggle in eloquent and prophetic terms. Others have marched with us down nameless streets of the South. They have languished in filthy, roach-infested jails, suffering the abuse and brutality of policemen who view them as "dirty nigger-lovers." Unlike so many of their moderate brothers and sisters, they have recognized the urgency of the moment and sensed the need for powerful "action" antidotes to combat the disease of segregation. 32

Let me take note of my other major disappointment. I have been so greatly disappointed with the white church and its leadership. Of course, there are some notable exceptions. I am not unmindful of the fact that each of you has taken some significant stands on this issue. I commend you, Reverend Stallings, for your Christian 33 stand on this past Sunday, in welcoming Negroes to your worship service on a nonsegregated basis. I commend the Catholic leaders of this state for integrating Spring Hill College several years ago.

But despite these notable exceptions, I must honestly reiterate   34
that I have been disappointed with the church. I do not say this as one of those negative critics who can always find something wrong with the church. I say this as a minister of the gospel, who loves the church; who was nurtured in its bosom; who has been sustained by its spiritual blessings and who will remain true to it as long as the cord of life shall lengthen.

When I was suddenly catapulted into the leadership of the bus   35
protest in Montgomery, Alabama, a few years ago, I felt we would be supported by the white church. I felt that the white ministers, priests, and rabbis of the South would be among our strongest allies. Instead, some have been outright opponents, refusing to understand the freedom movement and misrepresenting its leaders; all too many others have been more cautious than courageous and have remained silent behind the anesthetizing security of stained-glass windows.

In spite of my shattered dreams, I came to Birmingham with the   36
hope that the white religious leadership of this community would see the justice of our cause and, with deep moral concern, would serve as the channel through which our just grievances could reach the power structure. I had hoped that each of you would understand. But again I have been disappointed.

There was a time when the church was very powerful—in the   37
time when the early Christians rejoiced at being deemed worthy to suffer for what they believed. In those days the church was not merely a thermometer that recorded the ideas and principles of popular opinion; it was a thermostat that transformed the mores of society. Whenever the early Christians entered a town, the people in power became disturbed and immediately sought to convict the Christians for being "disturbers of the peace" and "outside agitators." But the Christians pressed on, in the conviction that they were "a colony of heaven," called to obey God rather than man. Small in number, they were big in commitment. They were too God-intoxicated to be "astronomically intimidated." By their effort and example they brought an end to such ancient evils as infanticide and gladiatorial contests.

Things are different now. So often the contemporary church is a   38
weak, ineffectual voice with an uncertain sound. So often it is an archdefender of the status quo. Far from being disturbed by the

presence of the church, the power structure of the average community is consoled by the church's silent—and often even vocal—
sanction of things as they are.

But the judgment of God is upon the church as never before. If   39
today's church does not recapture the sacrificial spirit of the early
church, it will lose its authenticity, forfeit the loyalty of millions,
and be dismissed as an irrelevant social club with no meaning for
the twentieth century. Every day I meet young people whose disappointment with the church has turned into outright disgust.

Perhaps I have once again been too optimistic. Is organized re-   40
ligion too inextricably bound to the status quo to save our nation
and the world? Perhaps I must turn my faith to the inner spiritual
church, the church within the church, as the true *ekklesia* and the
hope of the world. But again I am thankful to God that some noble
souls from the ranks of organized religion have broken loose from
the paralyzing chains of conformity and joined us as active partners
in the struggle for freedom. They have left their secure congrega-
tions and walked the streets of Albany, Georgia, with us. They have
gone down the highways of the South on torturous rides for freedom.
Yes, they have gone to jail with us. Some have been dismissed from
their churches, have lost the support of their bishops and fellow
ministers. But they have acted in the faith that right defeated is
stronger than evil triumphant. Their witness has been the spiritual
salt that has preserved the true meaning of the gospel in these
troubled times. They have carved a tunnel of hope through the dark
mountain of disappointment.

I hope the church as a whole will meet the challenge of this   41
decisive hour. But even if the church does not come to the aid of
justice, I have no despair about the future. I have no fear about the
outcome of our struggle in Birmingham, even if our motives are at
present misunderstood. We will reach the goal of freedom in Birmingham and all over the nation, because the goal of America is
freedom. Abused and scorned though we may be, our destiny is tied
up with America's destiny. Before the pilgrims landed at Plymouth,
we were here. Before the pen of Jefferson etched the majestic words
of the Declaration of Independence across the pages of history, we
were here. For more than two centuries our forebears labored in
this country without wages; they made cotton king; they built the
homes of their masters while suffering gross injustice and shameful
humiliation—and yet out of a bottomless vitality they continued to
thrive and develop. If the inexpressible cruelties of slavery could
not stop us, the opposition we now face will surely fail. We will win

our freedom because the sacred heritage of our nation and the eternal will of God are embodied in our echoing demands.

Before closing I feel impelled to mention one other point in your   42
statement that has troubled me profoundly. You warmly commended the Birmingham police force for keeping "order" and "preventing violence." I doubt that you would have so warmly commended the police force if you had seen its dogs sinking their teeth into unarmed, nonviolent Negroes. I doubt that you would so quickly commend the policemen if you were to observe their ugly and inhumane treatment of Negroes here in the city jail; if you were to watch them push and curse old Negro women and young Negro girls; if you were to see them slap and kick old Negro men and young boys; if you were to observe them, as they did on two occasions, refuse to give us food because we wanted to sing our grace together. I cannot join you in your praise of the Birmingham police department.

It is true that the police have exercised a degree of discipline in   43
handling the demonstrators. In this sense they have conducted themselves rather "nonviolently" in public. But for what purpose? To preserve the evil system of segregation. Over the past few years I have consistently preached that nonviolence demands that the means we use must be as pure as the ends we seek. I have tried to make clear that it is wrong to use immoral means to attain moral ends. But now I must affirm that it is just as wrong, or perhaps even more so, to use moral means to preserve immoral ends. Perhaps Mr. Connor and his policemen have been rather nonviolent in public, as was Chief Pritchett in Albany, Georgia, but they have used the moral means of nonviolence to maintain the immoral end of racial injustice. As T. S. Elliot has said, "The last temptation is the greatest treason: To do the right deed for the wrong reason."

I wish you had commended the Negro sit-inners and demonstra-   44
tors of Birmingham for their sublime courage, their willingness to suffer, and their amazing discipline in the midst of great provocation. One day the South will recognize its real heroes. They will be the James Merediths, with the noble sense of purpose that enables them to face jeering and hostile mobs, and with the agonizing loneliness that characterizes the life of the pioneer. They will be old, oppressed, battered Negro women, symbolized in a seventy-two-year-old woman in Montgomery, Alabama, who rose up with a sense of dignity and with her people decided not to ride segregated buses, and who responded with ungrammatical profundity to one who inquired about her weariness: "My feets is tired, but my soul is at

rest." They will be the young high school and college students, the young ministers of the gospel and a host of their elders, courageously and nonviolently sitting in at lunch counters and willingly going to jail for conscience' sake. One day the South will know that when these disinherited children of God sat down at lunch counters, they were in reality standing up for what is best in the American dream and for the most sacred values in our Judaeo-Christian heritage, thereby bringing our nation back to those great wells of democracy which were dug deep by the founding fathers in their formulation of the Constitution and the Declaration of Independence.

Never before have I written so long a letter. I'm afraid it is much too long to take your precious time. I can assure you that it would have been much shorter if I had been writing from a comfortable desk, but what else can one do when he is alone in a narrow jail cell, other than write long letters, think long thoughts, and pray long prayers? 45

If I have said anything in this letter that overstates the truth and indicates an unreasonable impatience, I beg you to forgive me. If I have said anything that understates the truth and indicates my having a patience that allows me to settle for anything less than brotherhood, I beg God to forgive me. 46

I hope this letter finds you strong in the faith. I also hope that circumstances will soon make it possible for me to meet each of you, not as an integrationist or a civil-rights leader but as a fellow clergyman and a Christian brother. Let us all hope that the dark clouds of racial prejudice will soon pass away and the deep fog of misunderstanding will be lifted from our fear-drenched communities, and in some not too distant tomorrow the radiant stars of love and brotherhood will shine over our great nation with all their scintillating beauty. 47

> Yours for the cause of Peace and Brotherhood,
> Martin Luther King, Jr.

COMPREHENSION

1. Martin Luther King, Jr., says that he seldom answers criticism. Why does he decide to do so in this instance?

2. Why do the other clergymen consider King's activities to be "unwise and untimely"?

3. What reasons does King give for the demonstrations? Why does he feel it is too late for negotiations?

4. What does King say *wait* means to blacks?

5. What are the two types of laws King defines? What is the difference between the two?

6. Why is King disappointed in the white moderates?

7. What does King find illogical about the claim that the actions of his followers precipitate violence?

8. What two forces does King say he stands between?

9. Why is King disappointed in the white church?

PURPOSE AND AUDIENCE

1. What is King's purpose in writing his letter? Why, in the first paragraph, does he establish his setting (the Birmingham city jail) and define his intended audience?

2. In the beginning of his letter, King refers to his audience as men of good will. What passages in the letter indicate that he does not really believe this?

3. What indication is there that King is writing his letter to an audience other than his fellow clergymen?

4. What is the thesis of this letter? Is it stated or implied?

5. Why does King so carefully outline for his audience the reasons why he is in Birmingham?

STYLE AND STRUCTURE

1. Where does King seek to establish that he is a reasonable person? Why does he open with "My Dear Fellow Clergymen"?

2. Where does King address the objections of his audience?

3. At what point does King introduce the problem his letter is going to deal with?

4. What facts or examples does King use to support his thesis?

5. As in the Declaration of Independence, transitions are important in King's letter. Identify the transitional words and phrases that connect the different parts of his argument.

6. Why does King use Jewish, Catholic, and Protestant philosophers to support his position?

7. King uses both induction and deduction in his letter. Find an example of each, and explain how they function in the argument.

8. Throughout the body of his letter, King criticizes his audience of white moderates. In his conclusion, he seeks to reestablish a harmonious relationship with them. How does he do this?

WRITING WORKSHOP

1. Write an argumentative essay in which you support a deeply held belief of your own. Assume that your audience, like King's, is not openly hostile to your position.

2. Assume that you are a black militant writing a letter to Martin Luther King, Jr. Argue that King's methods do not go far enough. Be sure to address potential objections to your position. You might want to go to the library and read some newspapers and magazines from the 1960s to help you prepare your argument.

3. Read the newspaper for several days, and collect articles about a controversial subject in which you are interested. Using the information from the articles, take a position on the issue, and write an essay in your own words supporting it.

Acknowledgments (continued from page iv)

Studs Terkel, "Brett Hauser: Supermarket Box Boy." From *Working: People Talk About What They Do All Day and How They Feel About What They Do,* by Studs Terkel. Copyright © 1972, 1974 by Studs Terkel. Reprinted by permission of Pantheon Books, a Division of Random House, Inc.

E. B. White, "Once More to the Lake." From *Essays of E. B. White.* Copyright 1941 by E. B. White. Reprinted by permission of Harper & Row, Publishers, Inc.

EXEMPLIFICATION

Richard Wright, "The Ethics of Living Jim Crow." Specified excerpt (pp. 3–4) from "The Ethics of Living Jim Crow" in *Uncle Tom's Children* by Richard Wright. Copyright, 1937, by Richard Wright.

Laurence J. Peter and Raymond Hull, "The Peter Principle." Chapter 1 of *The Peter Principle* by Laurence J. Peter and Raymond Hull. Copyright © 1969 by William Morrow and Company, Inc. By permission of the publisher.

Ellen Goodman, "The Company Man." From *At Large* by Ellen Goodman. Copyright © 1981 by The Washington Post Company. Reprinted by permission of Summit Books, a Simon & Schuster division of Gulf & Western Corporation.

Lewis Thomas, "Death in the Open." From *The Lives of a Cell: Notes of a Biology Watcher* by Lewis Thomas. Copyright © 1971, 1973 by Massachusetts Medical Society. Originally published in the *New England Journal of Medicine.* Reprinted by permission of Viking Penguin Inc.

James Thurber, "Courtship through the Ages." Copyright © 1942 James Thurber. Copyright © 1970 Helen W. Thurber and Rosemary T. Sauers. From *My World—And Welcome to It,* published by Harcourt Brace Jovanovich.

PROCESS

S. I. Hayakawa, "How Dictionaries Are Made." From *Language in Thought and Action,* Fourth Edition by S. I. Hayakawa. Copyright © 1978 by Harcourt Brace Jovanovich, Inc. Reprinted by permission of the publisher.

Malcolm X, "My First Conk." From *The Autobiography of Malcolm X,* by Malcolm X, with Alex Haley. Copyright © 1964 by Alex Haley and Malcolm X, © 1965 by Alex Haley and Betty Shabazz. Reprinted by permission of Random House, Inc.

Noel Perrin, "Falling for Apples." From *Second Person Rural* by Noel Perrin. Copyright © 1980 by Noel Perrin. Reprinted by permission of David R. Godine, Publisher, Boston.

Donald M. Murray, "The Maker's Eye: Revising Your Own Manuscripts." From *The Writer* (October 1973). Revised version reprinted by permission of International Creative Management, Inc. Copyright © 1973 by Donald M. Murray.

CAUSE AND EFFECT

COMPARISON AND CONTRAST

CLASSIFICATION AND DIVISION

S. I. Hayakawa, "Reports, Inferences, Judgments." From *Language in Thought and Action,* Fourth Edition by S. I. Hayakawa, copyright © 1978 by Harcourt Brace Jovanovich, Inc. Reprinted by permission of the publisher.

DEFINITION

Leo Rosten, "The Astonishing Talmud." Reprinted with permission from the September 1977 *Reader's Digest.* Copyright © 1977 by The Reader's Digest Assn., Inc.

Eileen Simpson, "Dyslexia." From *Reversals: A Personal Account of Victory over Dyslexia* by Eileen Simpson. Copyright © 1979 by Eileen Simpson. Reprinted by permission of Houghton Mifflin Company.

Neil Postman, "Euphemism." Excerpted from the book *Crazy Talk, Stupid Talk* by Neil Postman. Copyright © 1976 by Neil Postman. Reprinted by permission of Delacorte Press.

John R. Erickson, "The Modern Cowboy." Reprinted from *The Modern Cowboy* by John R. Erickson by permission of University of Nebraska Press. Copyright © 1981 by the University of Nebraska Press.

Margaret Mead, "New Superstitions for Old." From *A Way of Seeing* by Margaret Mead and Rhoda Metraux. Copyright © 1966 by Margaret Mead and Rhoda Metraux. By permission of William Morrow & Company.

ARGUMENTATION

Steven Muller, "Our Youth Should Serve." Copyright 1978, by Newsweek, Inc. All Rights Reserved. Reprinted by Permission.

William F. Buckley, Jr., "Capital Punishment." Reprinted by permission of G. P. Putnam's Sons from *Execution Eve & Other Contemporary Ballads* by William F. Buckley, Jr. Copyright © 1973–75 by William F. Buckley, Jr.

Isaac Asimov, "The Case Against Man." Copyright © 1975 Field Enterprises, Inc. Courtesy of Field Newspaper Syndicate.

George Orwell, "Politics and the English Language." Copyright 1946 by Sonia Brownell Orwell; renewed 1974 by Sonia Orwell. Reprinted from *Shooting an Elephant and Other Essays* by George Orwell by permission of Harcourt Brace Jovanovich, Inc.

Martin Luther King, Jr., "Letter from Birmingham Jail." "Letter from Birmingham Jail, April 16, 1963" from *Why We Can't Wait,* by Martin Luther King, Jr., Copyright © 1963 by Martin Luther King, Jr. Reprinted by permission of Harper & Row, Publishers, Inc.

cover art: *Beasts of the Sea* by Henri Matisse; Ailsa Mellon Bruce Fund, National Gallery of Art, Washington, D.C.

Index of Terms,
Authors, and Titles